WHO CAN'T HEAR MUST FEEL

My Angel Gabriel!

GABRIEL MOSES

REGINA

I longed for a baby son, my Prayers were answered, my Angel

As your Mum, my Angel, I hope you know how much I love you. Blessings the Lord has sent me. You are very gentle, humble and always smiling.
A Prayerful Son with Compassion heart.
I owe all my Gray Hairs to YOU!
Shine on Son! I love you Son!
Stay Strong my Angel!

Jesus Christ is Lord!

Prestel
MUNICH • LONDON • NEW YORK

FOREWORD
Gabriel Moses

From very, very young, my mum would speak life into me. She'd tell me how special I was and how if everyone was doing one thing, Gabriel you go do the opposite! It's one thing that stuck with me throughout my childhood. I fell in love with the concept of being an outsider. It's been the story of my life from my first day at school to now entering rooms as an adult. She'd always remind me of the Bible verse Joshua 1:3 where God says, "Every place that the sole of your foot shall tread upon, I have made your territory just as I promised to Moses." It has influenced the way I carry myself. It means that I step everywhere with confidence, and as an artist it allows me to give my perspective to viewers unapologetically, and leave it up to them to catch up if they feel like it.

There's a word throughout my career that I scream at every opportunity, and it's "Regina!" It means queen in Latin, while still sounding like the name of a woman. It was my way of expressing gratitude to the women who shaped the way I see the world – that's my grandmother, mum, sister, my nieces – they all shaped my approach and my values, despite going outside and seeing or being around things that weren't necessarily good for me, they always allowed me to see life in pink. When you see these images, I want you to understand that I work from a place of gratitude. I'm grateful for the opportunities, the trust, the angels that have come and gone in my life. It would be ignorant of me to believe that this is all by my power, because it isn't. My entire career has felt like a walk in the park, and I tell people I'd won the second I picked up a camera and gave my life some purpose, because I know how difficult it is to find that purpose and so many where I'm from spend their entire lives searching for that thing that wakes them up in the morning, so how can I complain? Till now, I work and dream like a child and just try to bring these things to reality. It's that same imagination that had me writing the craziest stories in primary school when asked by a teacher to write. I feel like life knocks the dreamer out of us, but I've stayed in touch with that madman that just wanted to do everything, and my life should be a testimony to that.

In this phase that I'm in right now, I understand all the accomplishments and the role I play in my community – as a Black artist entering spaces we ain't had much place in before, and I wear that like a tailored suit! I am now at a point where the legacy I'm trying to build has become an obsession, and God willing we continue to elevate while never losing sight of why we do this stuff!

REAL IMAGES
Federico Sargentone

You know I kept it for real / Walk around with it for real / You wanna bet that my money for real / For real? / For real.
— Lil Uzi Vert

For over a century, photographers and their apologists have argued that photography deserves to be considered a fine art.
— John Berger, *Understanding a Photograph* (1968)

I'm listening to seminal Italian rap crew Truce Boys' *Sangue* while I'm writing this. There's no "advantage" for me in that song that will be used in this piece – that's what they say in their opening track "Nessun Riscontro" ("No comparison / No advantage"). In Italian, it rhymes.

Yeah. No advantage. Why would you assume we got some?

"No advantage" means that you've never asked anything back from your peers. "No advantage" means that you talk about stuff the people around you don't understand. "No advantage" means that you do stuff your friends, at first, don't understand. Can't understand. "No advantage" means that you're an artist and no one recognizes it. It means "fuck you," but it also means "okay."

I have nothing in common with Mr. Gabriel Moses on a superficial level. He's successful. He's blessed. He's plugged. He's through. We're almost the same age though. We like stuff. I like stuff. Living in microscopic Italian provincial towns ruled by pseudo-fascist youth, and getting through only by "liking stuff." Liking stuff was essential to escaping one's surroundings. "Liking stuff" meant you were part of what you liked. Stuff transitioned from object-like status to behavior-like status. Through "liking stuff" you'd become what you are now. What we are now. What Gabriel is now, I think. And it seems we have more in common now. Not that it's important.

There's a lot to be said about pictures. About their form and their implications; about their interpretation and their intention. We won't say much about pictures. "Pictures," only in England. "Picture" is drill, "image" is trap. "Picture" is Gilbert and George, "image" is Andy Warhol. I only think about Andy Warhol, someone told me. In my work, in my writing, in my attitude. But Warhol, for me, was an entry point into an impenetrable art world.

For Gabriel I think it was Nike, technically. But I think it was Warhol too. Or someone close to that. In the sense that if you're not privileged, you're real. Real, as in what it means. As in real to people and things. In the age of image hegemony, reality assumes a whole new set of connotations: real images are not manipulated, not technologically enhanced, not staged, or not performative. In the words of John Berger, writing in 1968: "We think of photographs as works of art, as evidence of a particular truth, as likenesses, as news items. Every photograph is in fact a means of testing, confirming and constructing a total view of reality. Hence the crucial role of photography in ideological struggle." What Berger outlined in his classic book *Understanding a Photograph* is a conceptual paradox that is still applicable to today's image-making: a photograph is a document produced by the author's act of intentionality, a record of the world taken at a specific time, a fragment of a certain reality.

When Gabriel takes pictures they are visceral incantations that summon the specters of our own recollections. Through a lens that serves as both window and mirror he conjures a haunting, empathic relationship between subject and image, transcending the visual to embrace the emotional.

Memory, in Gabriel's hands, is a mercurial force, a thread that weaves together the past, present, and the ever-shifting contours of the psyche. Each photograph is a resonant chord struck on the strings of human experience, invoking a kaleidoscope of feelings that transcend the boundaries of time and space. His subjects are not mere figures caught in a tableau; they are vessels, their essence distilled and encapsulated in the very atoms of the image. The result is a visual poetry that pulsates with a profound, almost spectral resonance.

Gabriel's approach to image-making is an act of empathy – a ritual that invites the viewer not merely to observe but to participate in the emotional narrative. Through his lens we are drawn into profound communion with his subjects, experiencing their joy, sorrow, or vulnerability as if it were our own. His photographs are invitations to traverse the landscapes of the human heart, to navigate the labyrinthine corridors of memory, and to confront the fragility and resilience of the human spirit.

In an era where the digital deluge often desensitizes us to the world's emotional nuances Gabriel's work stands as a counterpoint, a reminder of our shared humanity. He compels us to confront the raw and tender underbelly of existence, to recognize that every life, every story, is a tapestry of memories and emotions. This is the case with his compelling film *Bal D'Afrique* for the Swedish beauty brand Byredo, in which a marriage is captured through the characters of an intimate, familiar celebration.

A mental image, by definition, is not real. A mental image is not a photograph, but a cognitive artifact. In Gabriel's work, any image is a mental image – crafting narratives of people, identities, and bodies through the filter of memory. Scenes that reside in the realm of the real although constructed and purely intentional. In his work mental images become real not because of their form, but because of their subjects, their own perfections and imperfections. "Painting is an art of arrangement: therefore it is reasonable to demand that there is some kind of order in what is arranged," once again John Berger. "Every relation between forms in a painting is to some degree adaptable to the painter's purpose." This is how Gabriel, I think, operates. An act of arrangement.

Gabriel makes classics. Reverence and rebellion. He pays homage to the visual canon by channeling its elegance and familiarity, but then he takes an audacious leap into the avant-garde. He deconstructs the established, disrupts the traditional. "Images last longer than humans," he said to me, as if his pictures are a testament to something bigger, something divine and not mundane, something that elevates the picture to a higher state. It's as if his photographs become bridges spanning epochs. The thick grain in the (mostly) black-and-white music video for Little Simz's "NO THANK YOU," for example, or in the extremely moving work of introspection that is *IJÓ*, is his way of conveying this approach to classicization in the formal arena. Again painting comes to mind – especially in the latter, which follows a group of young ballet dancers in Lagos, Nigeria. One is tempted to compare Edgar Degas's ballet paintings to this film, but in Gabriel's work the subjects are not aestheticized by the artist's gaze as are Degas's highly stylized, fetishized dancers. In *IJÓ* the cultural context is more important than the subject, or at least as relevant. The film's storytelling thrives on the reinterpretation of a "classic" trope – that of the ballet dancers – although it is clearly infused with emotional layers that complicate a linear reading, rendering it a suspended image of intimacy.

Gabriel is self-taught. He didn't come from an "art" environment but from South London. In South London he still is. And in an "art environment" he now is. Facts: at eighteen he was the youngest photographer to shoot a cover for *Dazed*. Gabriel wants to portray everyday people and their emotional worlds, he said. He juggles art and commerce with ease because he's aware of how much certain commercial projects can amplify his vision and bring it to as many people and their emotional worlds as possible. Gabriel goes to the studio every day, but he doesn't shoot pictures there. There he hangs out with his friends, family, and loved ones, every day. Thinking of images. Or pictures. Real things. "Images that last longer than humans." Images that don't Tik-Tok. Images that aren't loud but that break silence. Images of people. Images that not only tell a story but make one. Images that are of today, of yesterday, and of tomorrow. Images that are painted. Images that are us. Mental images. Real Images.

CONTRIBUTORS

edited by
KATJA HORVAT

conversations with
SKEPTA † NICK KNIGHT

essay by
FEDERICO SARGENTONE

impressions from
MUMSY ‡ CLINT ‡ SLAWN
KATJA HORVAT ‡ ARI CHANOUX ‡ SAMUEL ROSS
CIESAY ‡ MATTHEW WILLIAMS

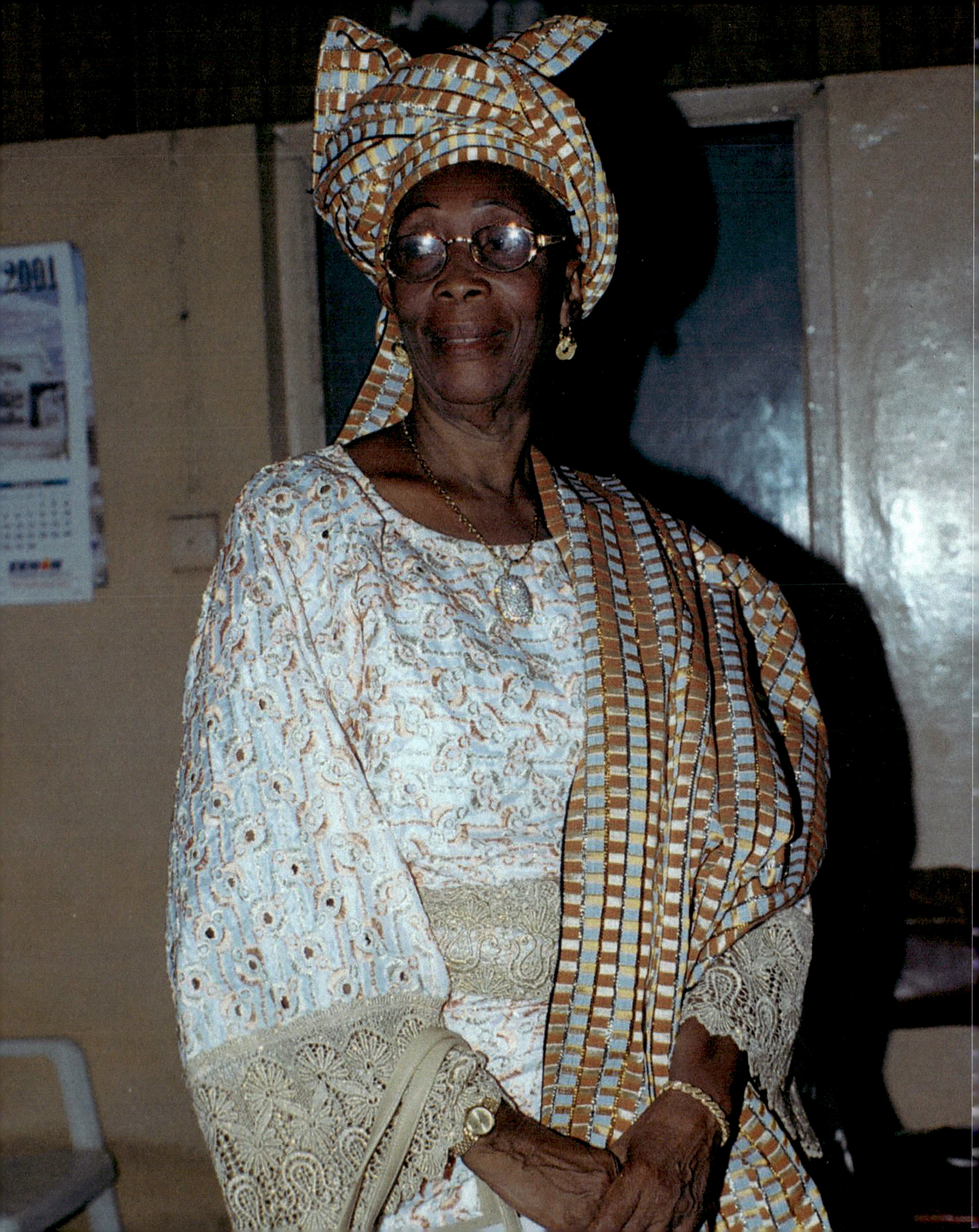

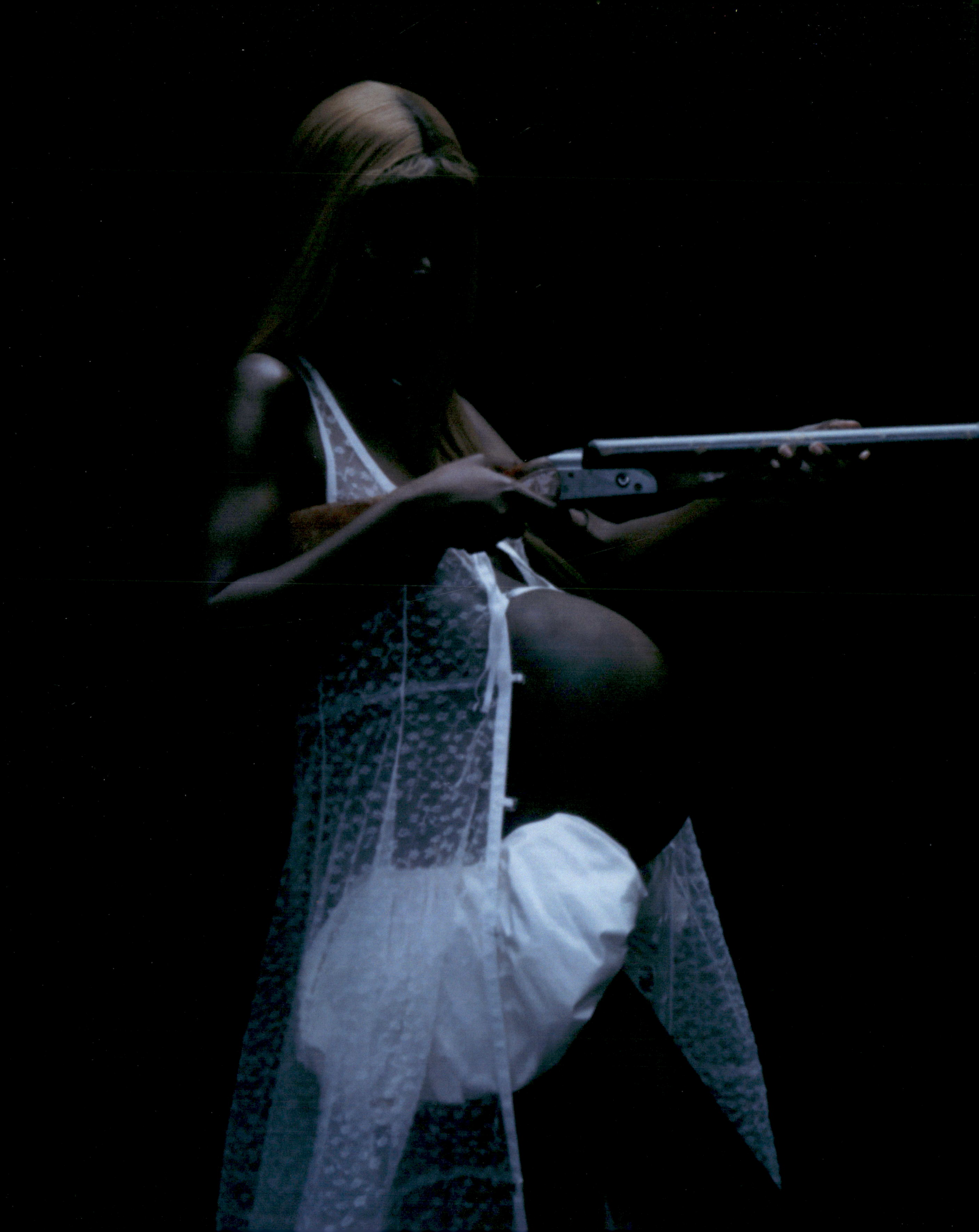

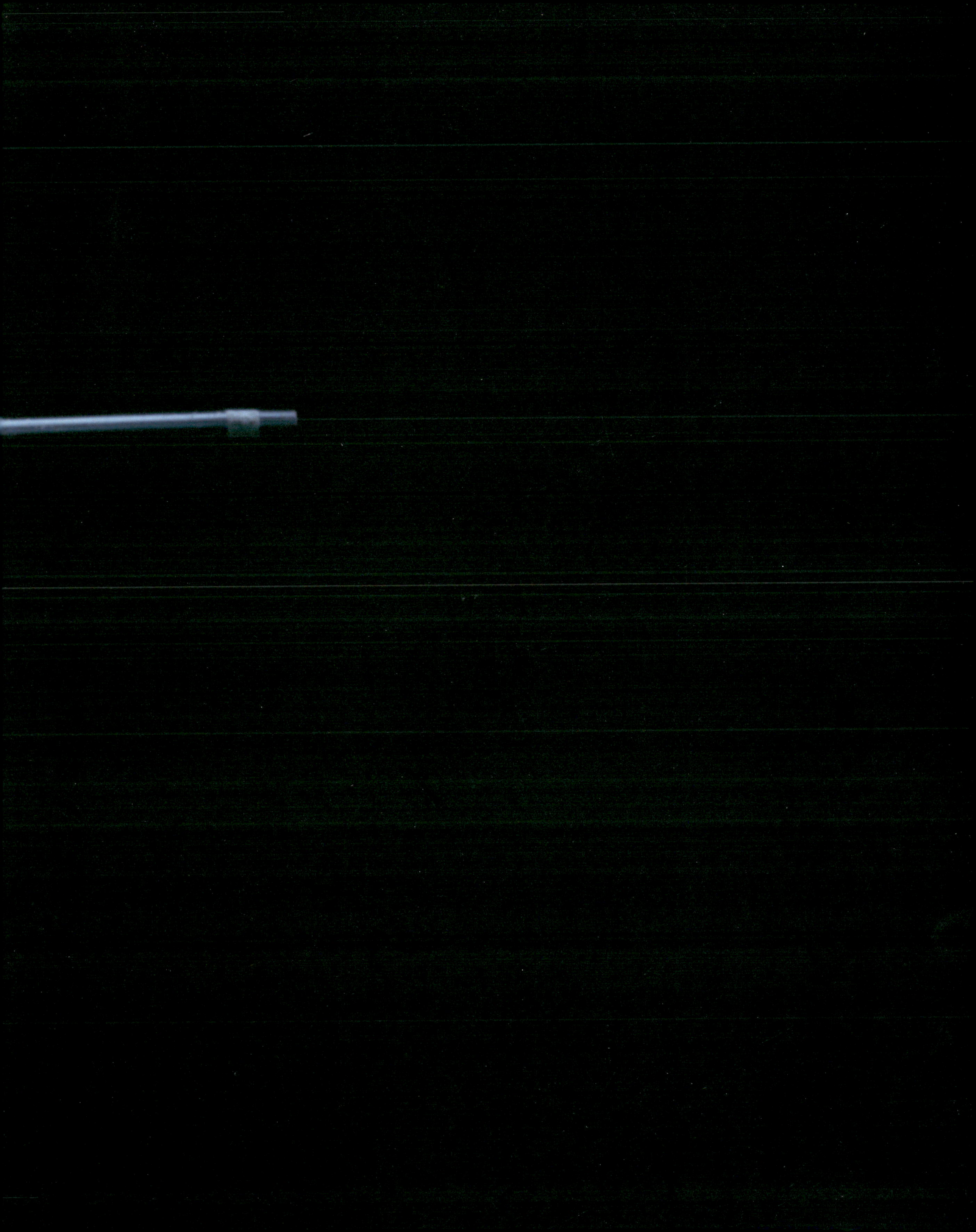

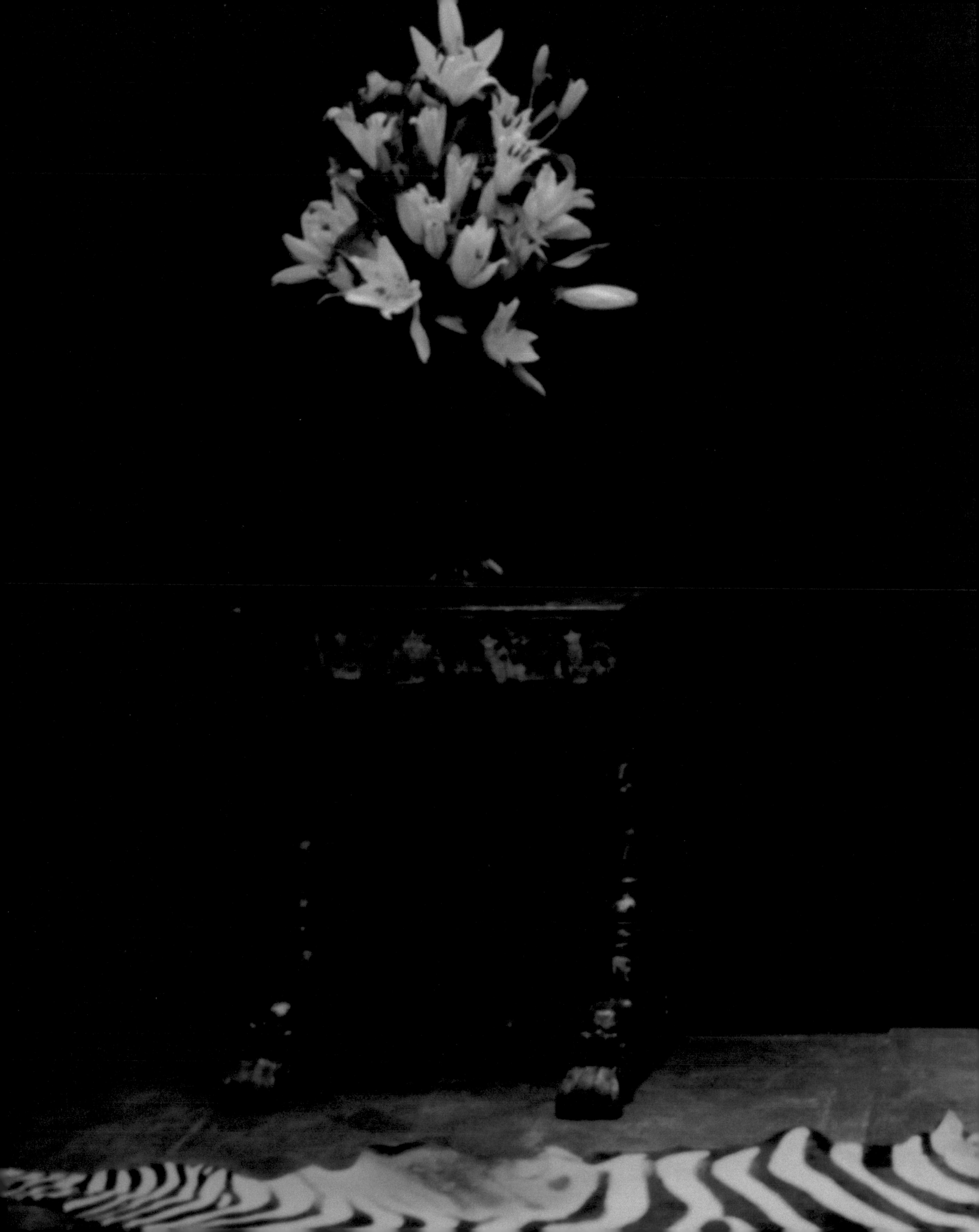

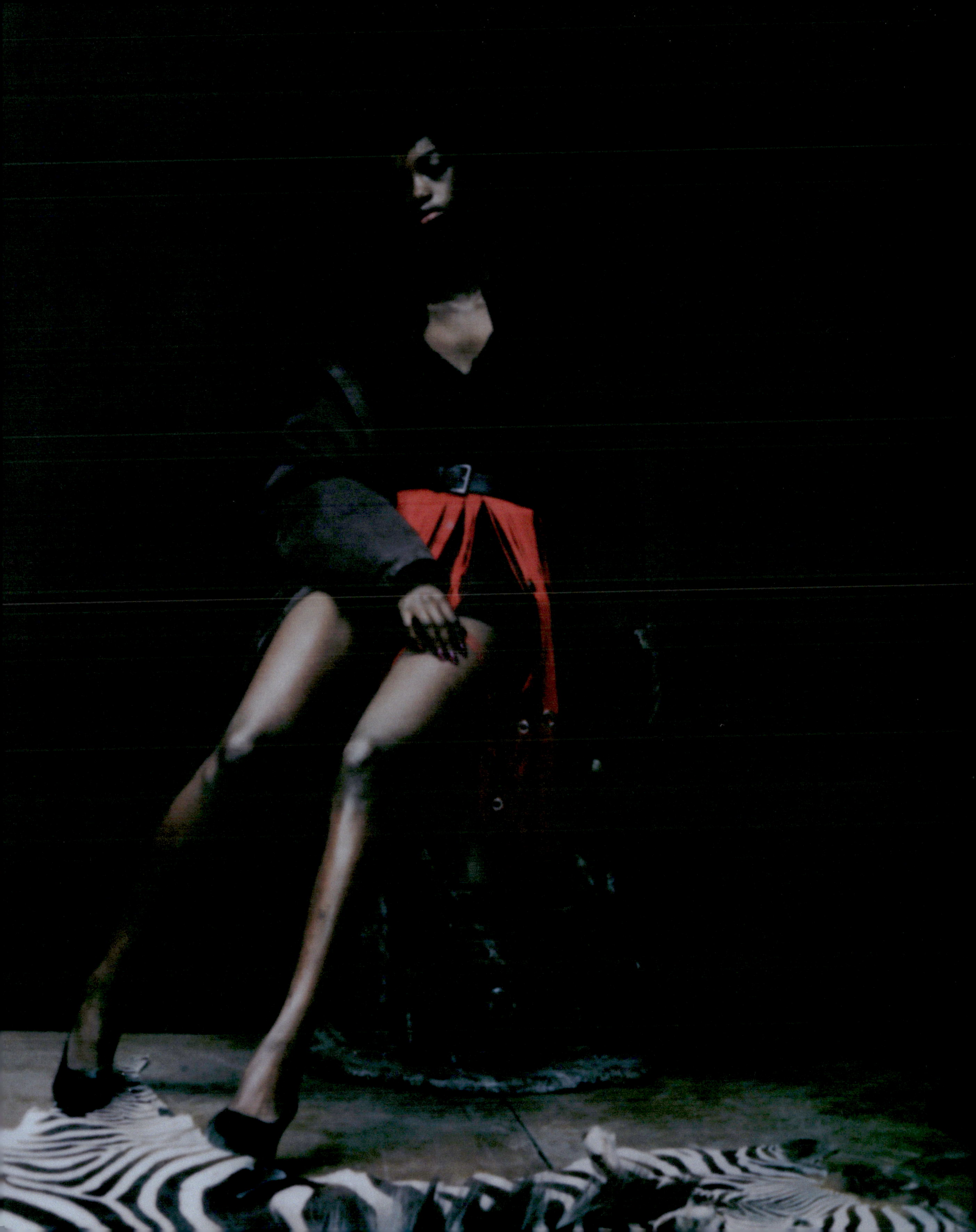

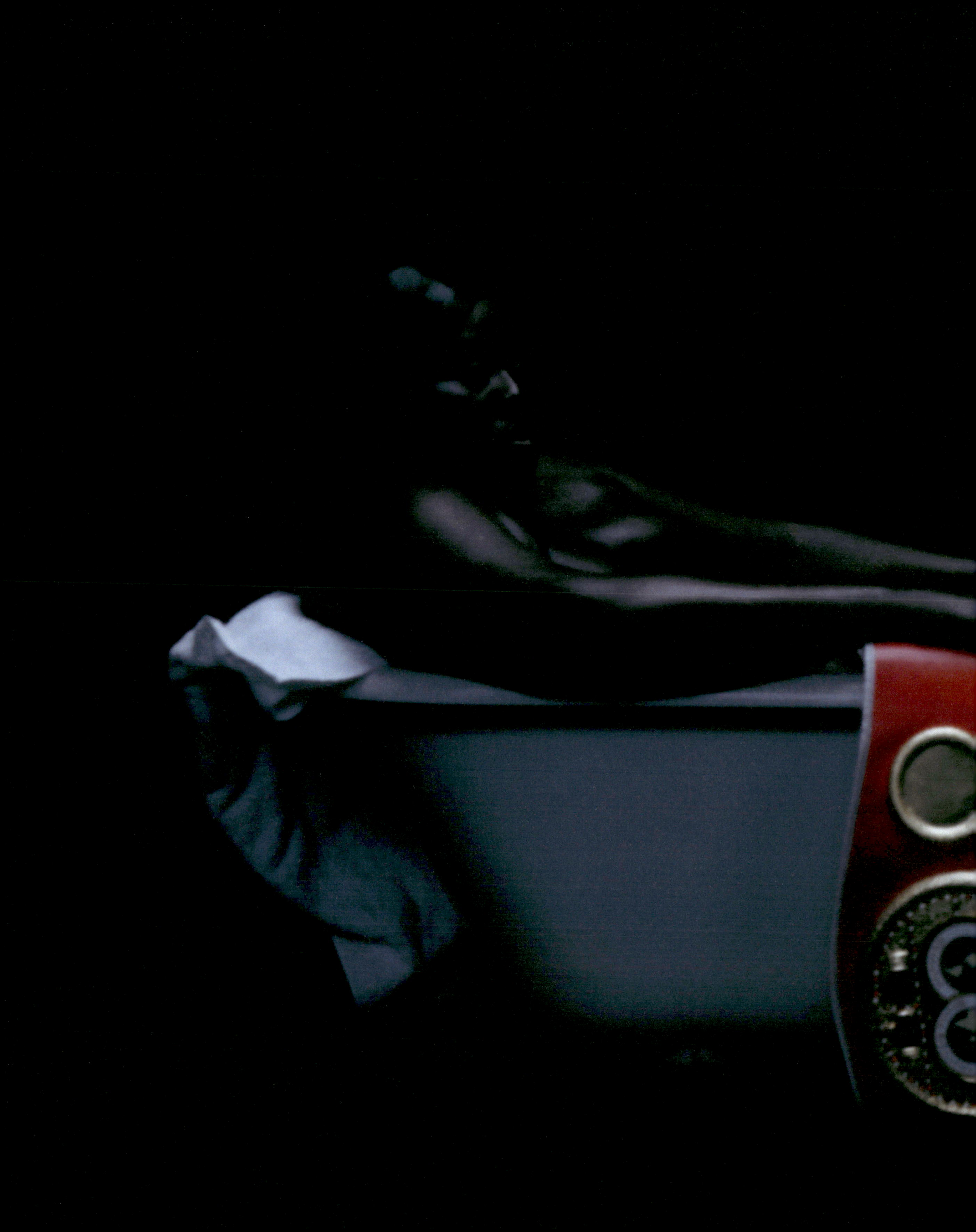

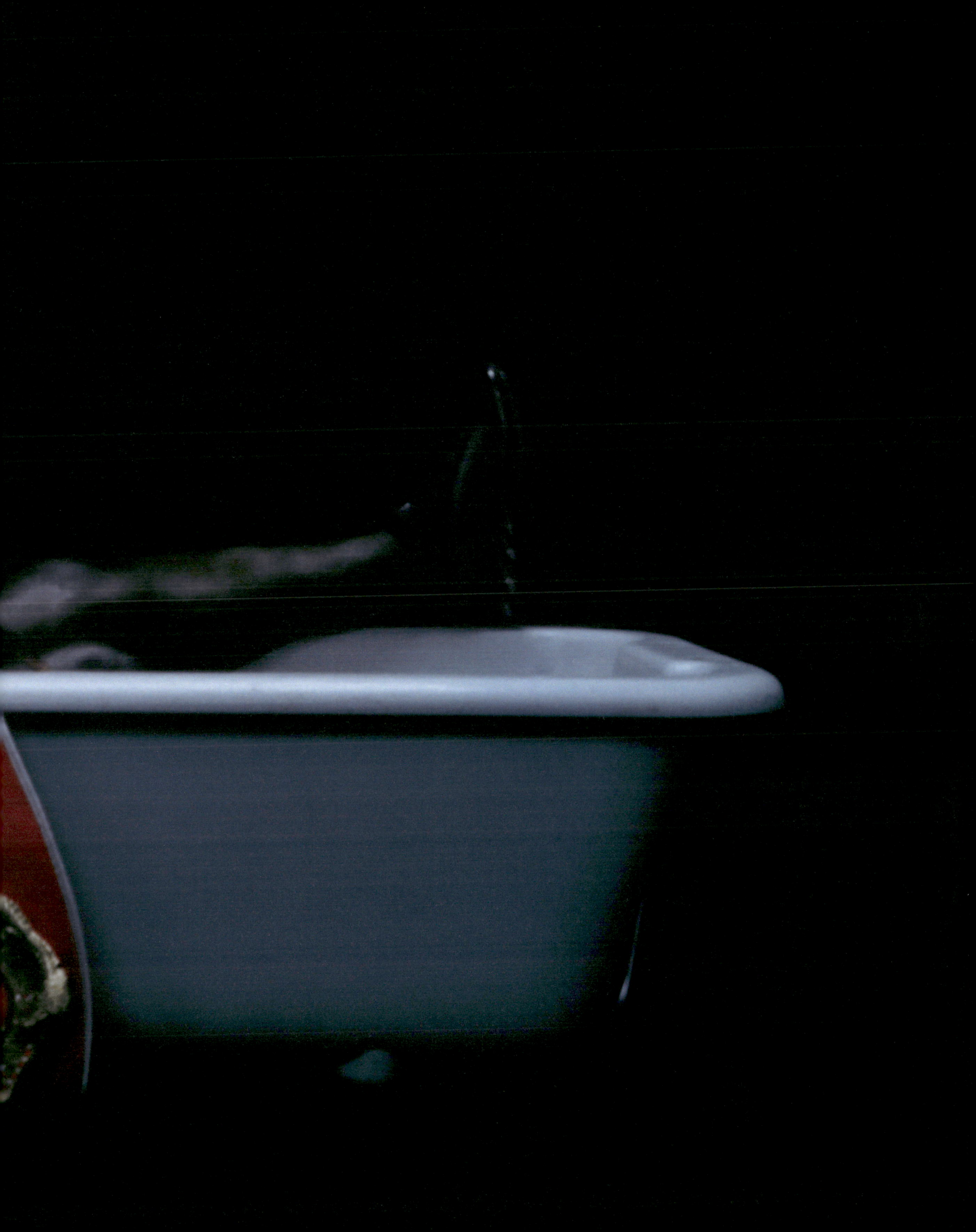

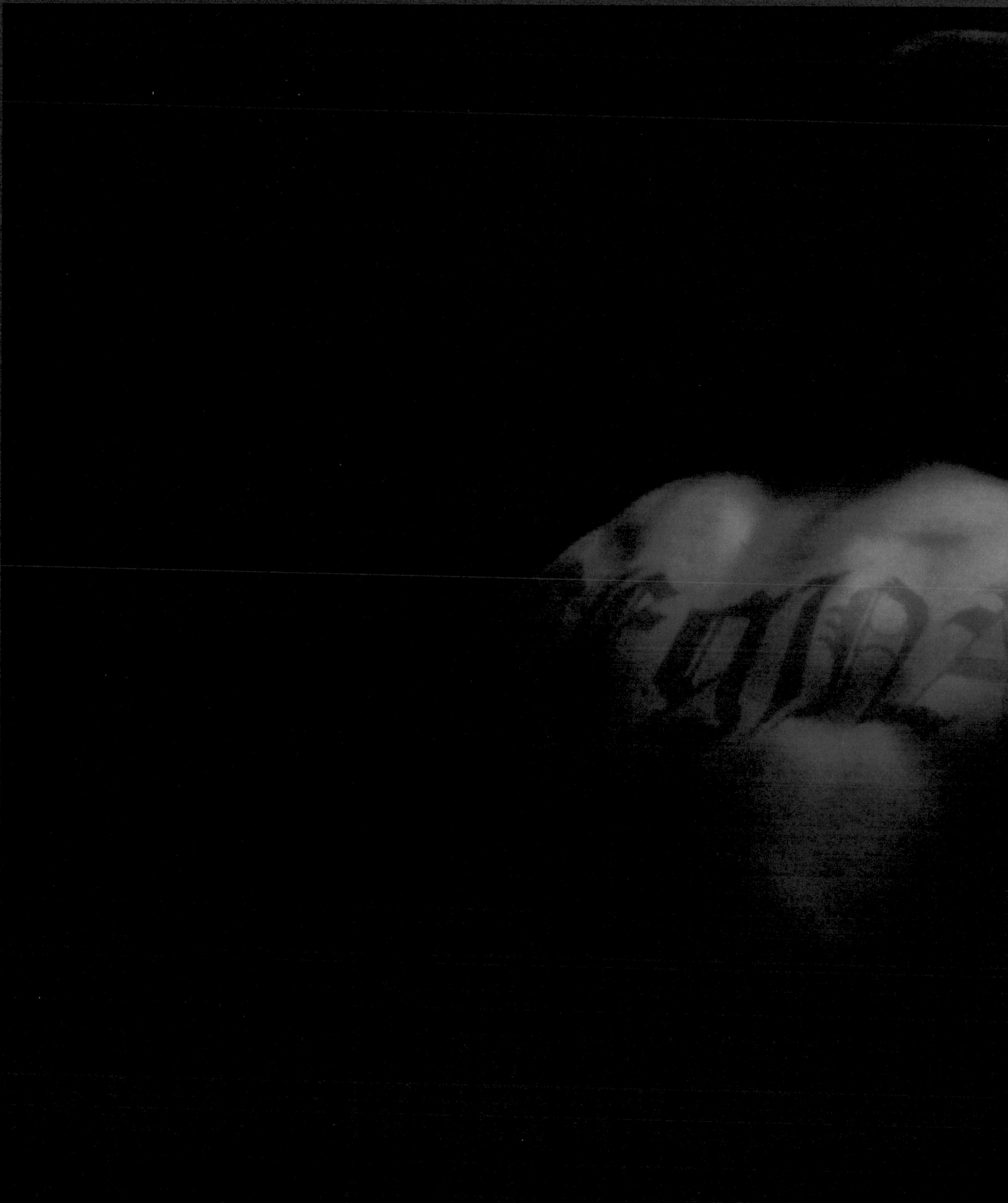

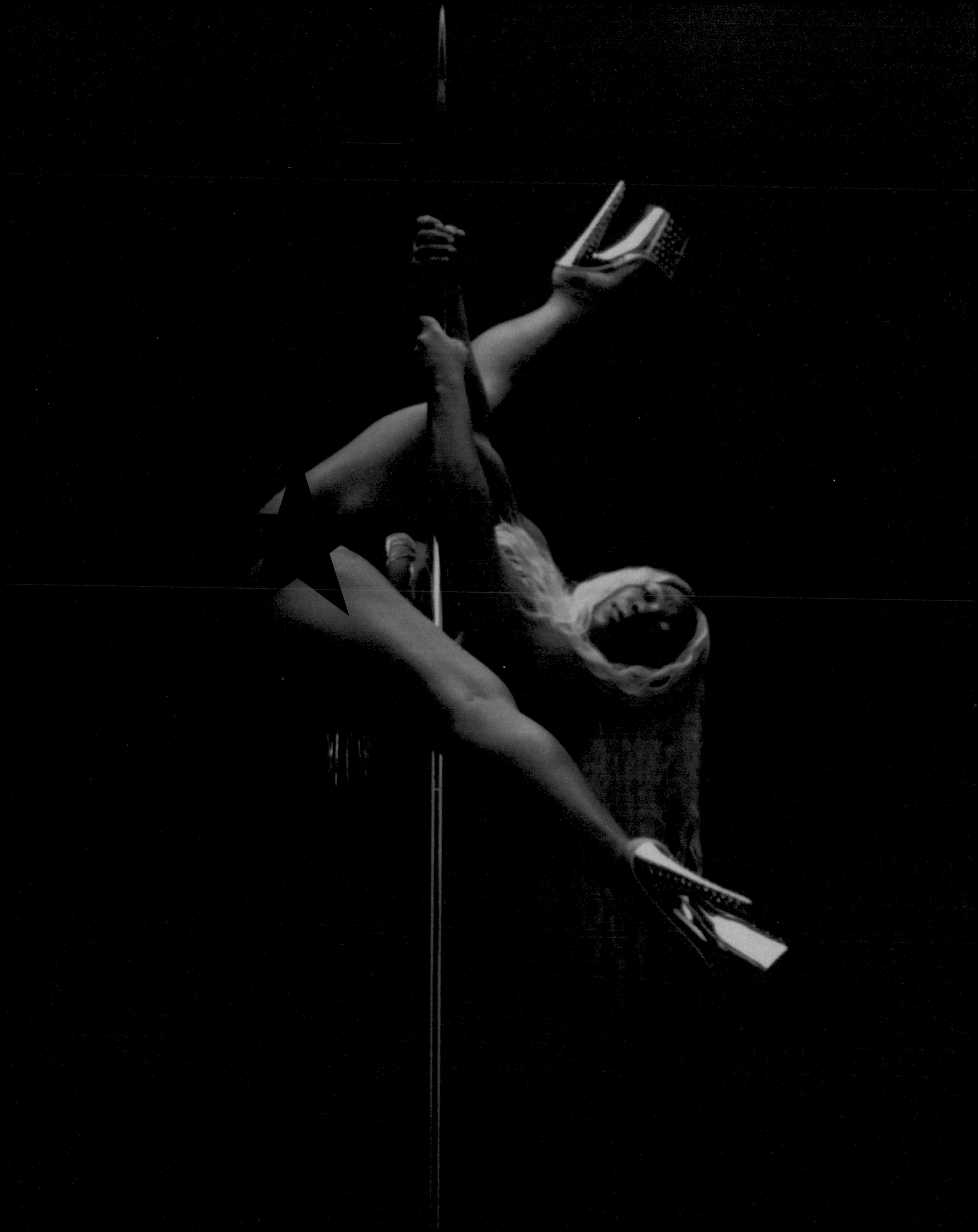

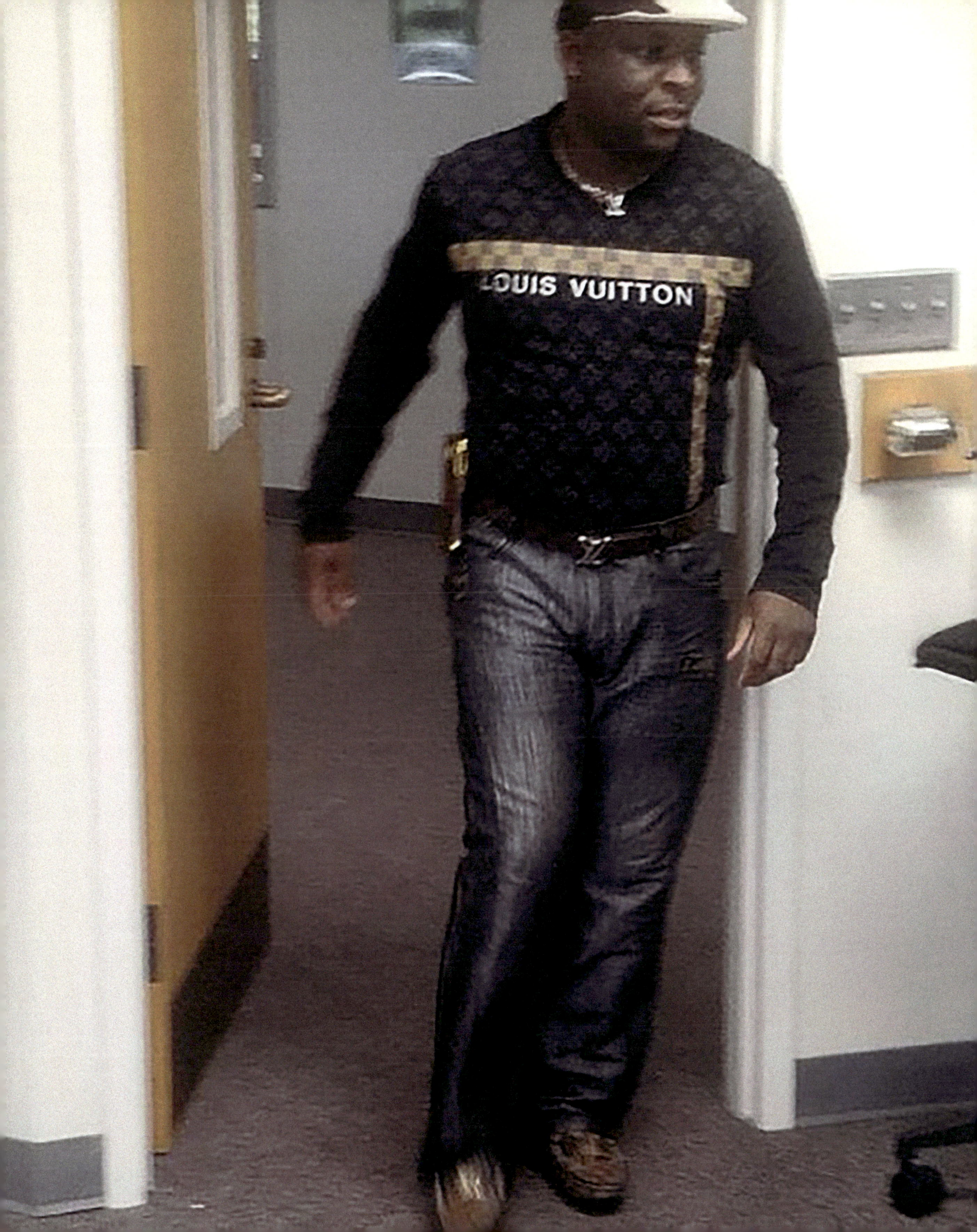
LOUIS VUITTON

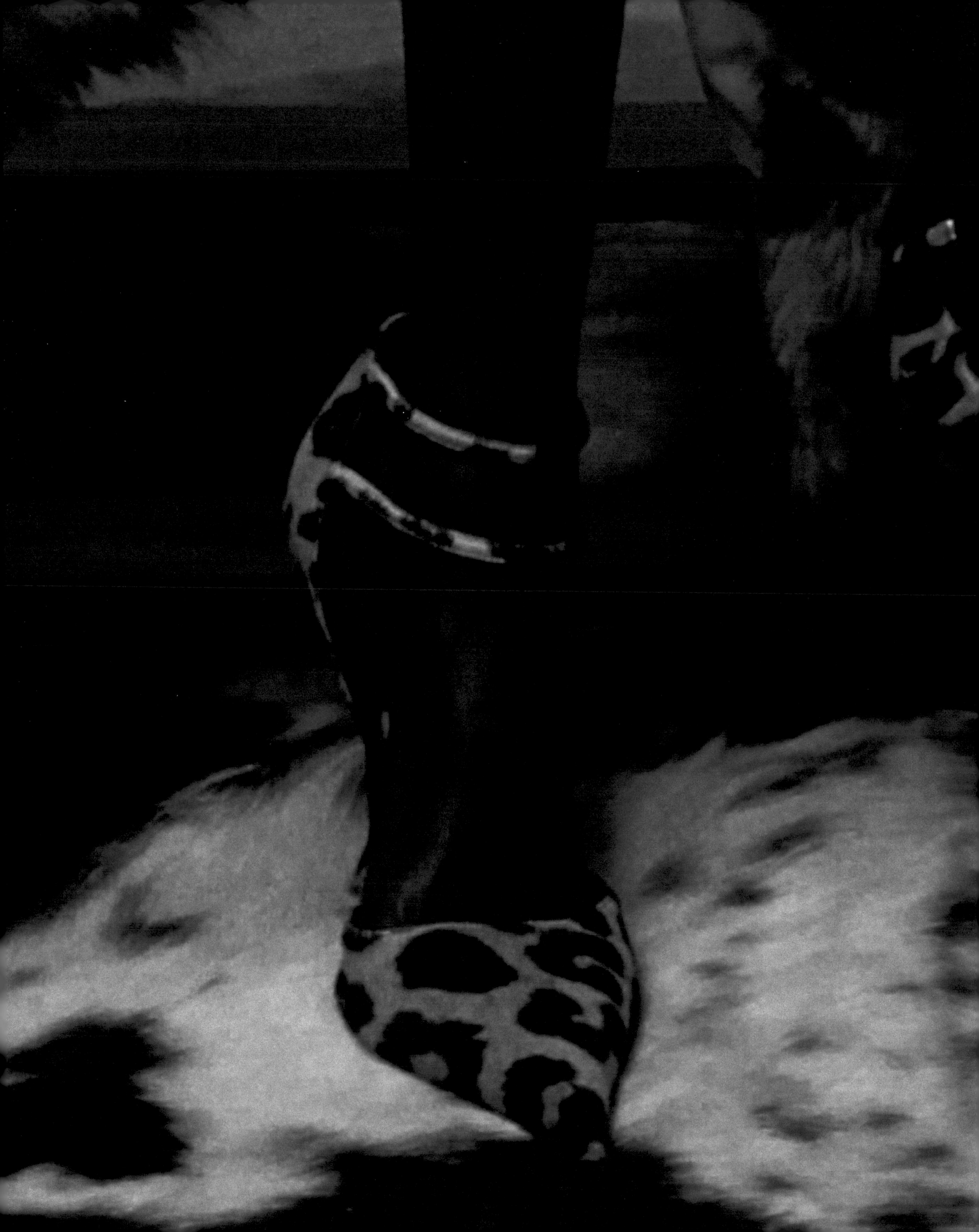

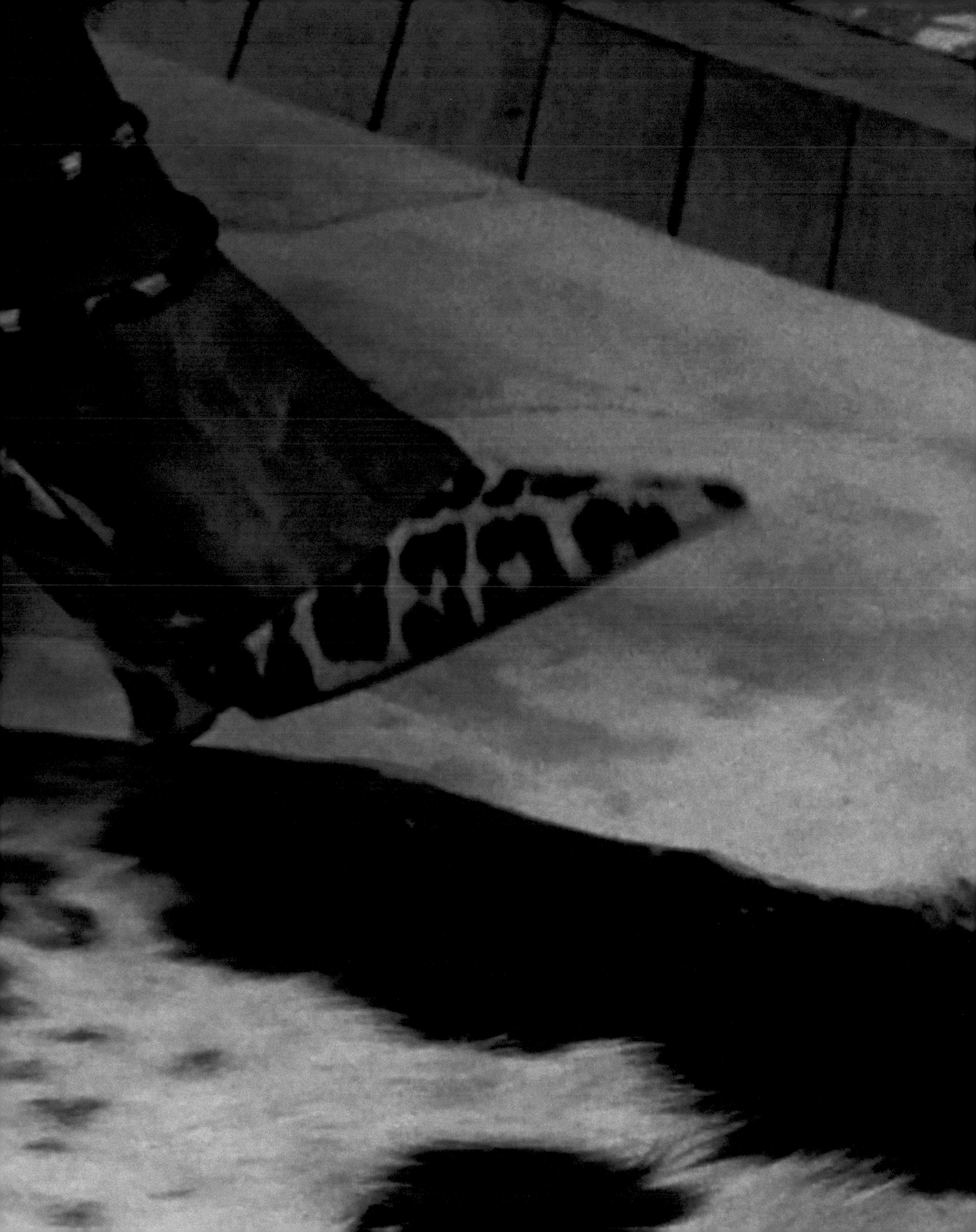

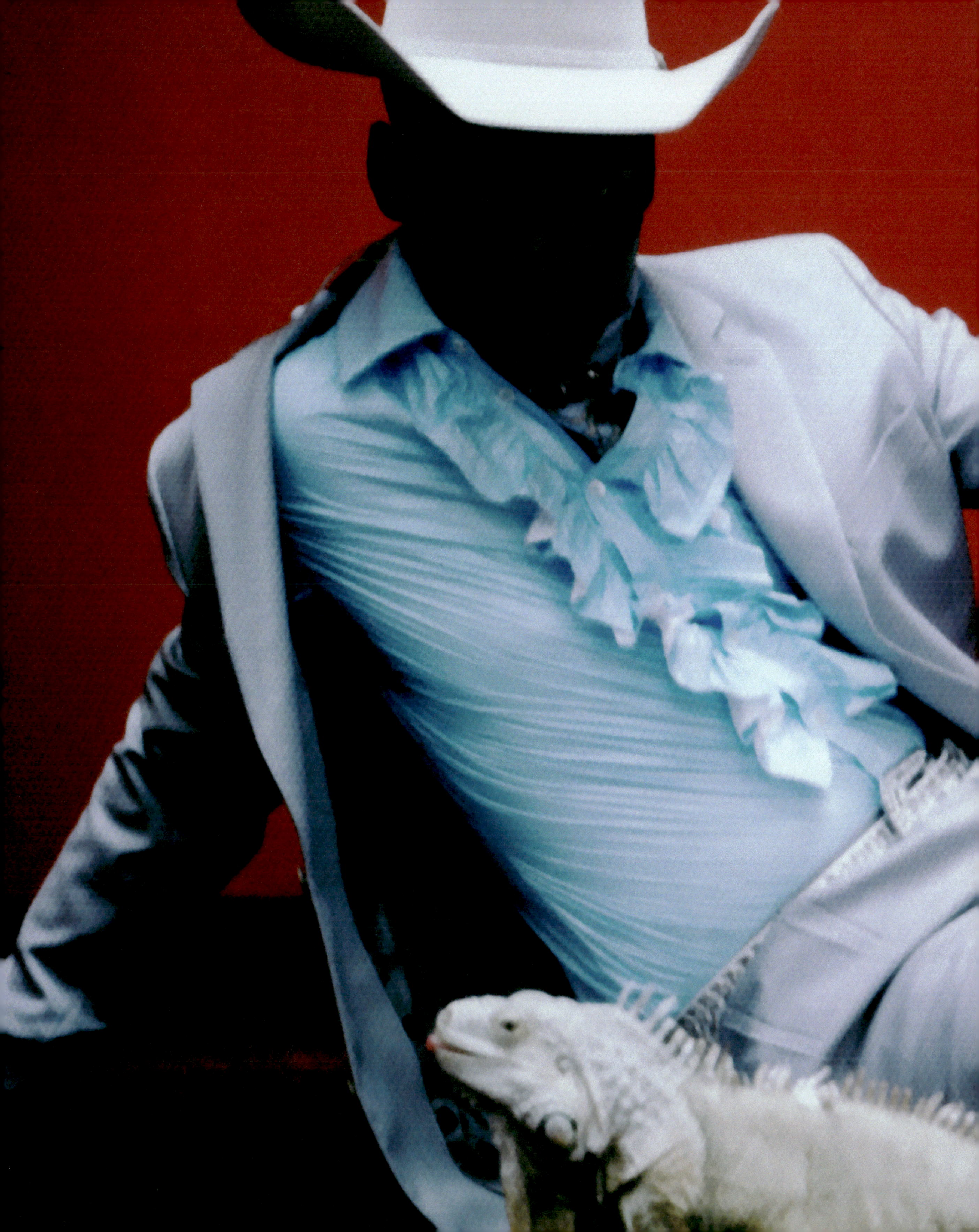

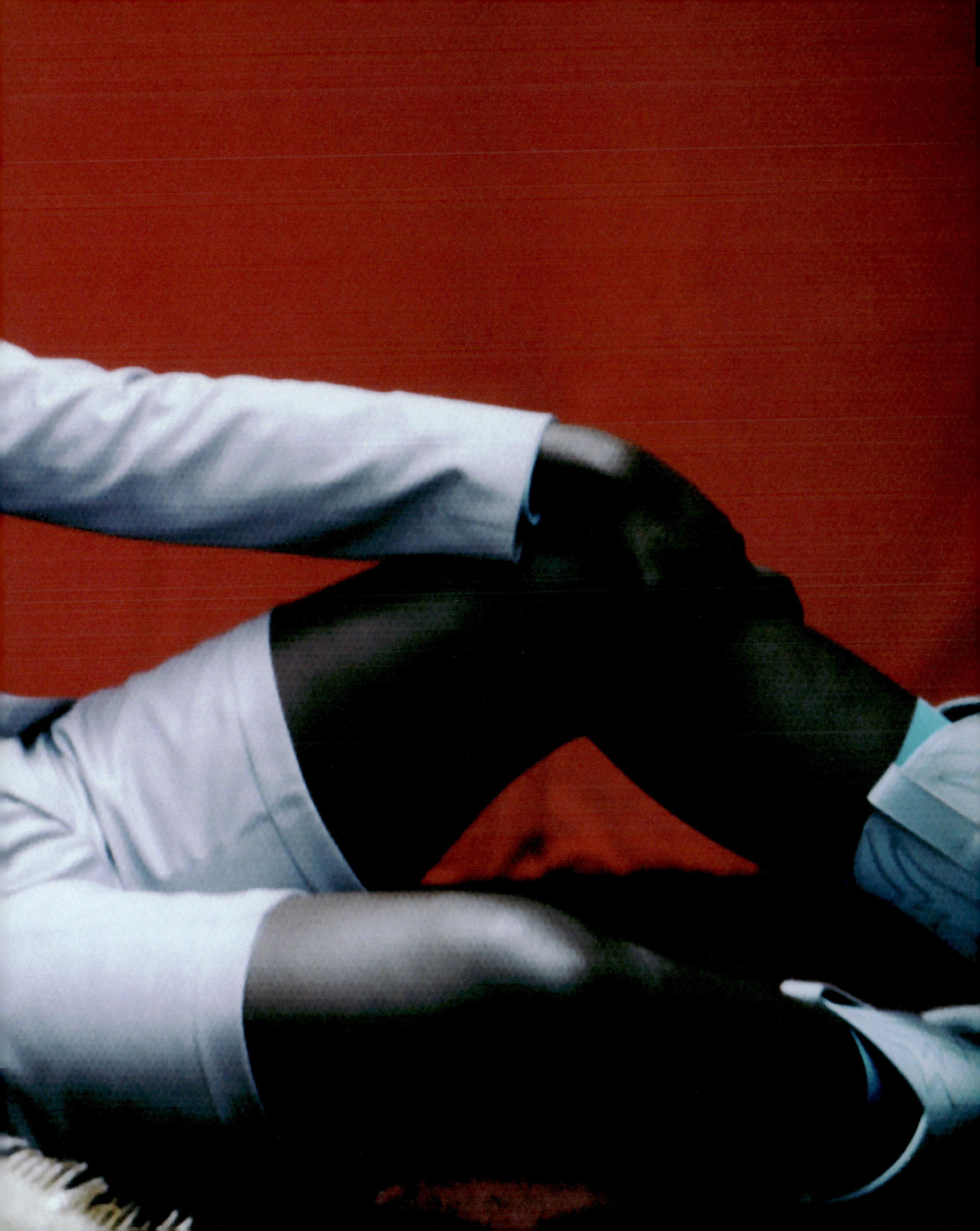

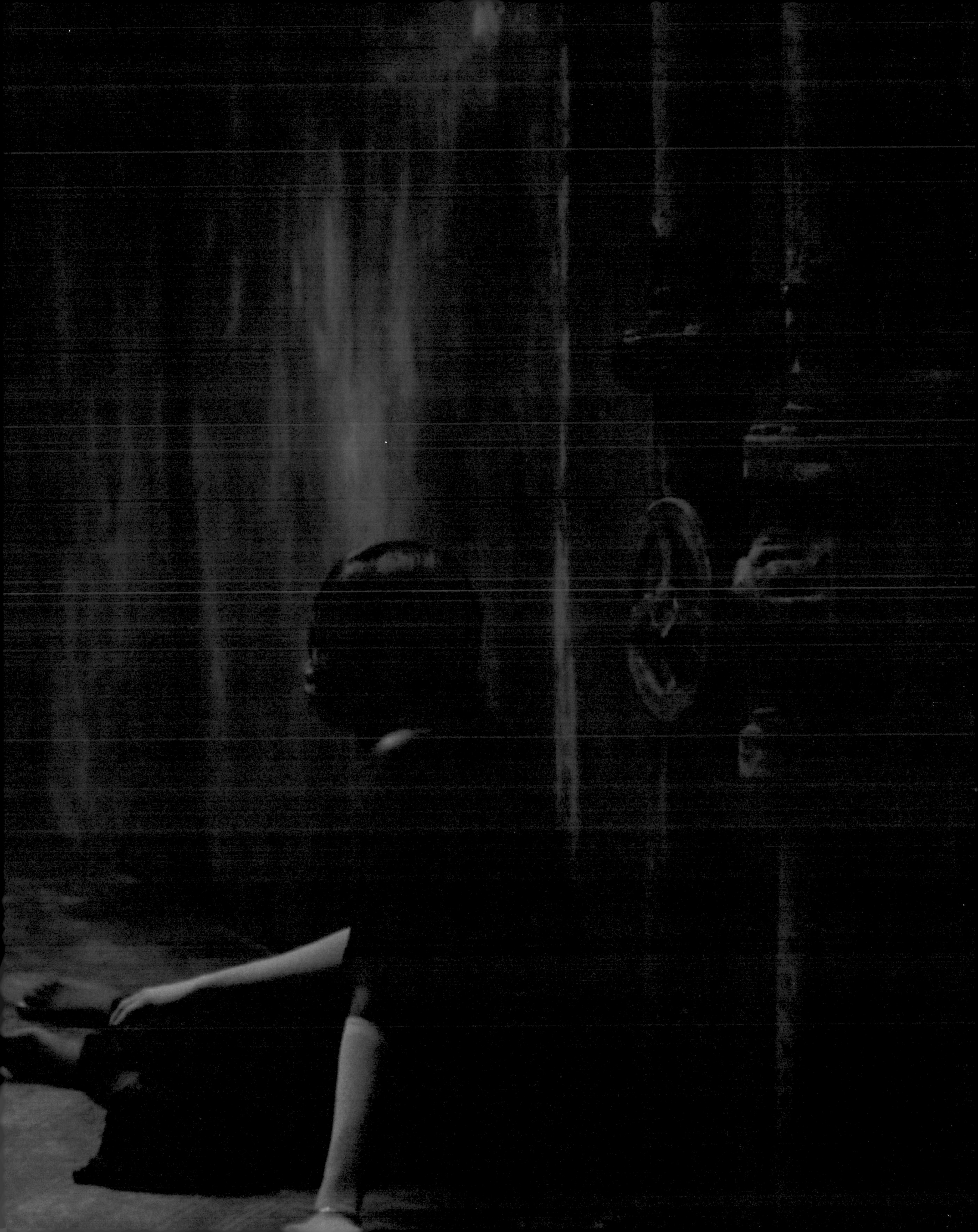

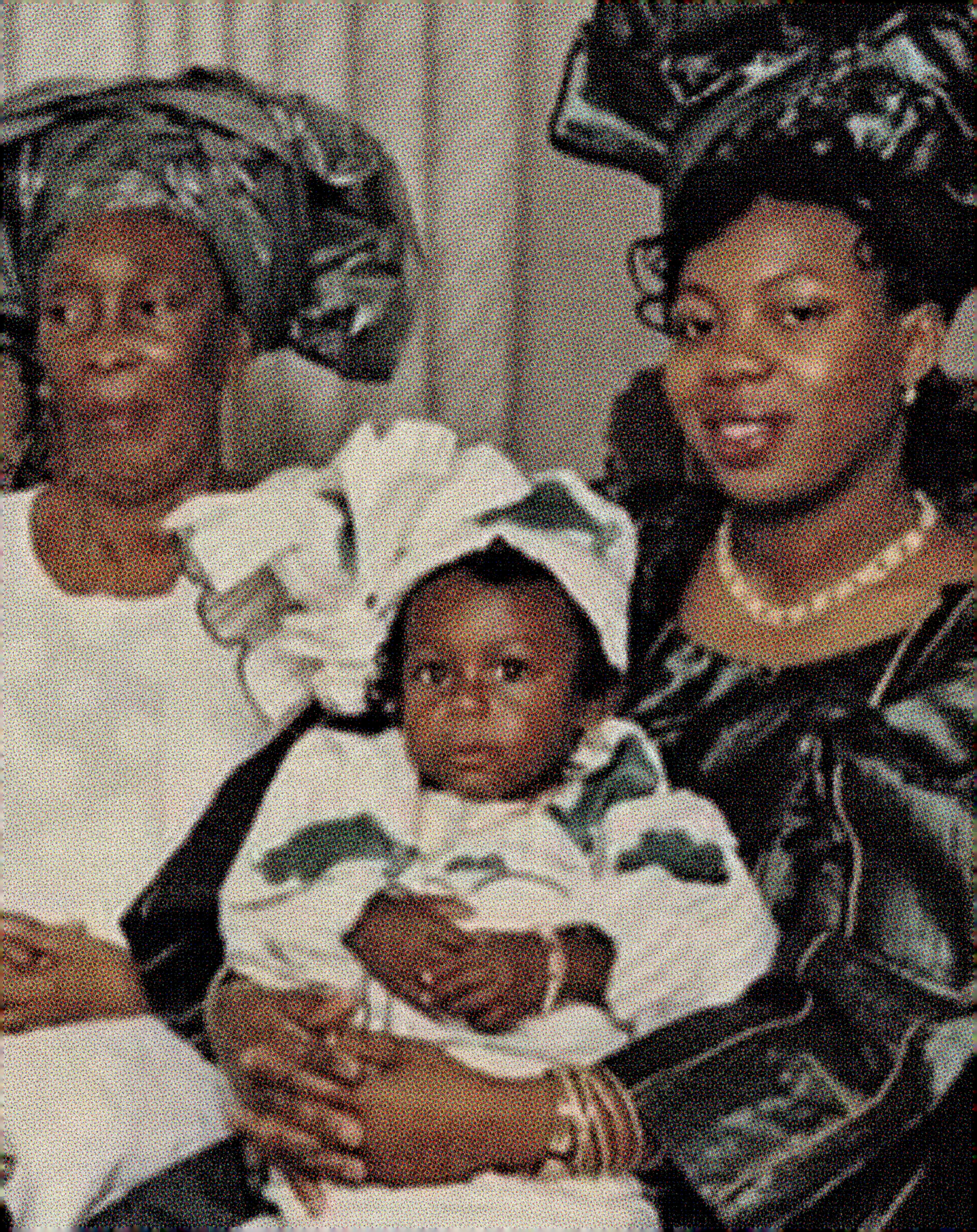

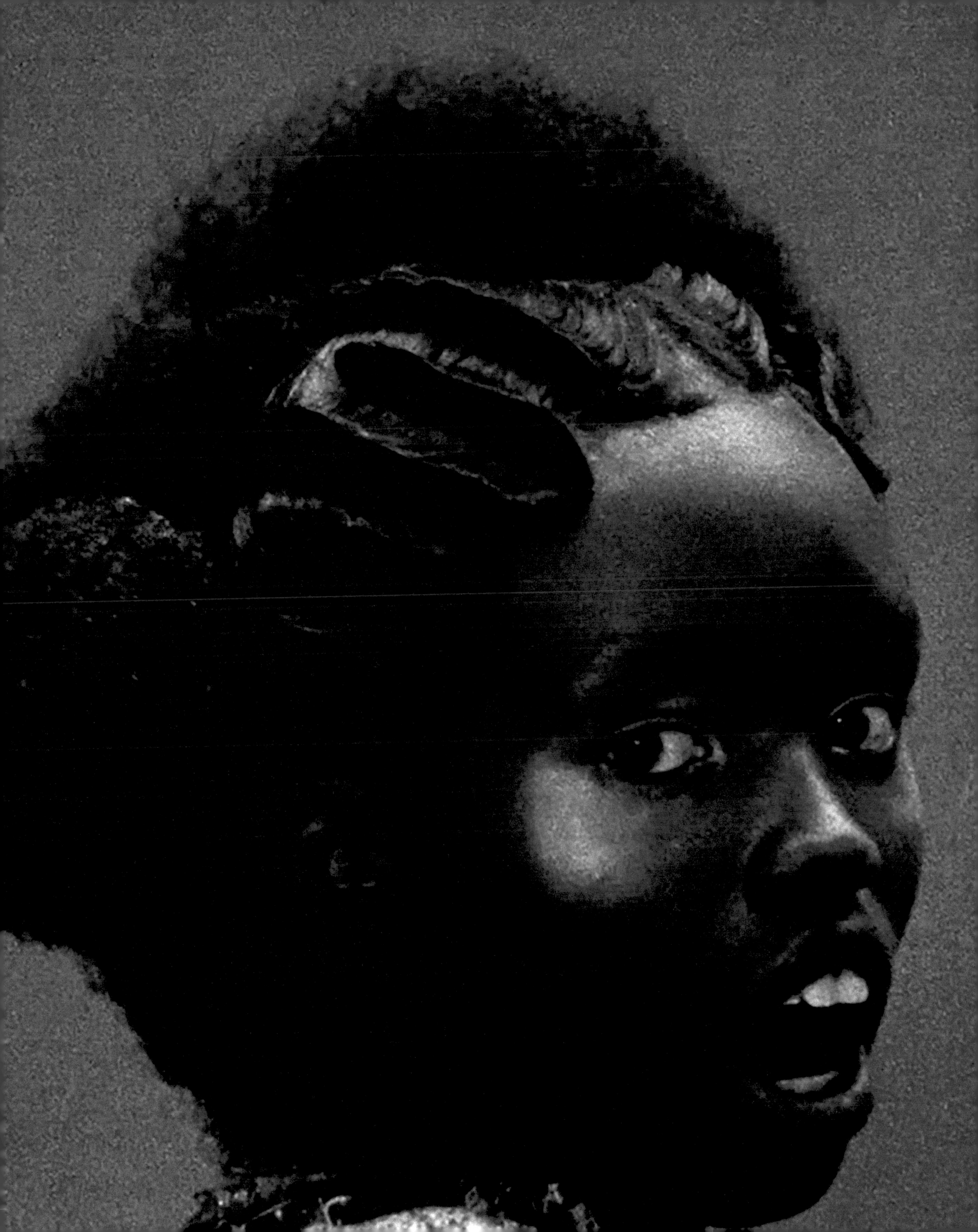

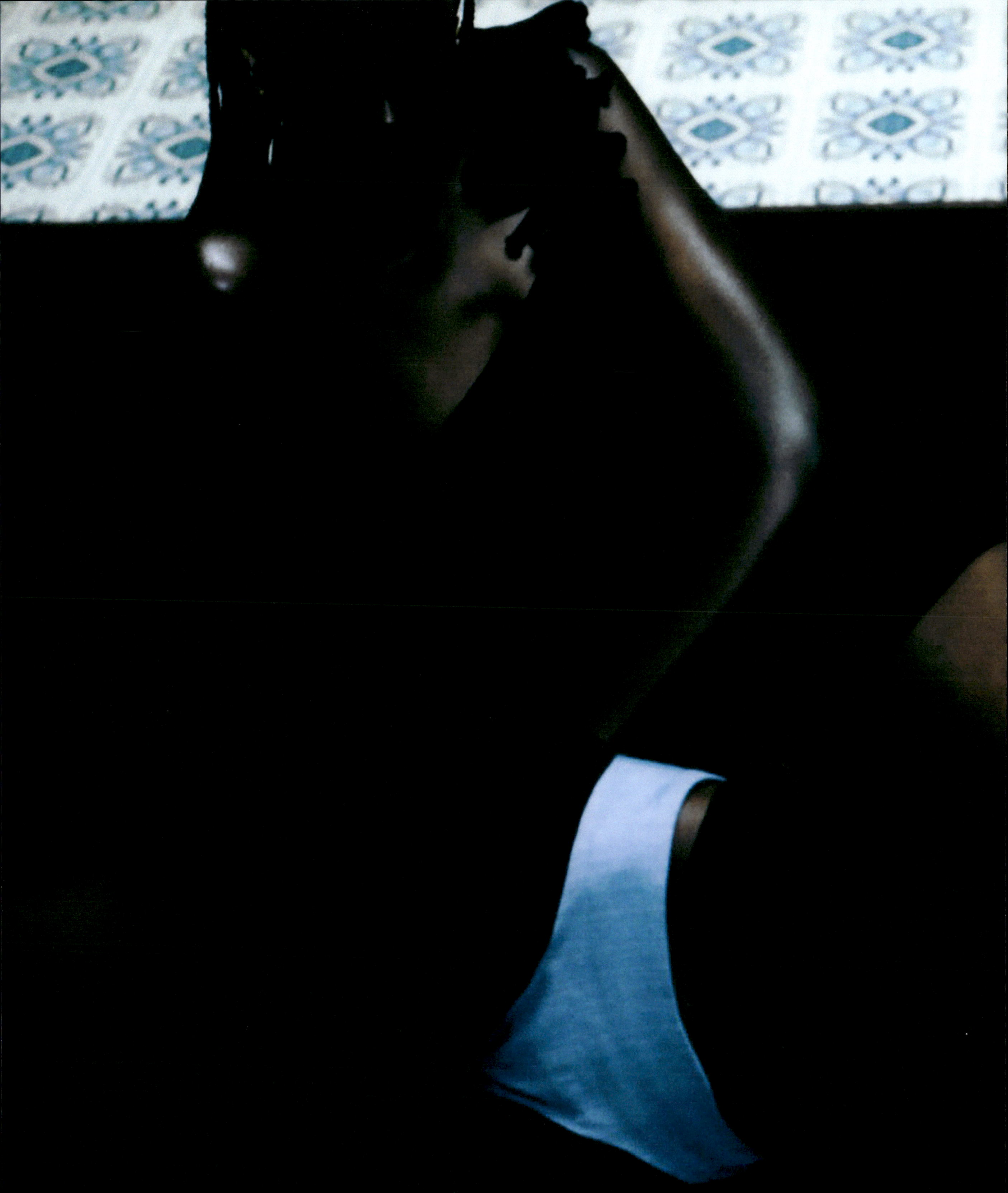

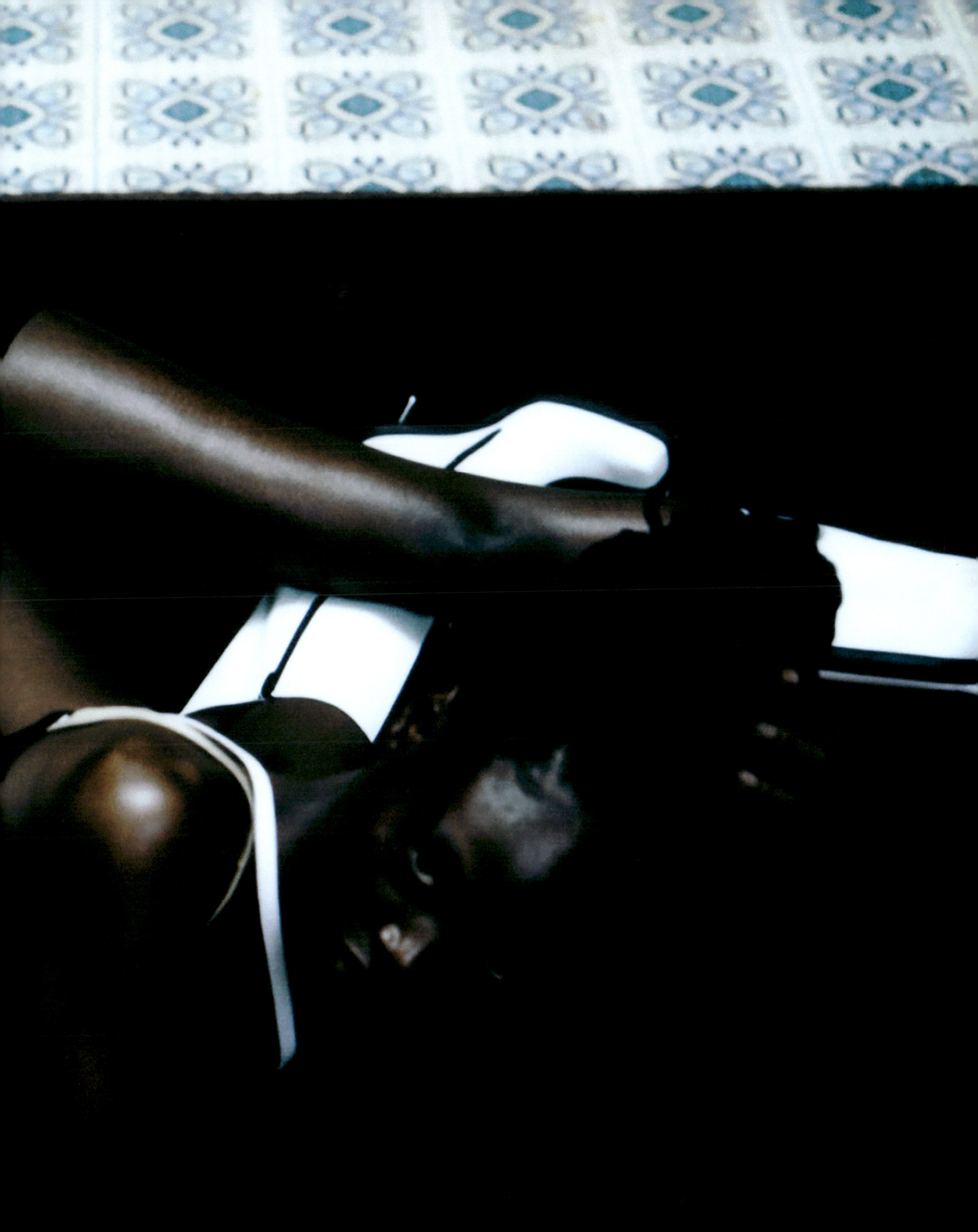

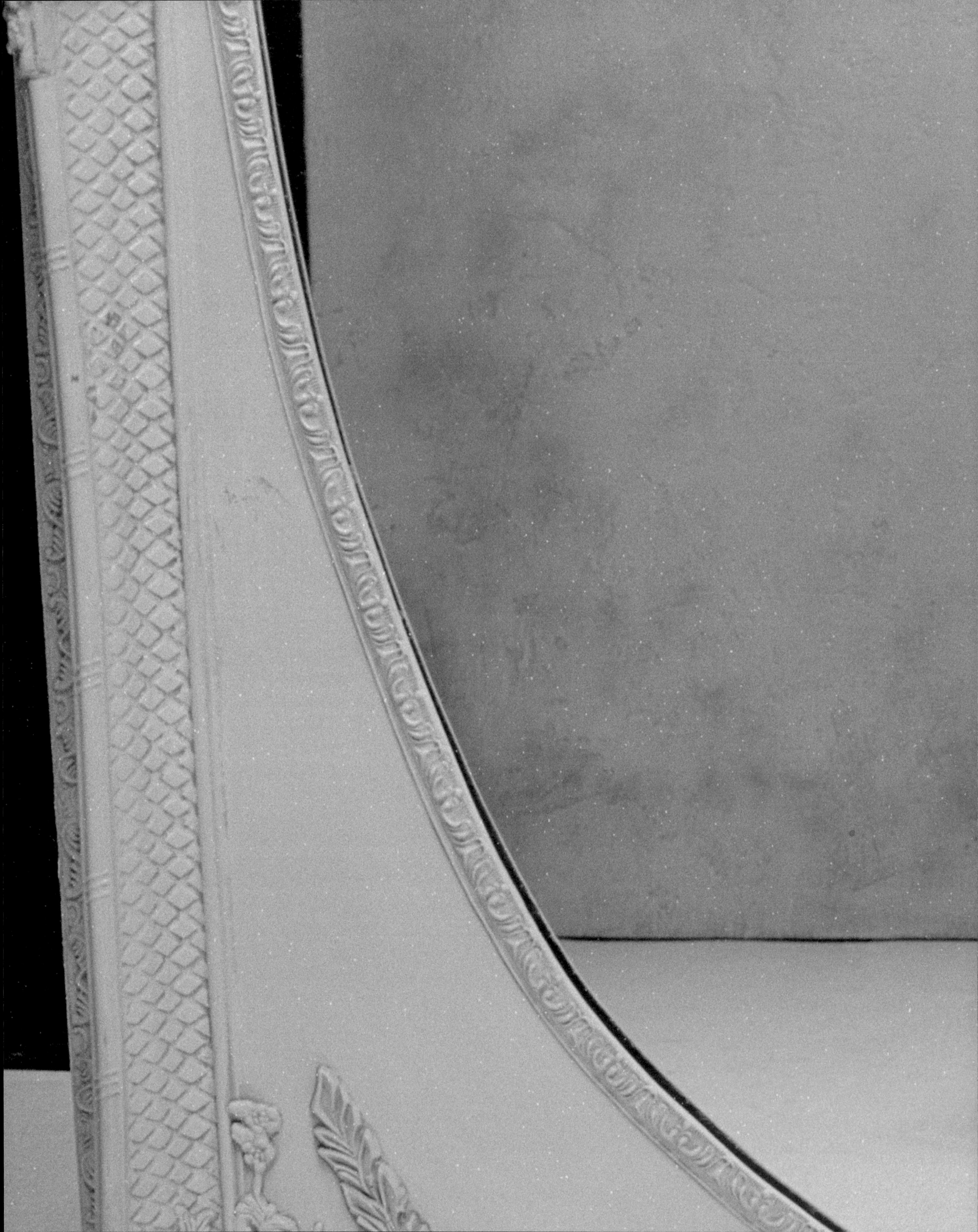

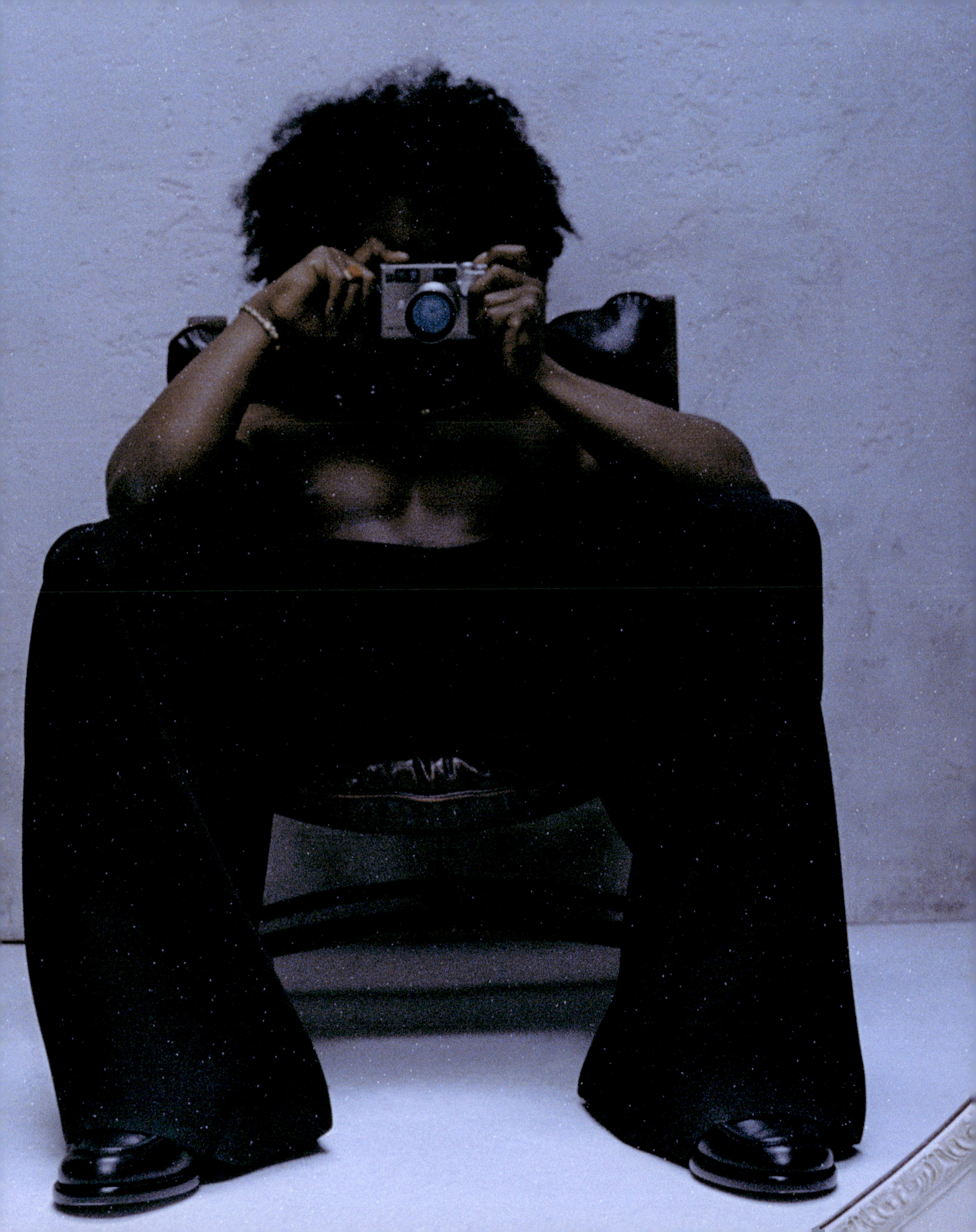

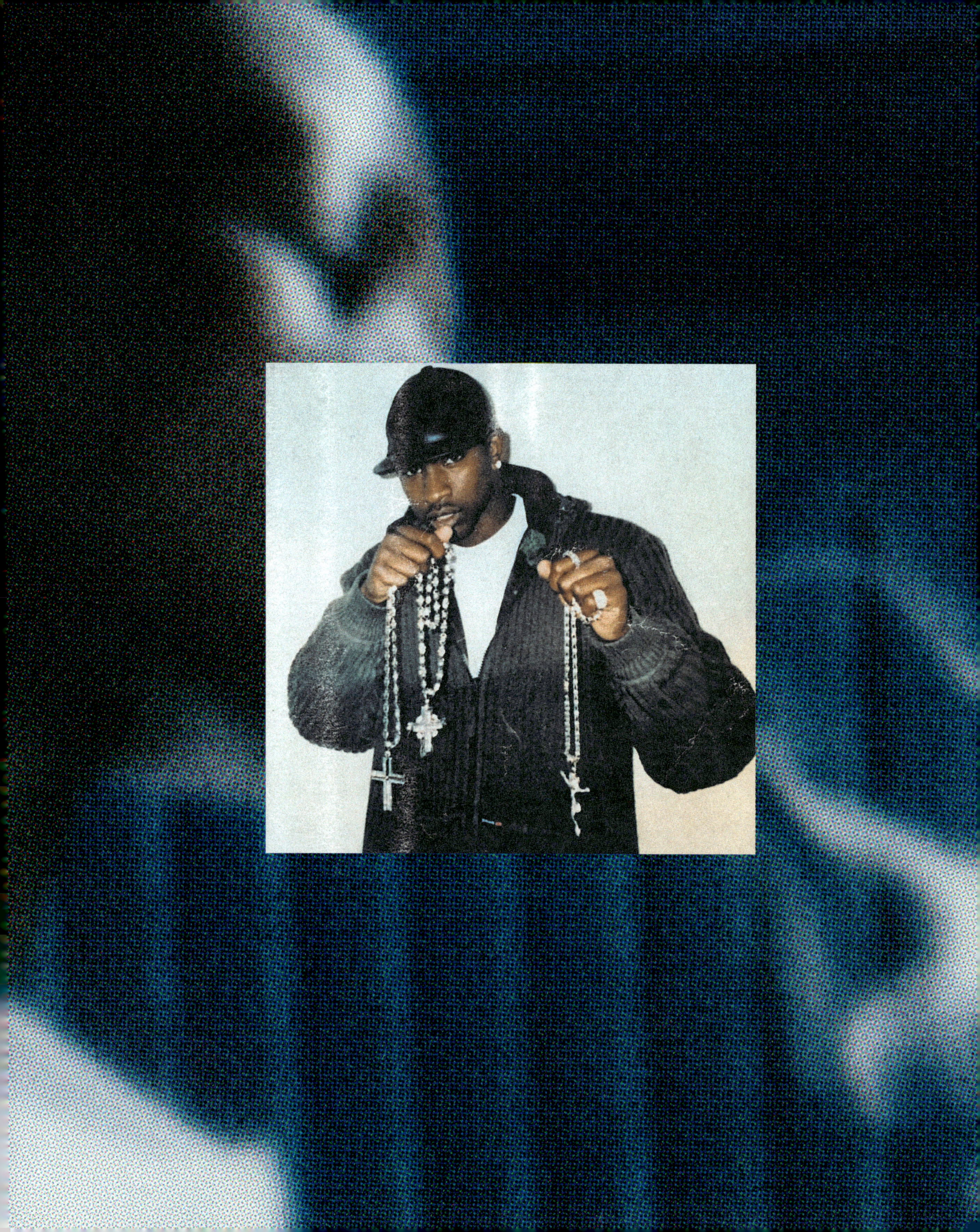

In Conversation: Skepta & Gabriel Moses
Interview by Katja Horvat

September, 2023. London.

K *(Katja Horvat)* Let's start at the beginning, how did it all start?

G *(Gabriel Moses)* My sister studied fashion, and she had ripped up pages from *Vogue* and *Dazed* on her walls. My PlayStation was in her bedroom. I would be playing it and subconsciously look at those images. It's crazy how childhood defines the way you see the world as an adult. She had lots of Nick Knight on her walls, so when I picked up a camera at the age of 18 I just naturally had a taste for that, as that, to me, was beautiful and familial. And then my family photos, my mum was big on dressing us all nice, looking aligned, taking family pictures. And one thing about Africans, everyone just has a natural steeze about them, the way people dress, the way they stand, and I always saw beauty in that, so it all kind of boiled up in me and now comes out in my photographs.

S *(Skepta)* My dad used to DJ, and whenever there would be a party my mum and a few of my aunties would go to a local seamstress to make them clothes from the same material. So when you went to a christening, a wedding, or a party, my mum, the aunties, and even we kids would all have the same attire, head wraps. So music and fashion were something I was just thrown into as a kid, unknowingly. But I realised later that I was almost being programmed.

K At what time did it click?

S With age. When I was younger, I almost shied away from being African. Growing up in London, people would make fun of you for being Nigerian or African in general. I almost lived a double life. But yeah, the older I got, the more I realised that when I am creating something, I am really looking at my identity first and my earliest influences.

G Same, it's almost like backtracking.

K I feel like as kids we really think we have something to prove, and usually that lies in going the exact opposite direction of the norm we know, just to prove a point.

G When I stepped into this industry, talking how I talk and dressing the way I do, I was like, what the hell is going on. It took me seeing, also I always say, "Seeing is believing," but yeah, took me seeing Virgil at Off-White, just working in the studio, and at the time I didn't even know his story, but I just saw this Black man heading his brand, his studio, and it made me way more comfortable to just be myself. And for that to be my introduction to fashion, it truly was a blessing.

K So when you put your work out there, whether an image or a song, whatever the medium may be, you are putting a piece of yourself, your personality, out there for people to see and know. How does that feel? Is it like, okay, the work is done, do whatever you want with it, or do you feel a little bit like. . .

S That one, the first thing you just said! It's out there, now people can do whatever they want with it. I used to judge what I did off the feedback, because good feedback of course is nice, and essentially you are putting your work out for people to enjoy, critique, or hate it. But I grew to understand that creation and success are subjective. Also, once we decide to put work out, that simply means we are done with it, we are finished. But funnily enough, the reaction is most of the time different from what you thought it was going to be. Also, I don't want the public to depict the success of something. This shit is personal! Our work is us, and the reaction should not be seen as a measure of something being successful/good or not.

K Anaïs Nin once said something along the lines of, "We don't see things as they are, we see them as we are." And with that in mind, all reactions are subjective, as you say, so therefore they should not determine the success of something, as one's reaction is merely just a reflection of one's mood in that exact moment, good or bad. Just wish the majority had their egos more in check to understand that their truth is not everyone else's truth.

G I second that! And because of everything you just said, I don't overthink the process, the reactions.

S You really own your identity, and I respect that greatly. I love how you also chose the slower approach and are creating images that last, whereas with social media and TikTok you could easily just create something banal and put it out and get that instant success. But to be consistent with your imagery and your identity the way you are, you've done it, and it's been amazing to see.

G Bruv, thank you! Also, Skep, I remember watching your #UnderdogPsychosis no.1 video, and you talking about how teachers misunderstood you. I related to that a lot as my parents would get called into the school all the time, but now schools are calling me back to do an assembly. It's like wait, you never facilitated my ideas back then, but now you want me to come and talk about my creativity?

K Same! I even lecture at university sometimes, but back then I put my mum through hell with all the school stuff. But just think how much trust our parents must have had in us. They are called to school for shit we did wrong, but somehow they still just let us be. I am sure we all had momentary consequences, but in the long run, we now all work in the creative industry, which I am sure all our parents would agree is not something they probably wanted us to do back in the day. Everyone just wants safety and stability for their kids, so when you combine school stuff with pursuing creativity, I mean . . .

S I mean. . . (Laughs) My parents, yeah, they really didn't want me to be a musician. If you asked them today, they would surely say they always supported me, but I think because my dad used to DJ, he was really into music; he had a kind of understanding, but even he would hypocritically still say to me, "Get a job so you can do your music on the side." But also, he is coming here at a different time. He came to London from Nigeria. The main thing for him was education for his kids, a good job, and taking the money back to the village. That's all he knew, but for me, I was born spoiled. I was born in the UK, but they installed that drive in me. My mum, if you see her, you would see she is relentless! Big mouth, talks loud, doesn't give a shit, would shout and curse anybody. And then my dad is very meticulous with anything he is creating, so I truly am a mixture of both of them. But they definitely wanted me to get a proper job, but now they are cool.

K They seem very cool with it! I remember back when you won the Mercury Prize for *Konnichiwa*, and your mum was with you on stage acting like she won it herself. (Laughs)

S Right!!!! (Laughs) Thank you for saying that! She was dancing up there, having the best time, like she won, for sure.

G Mums are just about excellence. Mine always said, whatever you choose to be, be the best at it. Even if it was a postman, she would be like, "Be the best postman there is." She showed me so much trust and gave me so much freedom to pursue what I envisioned. I even dropped out of school, took a year off, lived with her and off her, and she would just let me be.

S Freedom yes, but I am a bit of a spiritualist, so I always think we are these little computers that our parents designed and we are just running around doing, not exactly what they wanted to do, but what they started, in a weird way. We are the manifestation of whatever they were thinking and doing.

K I agree, there was nothing else to know. Our world was our home. Then it all just came down to whether we chose to utilise it or do the exact opposite.

G I would say that, yes, and people we chose to look up to. Skep, who were some of your role models growing up? Was there a blueprint?

S Growing up, Bob Marley, and later on Fela Kuti. First, they were musicians, and then also just how they both moved in the space they were occupying. They were so aware of what was going on but they were not being aggressive about it. Their art was their medium, they said what they had to say through their work, but they were so soft in their ways that they were cutting through.

K They had the world singing their lyrics word by word with many not even realising how socio-politically charged it all was. They got into everyone's subconsciousness!

S Exactly! That's hard!

G I also always loved Nina Simone and Lauryn Hill. I love extremely talented people who don't care about the industry.

S But oftentimes with these extreme talents and going against the industry you get someone who destroys themself for the message. Anger gets them, and when you get angry is when you lose! If life were a computer game, anger, when you press that button, is like jumping off the ledge into a fire, because you want to start the game again. Anger has never won or done anything for anyone. So with people like Marley, people like Fela, people like Virgil, they were still able to put the messages through without succumbing to the anger.

K But also, each of them is a very specific type of artist. These people had a goal before they had a product, a song. They had a message, and then they found and created the way to get that message out to the world. I feel like they were hyper-aware of the environment they were in, and also extremely intelligent, or just emotionally and socially mature. They moved in a very particular and precise way!

G The achievers! I am also football obsessed, so seeing, let's say, Kylian Mbappé do what he does, and we are the same age, I would be amazed how even as just a yute he would be performing on the level he was. Or Messi as well. Look at what he has been doing consistently. I want to achieve that! I want someone to see Gabriel Moses and say he has done it again and again and again.

S But all the people you're naming, yeah they got the talent, but do you actually think what's getting them where they are is talent? It's who they are as people. It's how they deal with things. Their will and how they go about things is what makes them great. They are unfazed by the environment and what people are saying. That's the game I play nowadays too. I am just very aware of who I am letting in and how I react to things. I don't want to be completely emotionally unavailable, but I'm very cautious about who and what I let affect my day to day. Obviously, I care about people's emotions and life is about balance, but I am just trying to be really mindful of who I let in, every day!

G 100%! Talent plus personality, can't just be one.

K Accessibility, fame, and talent are a tricky combination. You get famous for your talent and all this, by default, comes also with accessibility to millions of people who all have an opinion and think they know you based on what they have chosen to see and believe from the media. But anyhow, that is a whole different conversation. Let's maybe hit a few Freudian ones now, so we can all actually get to know you, but just a little bit.

So. . . What do you fear?

G Being my own worst enemy. Finding myself working against myself.

S I fear that art is a curse. I fear that I will die and in the end realise that creating things is evil. That we are all just trying to play God! For example, sometimes I would just sit there, create a melody out of nowhere, and I would be tripping, thinking where is that coming from? Why am I able to do that? And then I put it out, that trip goes everywhere, people follow it, and I am just like wait, should it even be like this? But yeah, I can handle a lot of things, but the fear that our creation is a curse gets me sometimes.

K Losing your body or losing your mind?

G Body!

S Body, for sure!

K If you could pick a song that would serve as a soundtrack to your life, which would it be?

S I hate that I am saying this because he stormed the capitol, but John Maus, "I'm Only Human."

G "Smile" by Nat King Cole.

K Favourite memory?

G Probably when I made my first film. The feeling was unmatched, but more in a sense, this is just the start and it felt like I had just given myself a purpose. Because as a kid, I would, of course, have an identity crisis not knowing what I wanted to be, and when I made my first film, it all made sense.

K Gabs, you are still going to have a few of those [identity crises], it comes with age. I feel like I have one every year. (Laughs)

S She's right. (Laughs)

K Yeah, it's coming. Anyhow, but even in a crisis, do you ever fistbump yourself? (Laughs)

G Oh, for sure. I'm my biggest hater but I still gas myself up more than anyone.

S Same, man! Biggest hater but I would gas myself up like there is no tomorrow. But you have to! Sometimes I would be gassing myself up, and I would think, stop that! (Laughs) Anyhow, what was the question again?

K Favourite memory?

S Seeing my kids being born, by far!

K Favourite colour?

S Green.

G Klein Blue.

K Favourite film?

S *Natural Born Killers.*

G *Prince of Egypt.*

K Lastly, hit me with some words of wisdom...

G Everything starts somewhere.

S It is exactly what you say it is.

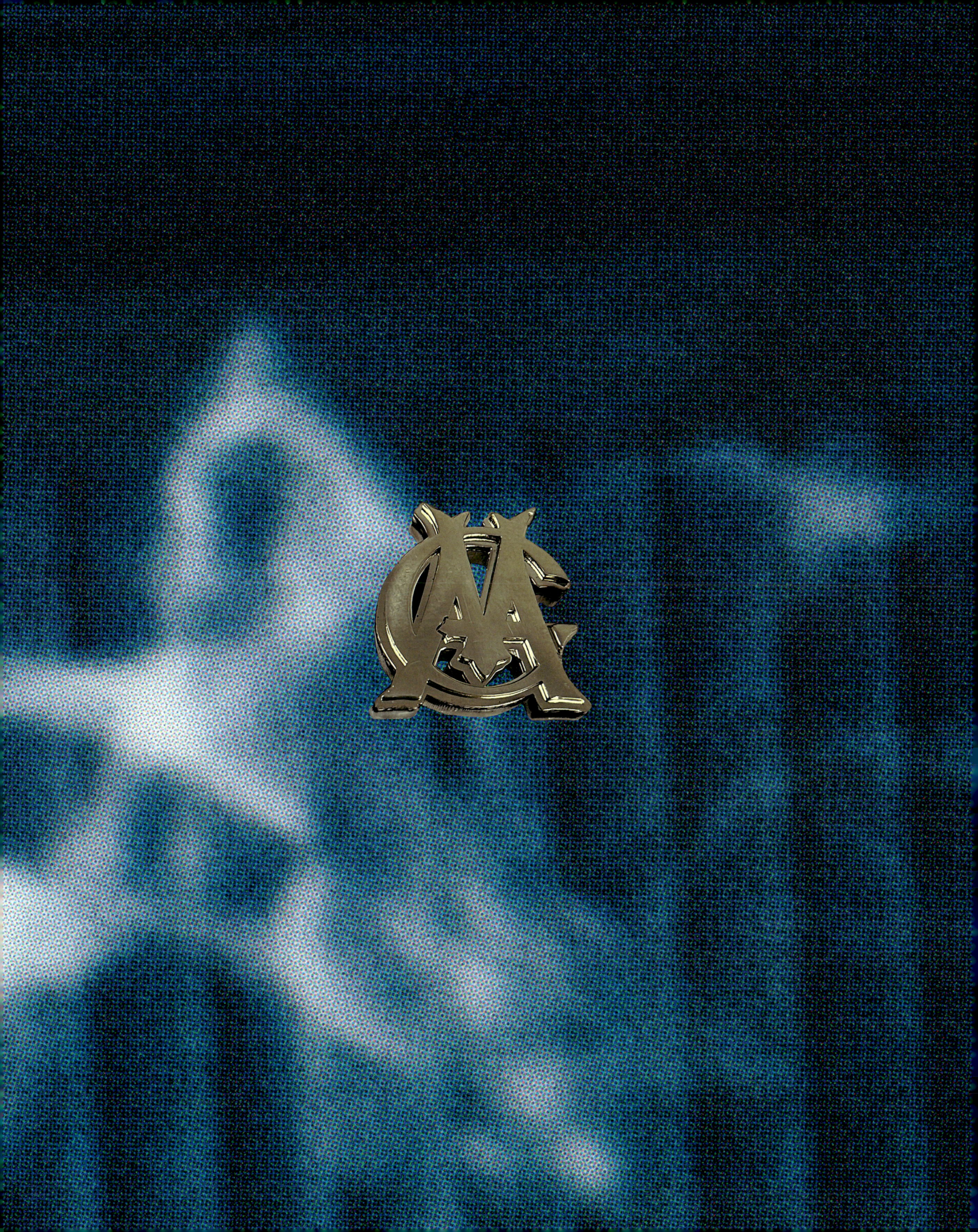

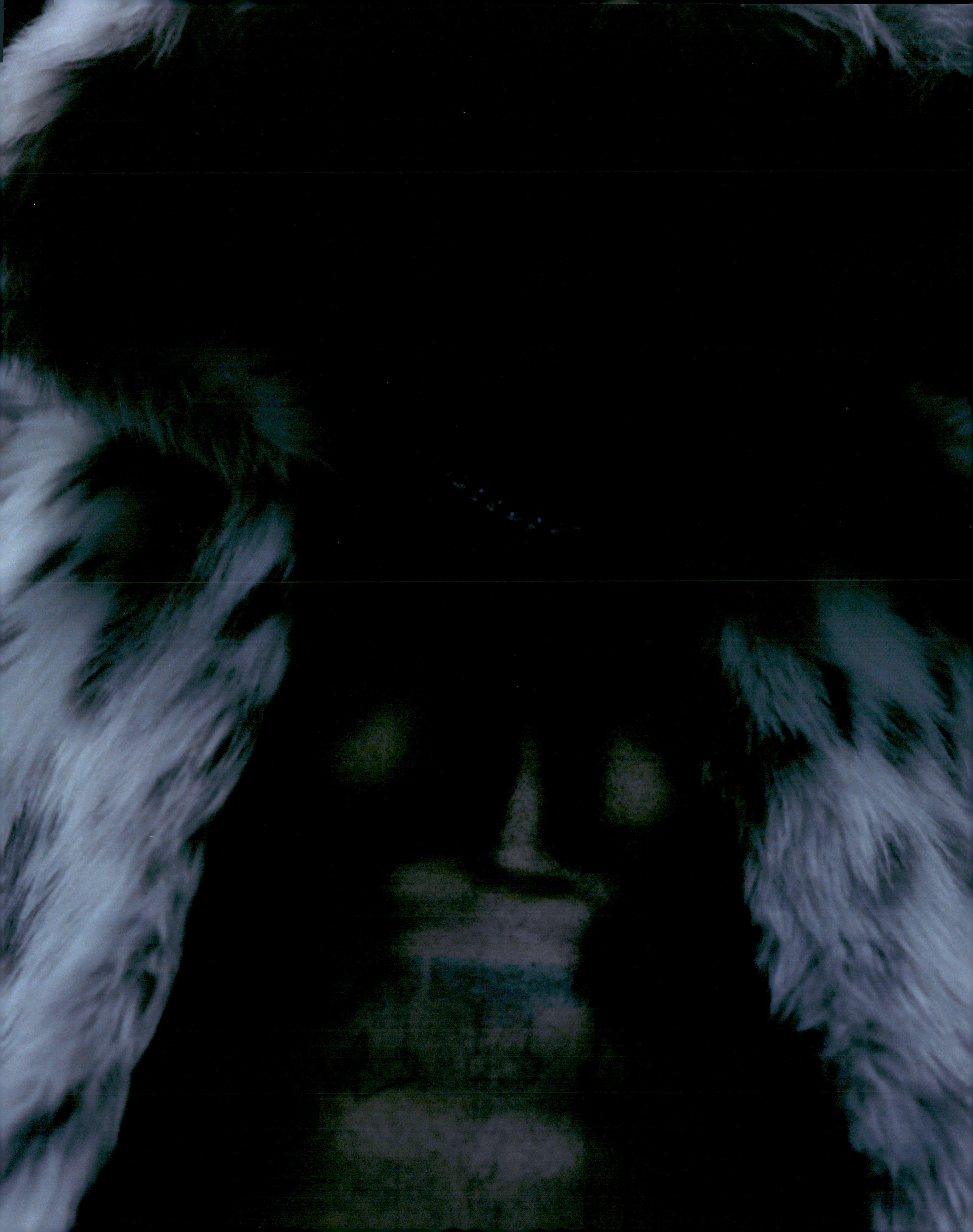

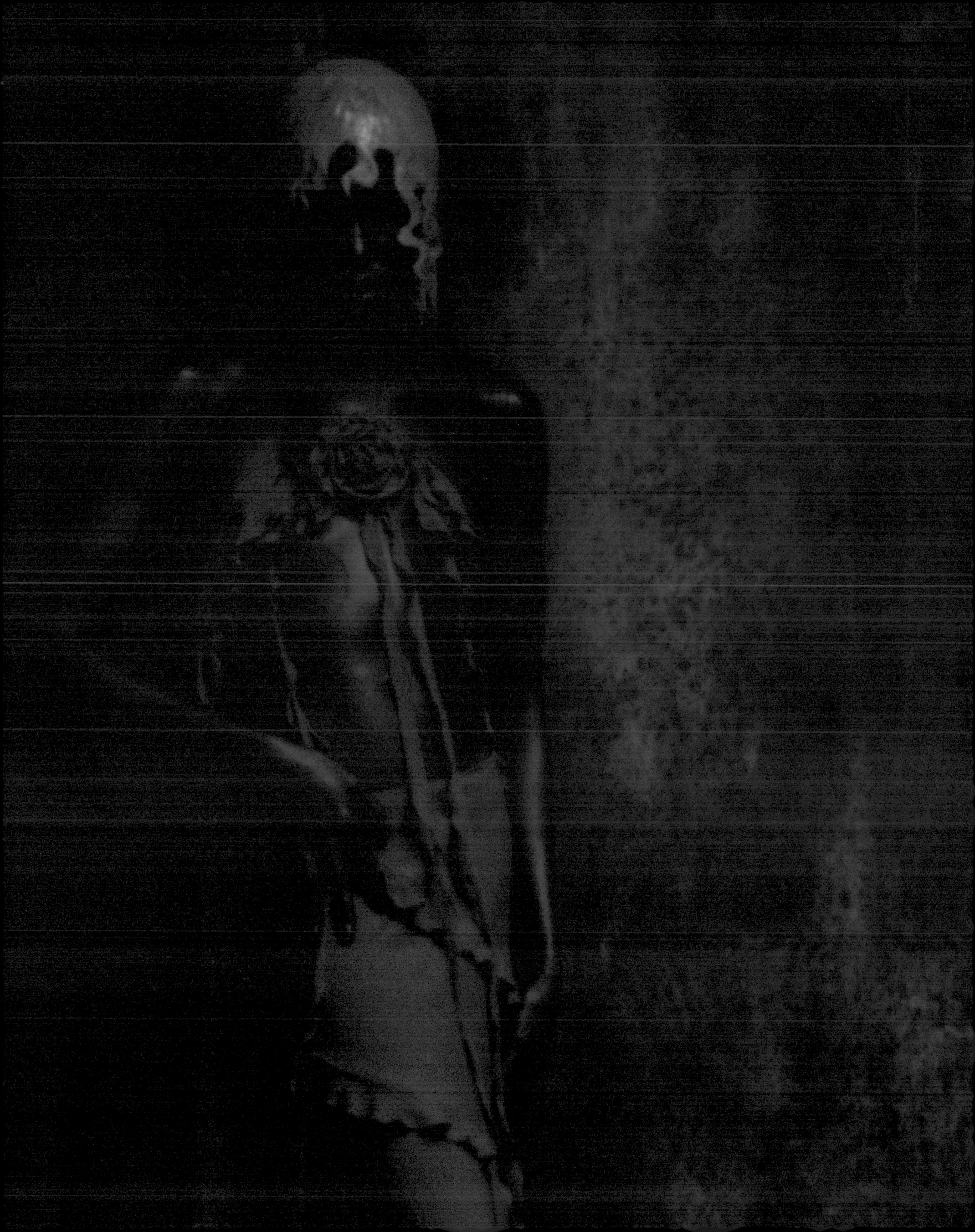

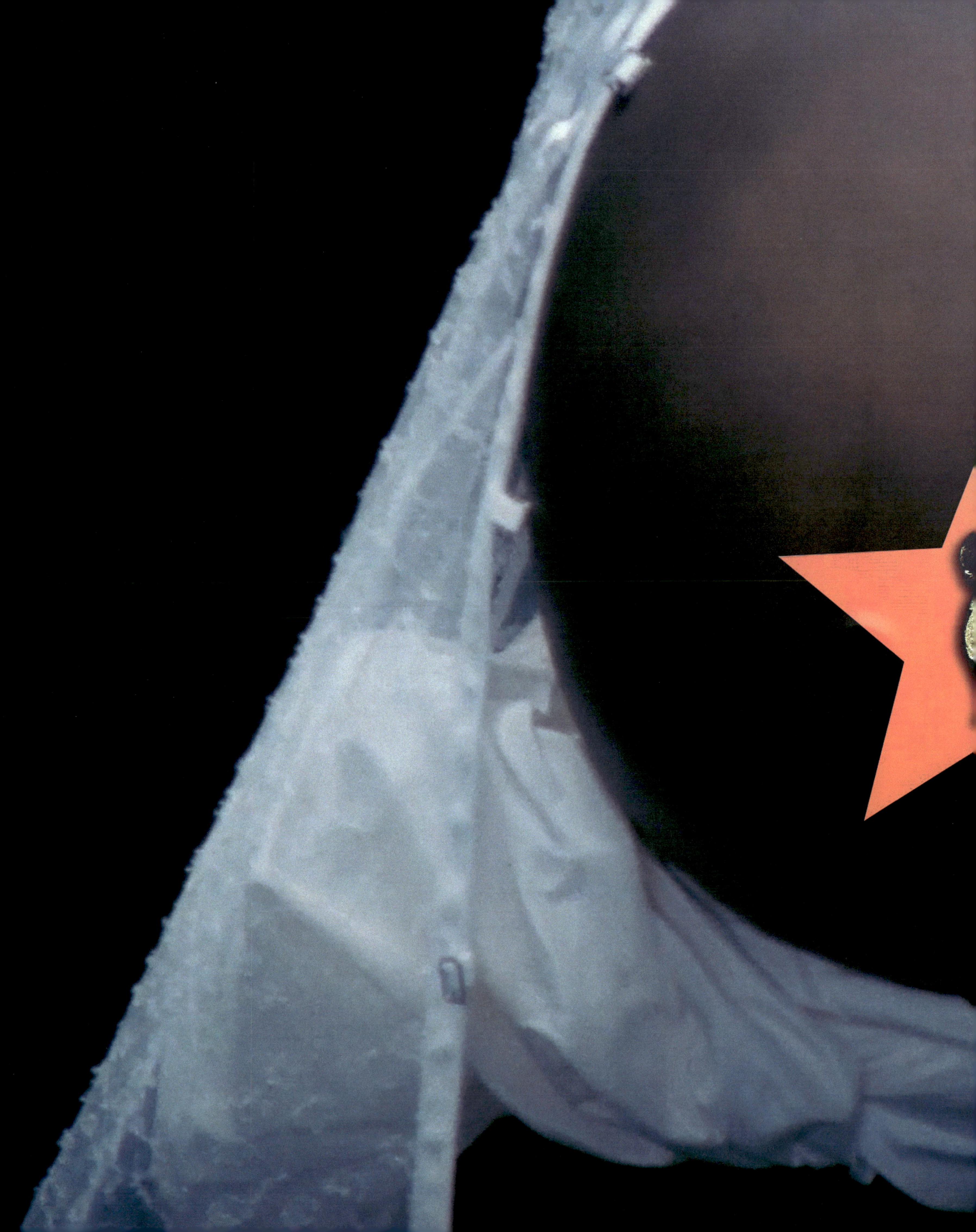

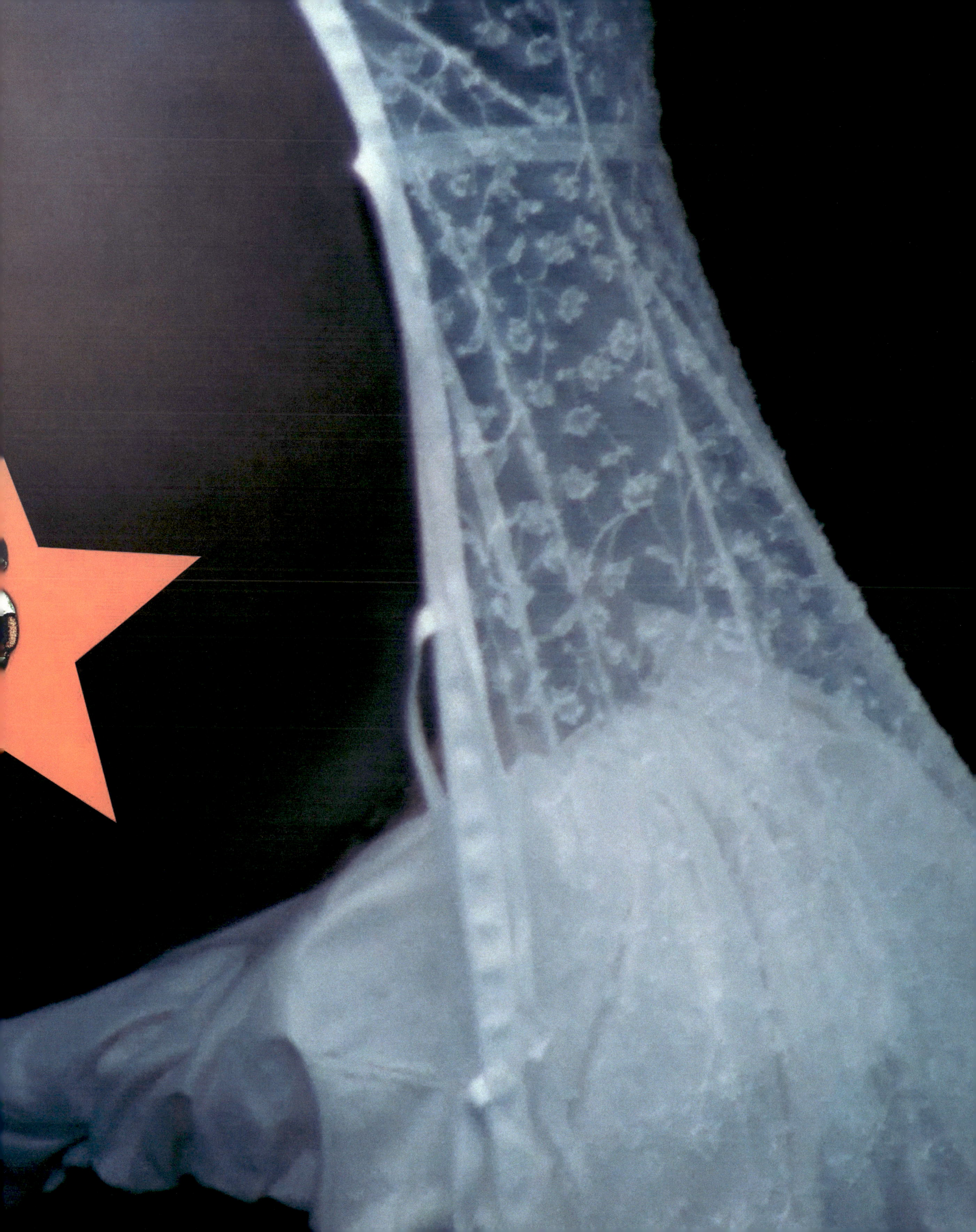

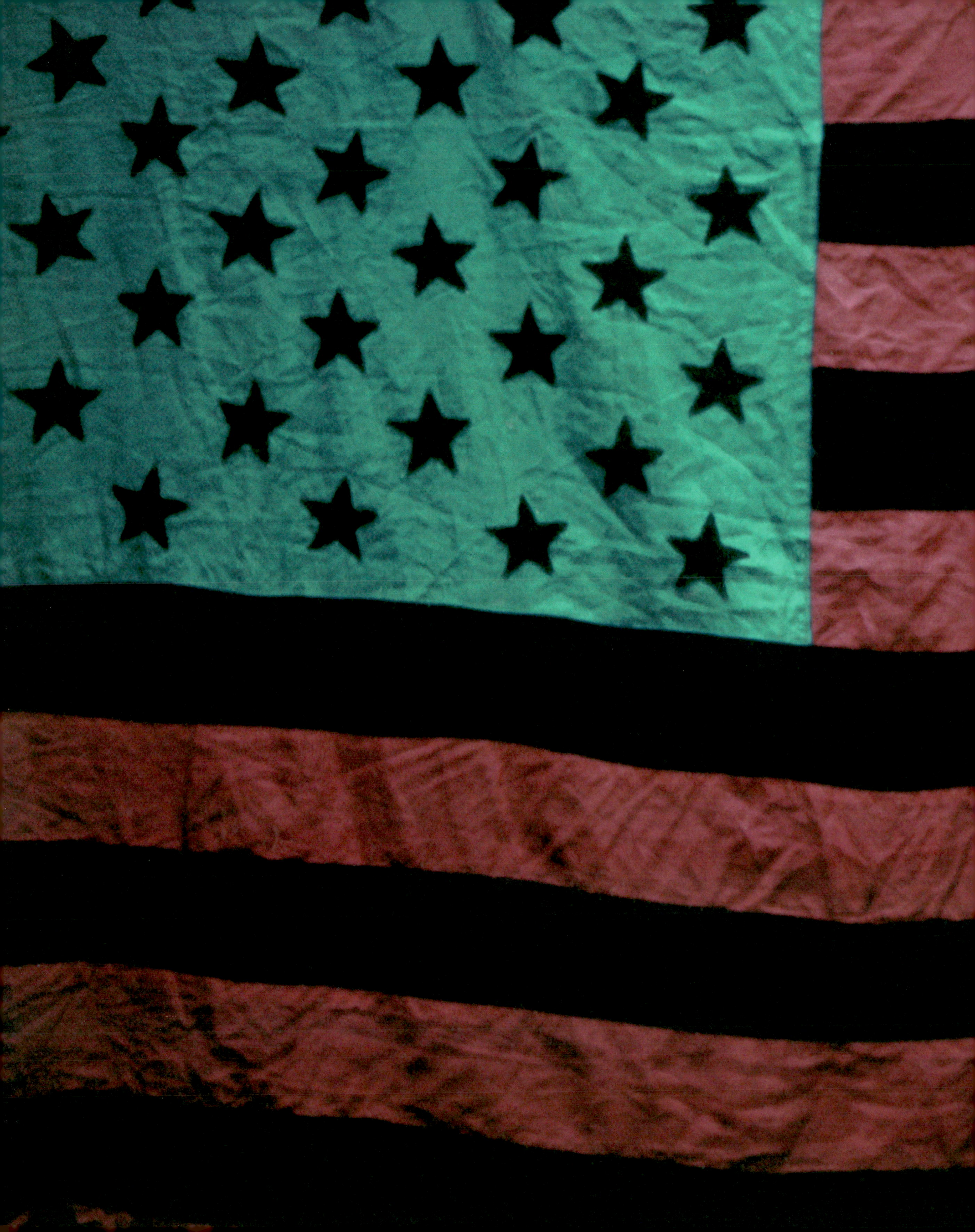

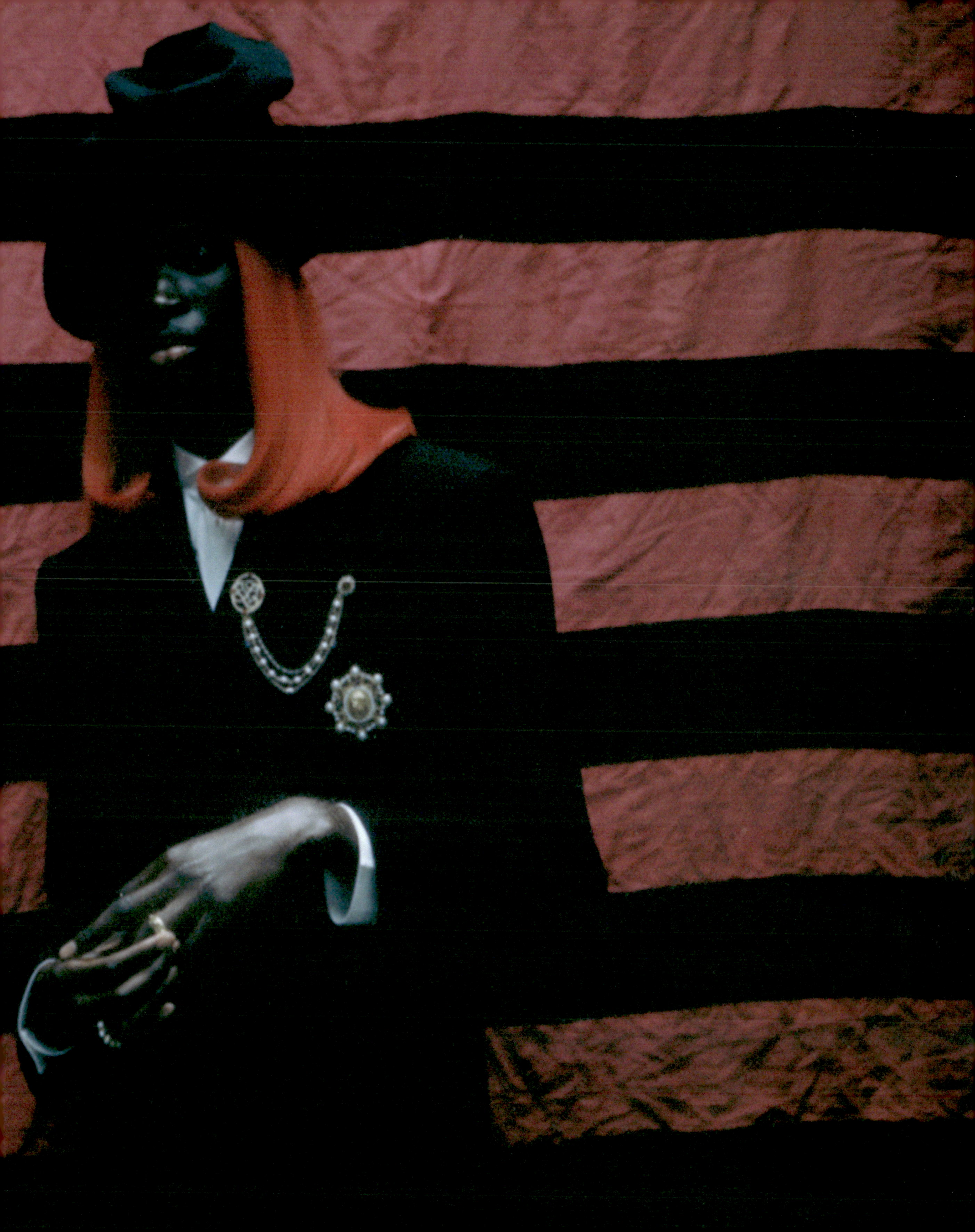

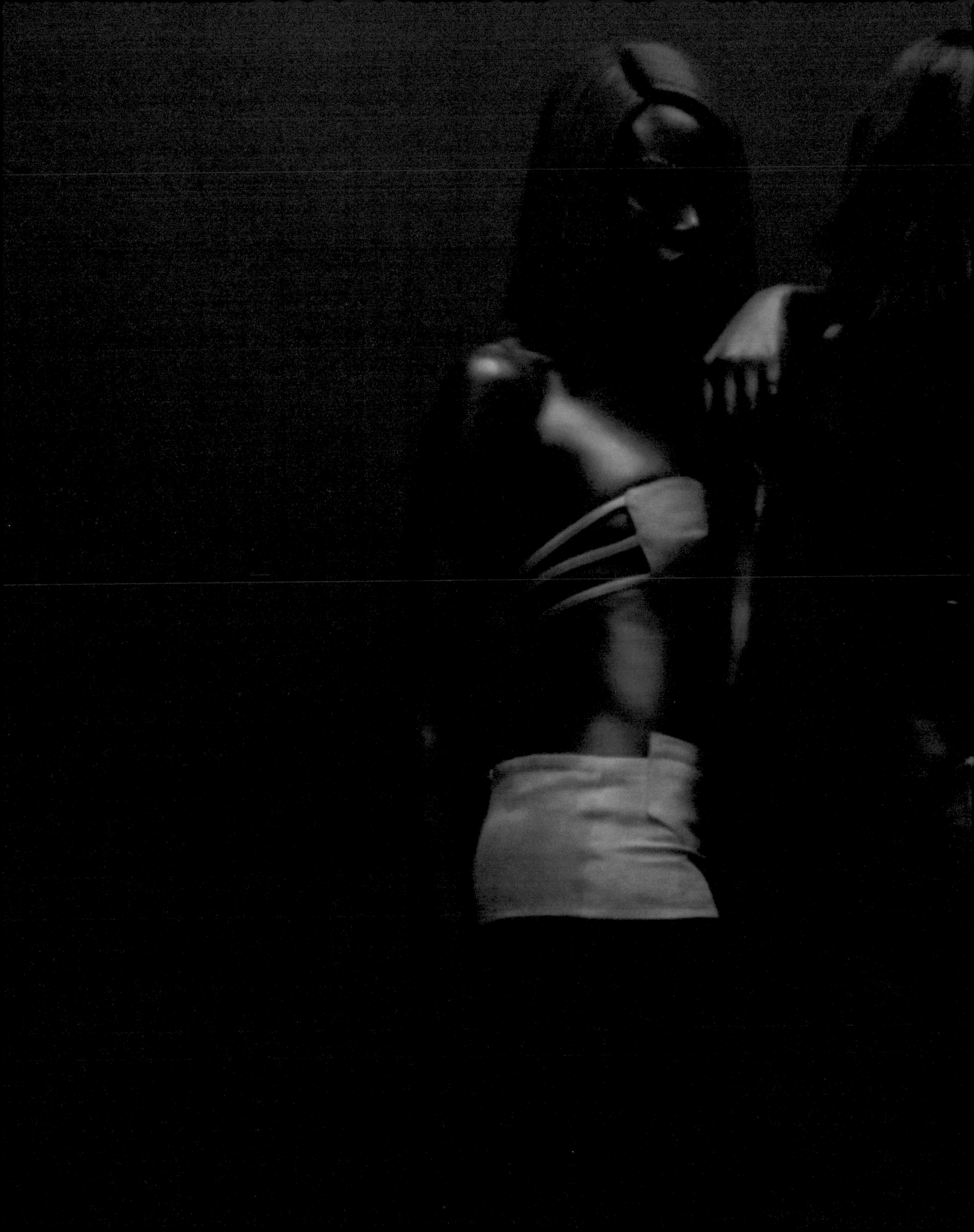

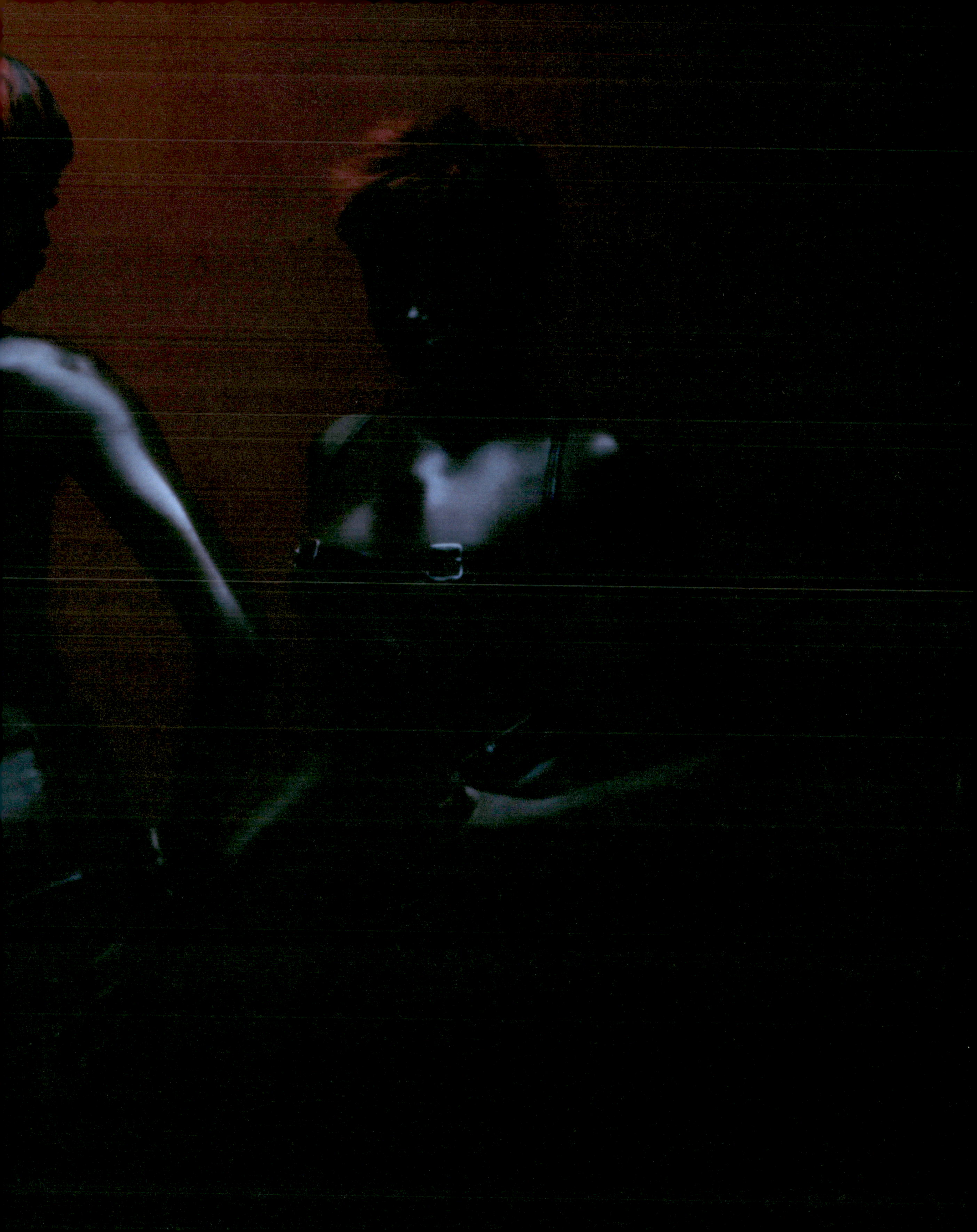

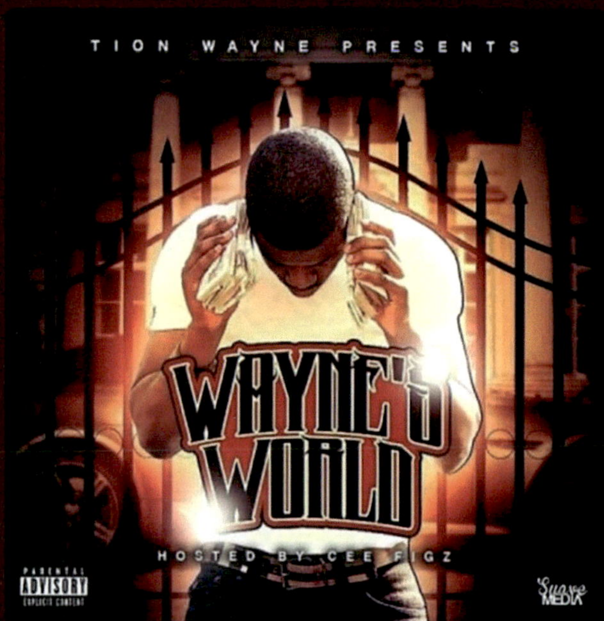

Getting Dough

Tion Wayne

Spotify

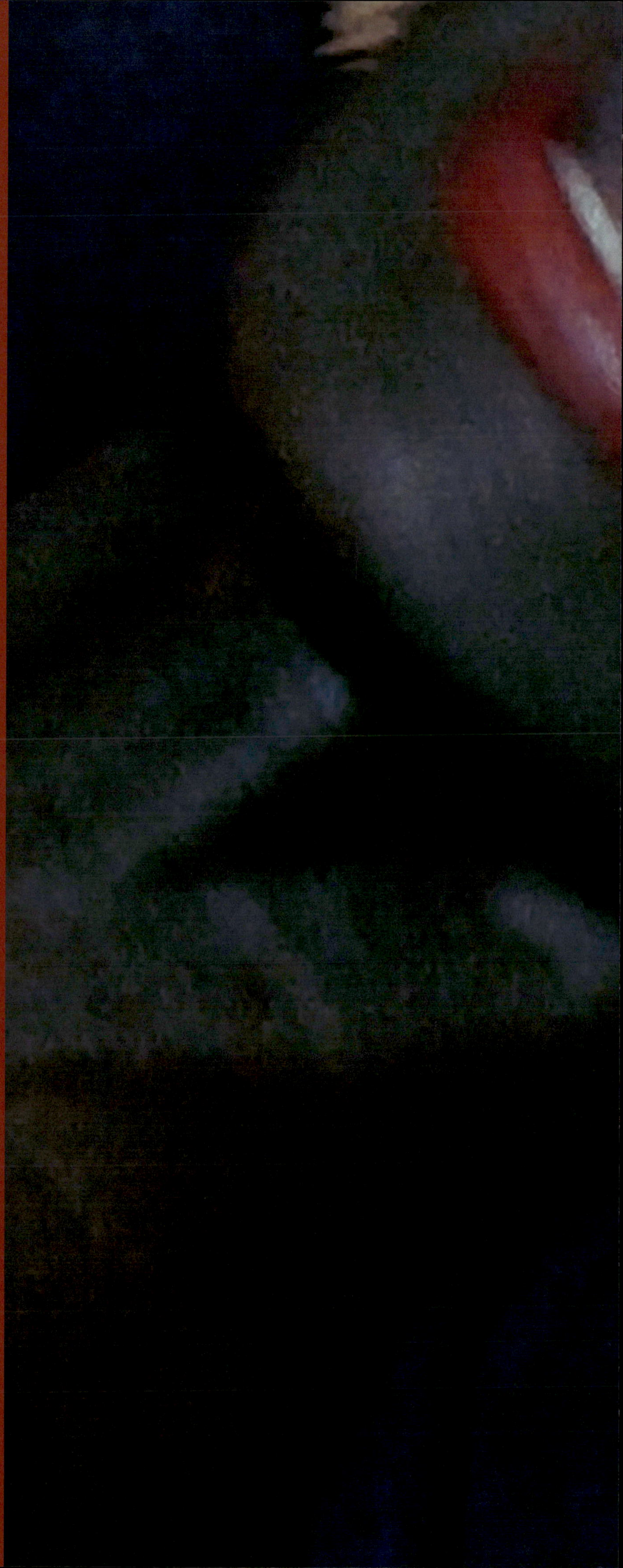

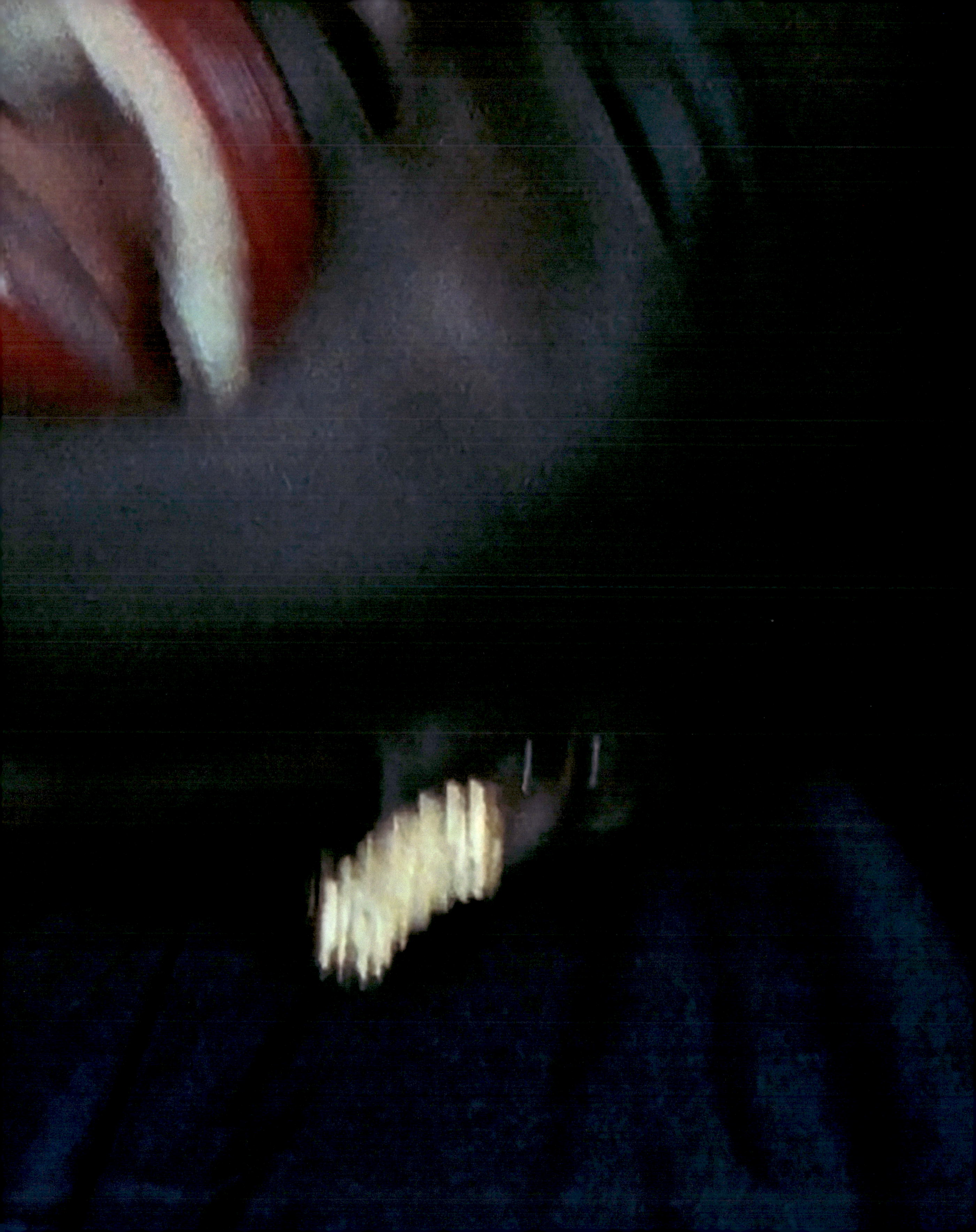

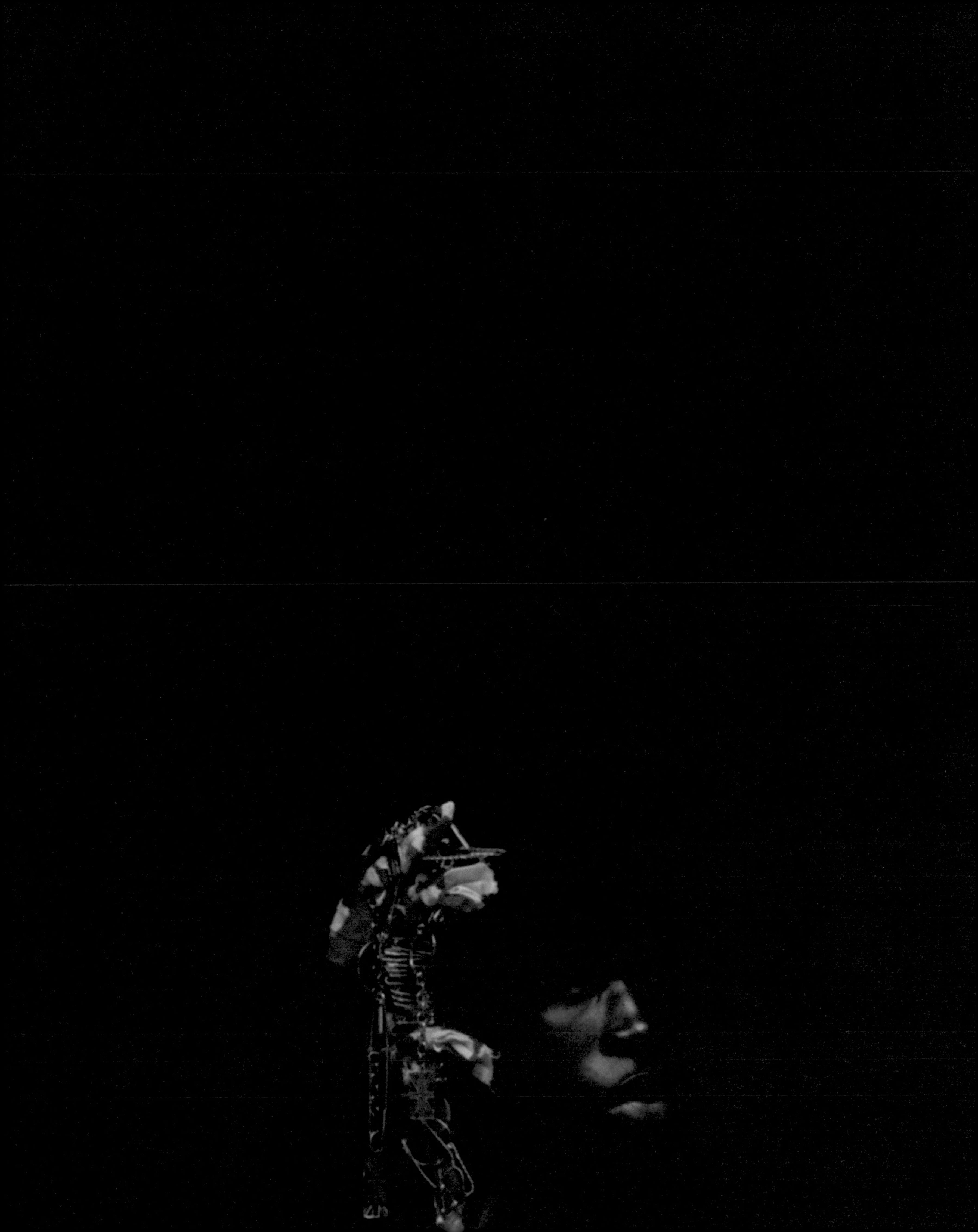

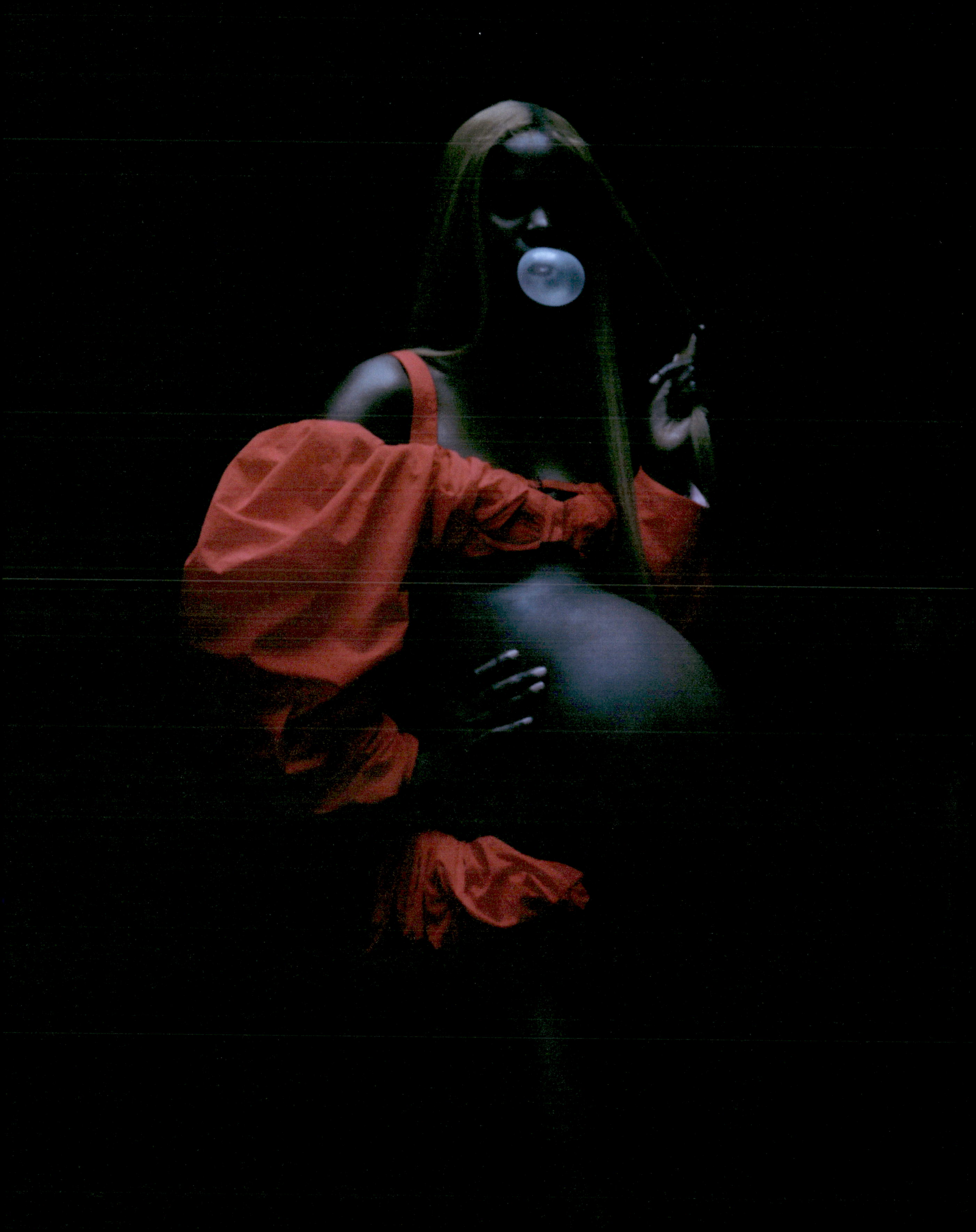

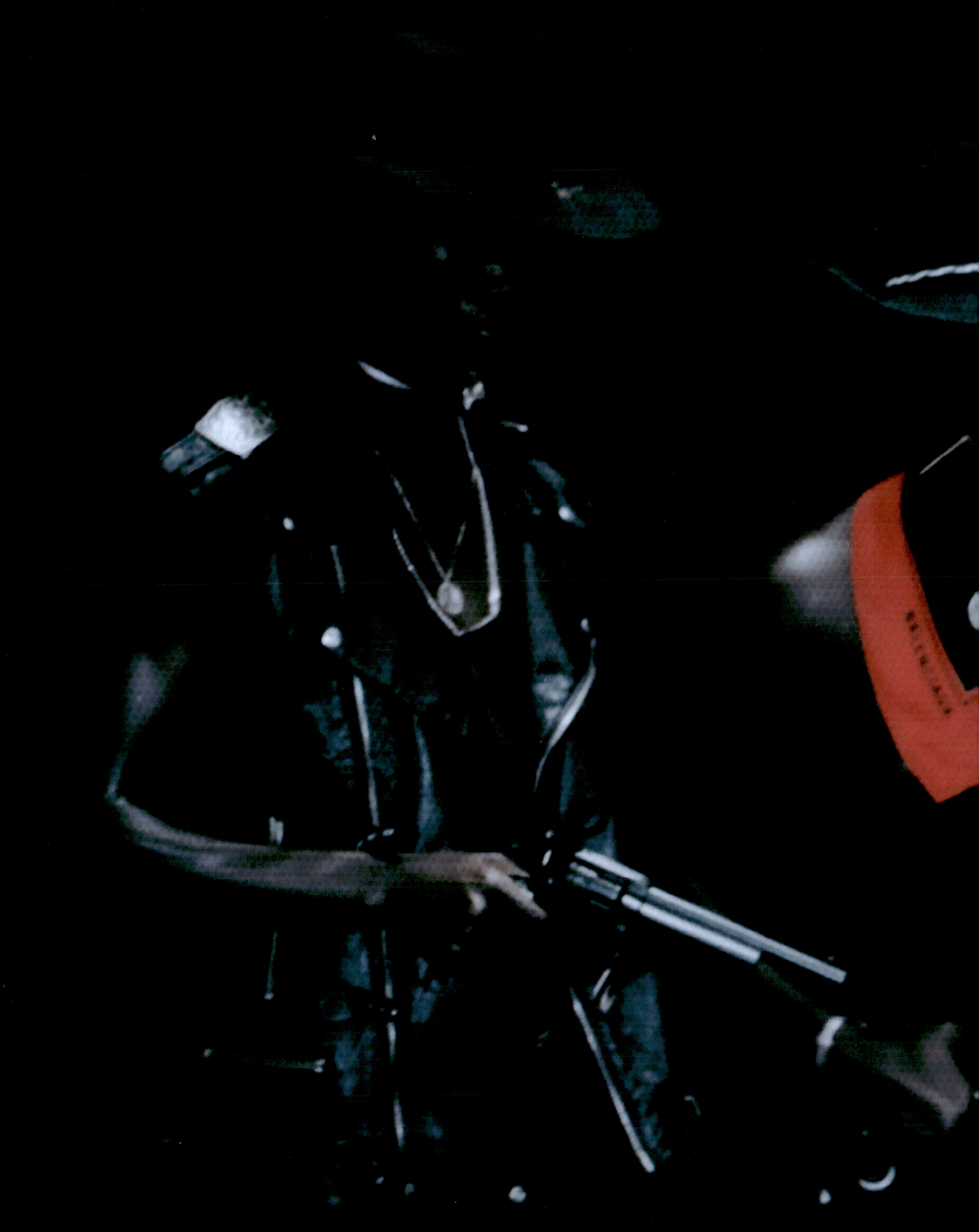

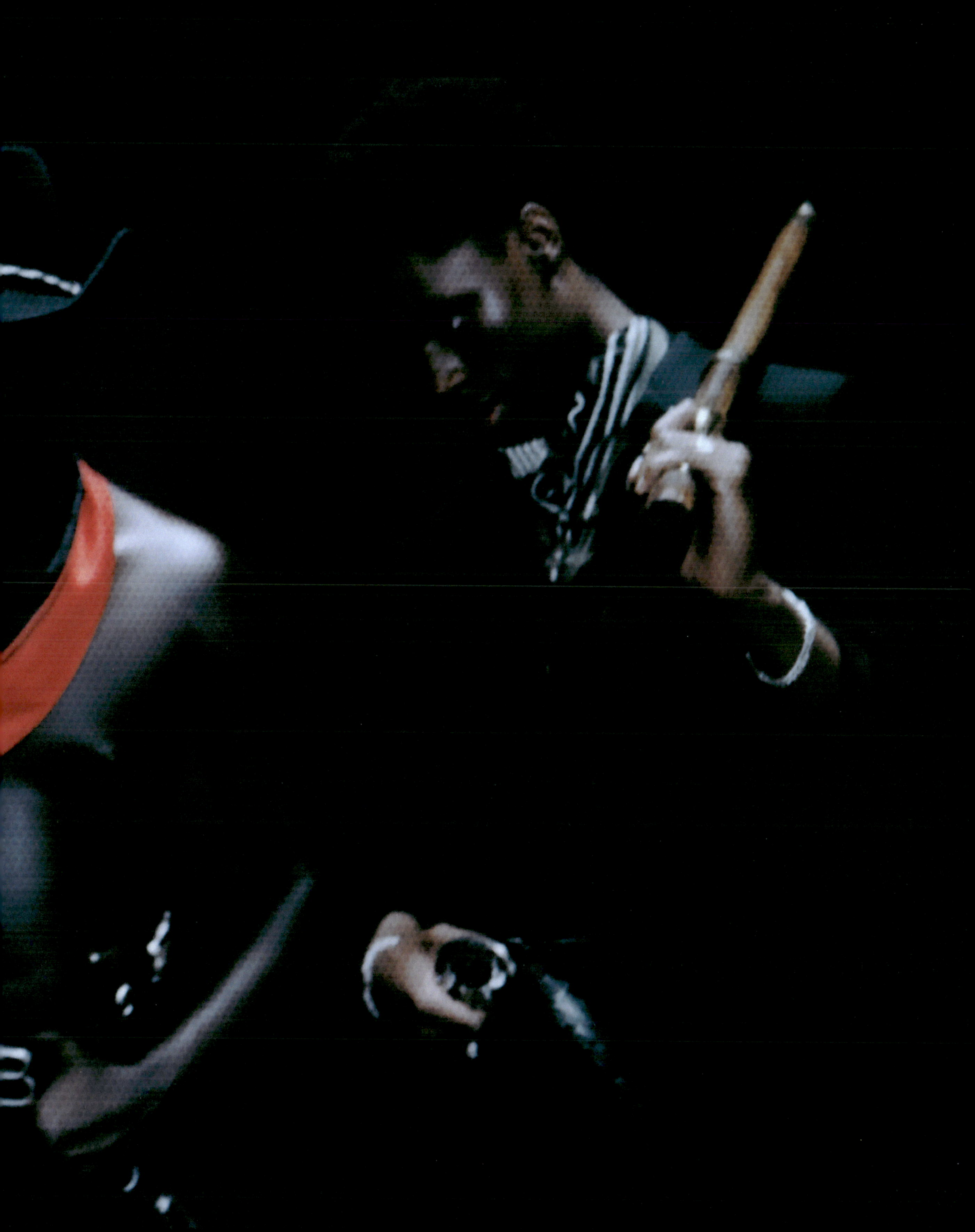

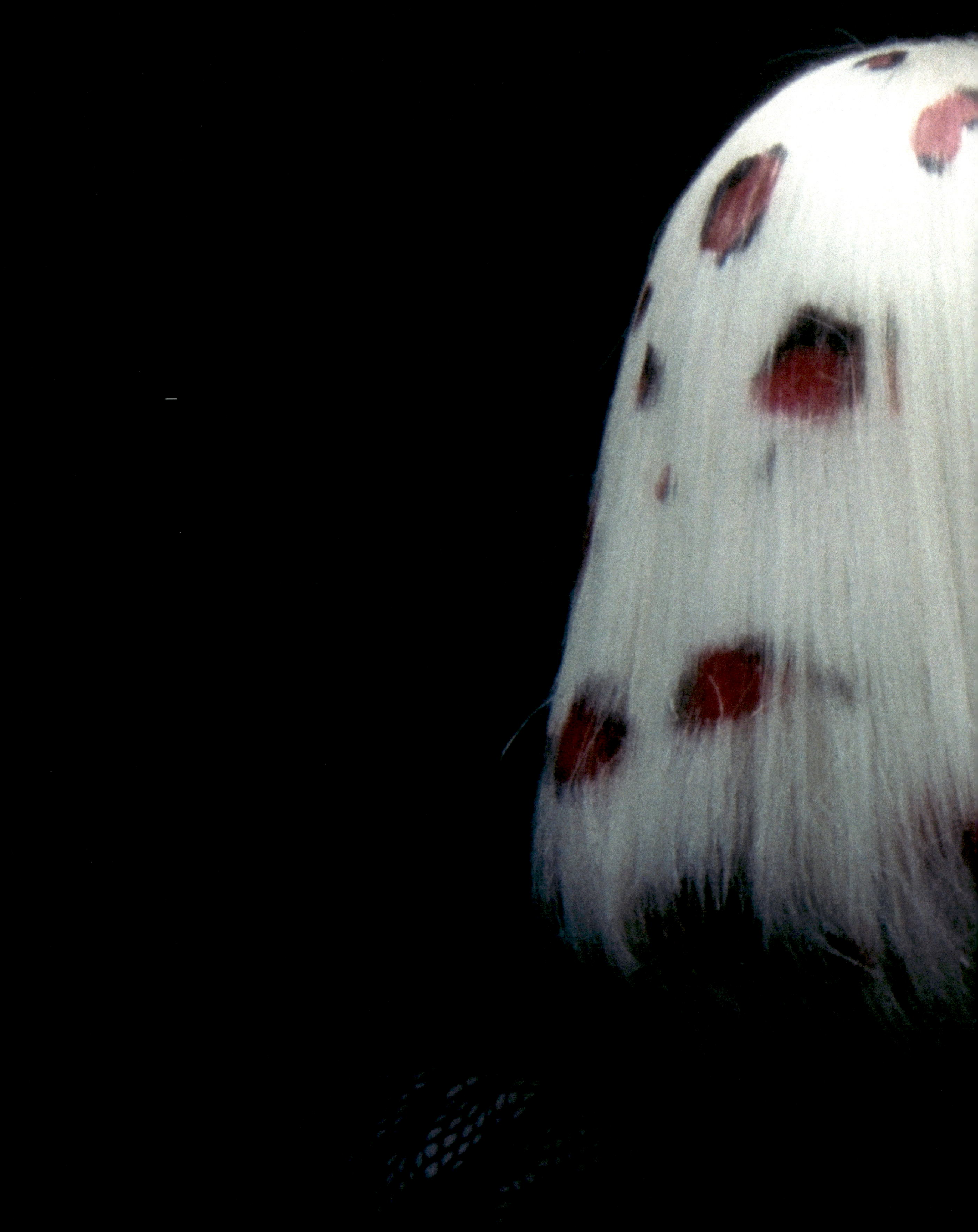

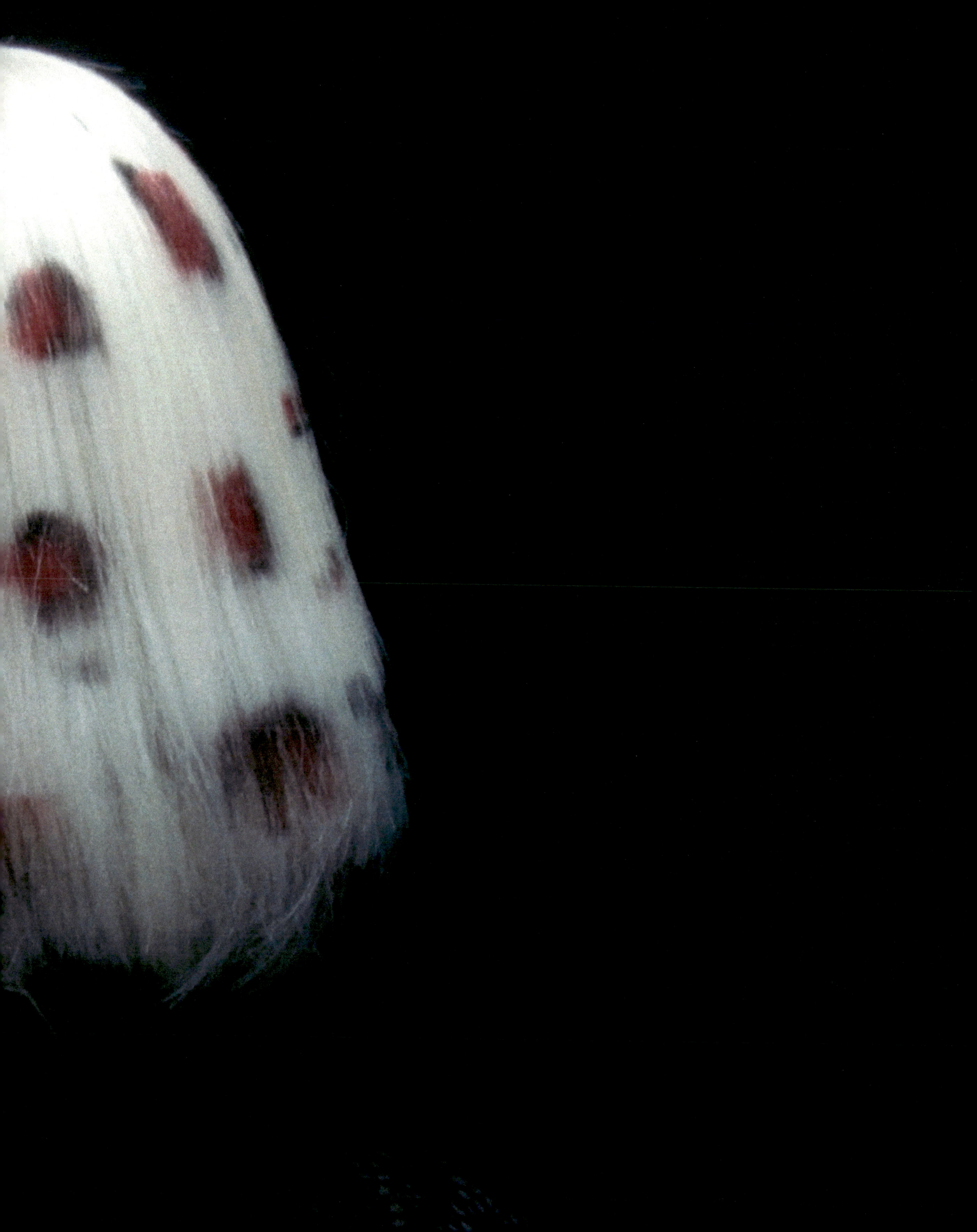

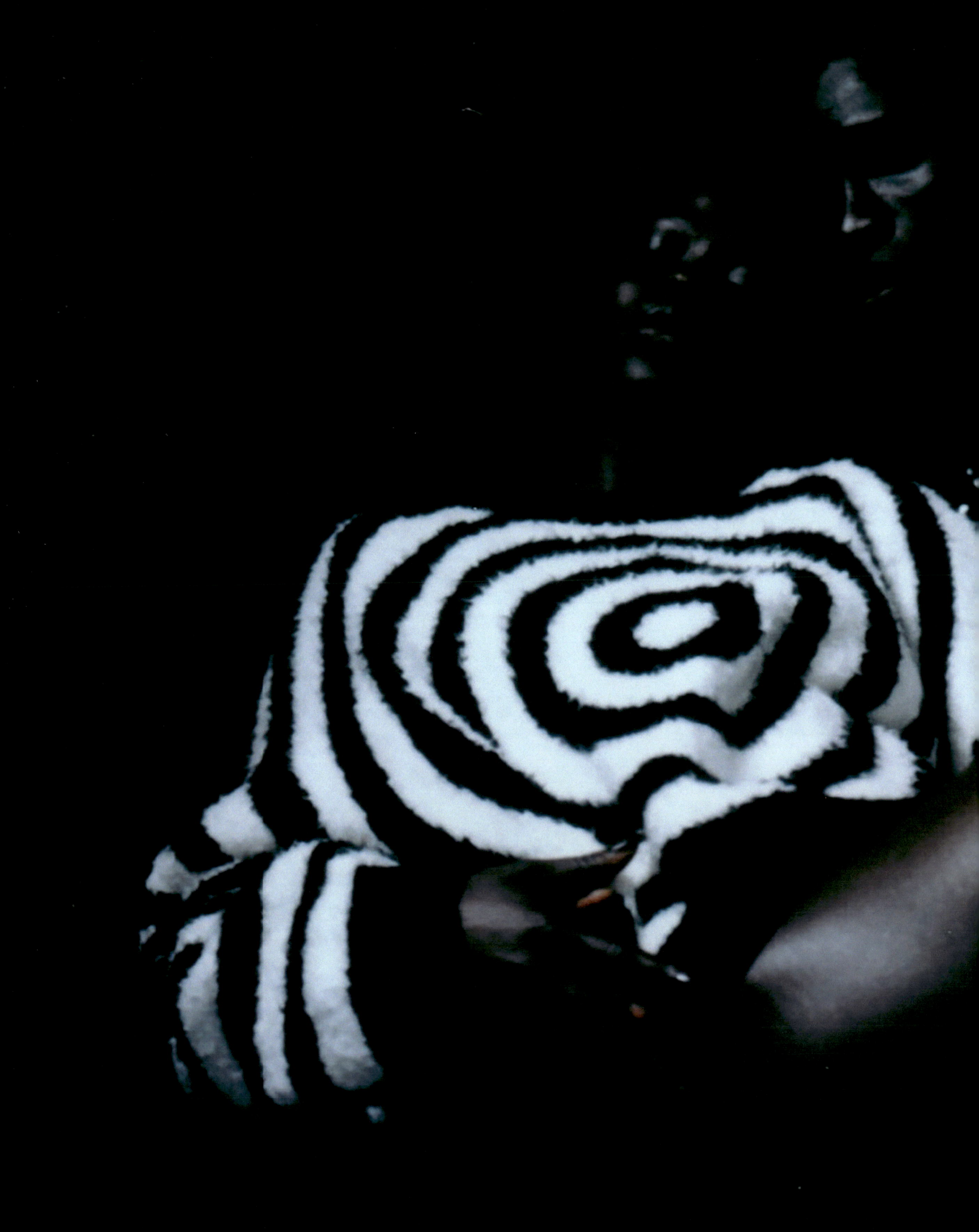

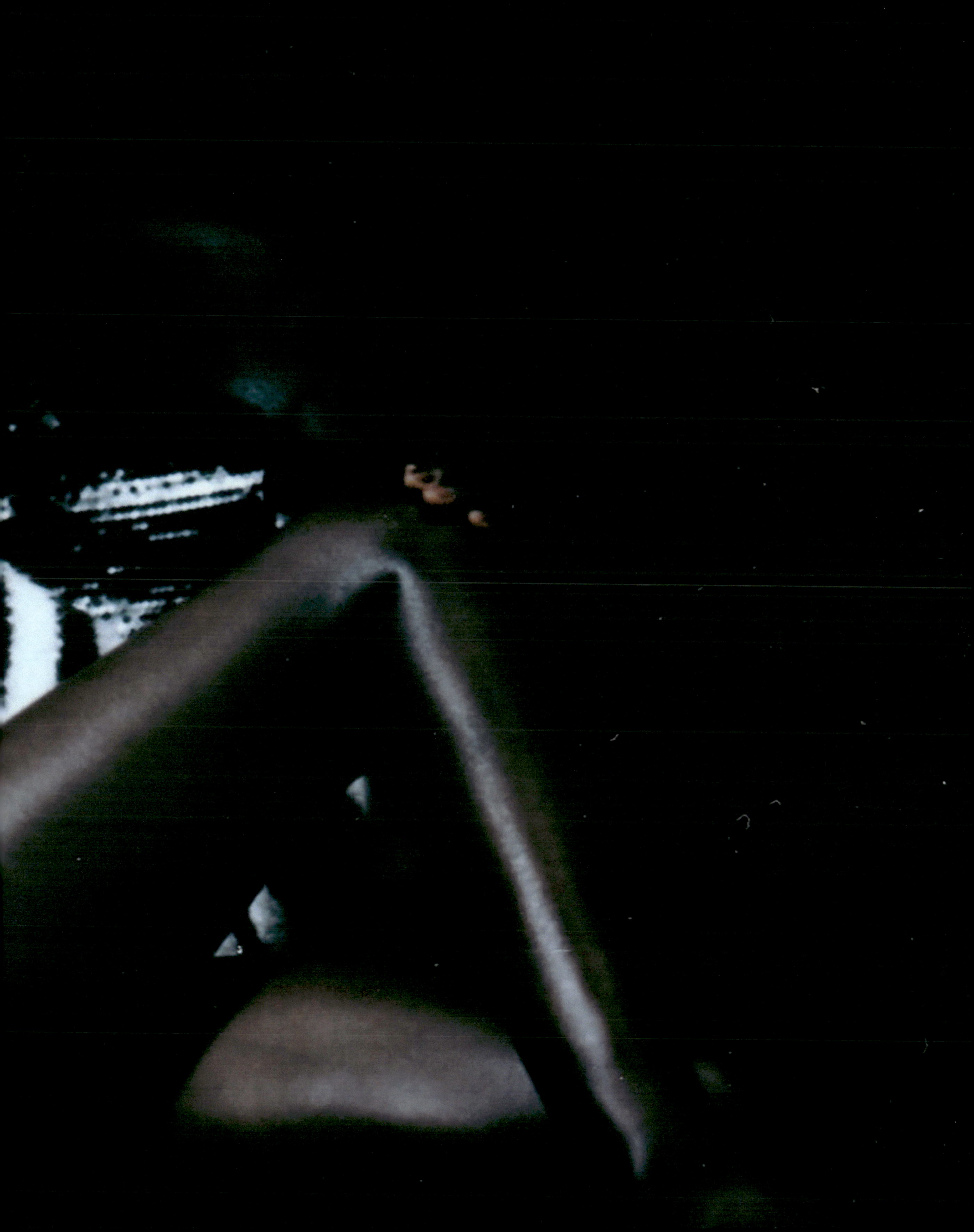

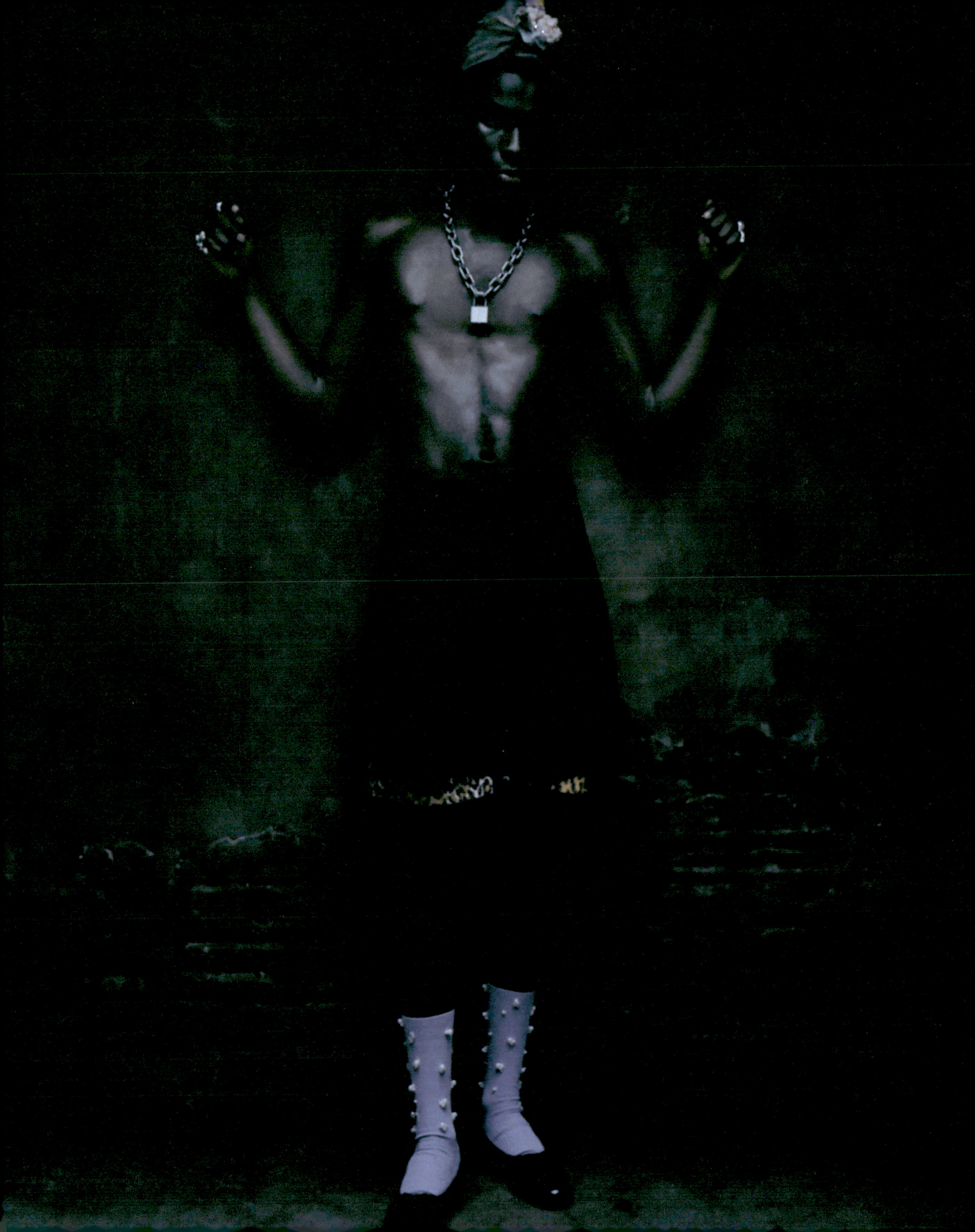

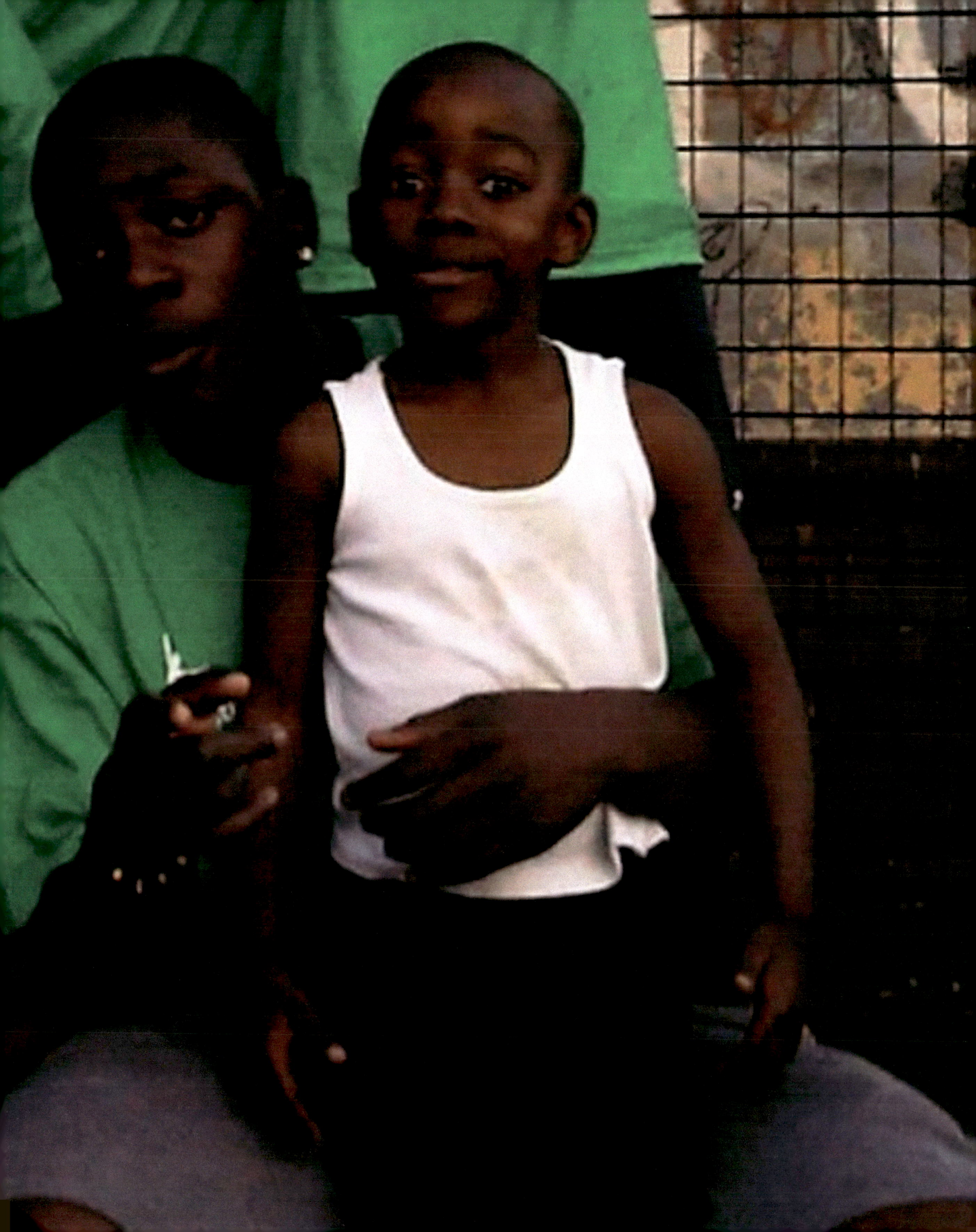

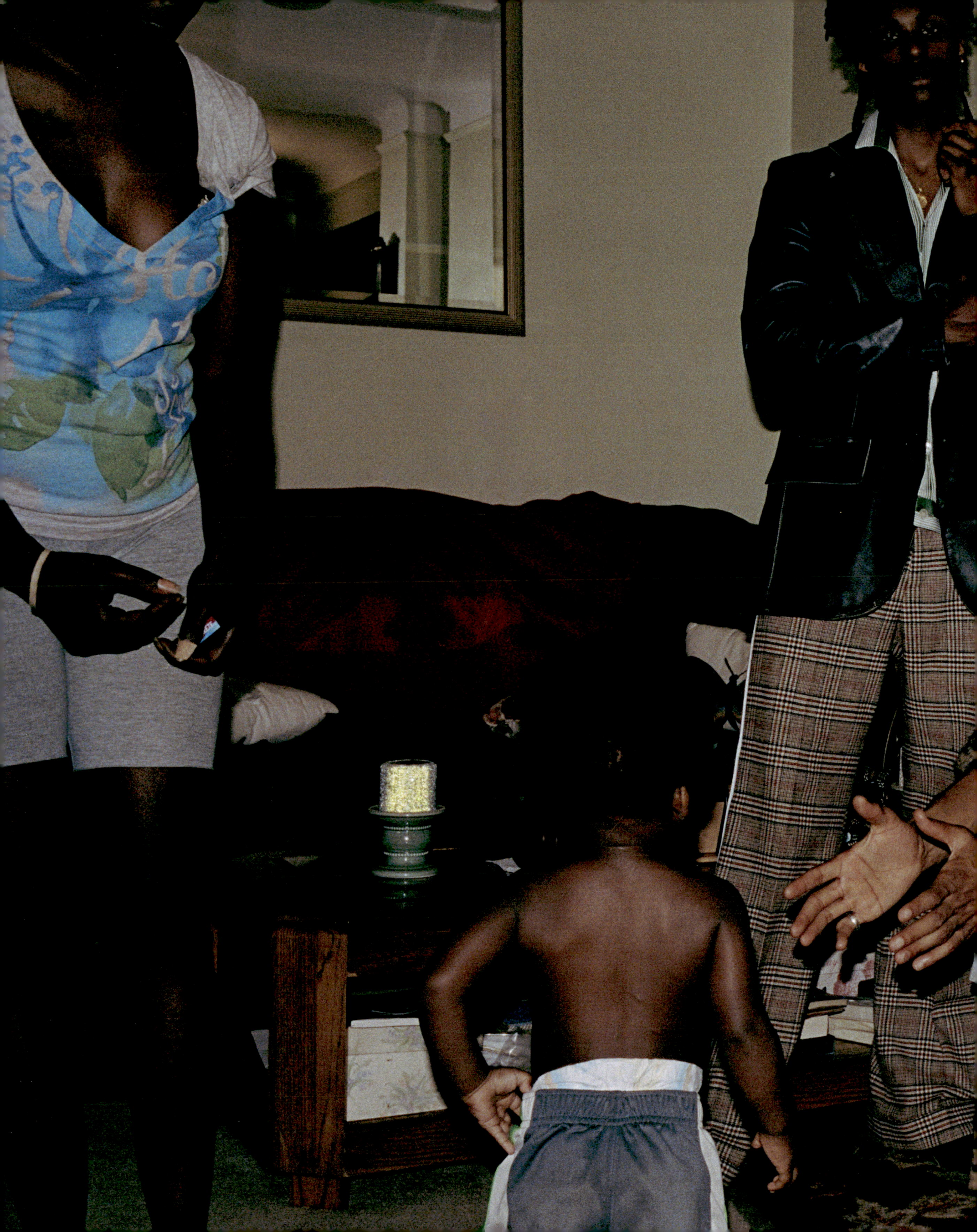

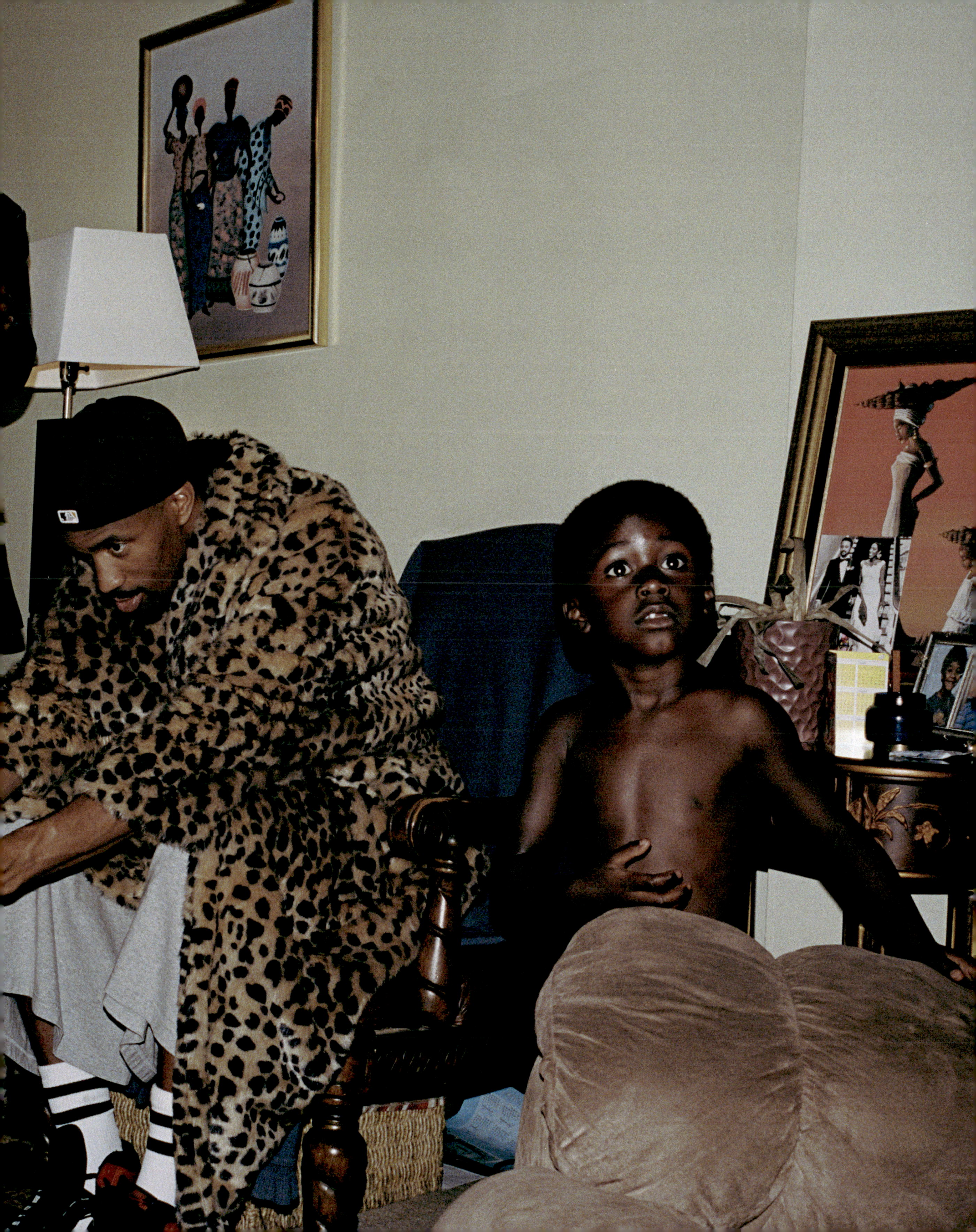

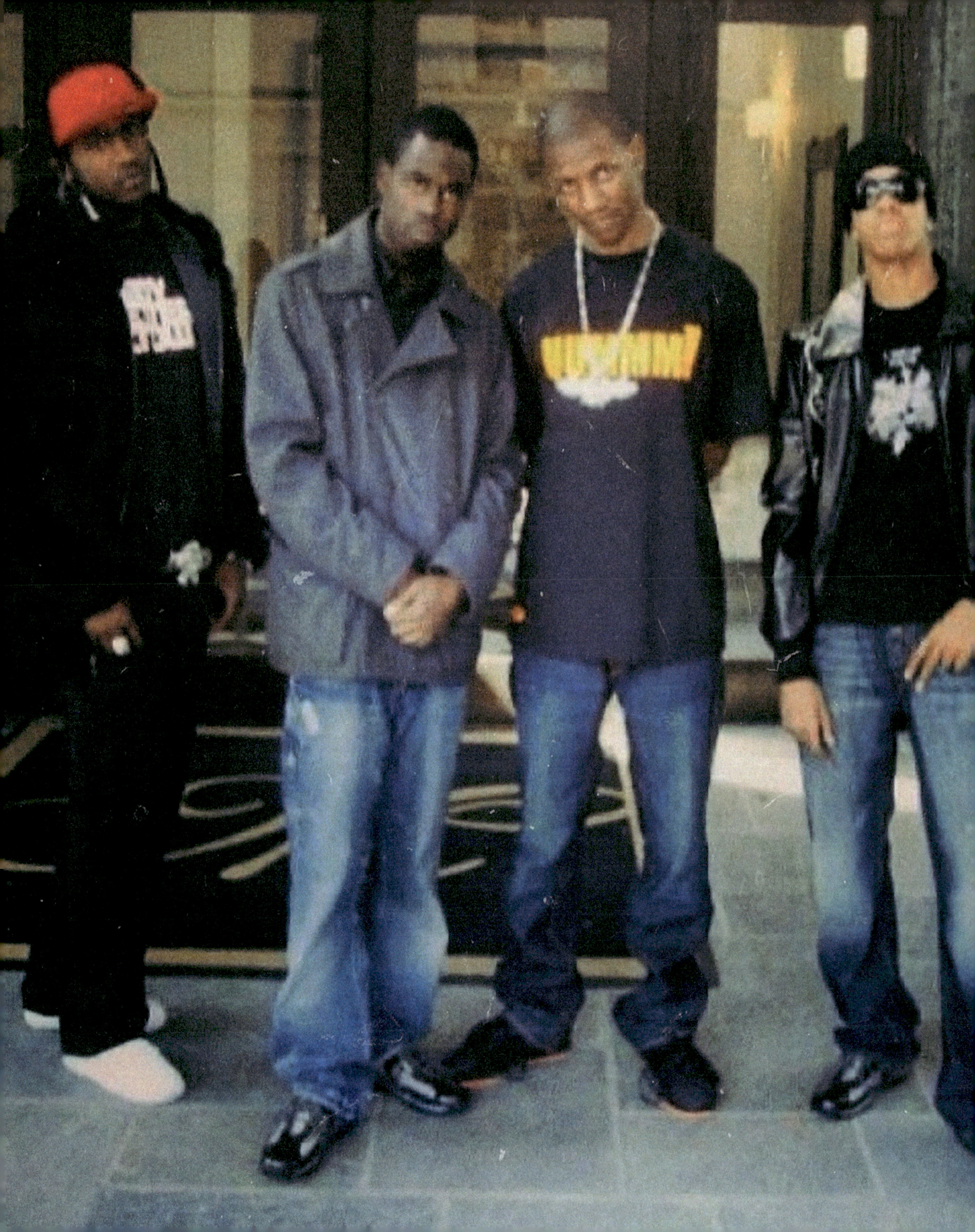

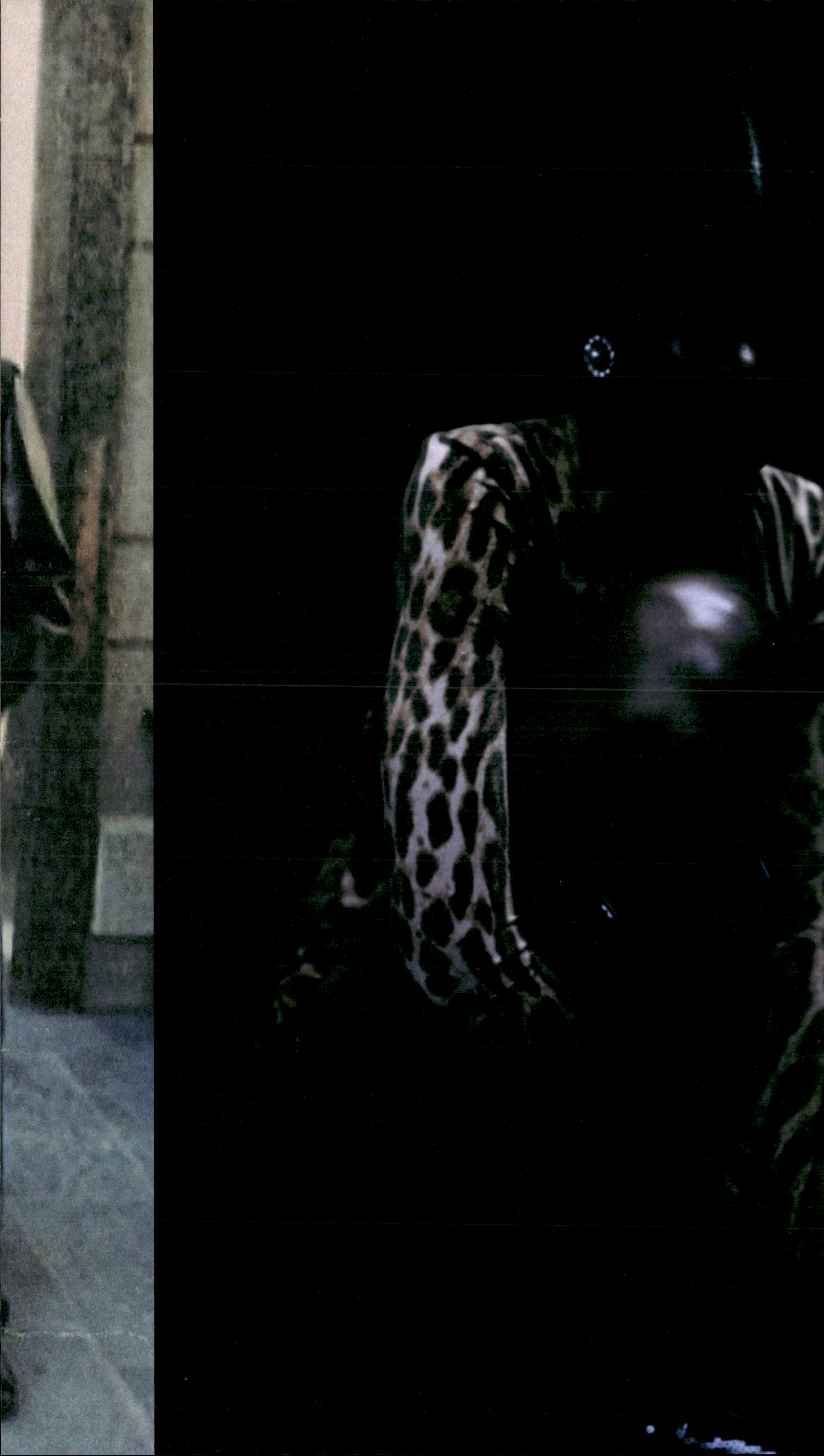

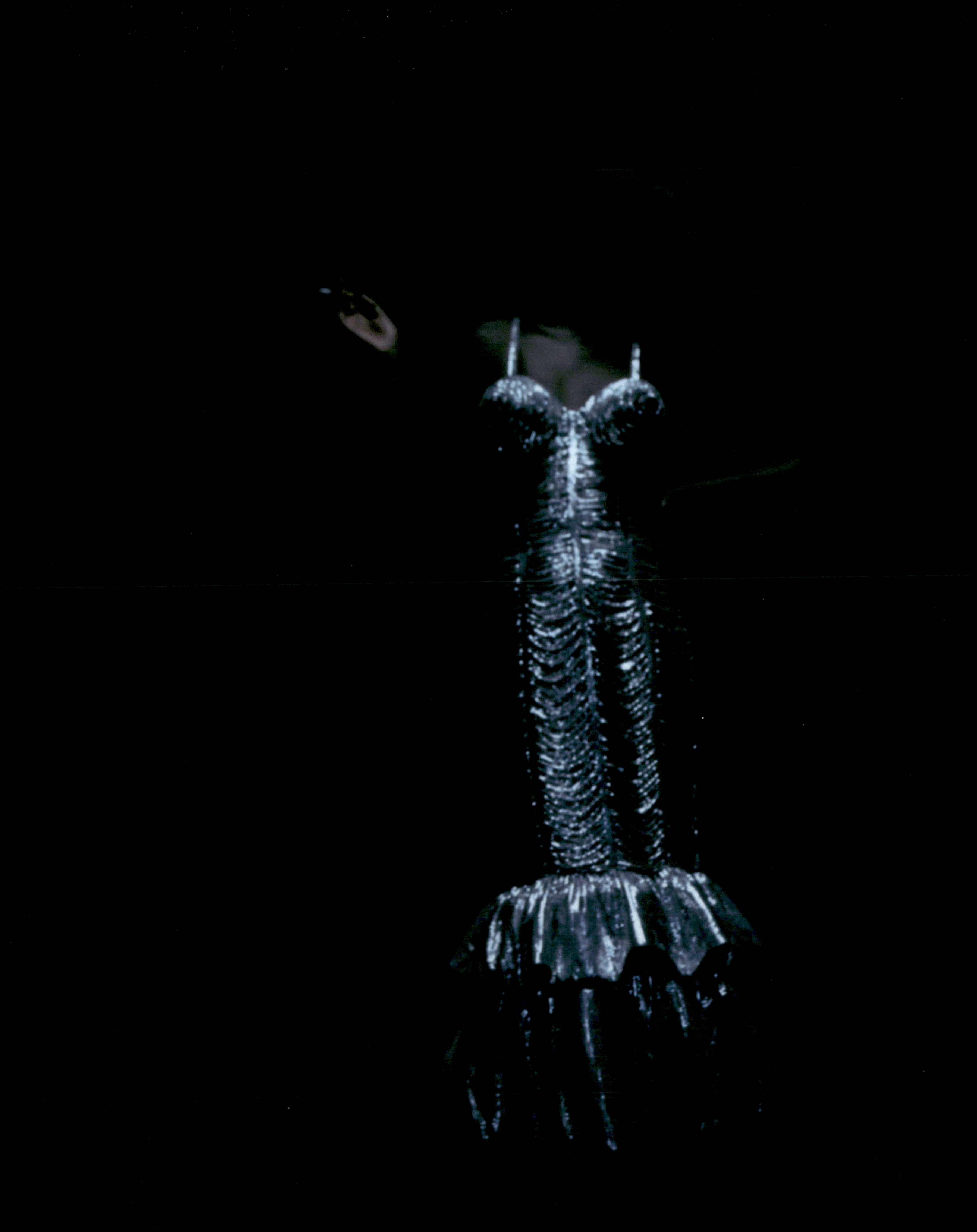

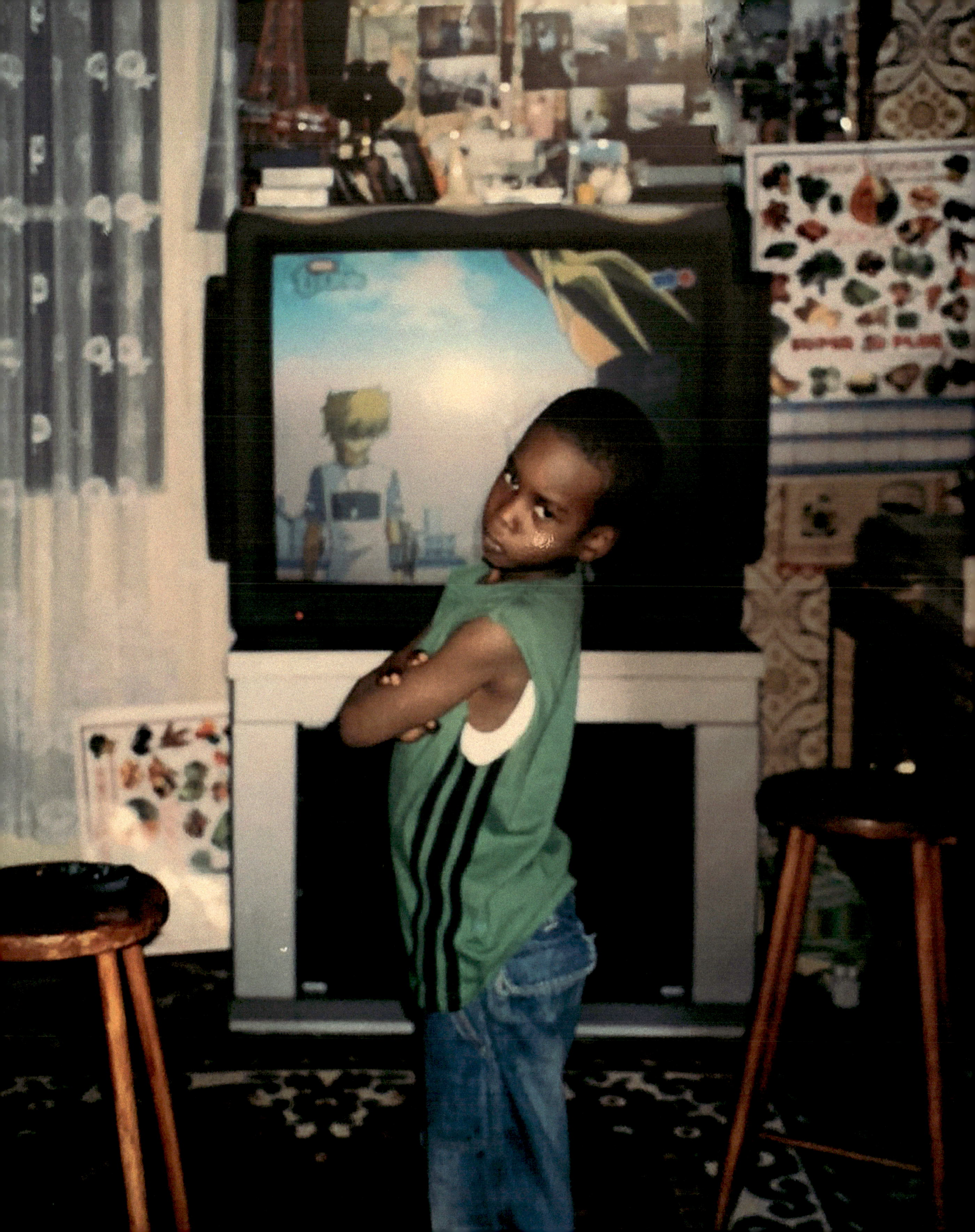

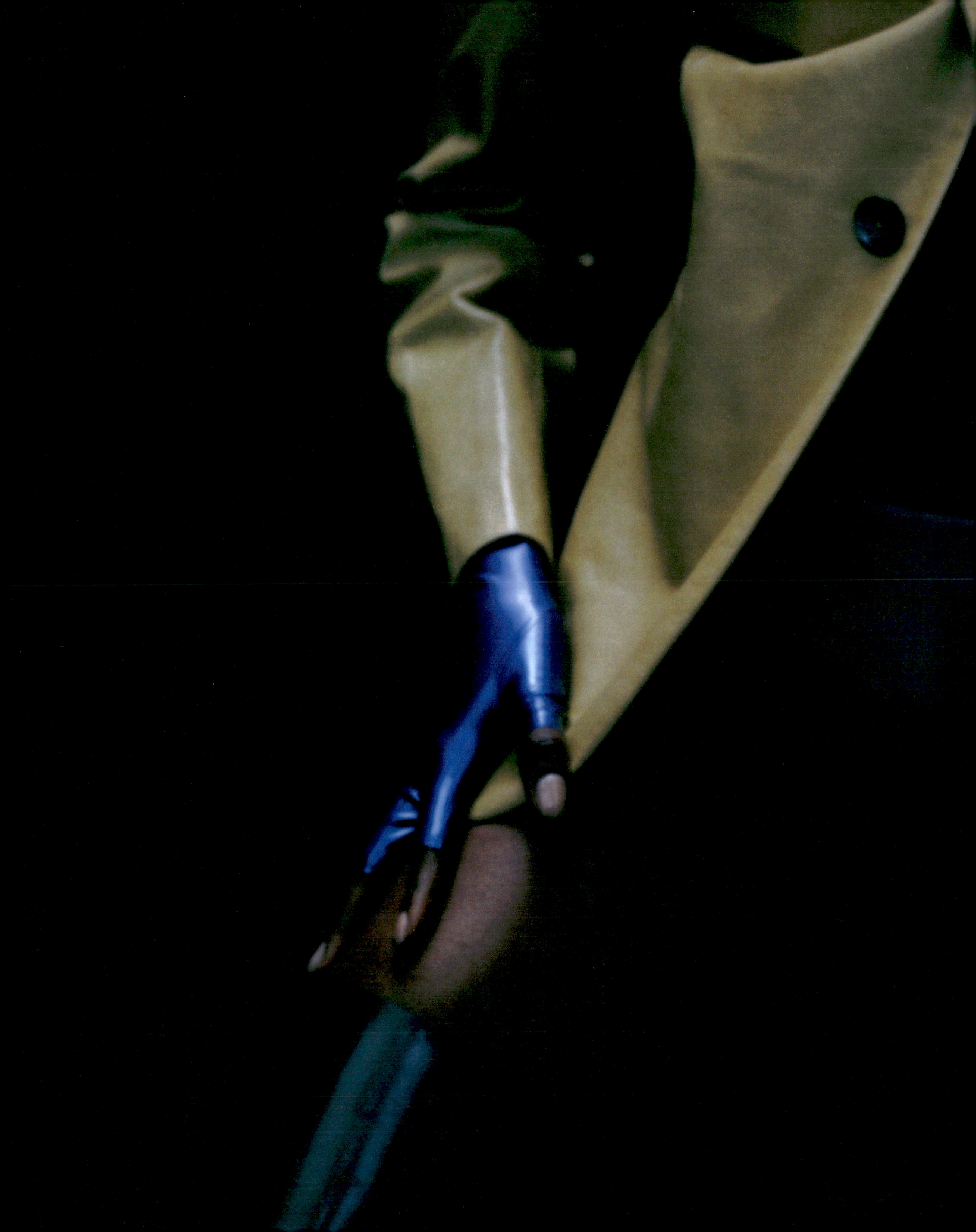

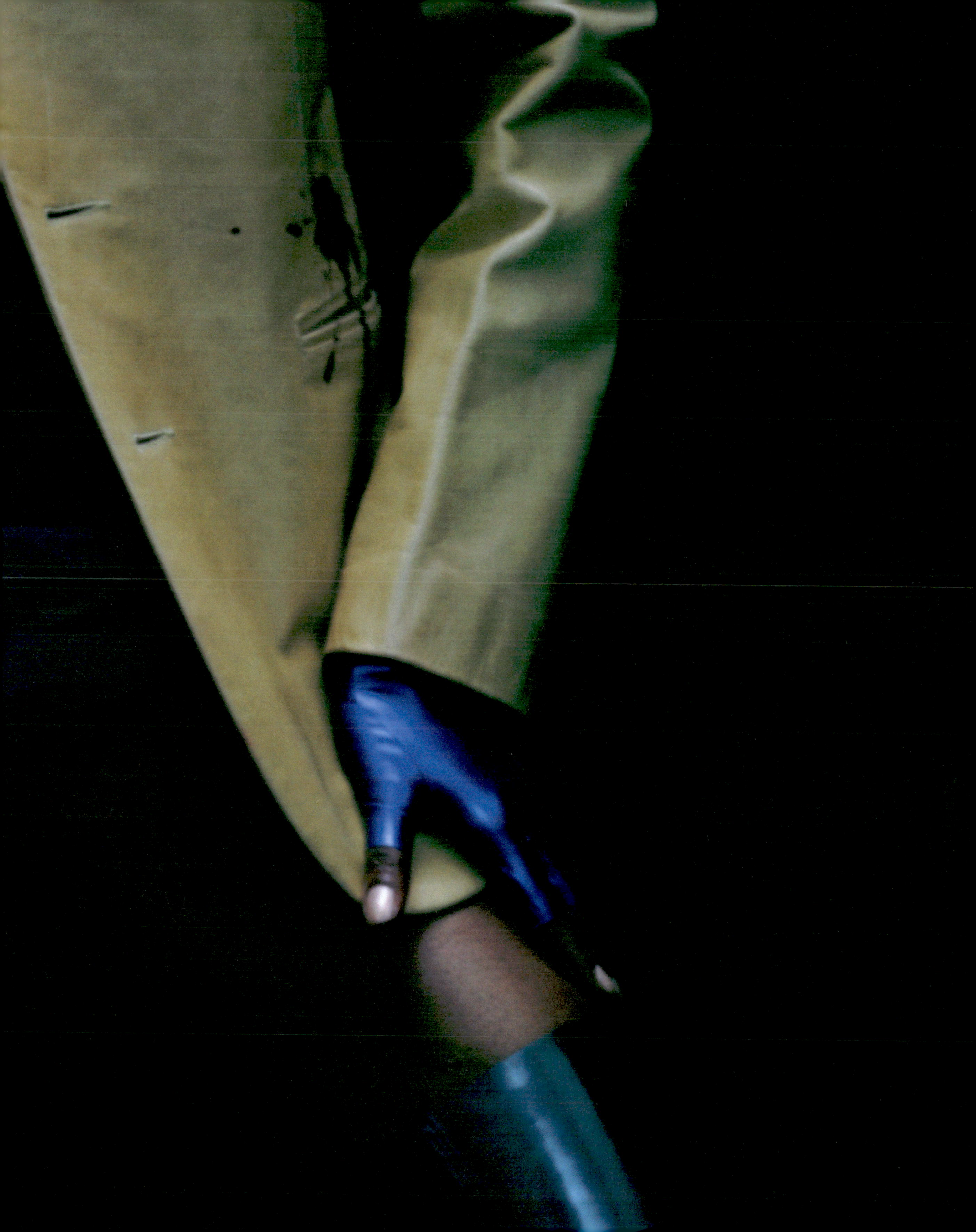

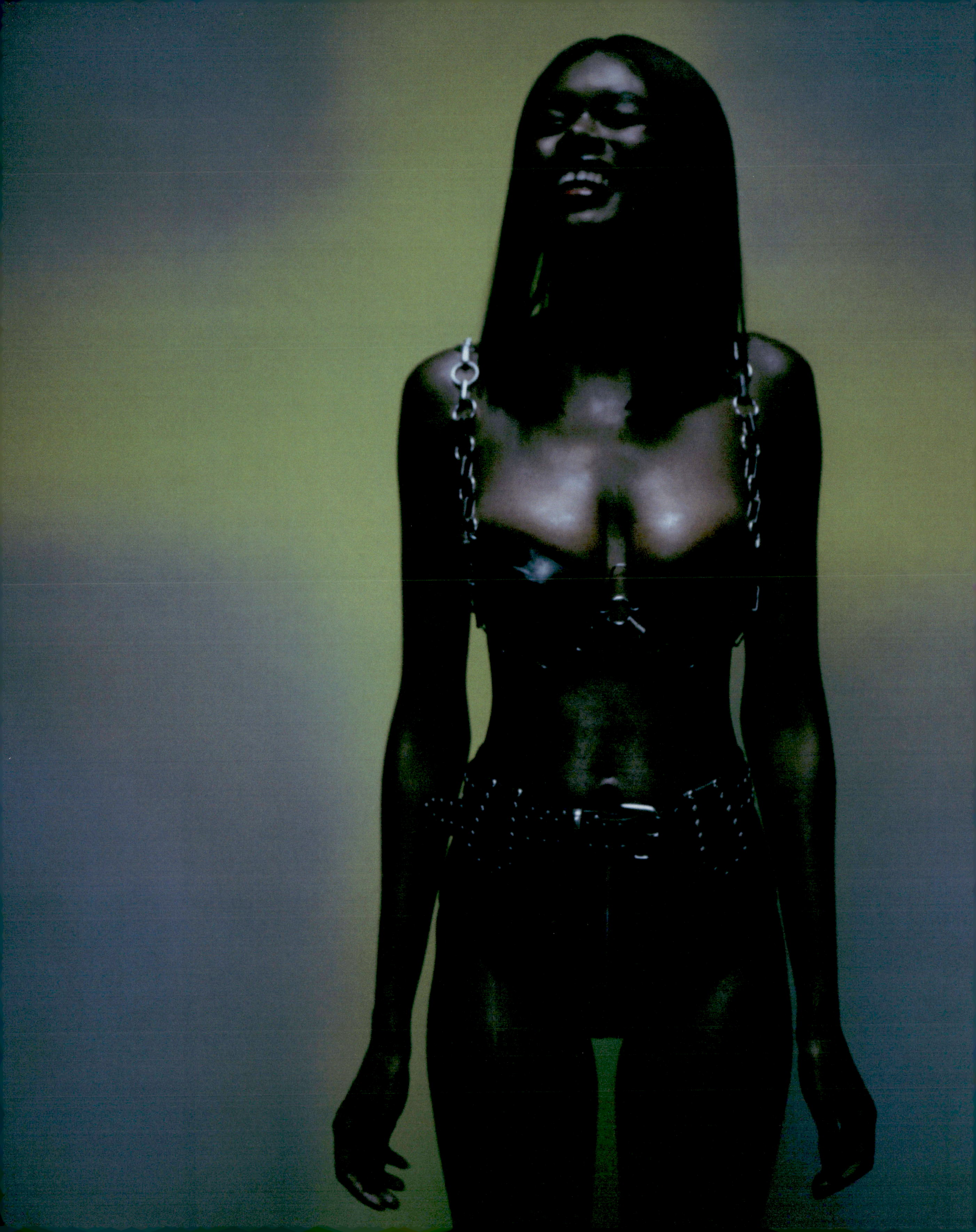

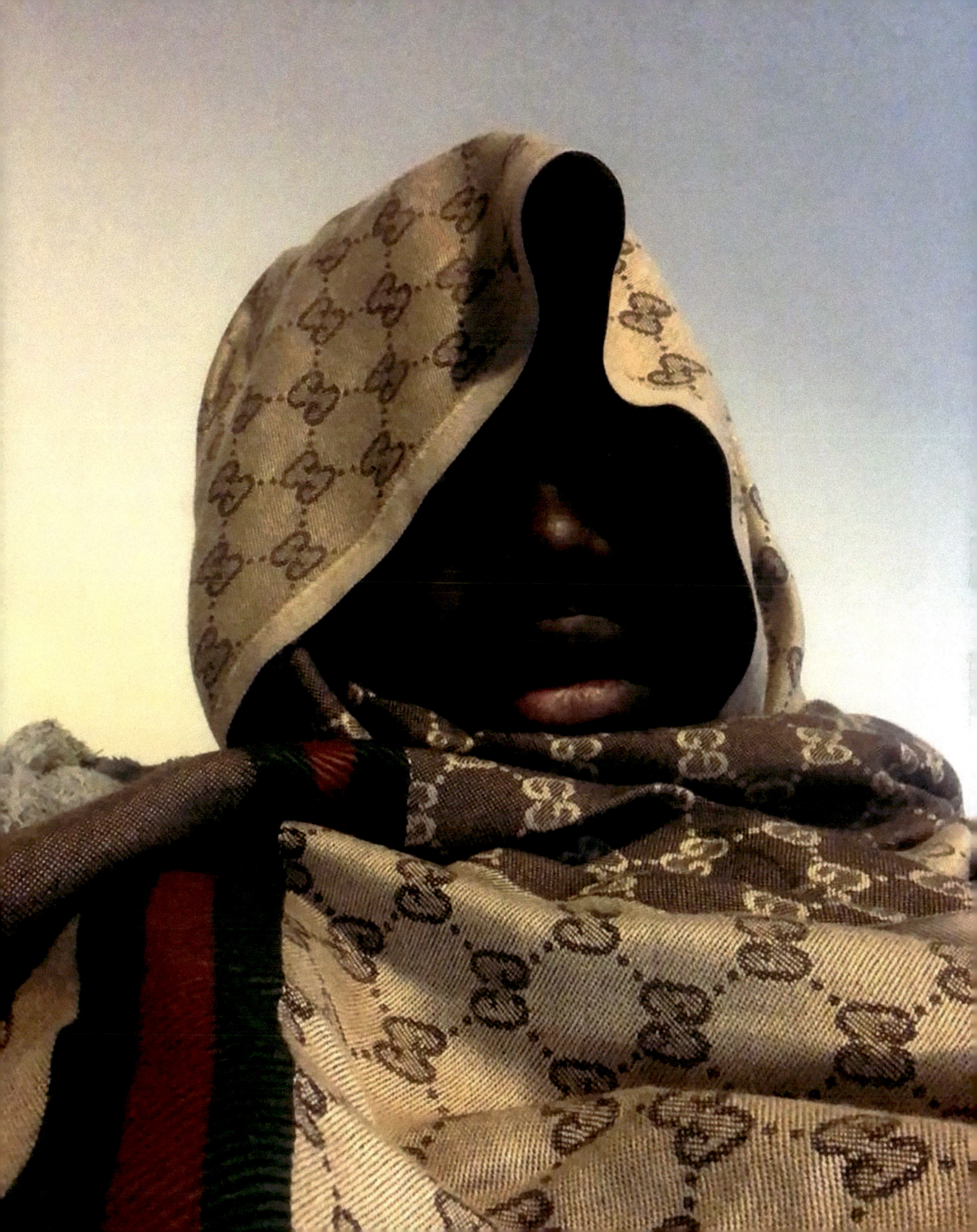

CLINT

Gabriel is such a real person, man! I feel like in this industry that we're in, especially in fashion and arts, a lot of people are social climbers, but with Gabs, his energy has always been straightforward, he isn't going to fake fuck with you! I feel like he doesn't really have the time or energy for that. Gabs has always just been real innit, and I have great respect for that.

I feel that with our current friendship group, we're all kind of doing our own thing, in our own way, and elevating simultaneously. I just want to be able to remain friends with these people beyond everything, but also to set out a blueprint for a kid who looks to us in the future and is like, "Oh this man, Gabriel, was doing big boy things for all these people, all these campaigns and shit at the same time he's also friends with Clint, and Clint was doing his thing." I just want all my friends to be on some real shit. It's just sick how we are all trying to elevate and extend our legacy, but also get other young creatives on, show them how real is done, and that it can be done.

I feel like Gabriel is a dime in a dozen and we're not gonna have someone like him for a long time, or you know what, maybe after Gabriel, we will have more people like him that come from where he comes from, South London, having a specific perspective. First he was fucking around with his creativity making videos of Dele Alli on a Sony A7 or whatever, just trying to make art, and then the next thing you know, he is shooting campaigns for Nike, Pharrell, A$AP Rocky, Mercedes. . . . He's doing his thing on a whole different type of a level, but he's staying true to himself through it all. I've never seen someone wear one pair of Corteiz joggers for a week or two weeks straight the same way Gabs has. That's some real shit – I be wearing my shit for like a week as well man, but it's mine, for him to do it. I don't have a lot of friends in this thing, only a few people have my phone number, and Gabriel is just one of them. I am excited to see him grow and extend his creative vision, his voice. We need more people like him, like us, being represented in spaces where we used to not exist. Our views are just as important as anyone else's, and Gabs is one of the voices we all need(ed).

SLAWN

God's own given gift, literally!

And that's coming from someone
who's joking all the time.

I mean this with all seriousness!
With every bone in my body!

Only one Gabriel Moses!!!!!

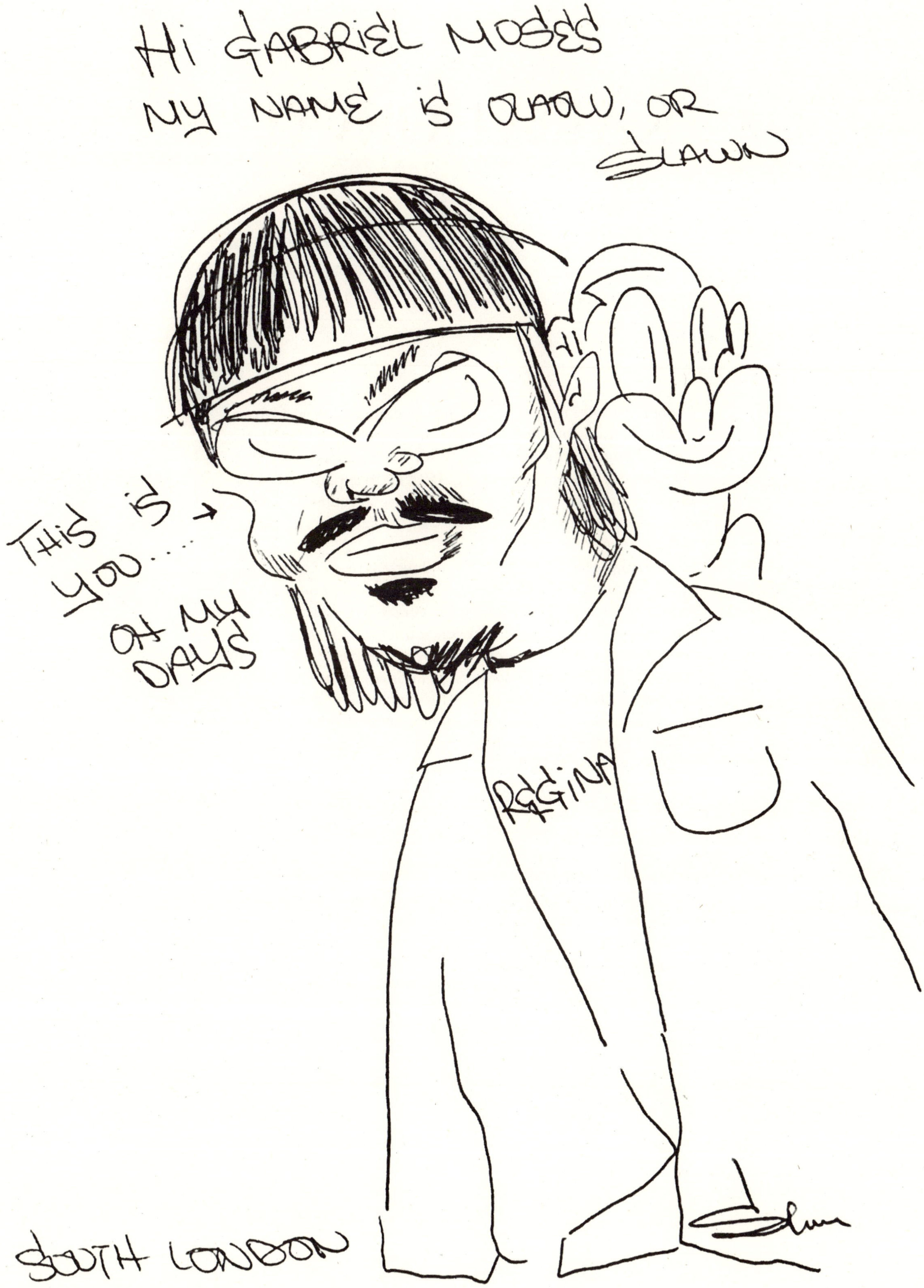
HI GABRIEL MOSES
MY NAME IS OLAOLU, OR
SLAWN
Hi
THIS IS YOU.....
OH MY DAYS
REGINA
SOUTH LONDON

KATJA HORVAT

There is everything to say, but at the same time nothing. Gabs is family! He is my brother! He is also someone I met a few years ago, working together on a shoot. Ever since our first brief, first call, we were in this, whatever it is. It's hard to explain why him, why this connection, why the friendship we have. It all, kind of, makes zero sense but it also makes all the sense in the world.

There is magic to Gabs as a person, and there is magic to his work. I don't even know where the line is. His demeanour is subtle and shy yet so strong, just like his imagery. When you encounter him, you will remember him. When you see his image, you will remember it. He is a generational talent, the chosen one! Not many people can convey so much in an image or a frame as he can. Not many people stay so true to who they are regardless of the environment they are put in. Not many people carry themselves so unapologetically honestly the way he does. Not many people have the determination he has.... I mean, again, I could say everything and nothing, I will just let his work speak for itself.

But I do want to say one more thing, to Gabs . . .

Thank you! Thank you for everything you do. Thank you for being there. Thank you for keeping up. Thank you for all the respect, patience, and understanding you show me every day. I love you and I am so proud of you! I am proud of all the work we did and will do together. I am so proud of this book! Gabs we did it!!!! We made a book! This is just the beginning, and I can't wait to see what is next.

Love always!

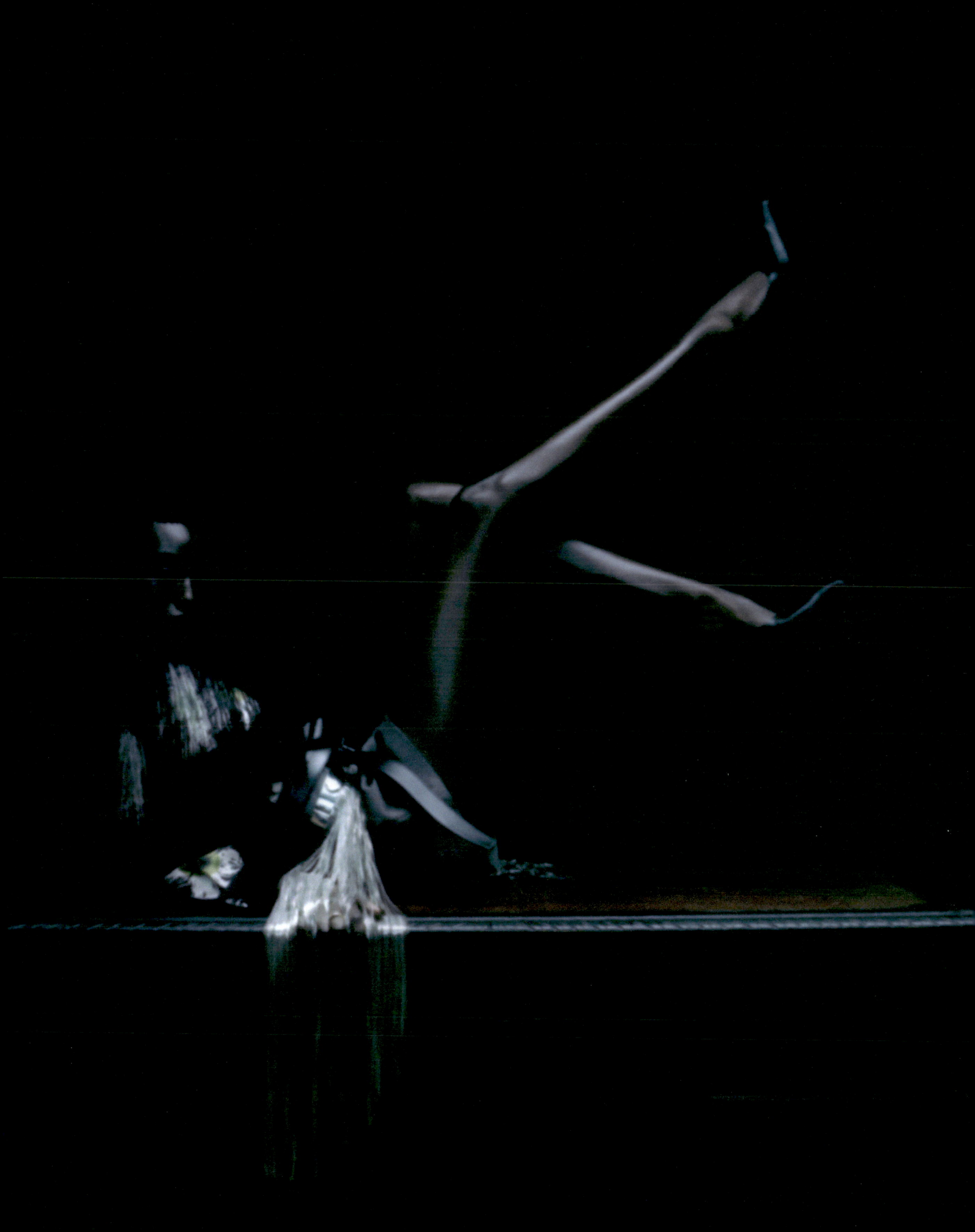

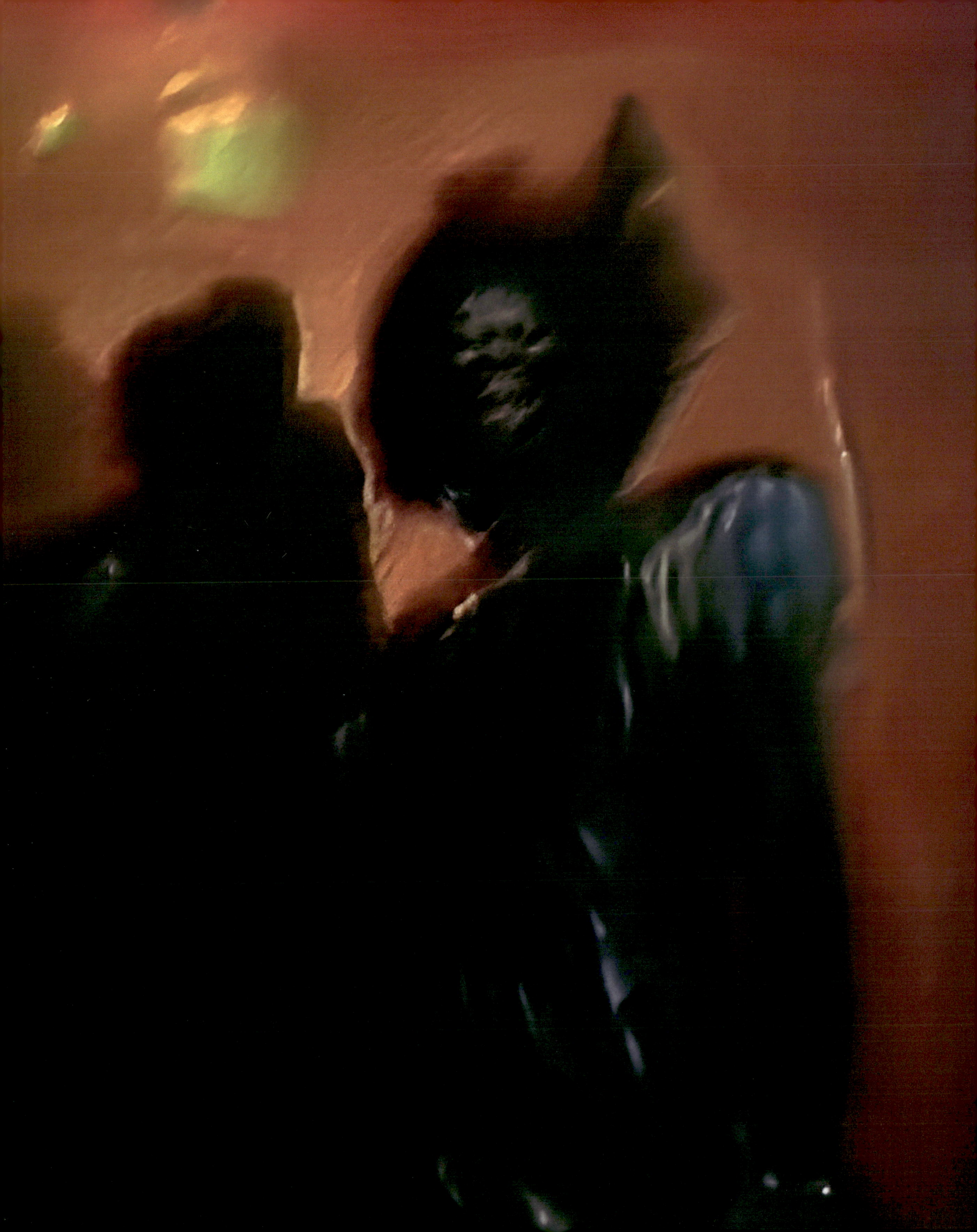

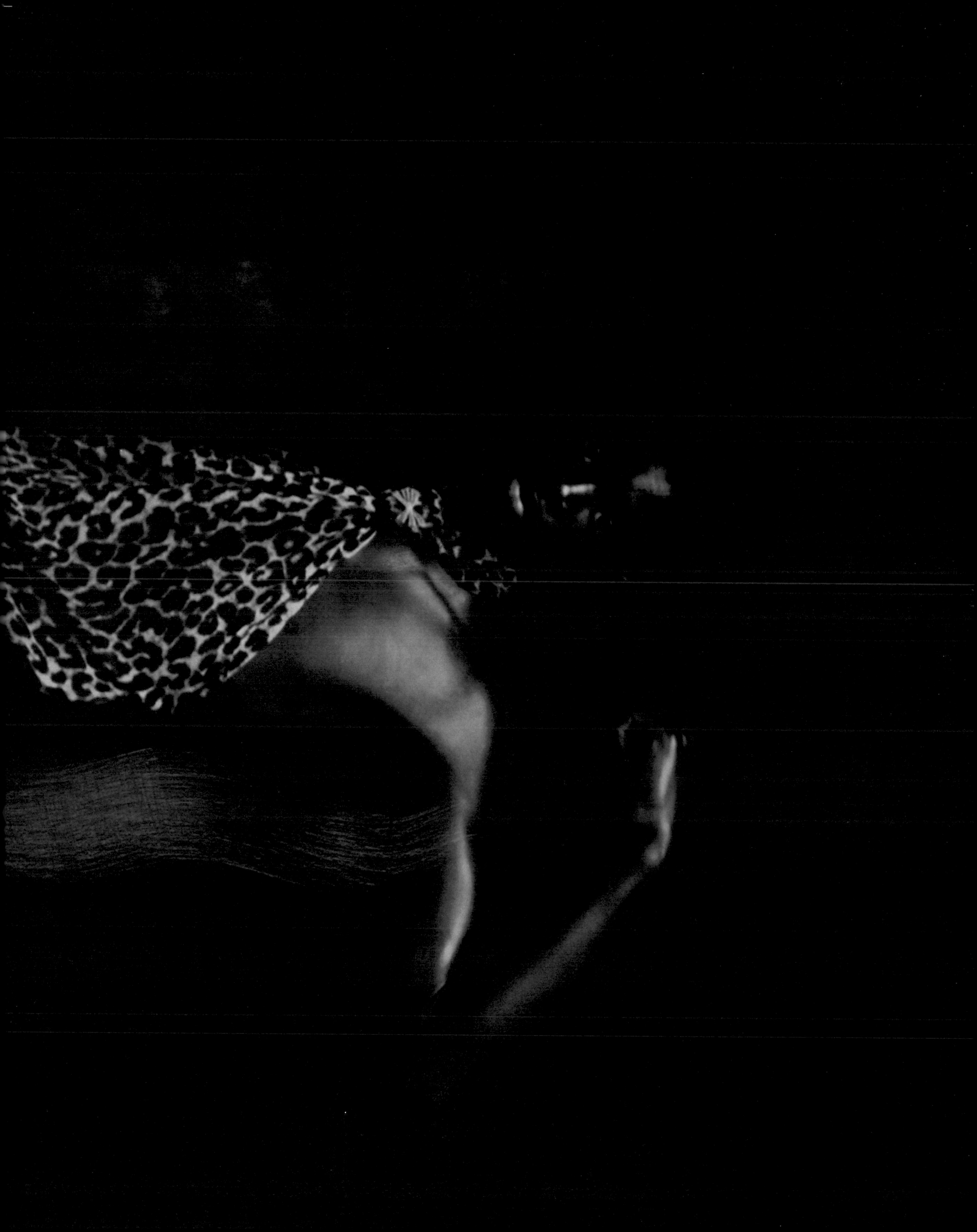

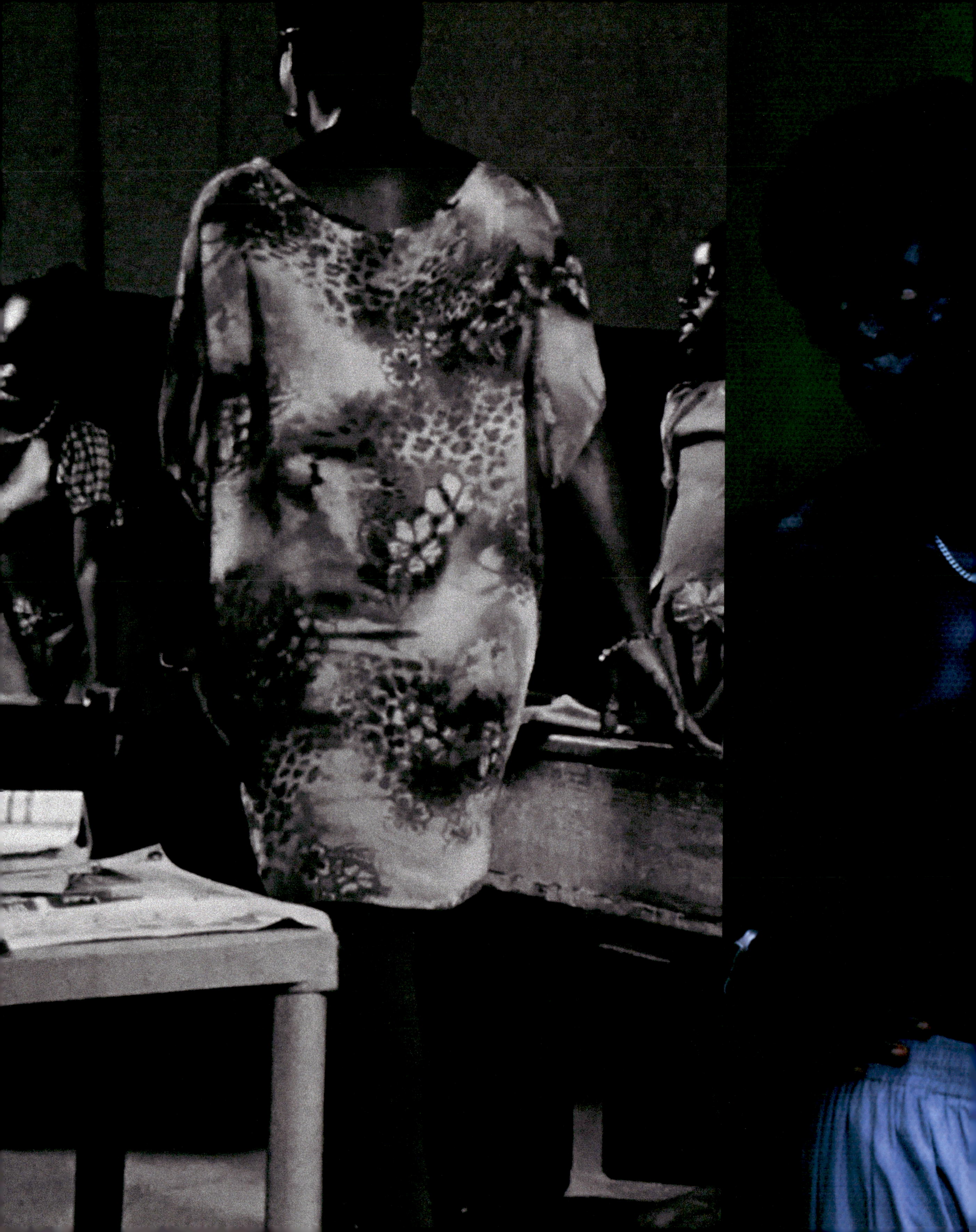

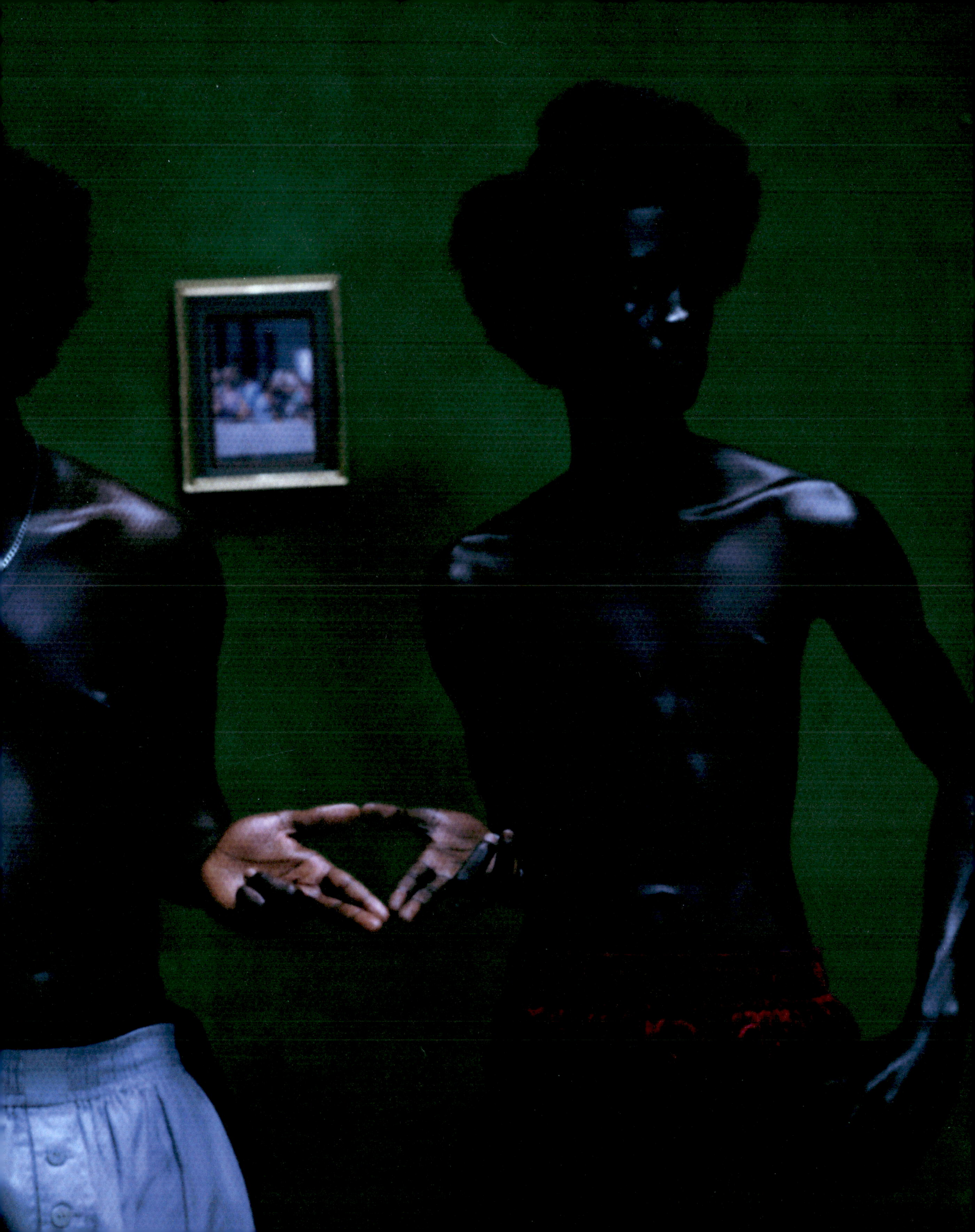

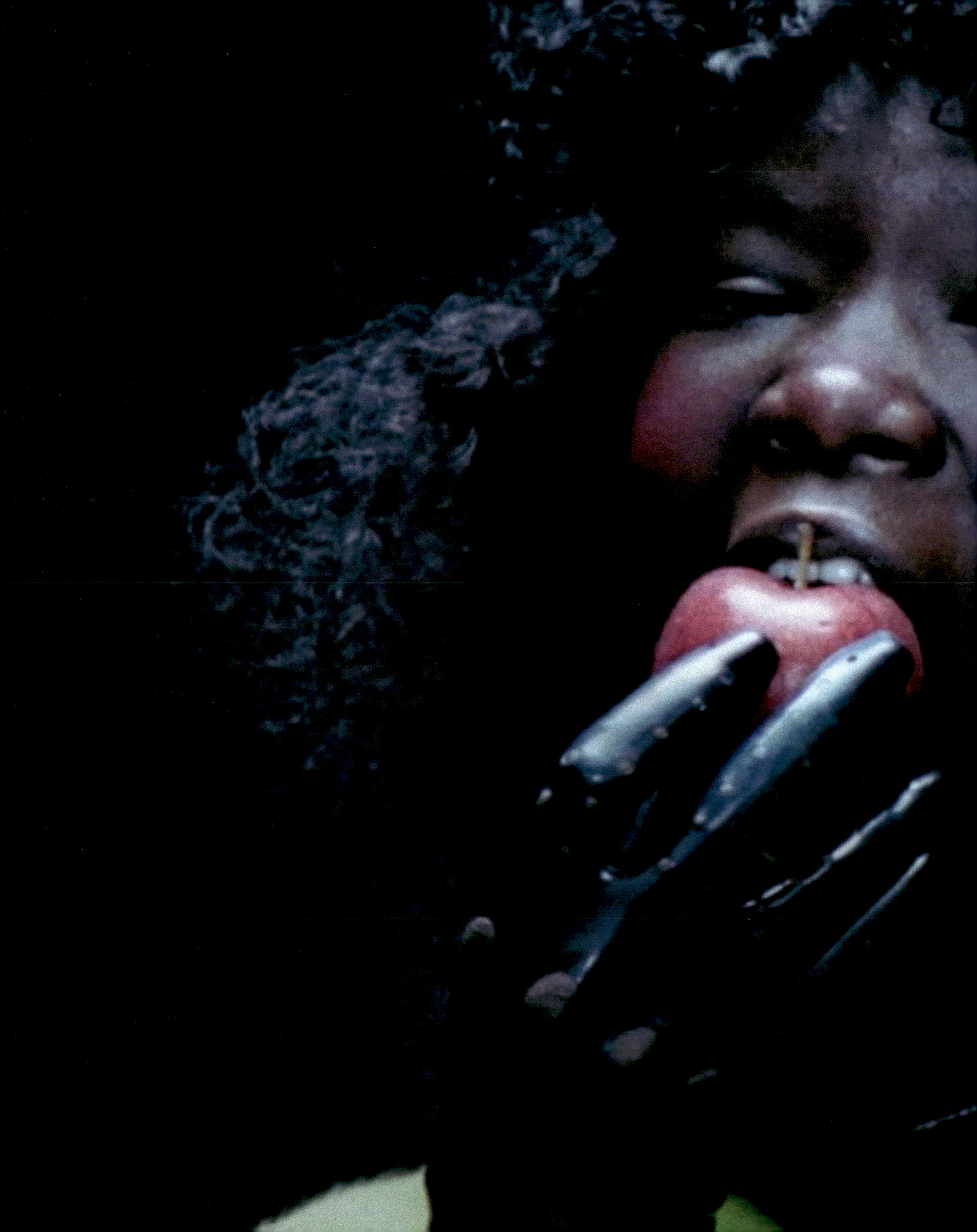

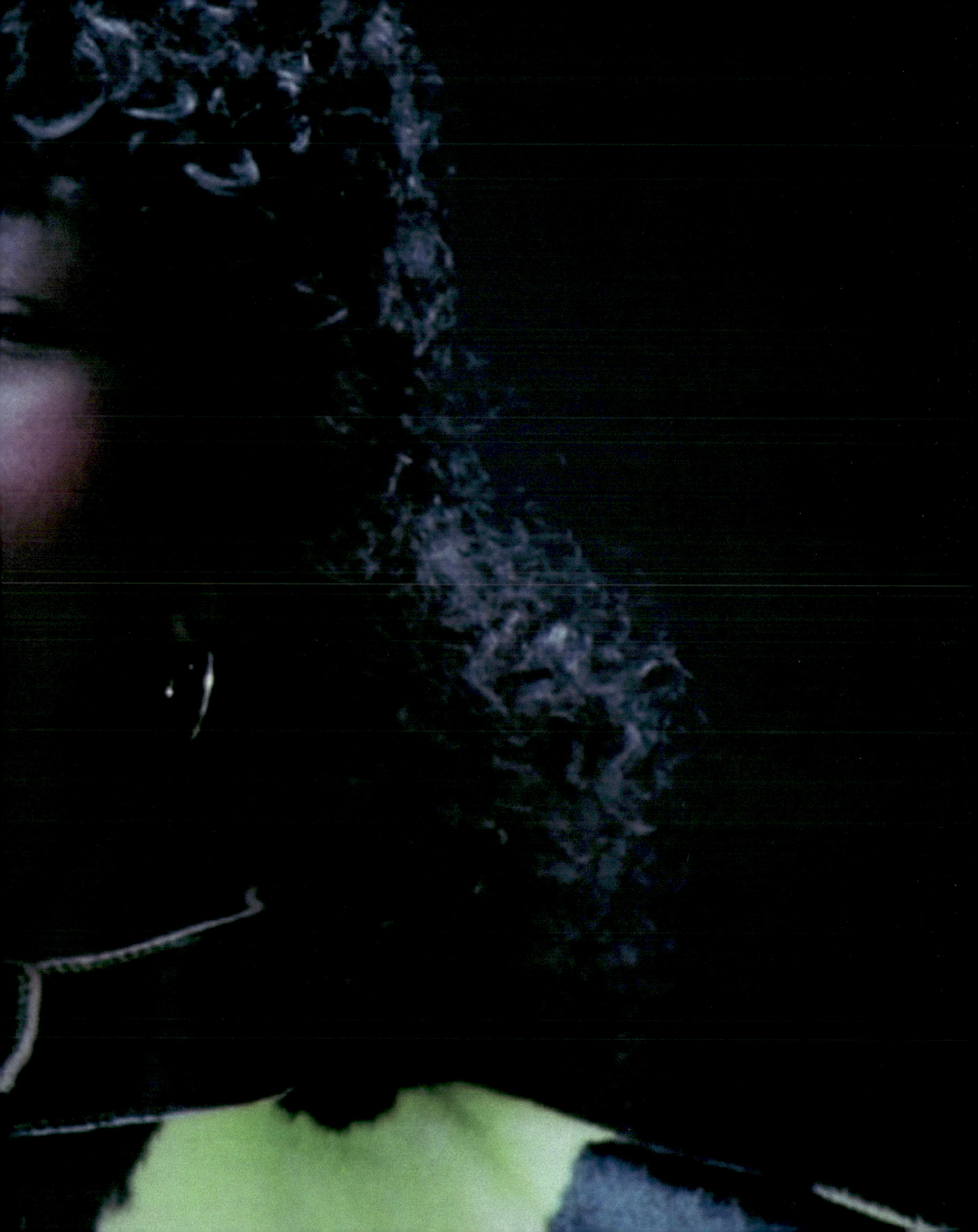

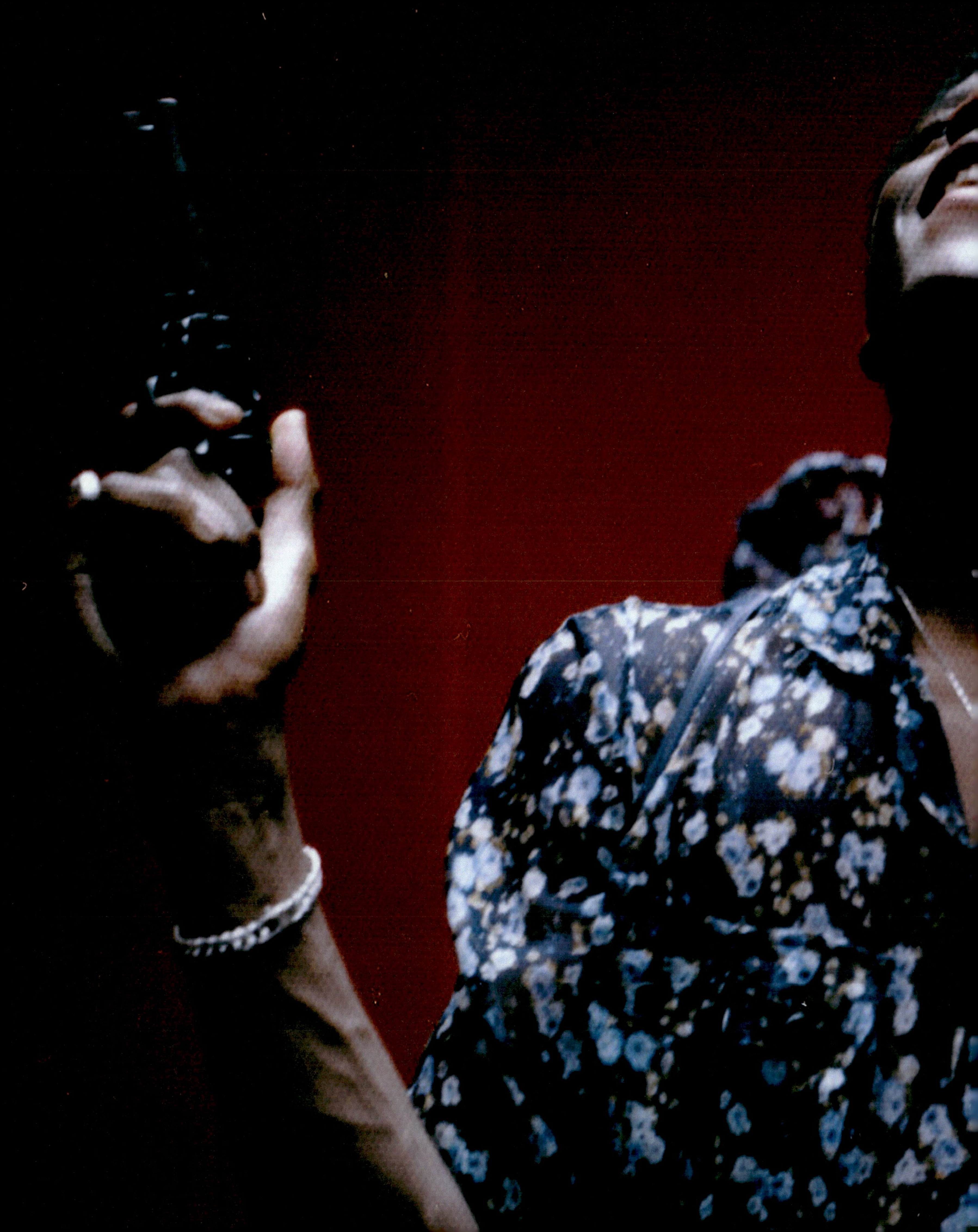

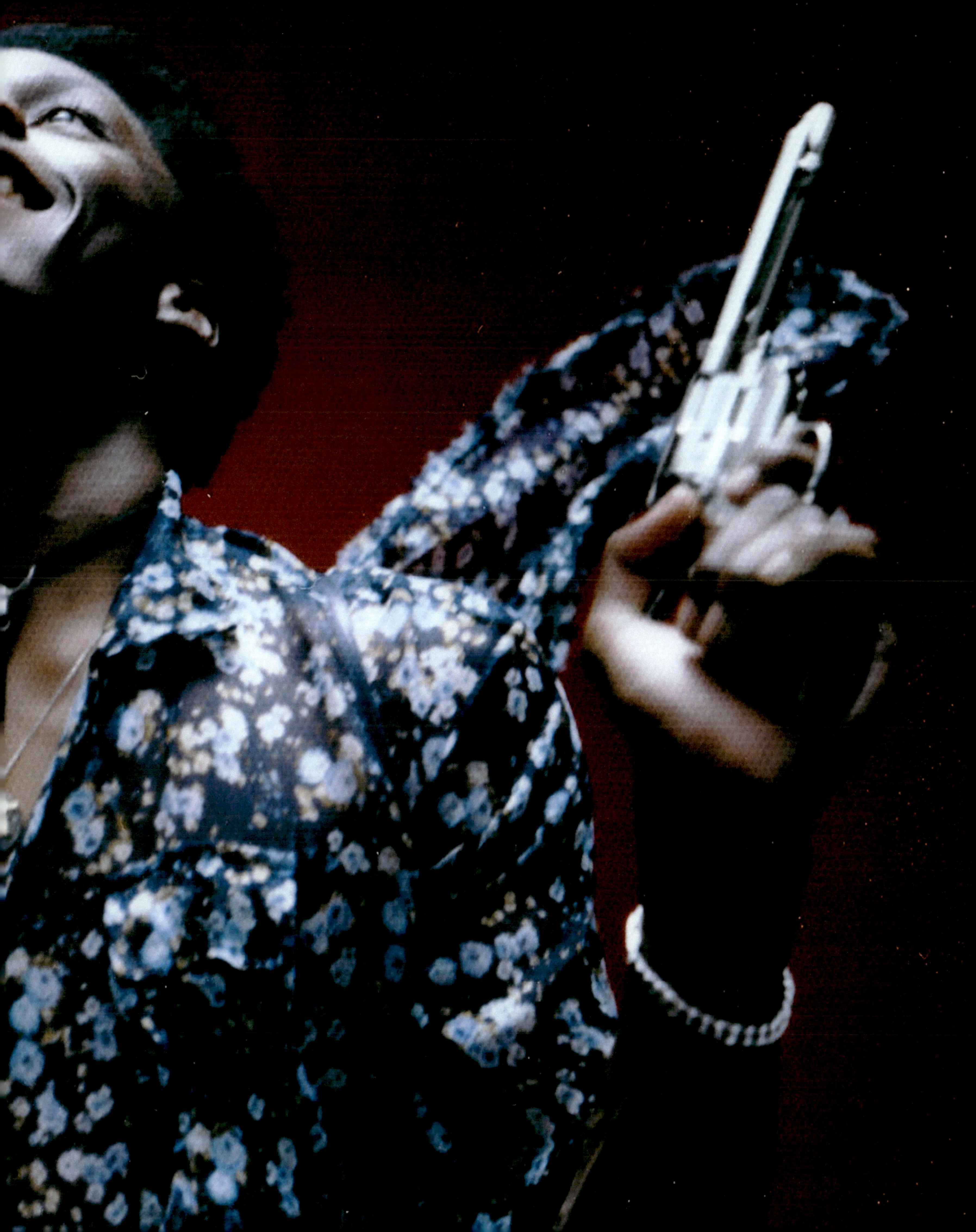

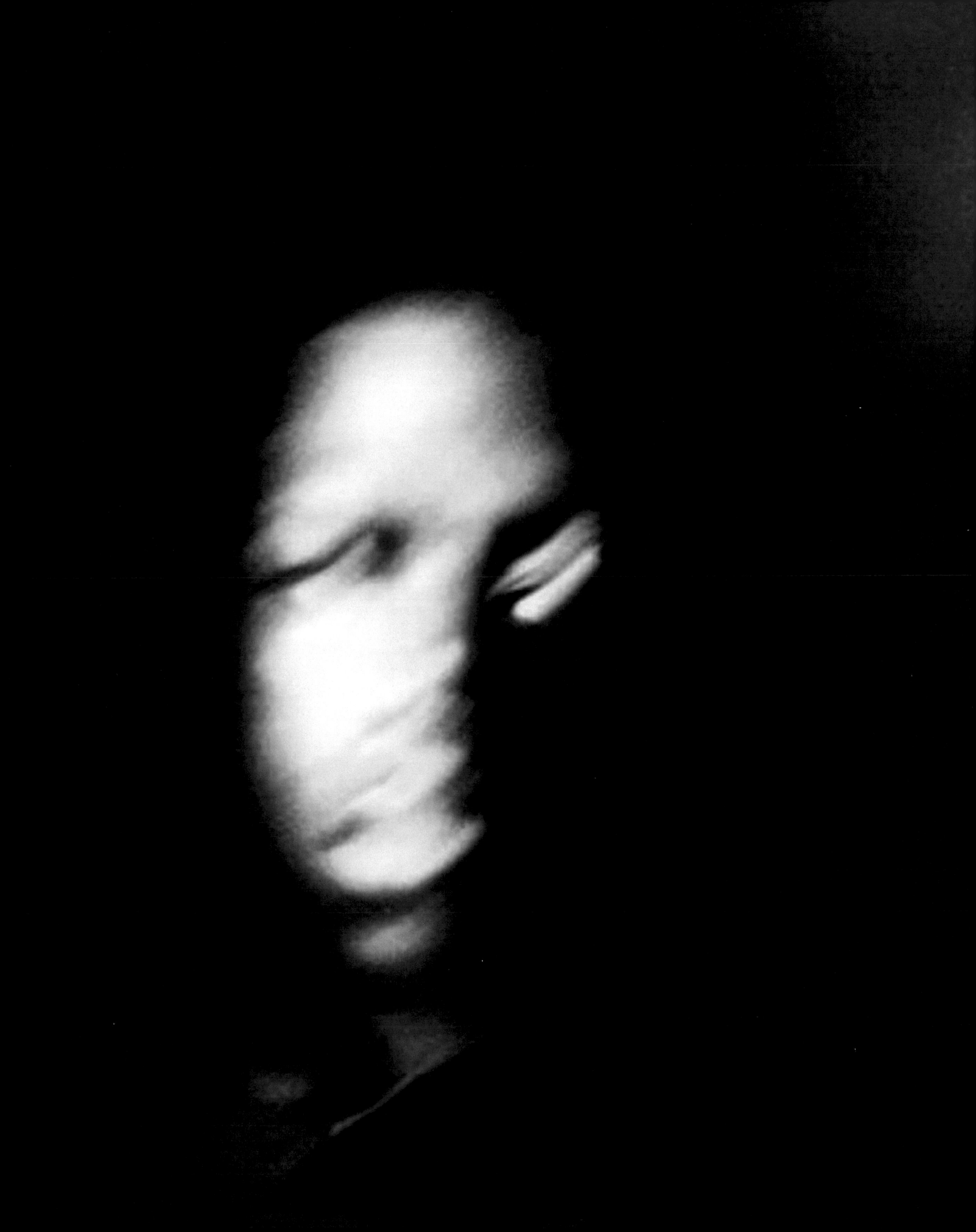

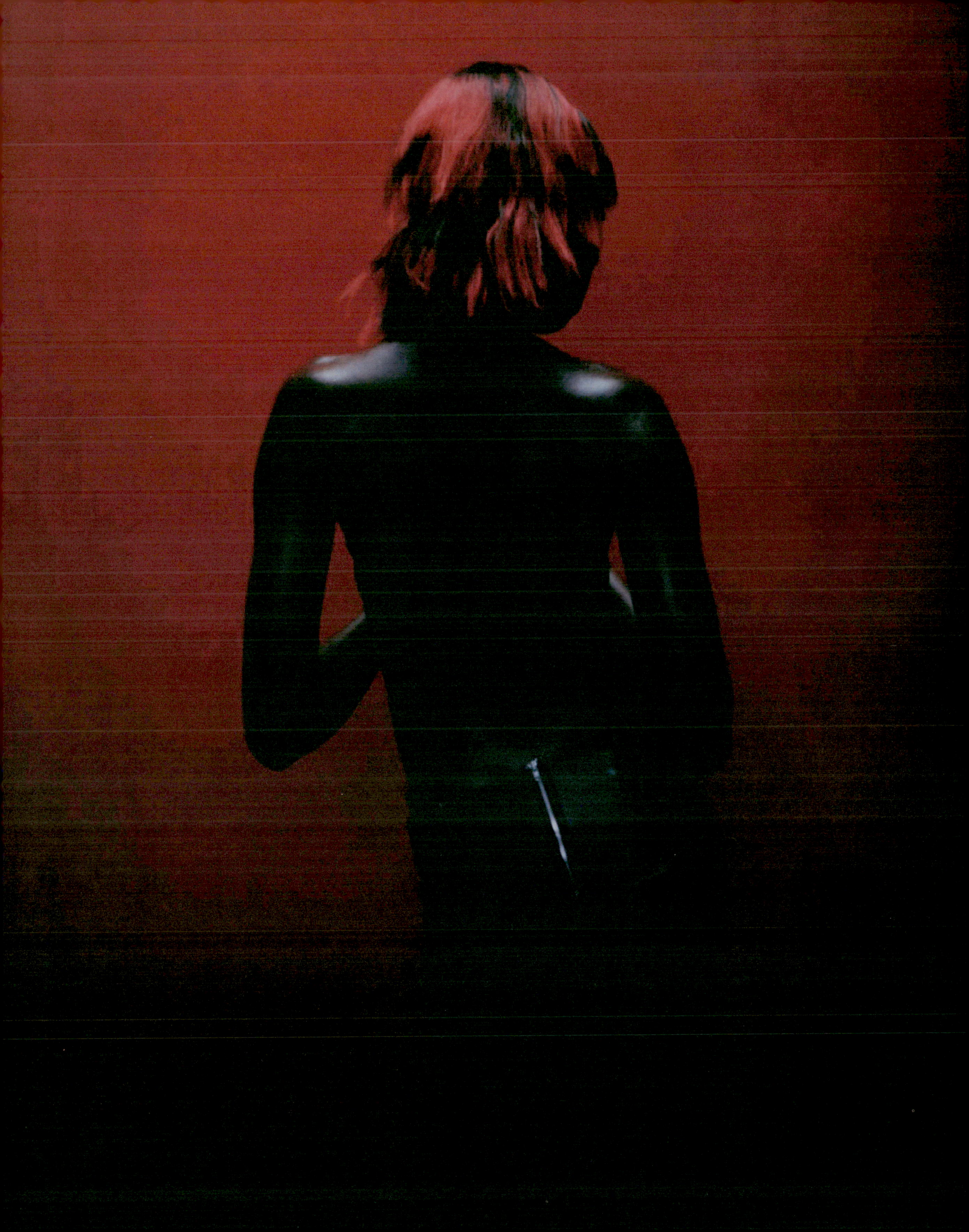

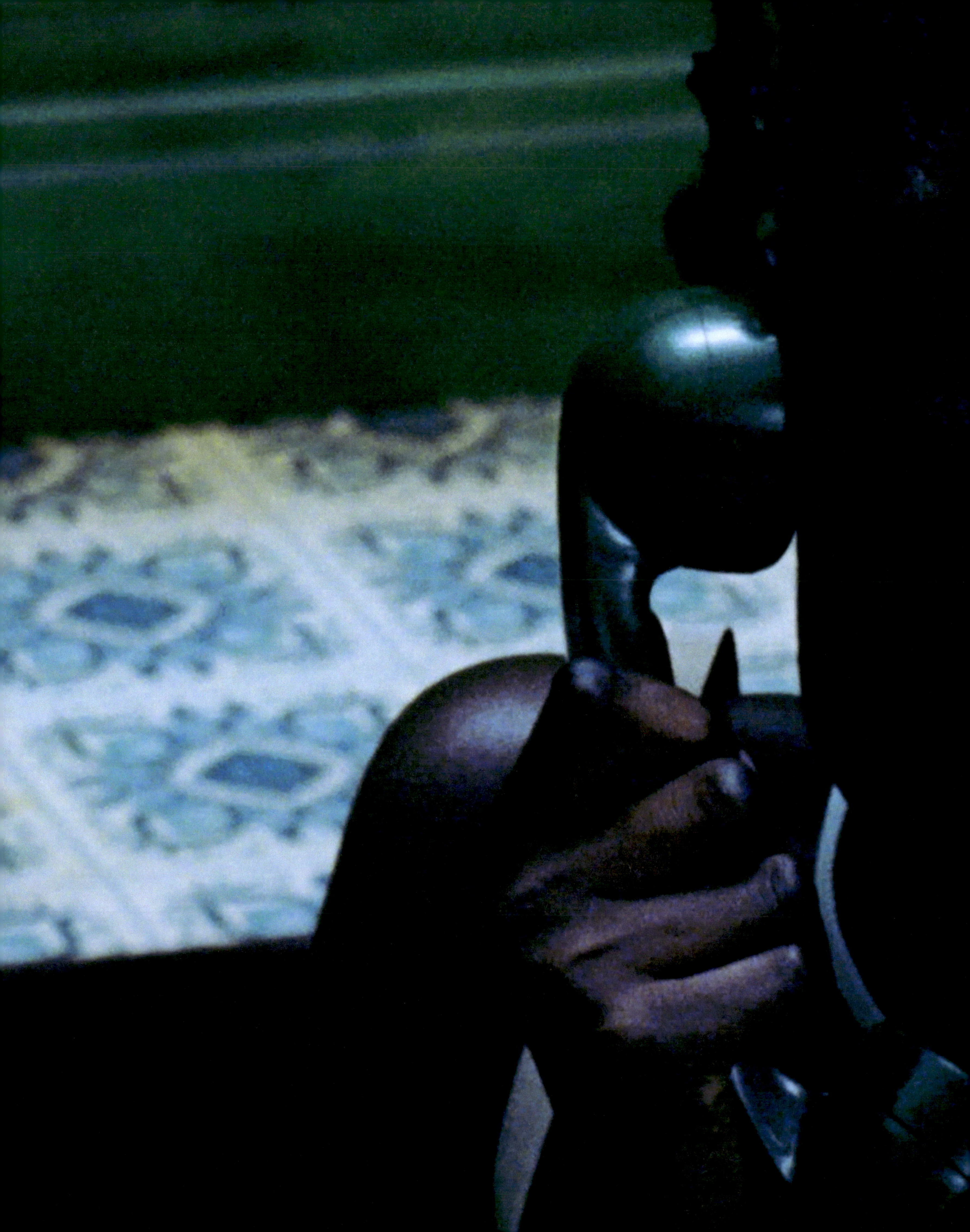

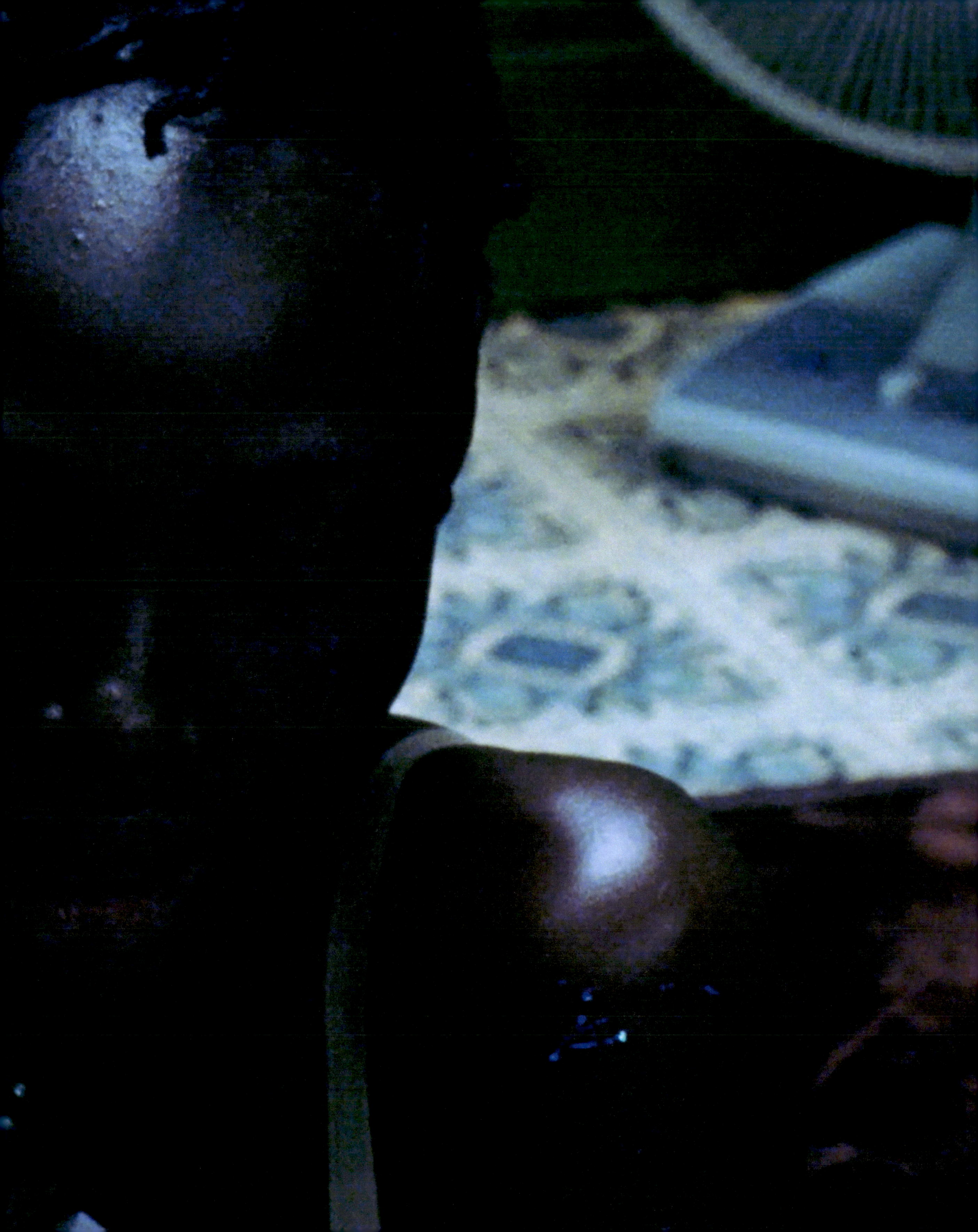

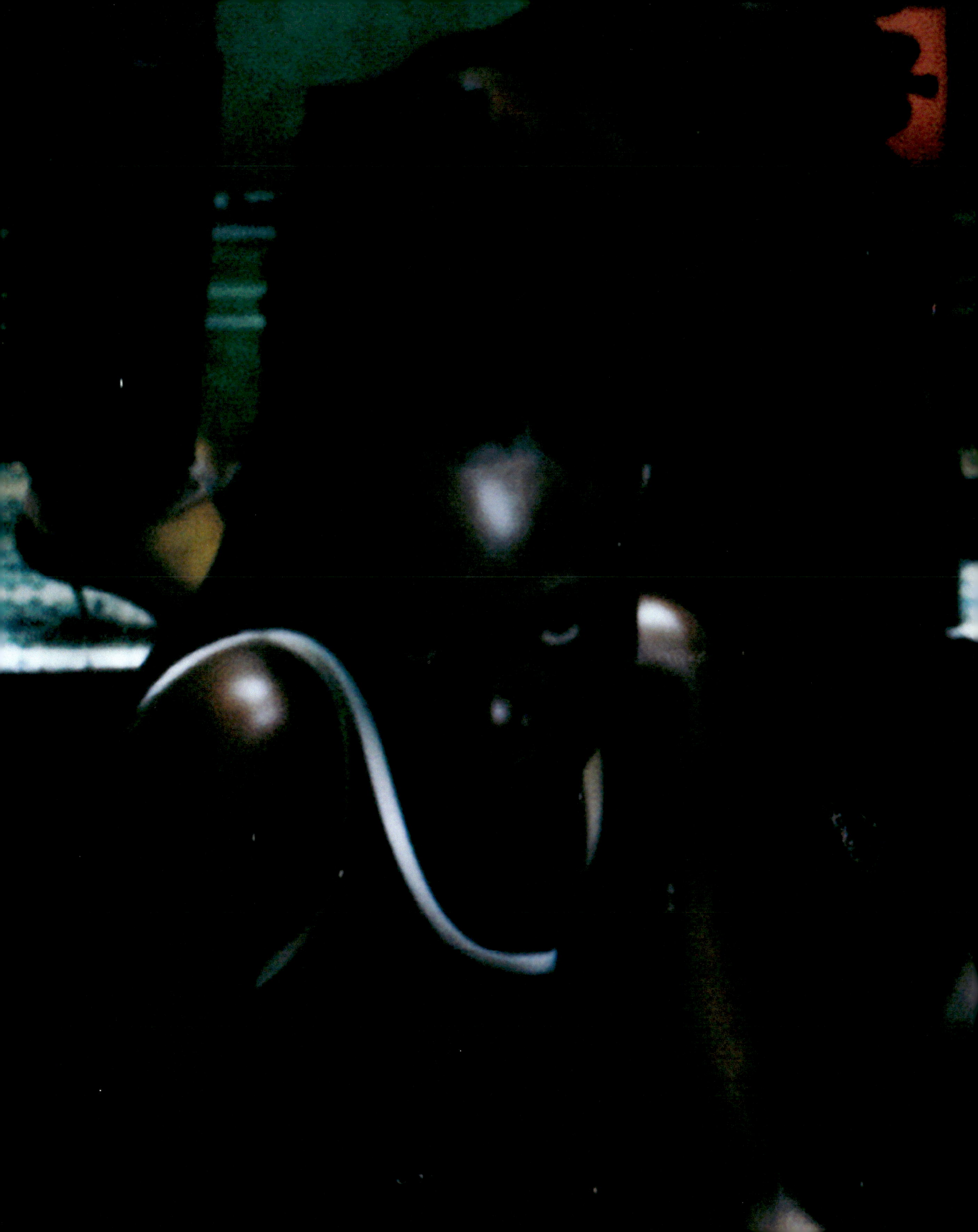

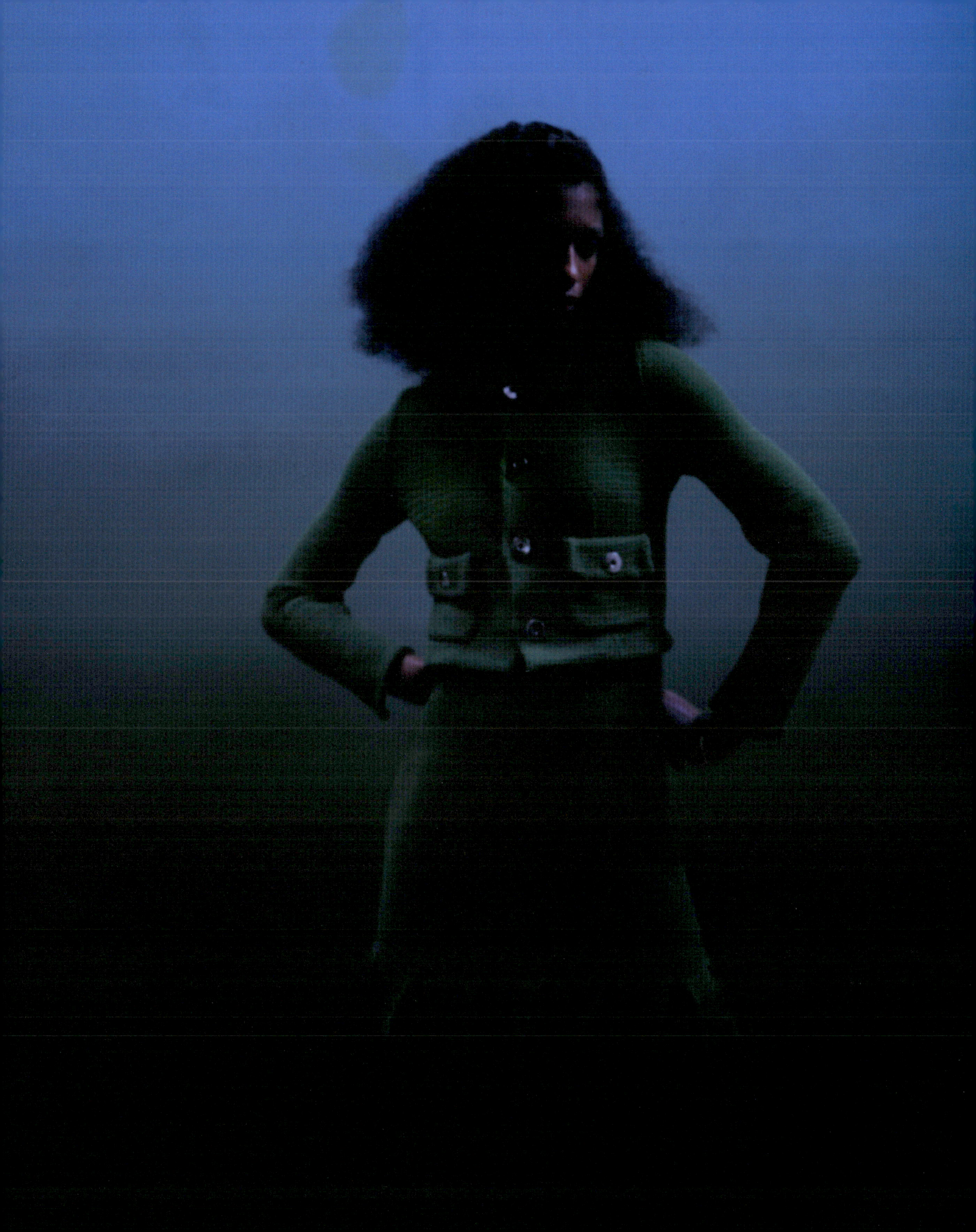

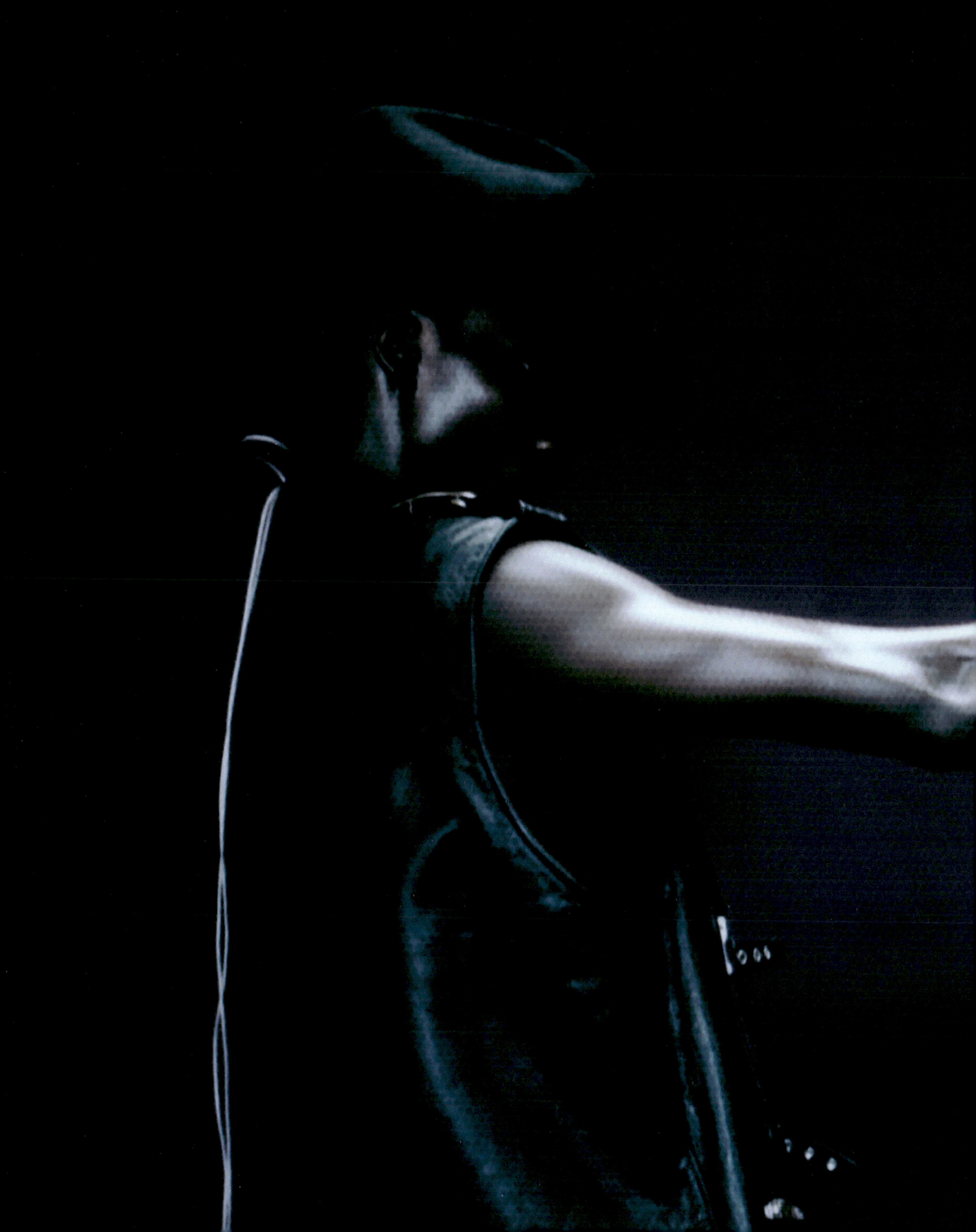

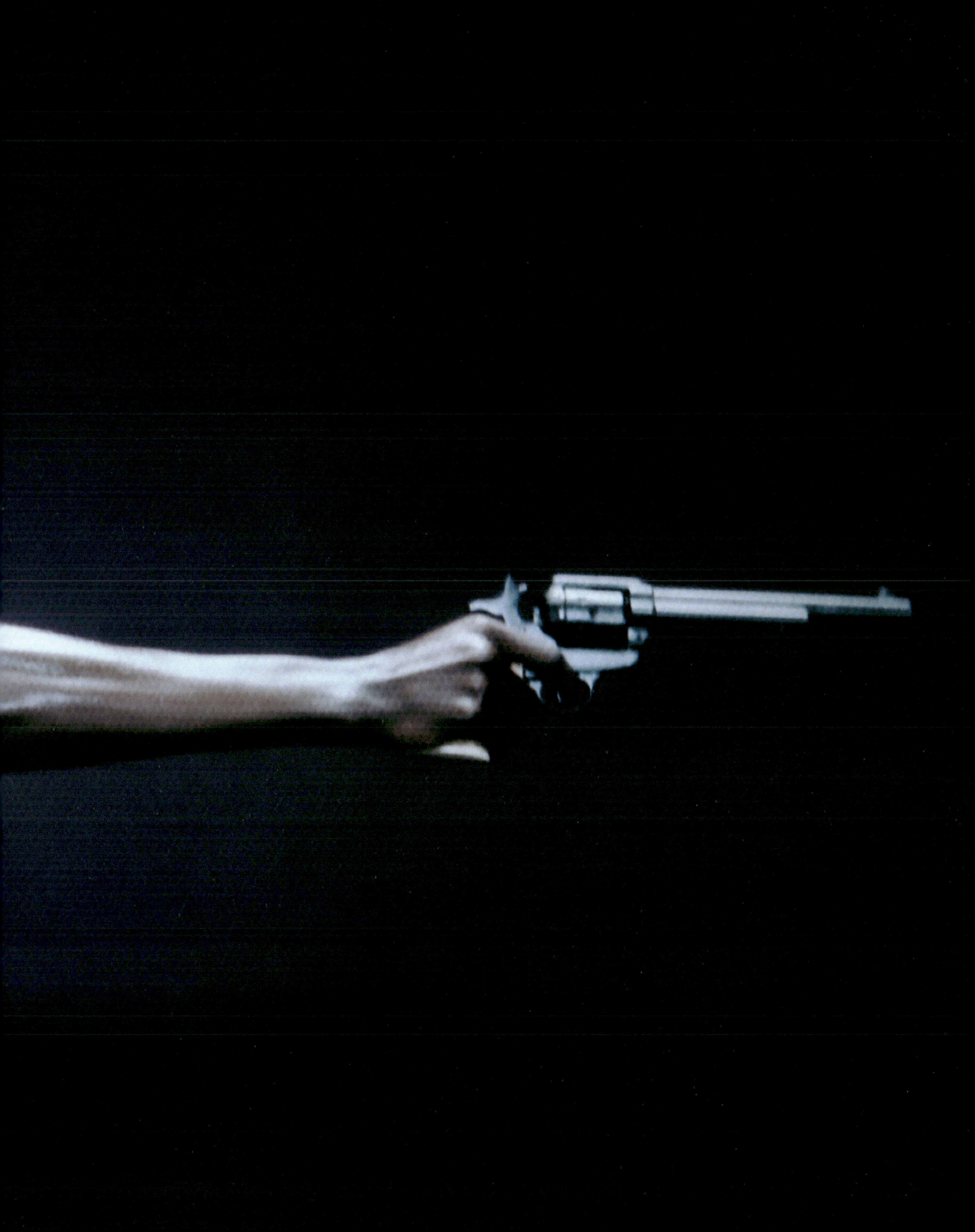

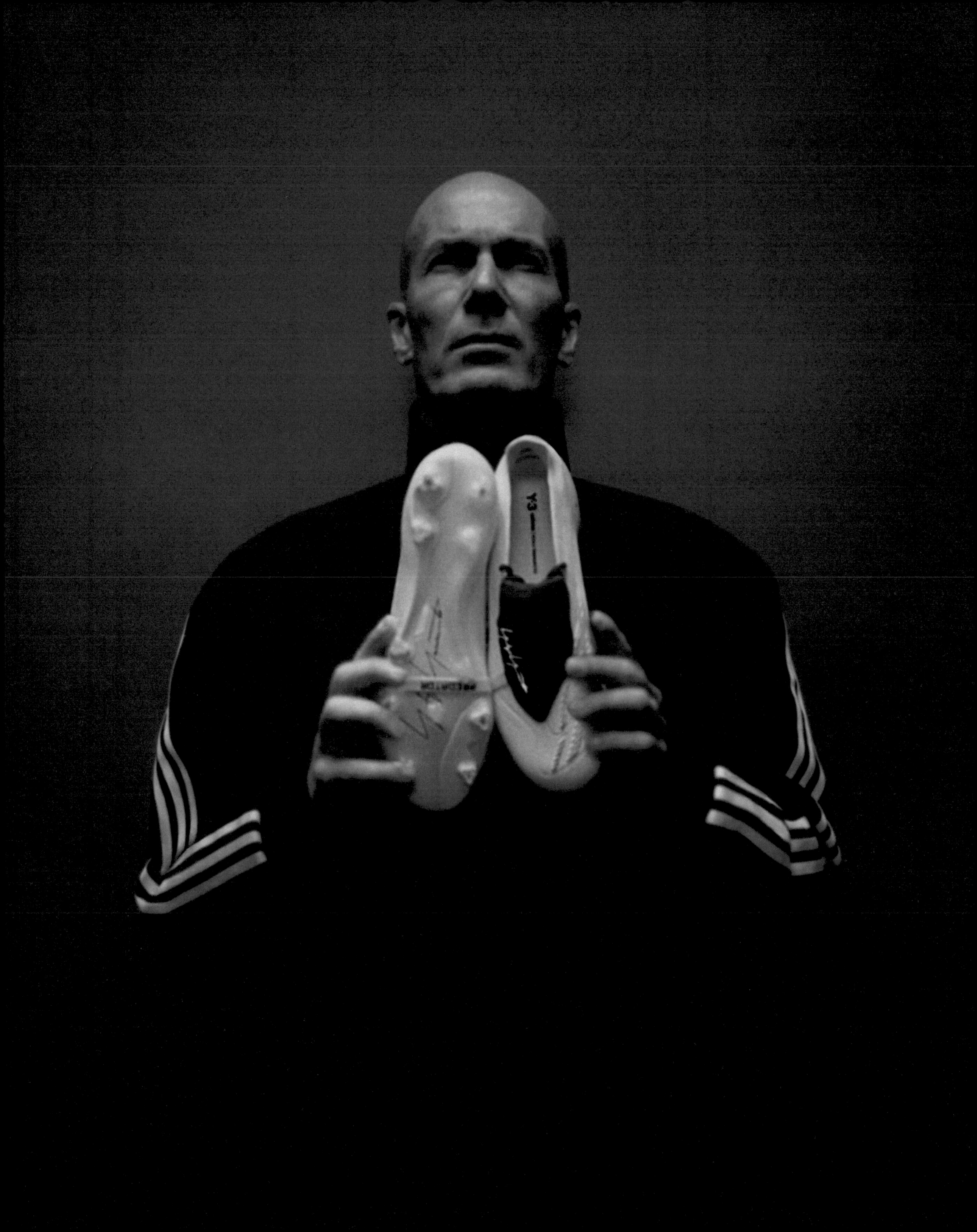

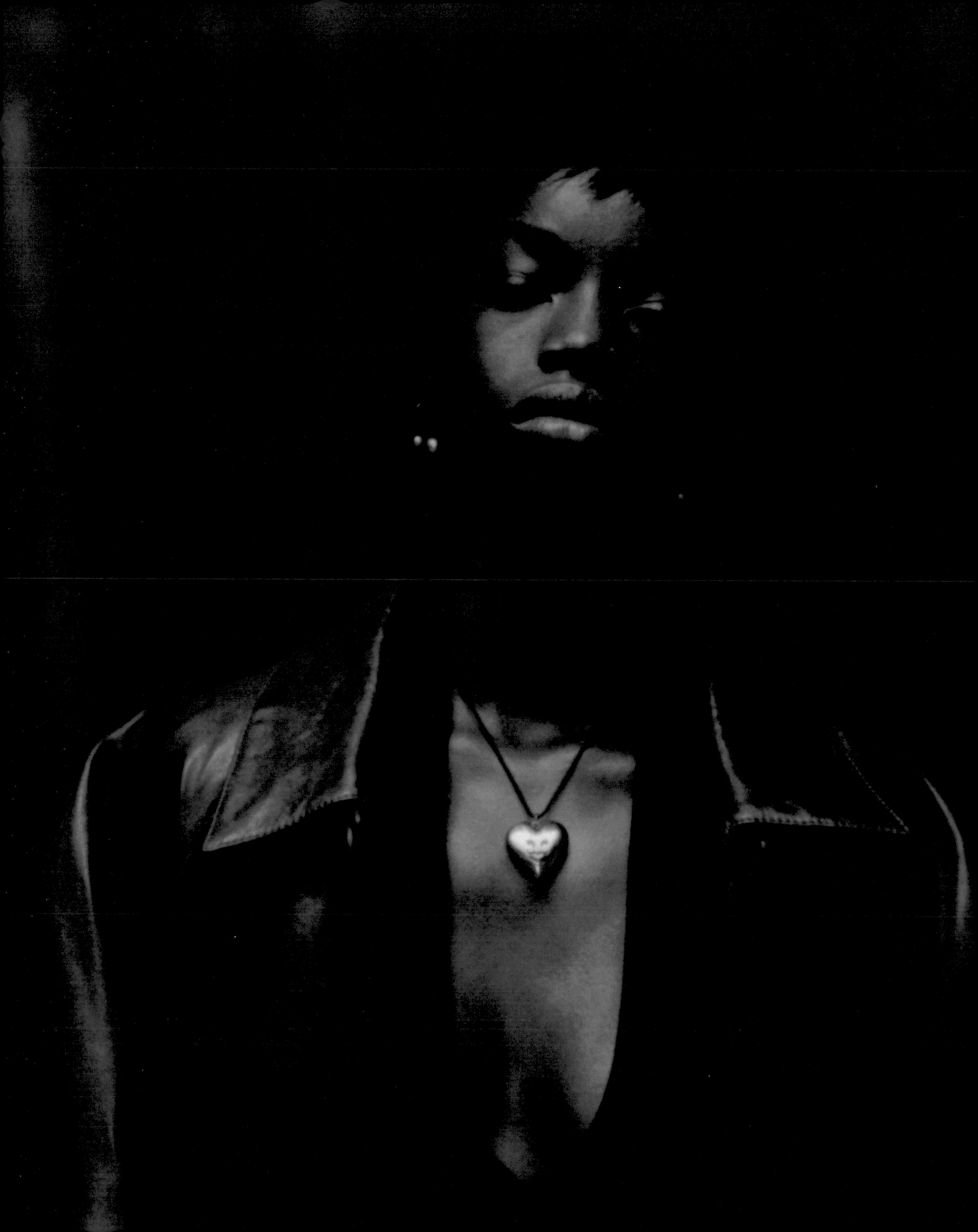

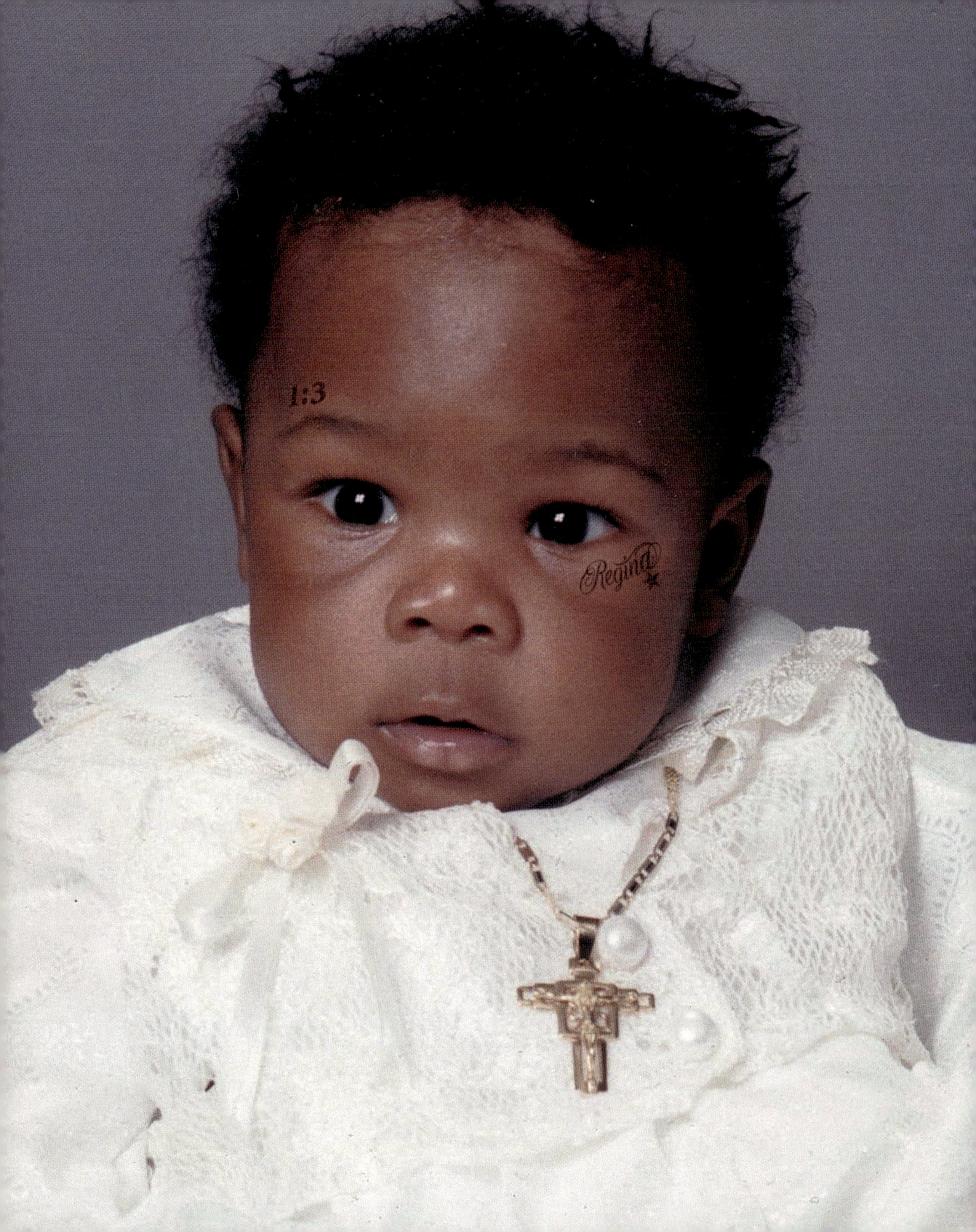
1:3
Regina

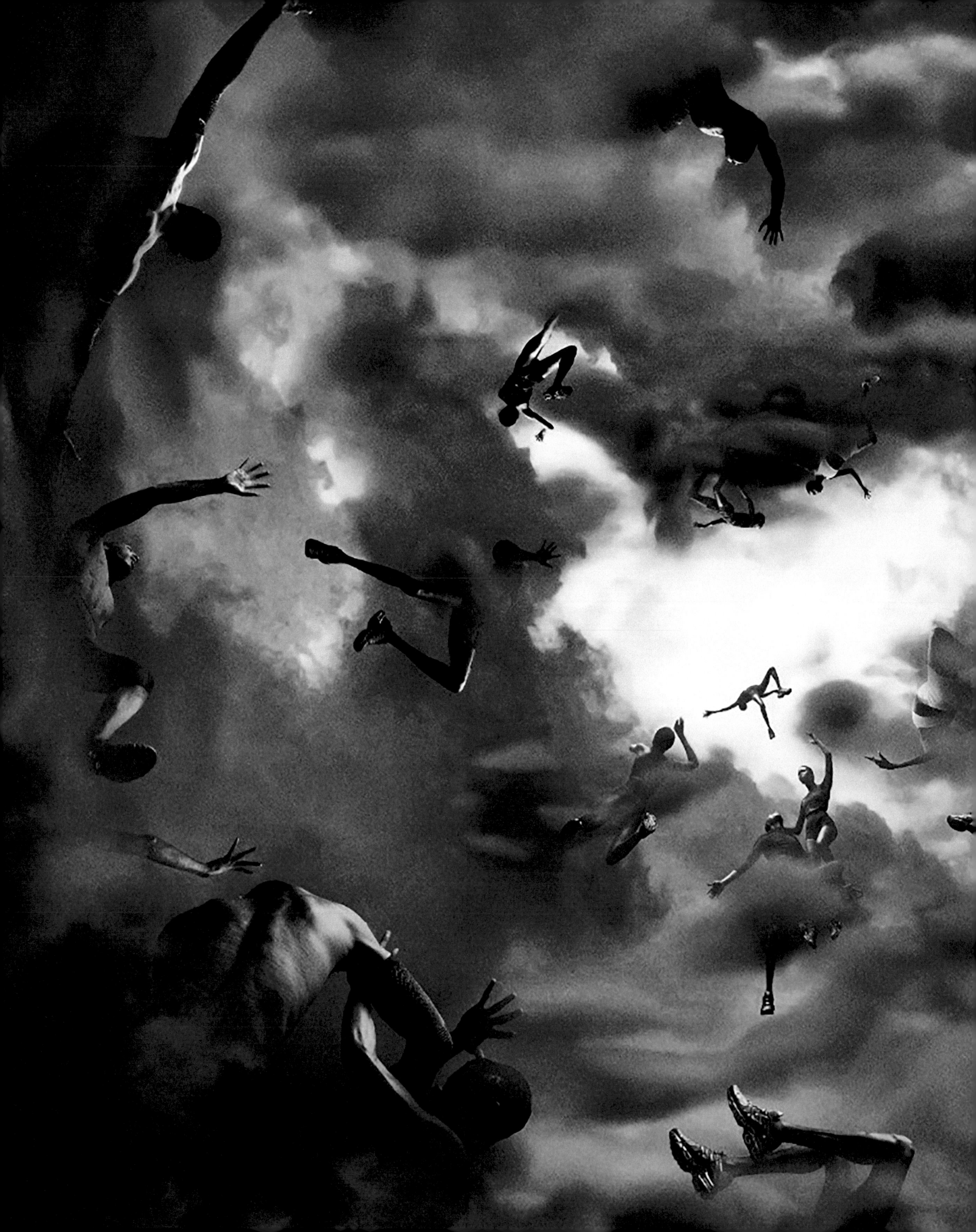

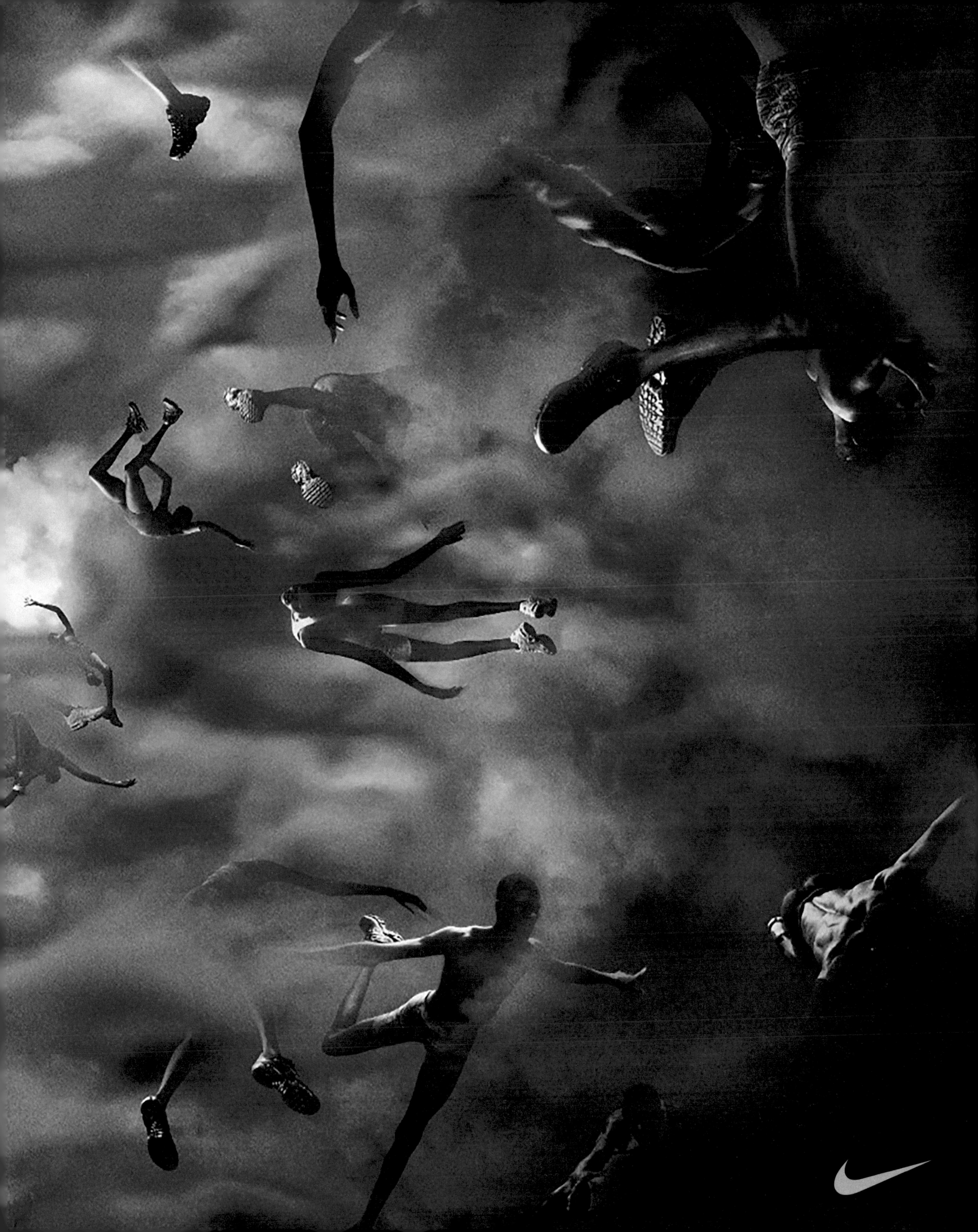

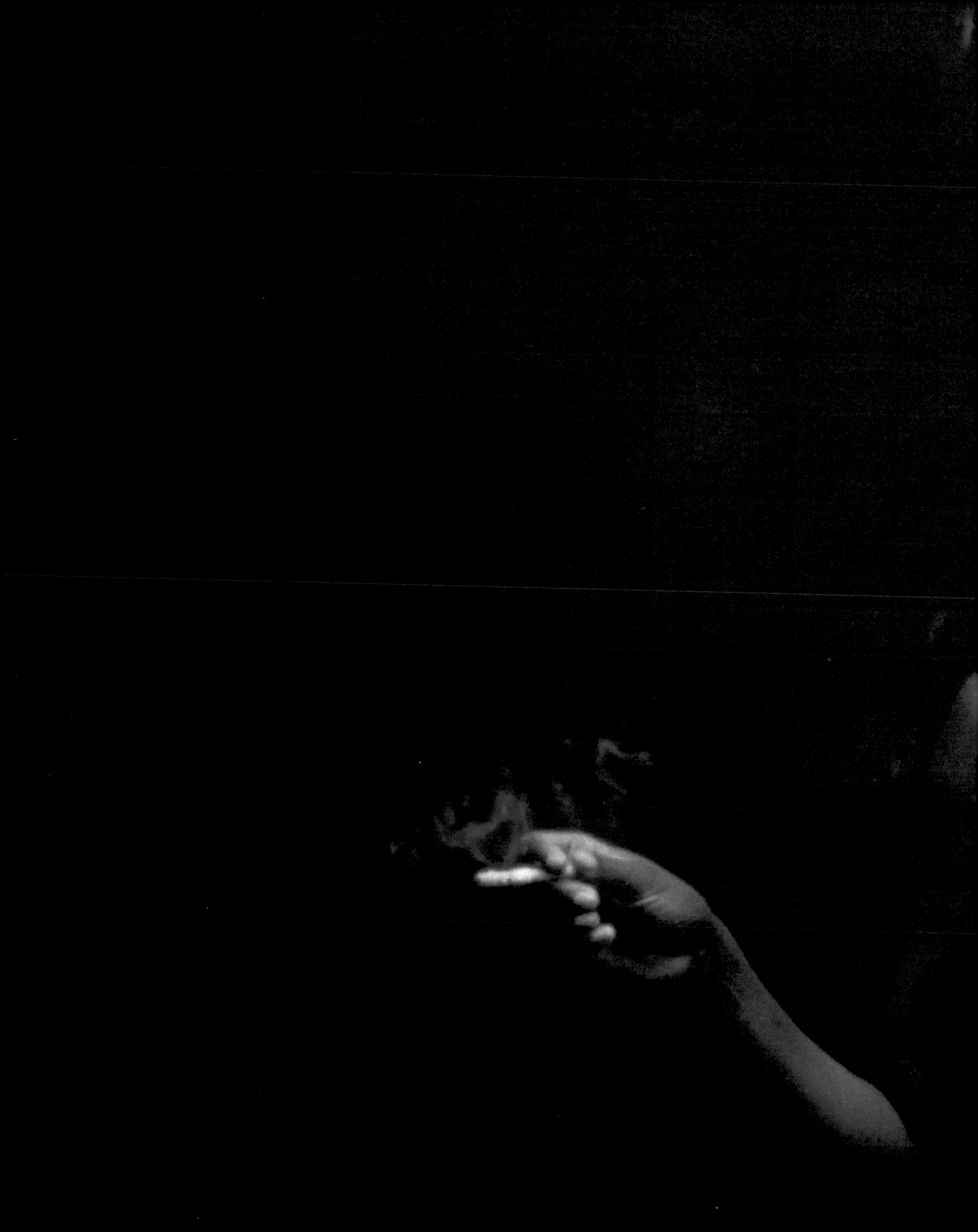

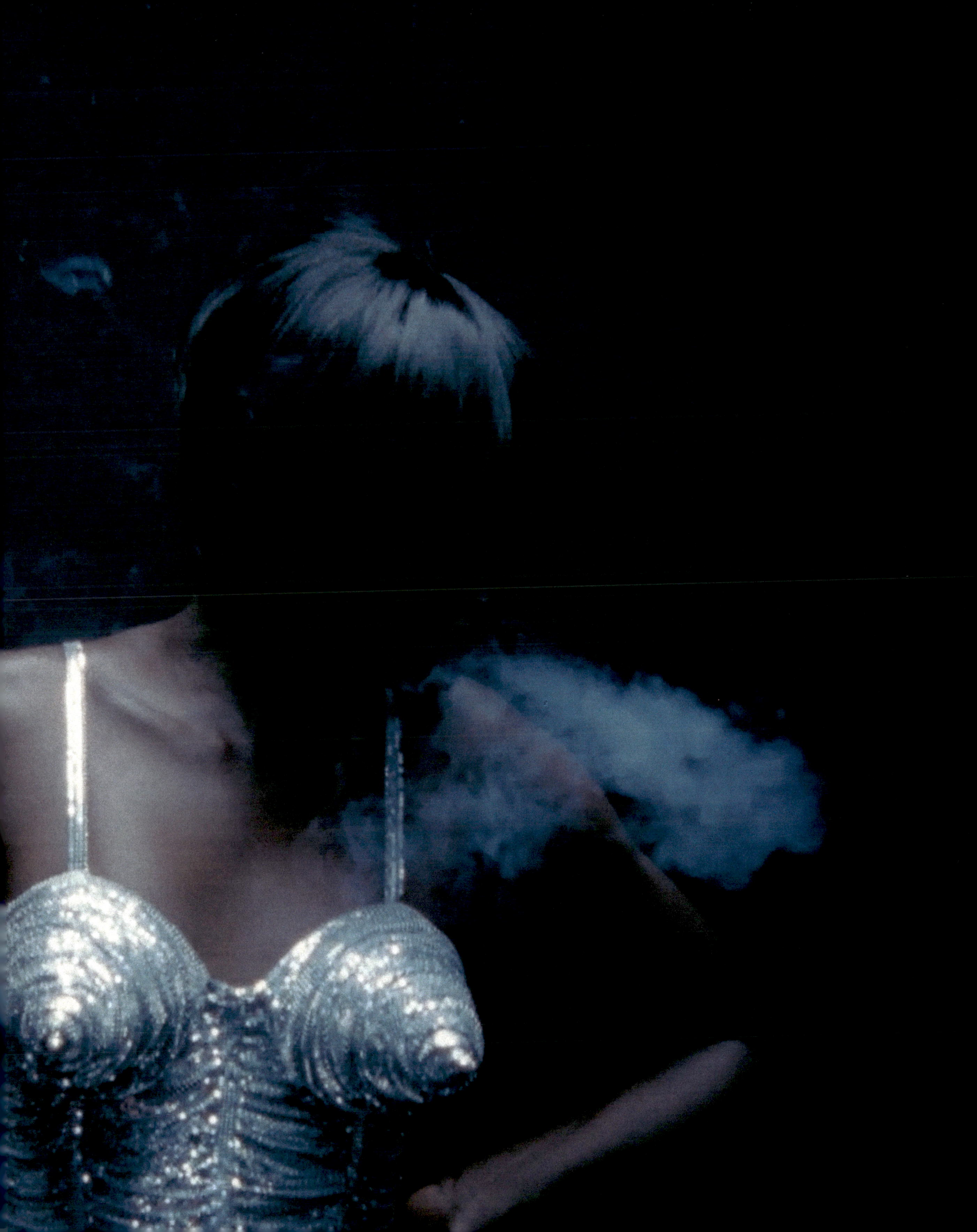

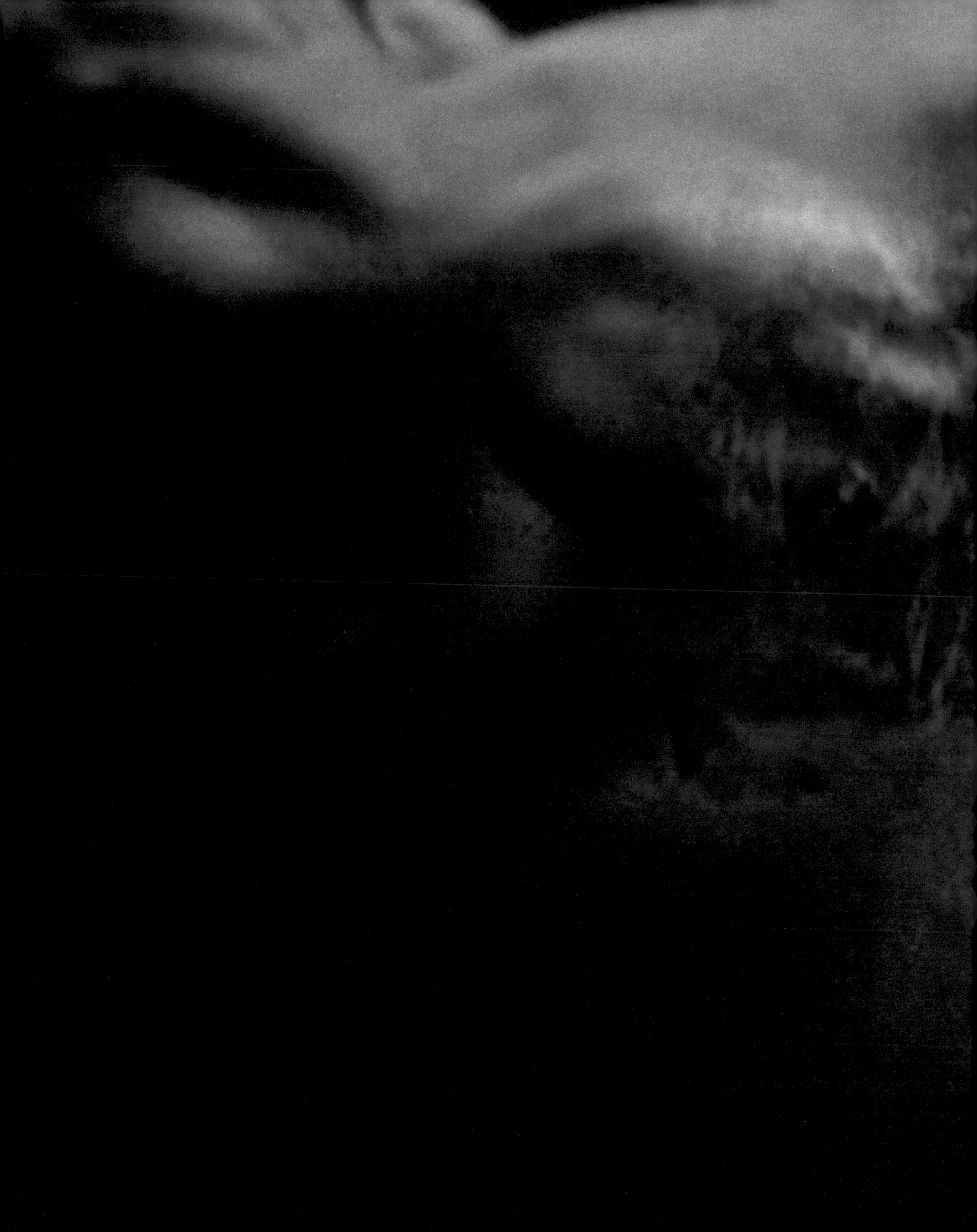

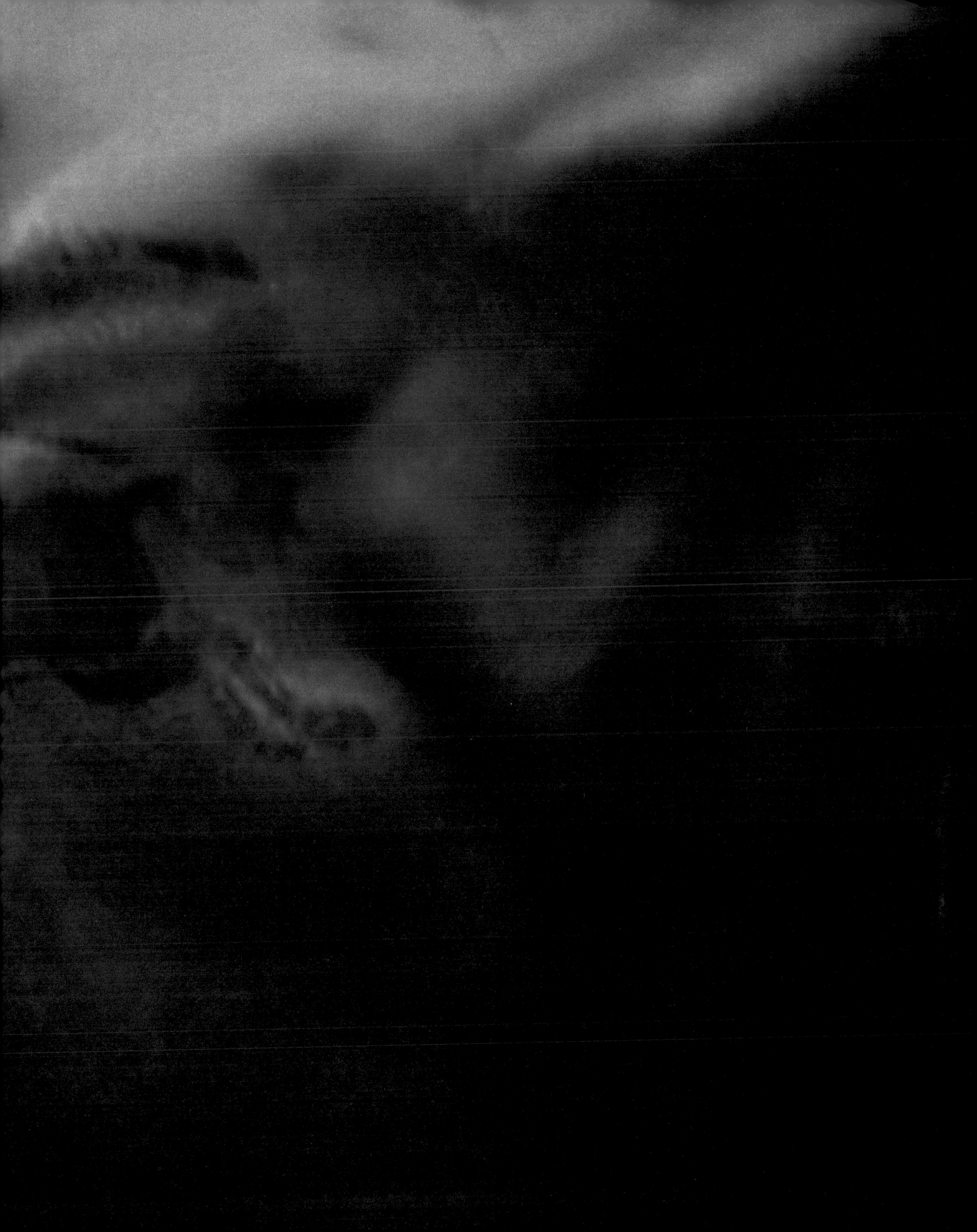

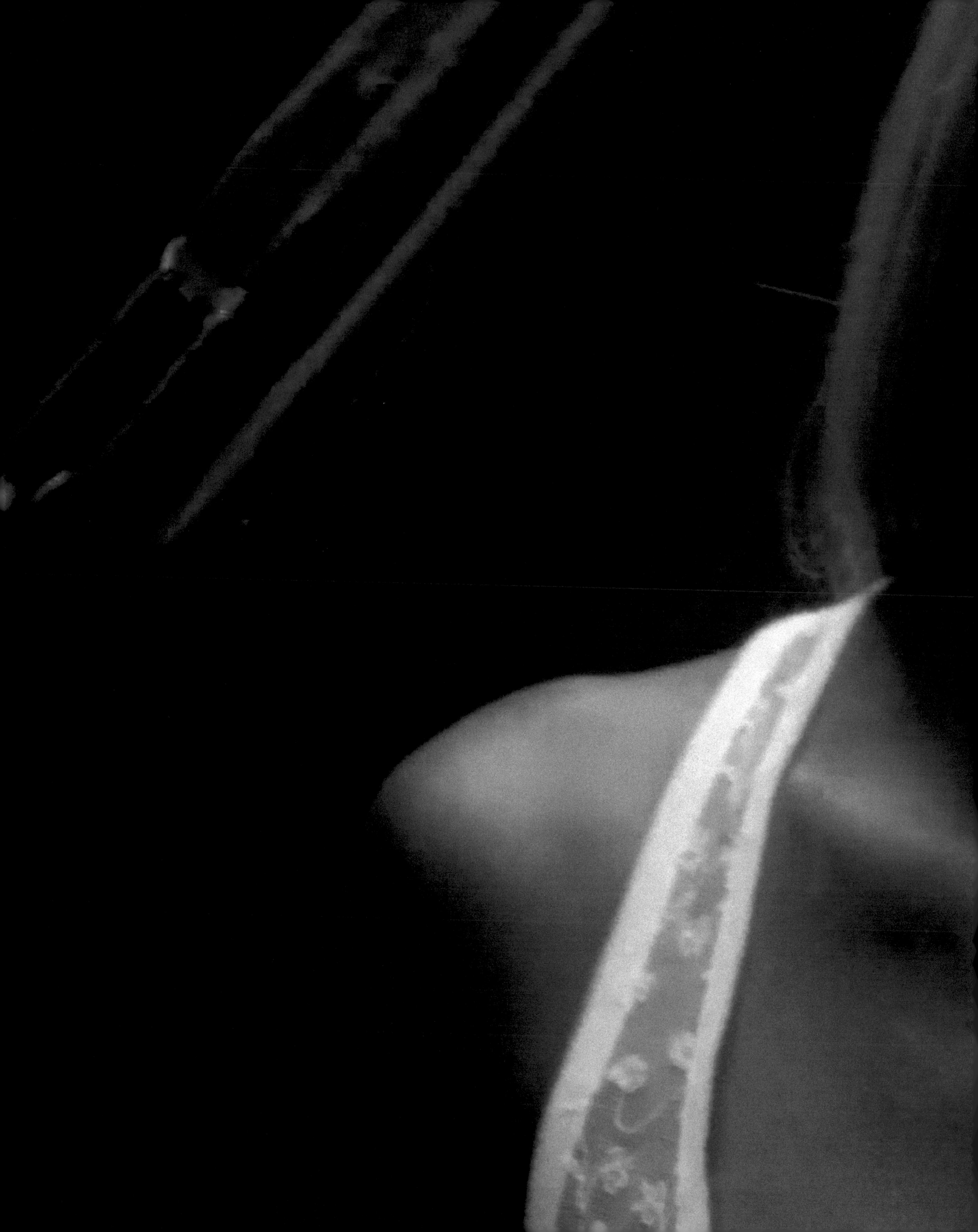

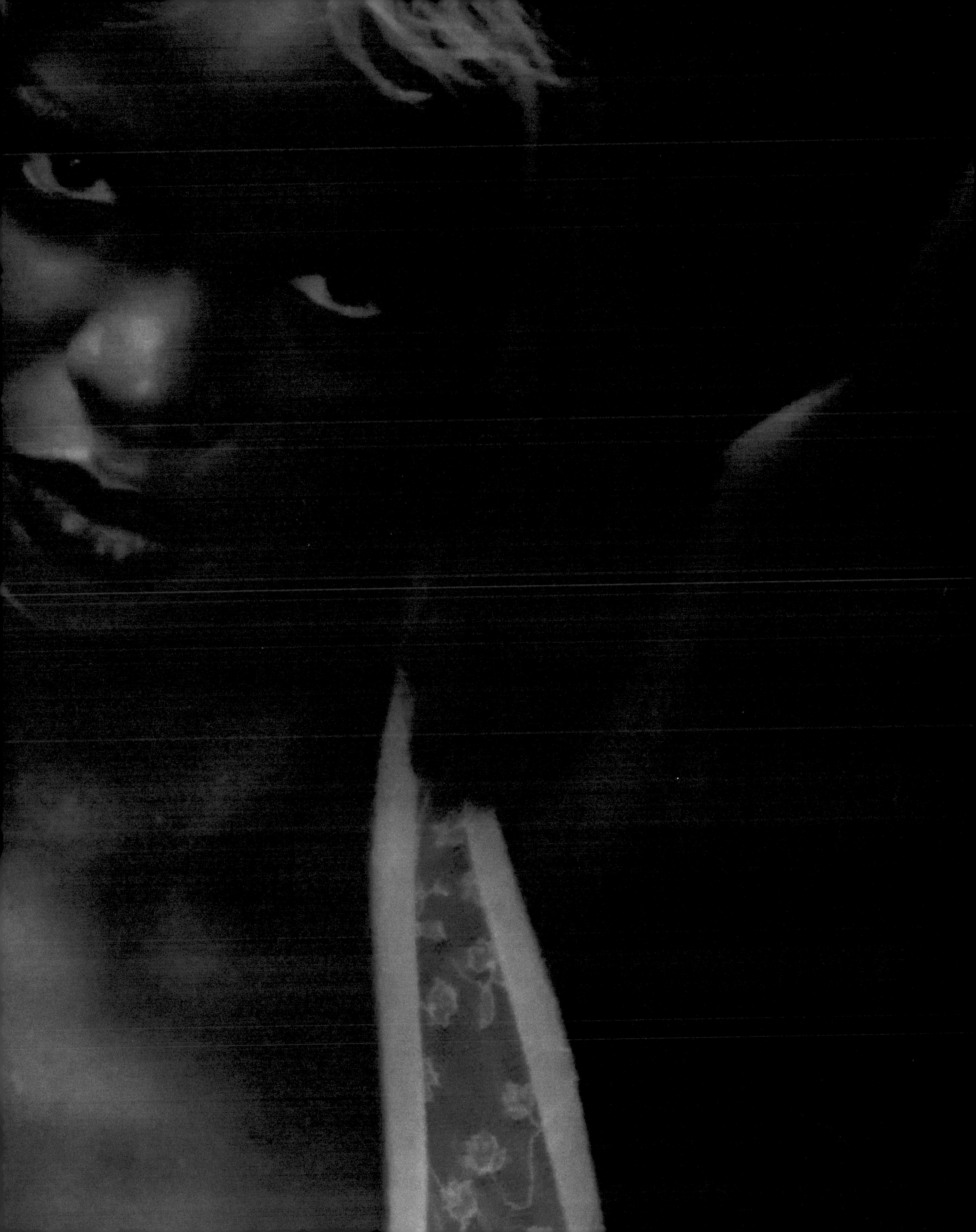

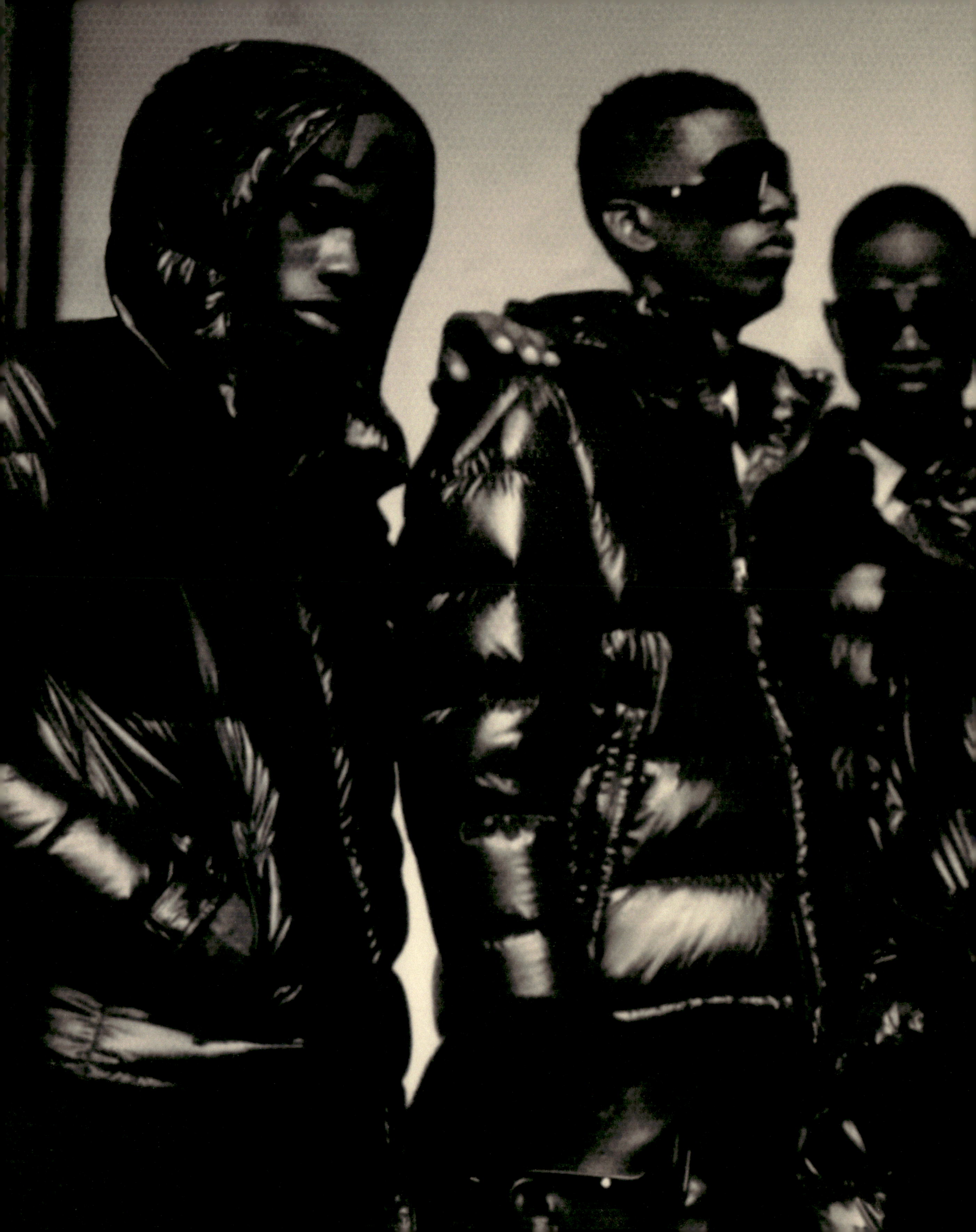

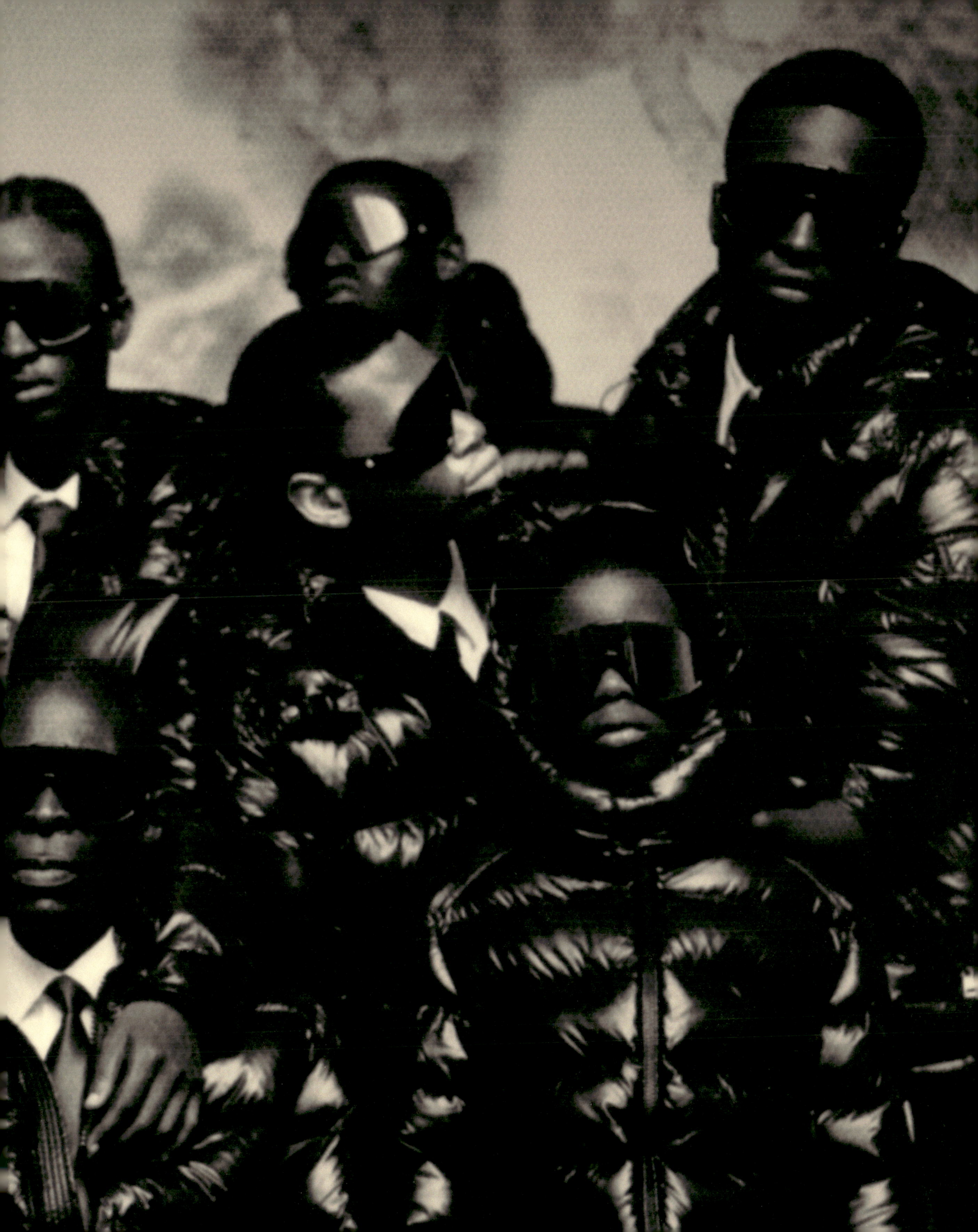

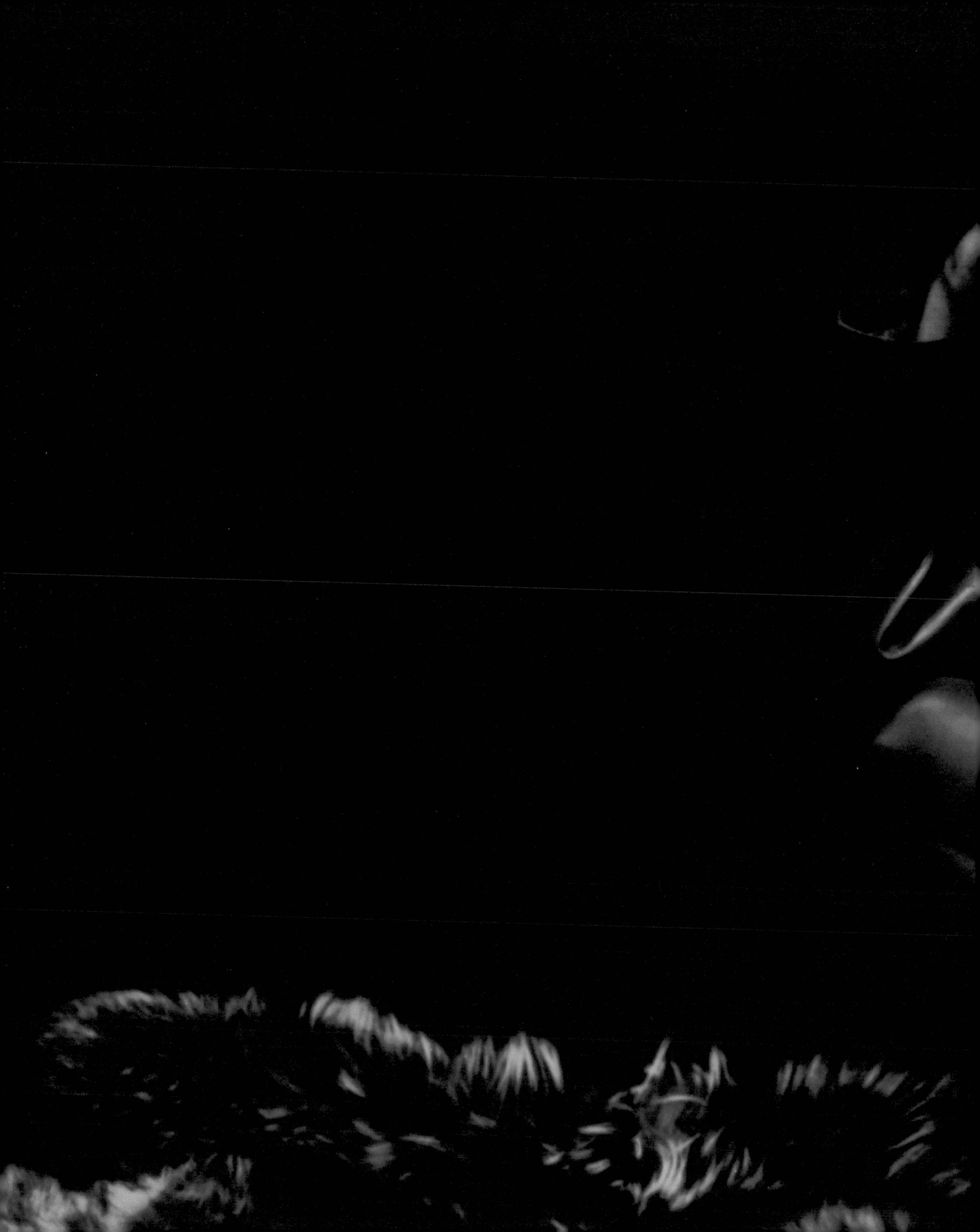

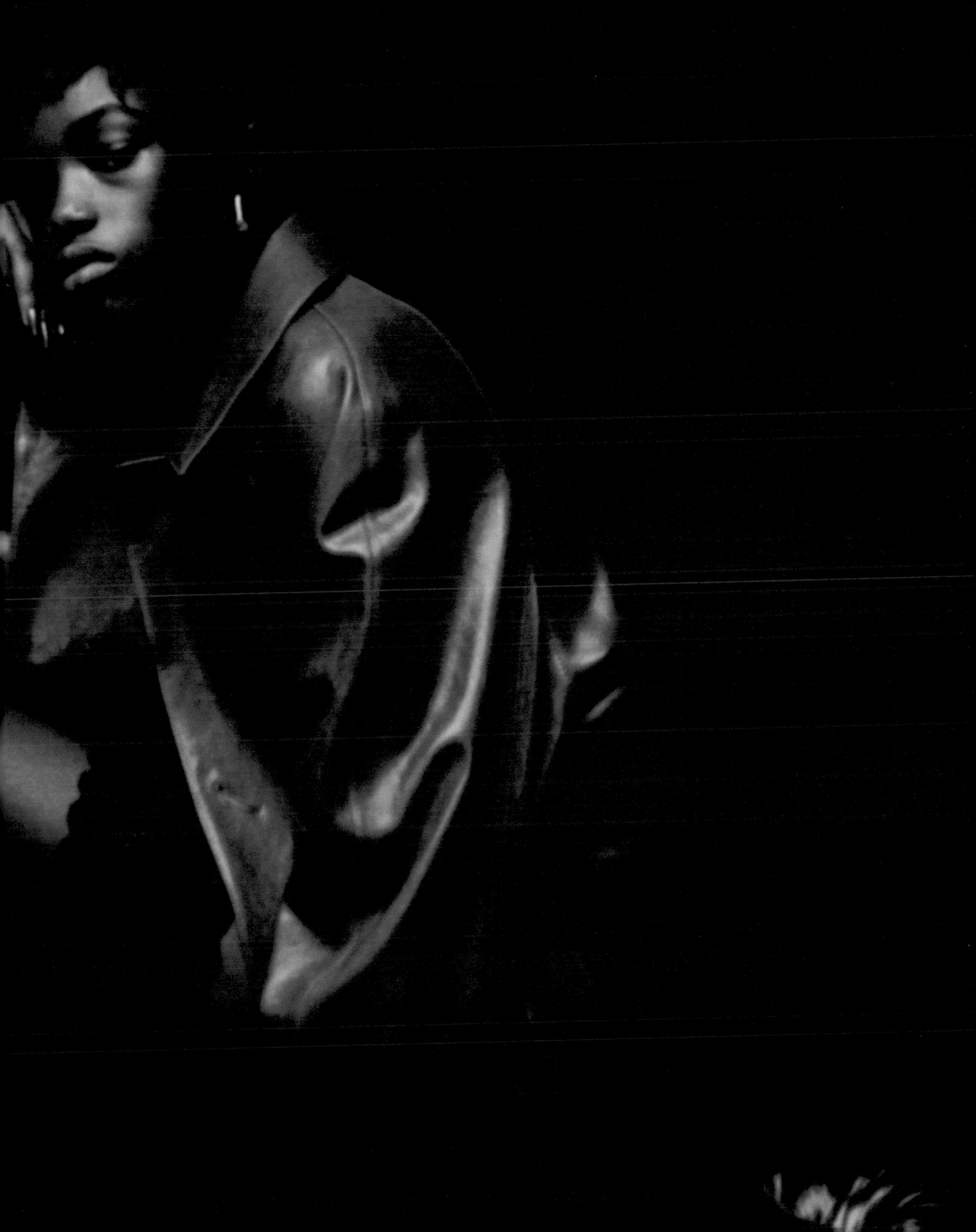

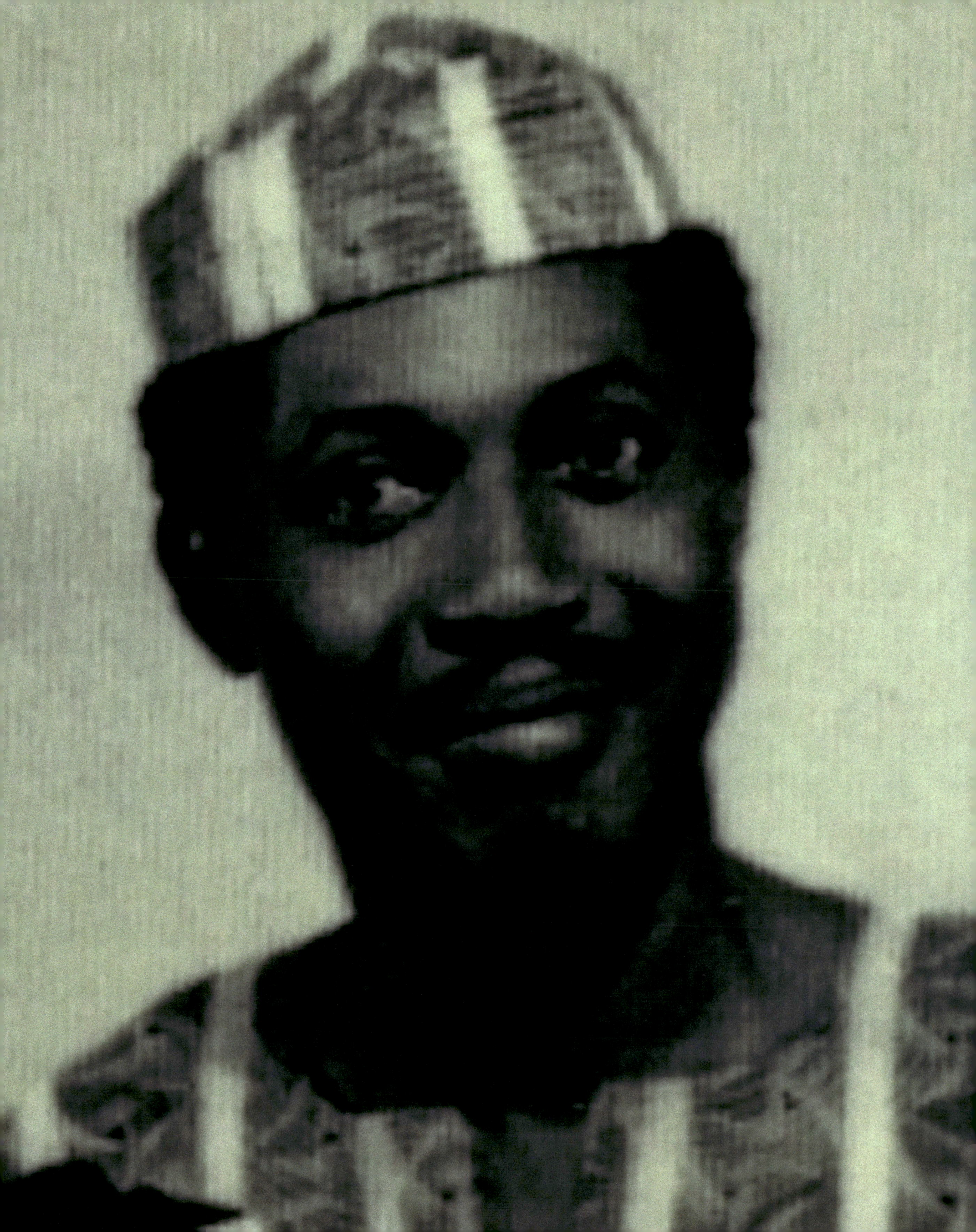

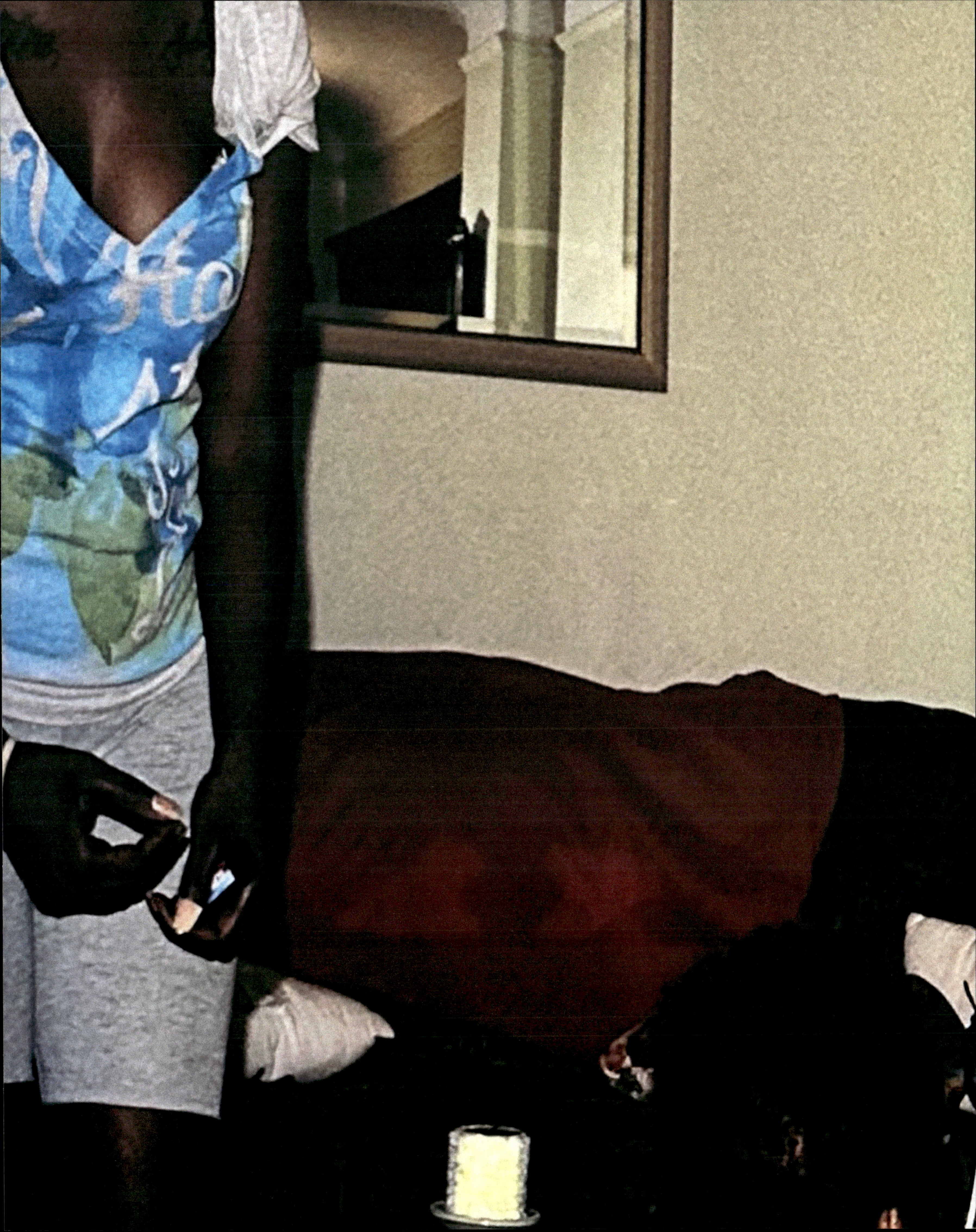

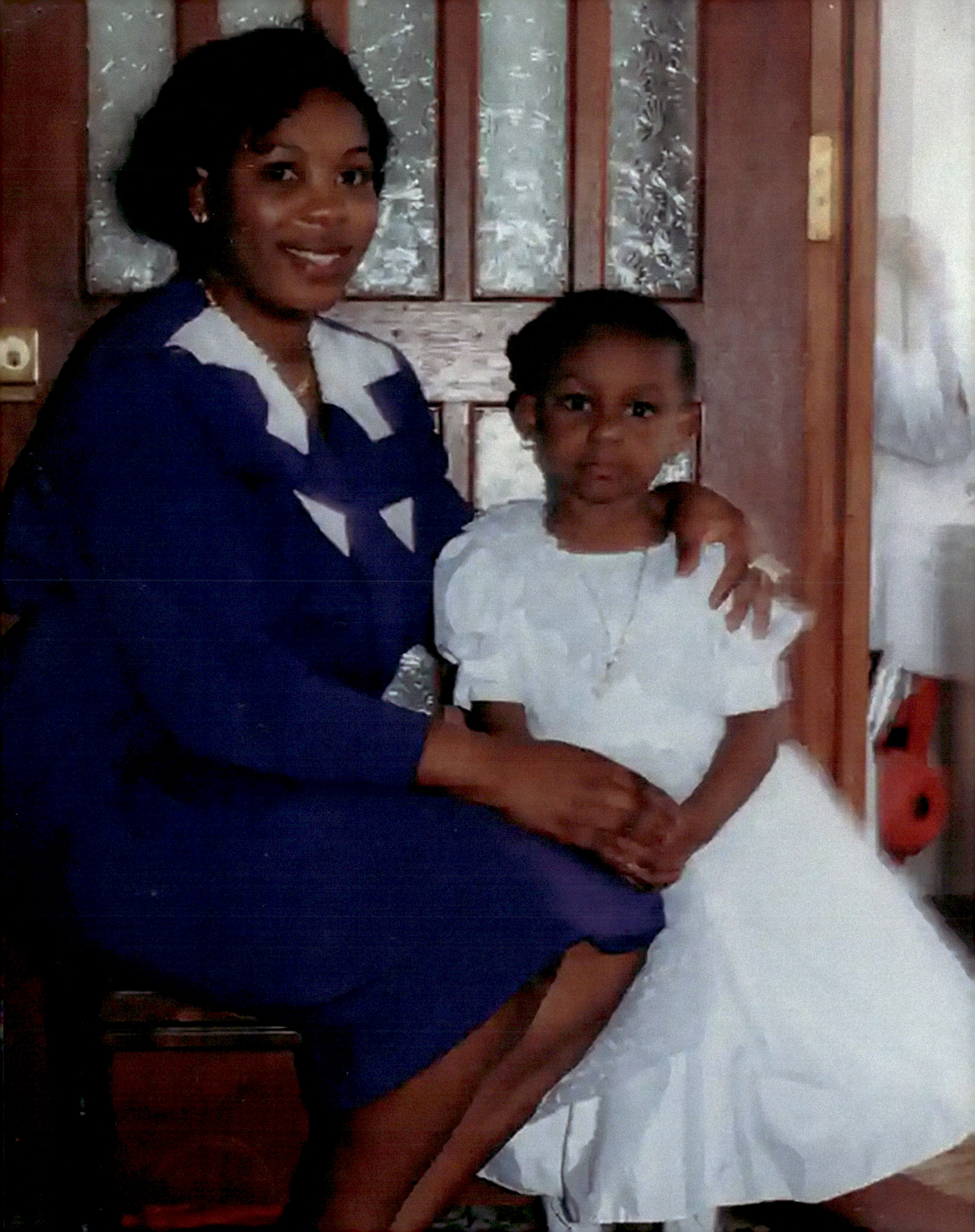

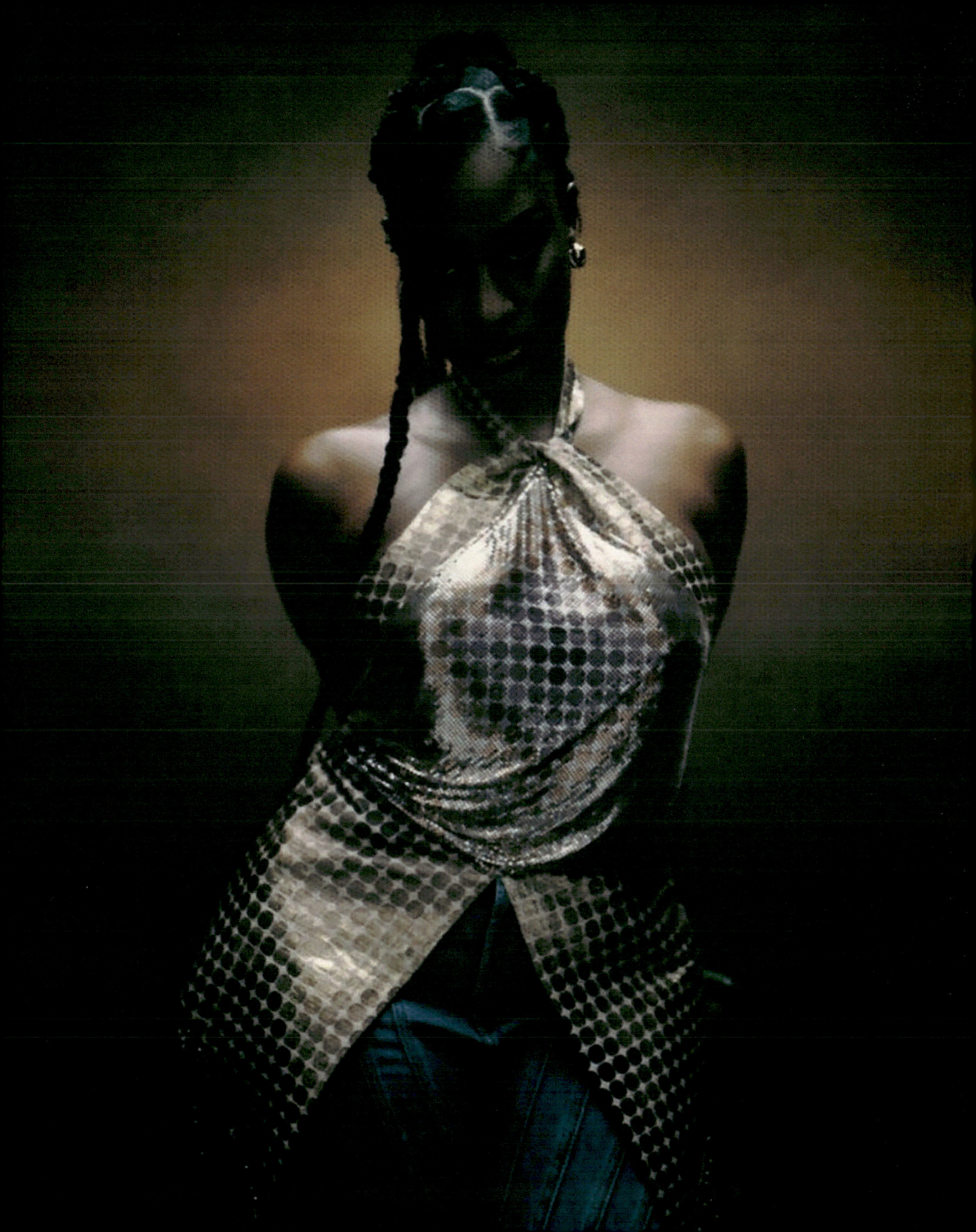

EVERY PLACE
THAT THE SOLE
OF YOUR
FOOT SHALL
TREAD UPON,
I HAVE MADE
YOUR TERRITORY,
JUST AS I
PROMISED TO
MOSES.

JOSHUA 1:3

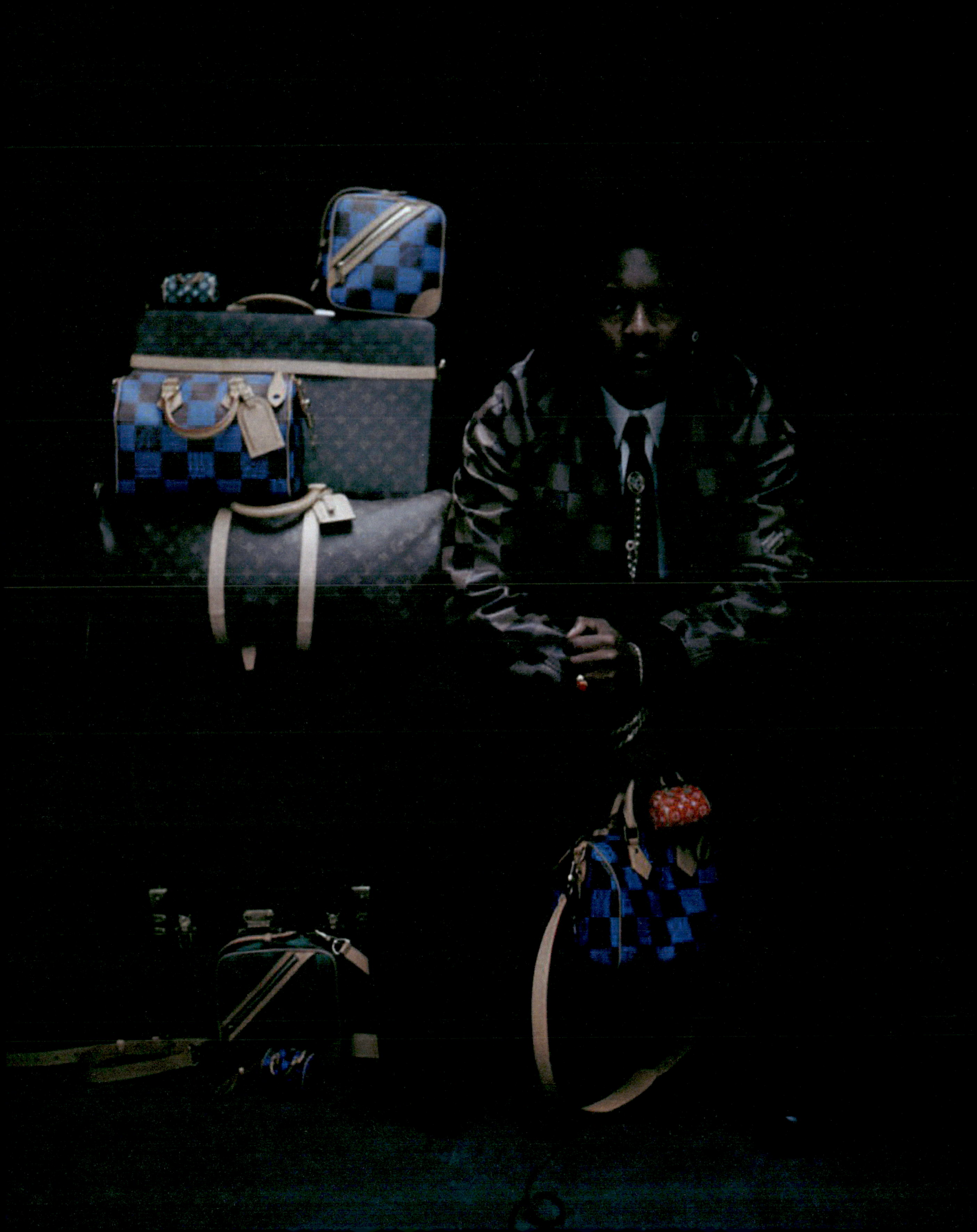

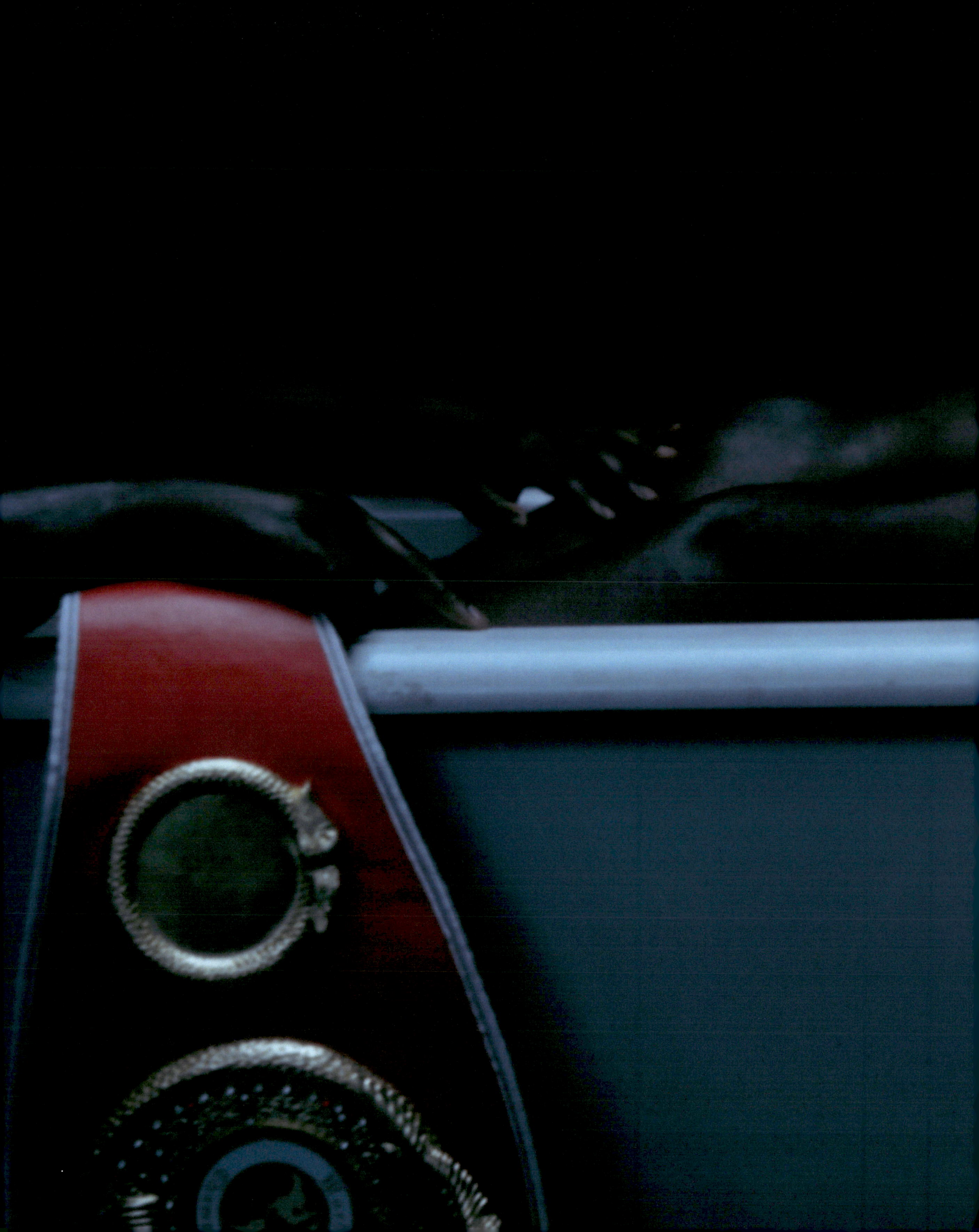

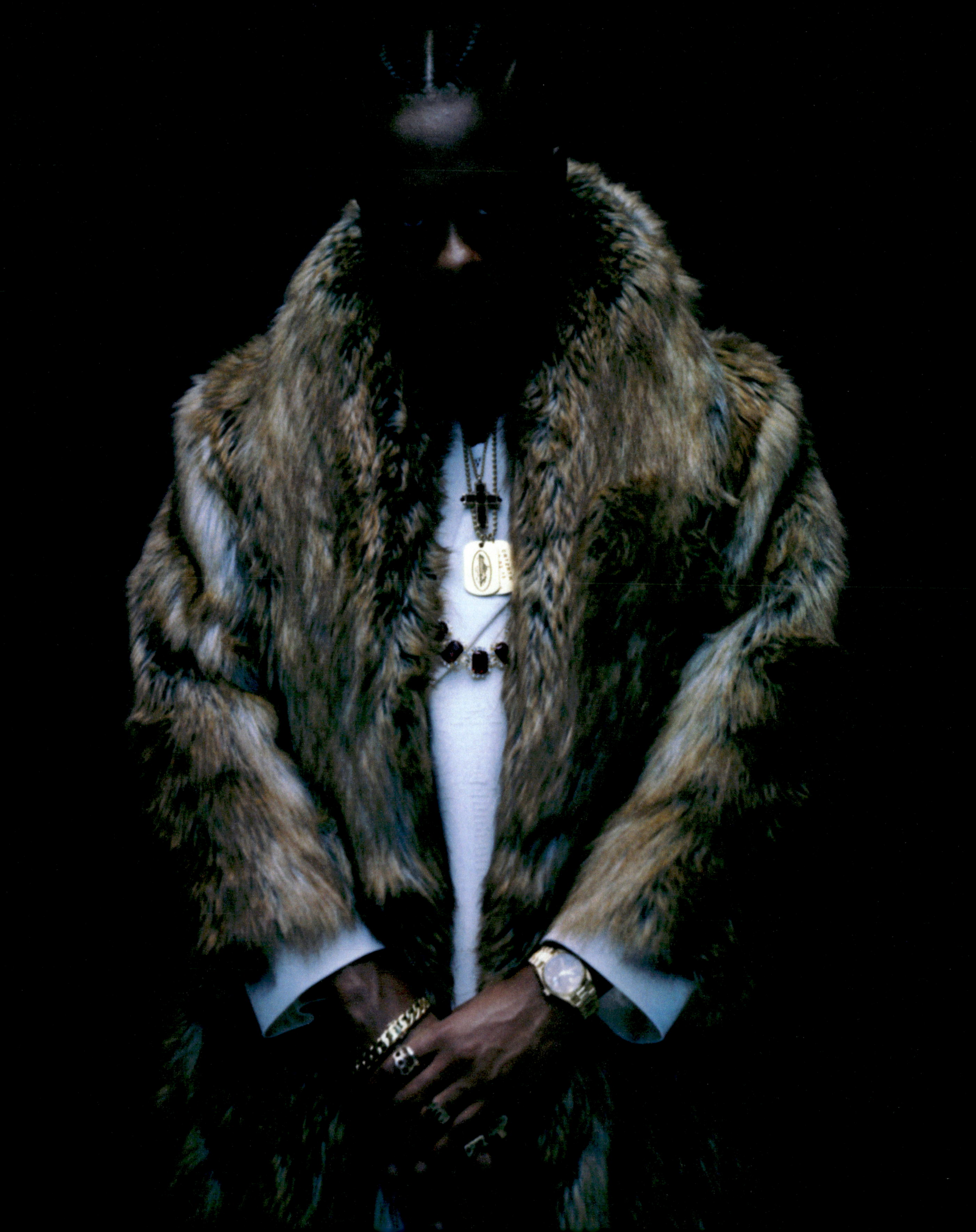

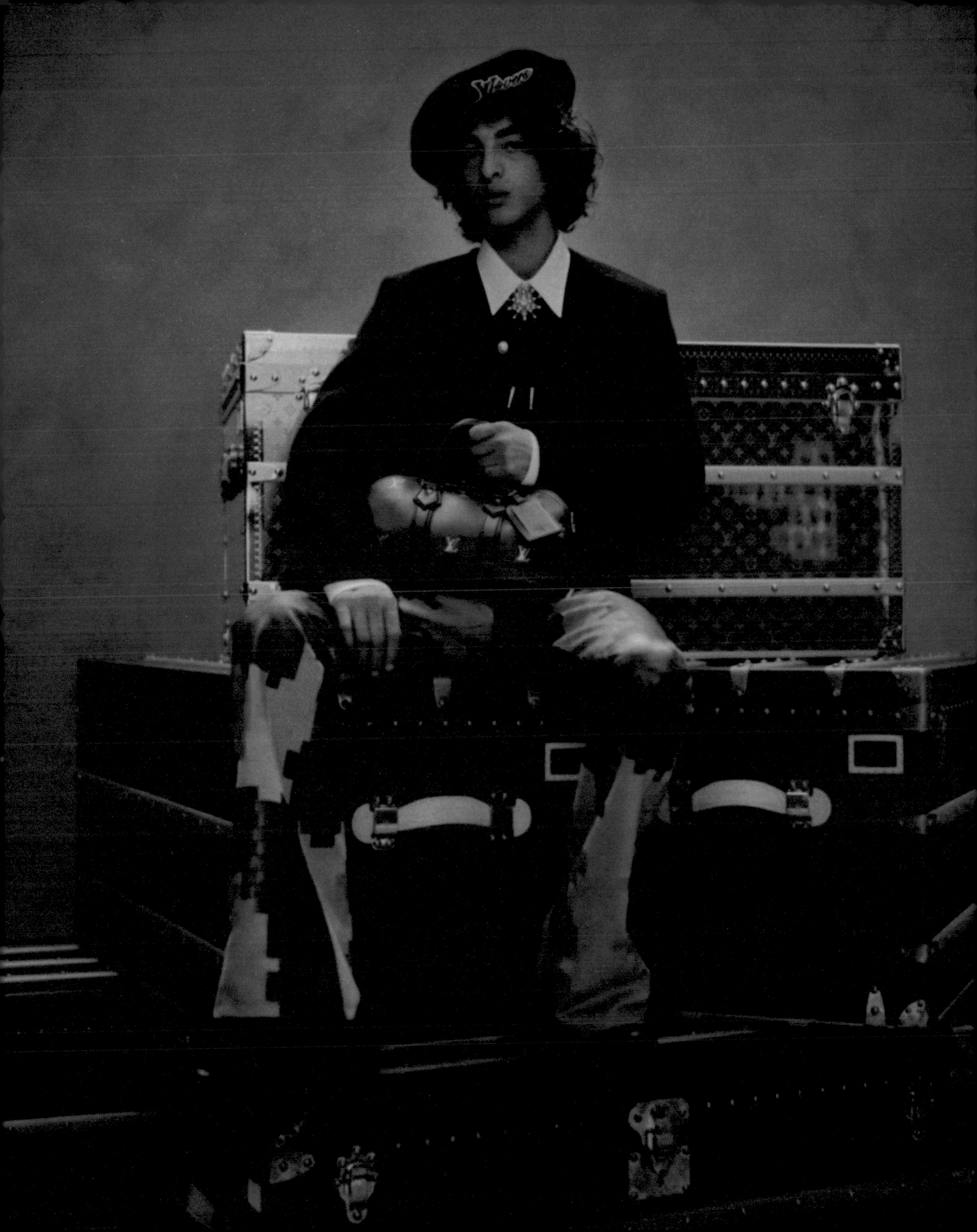

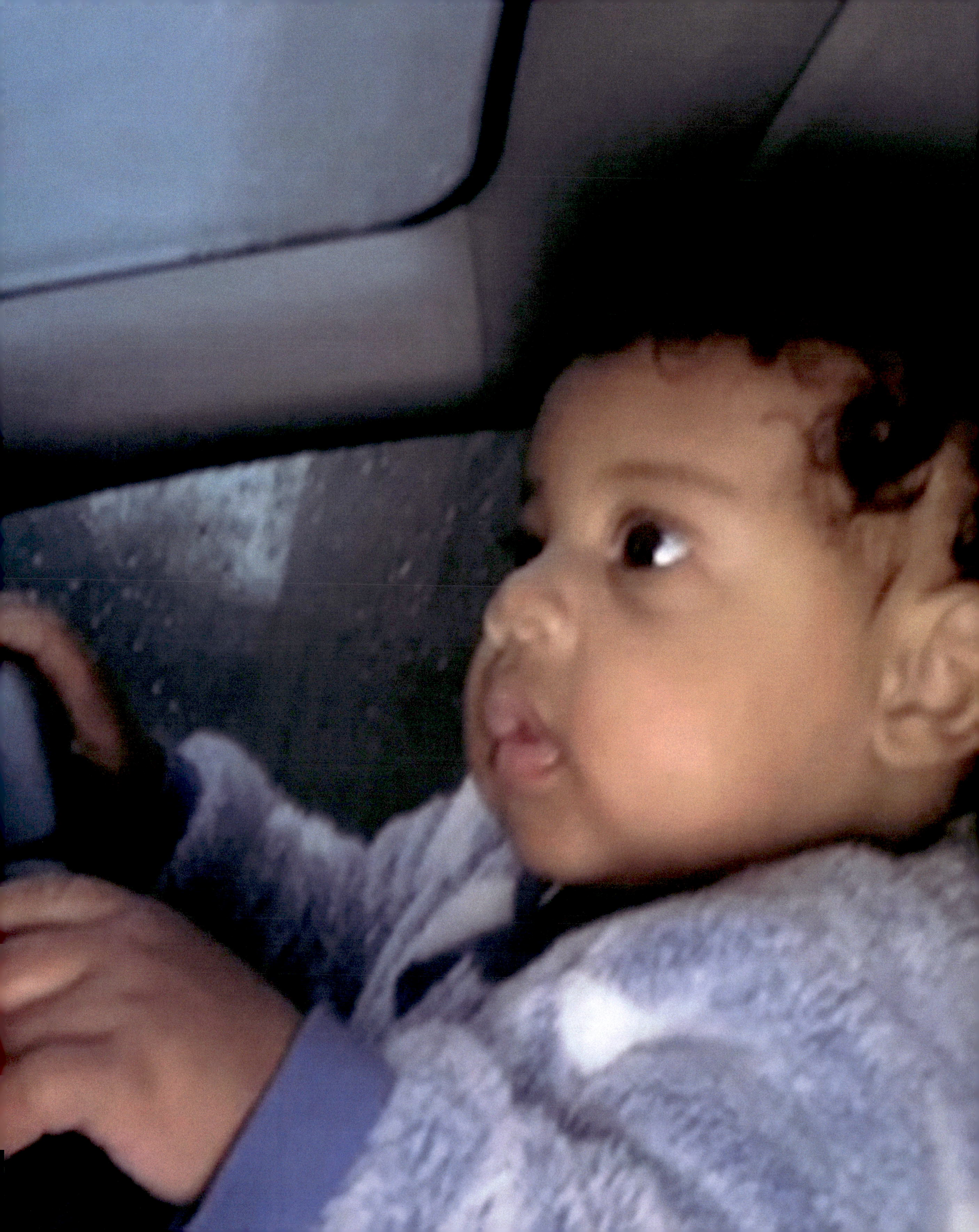

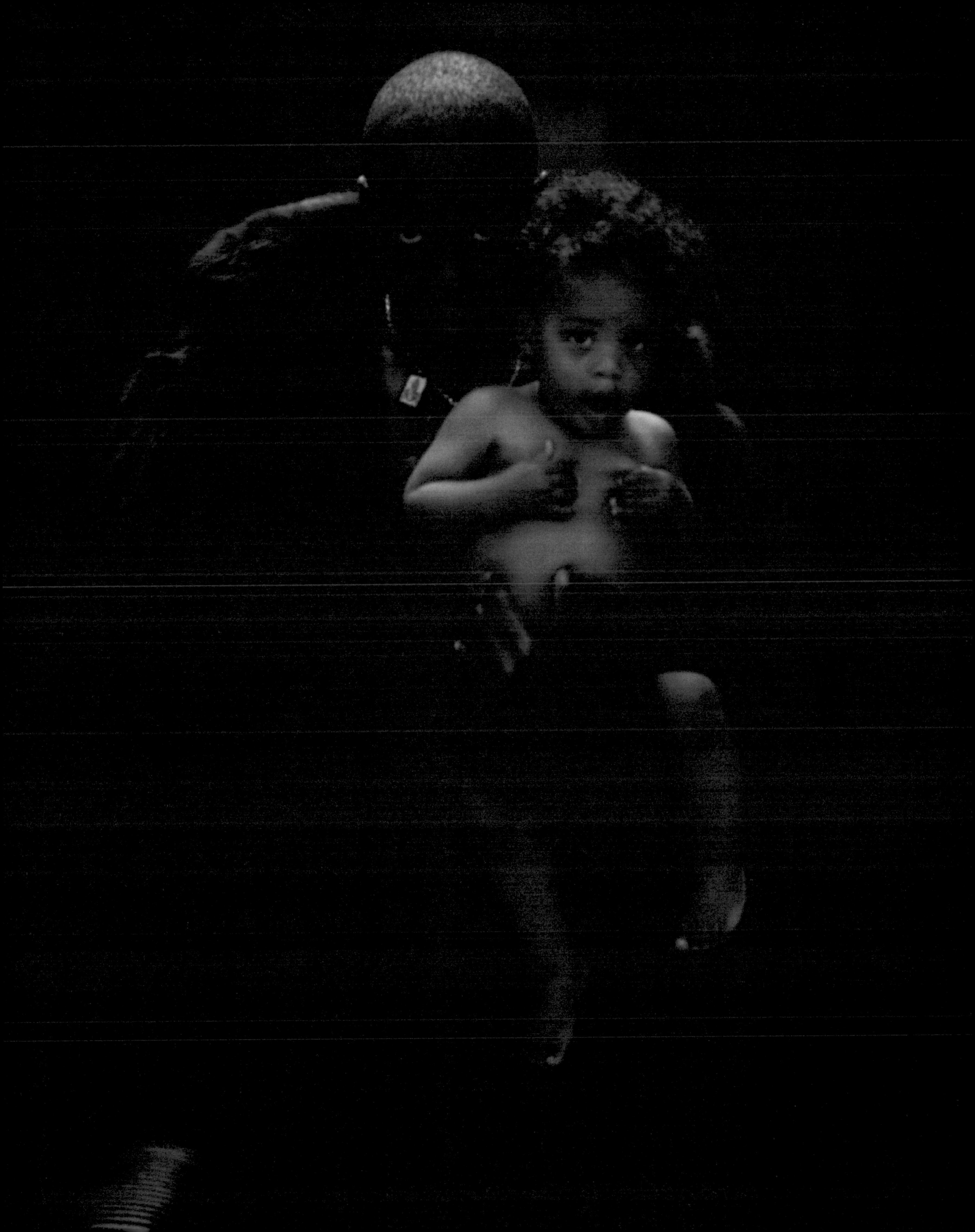

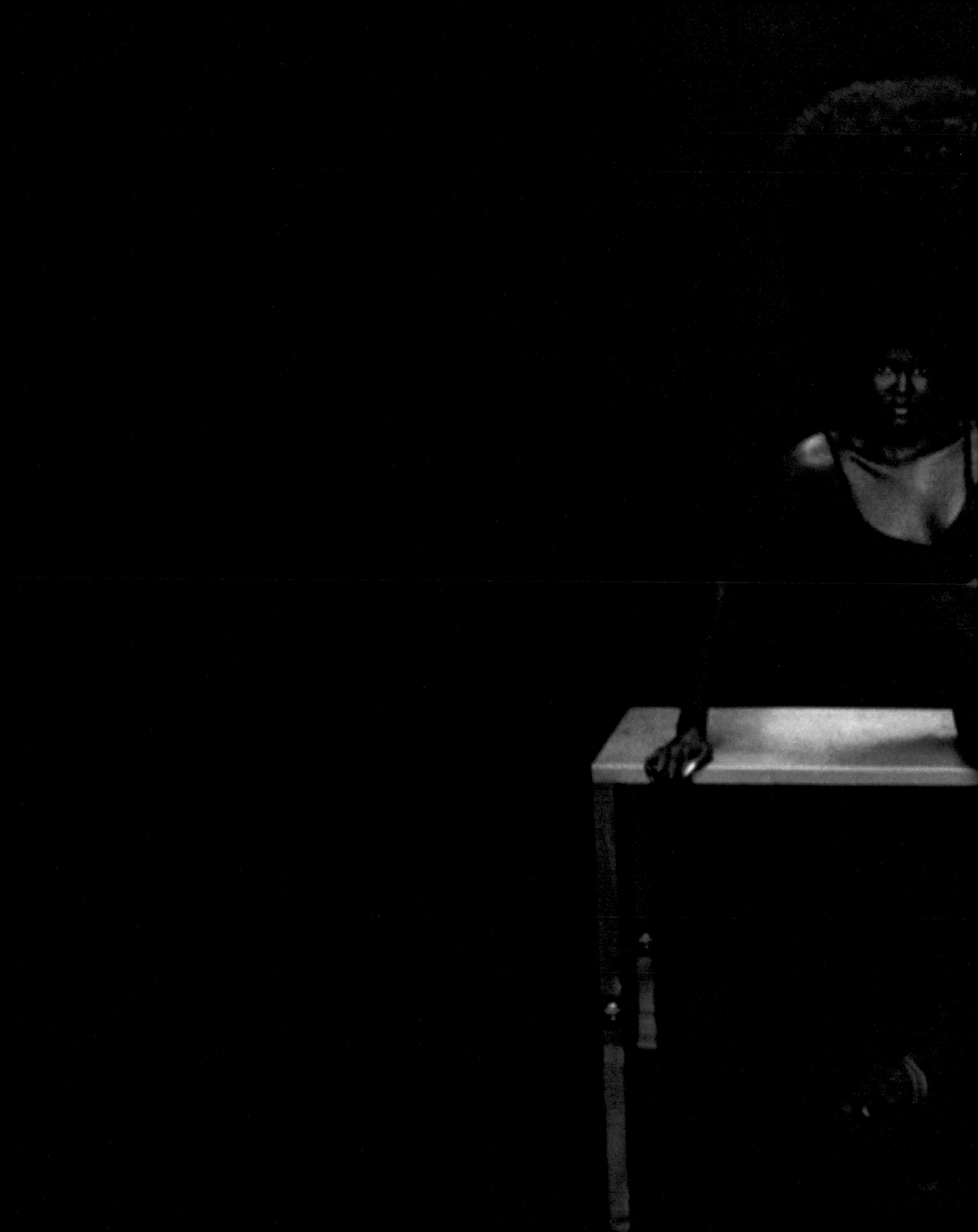

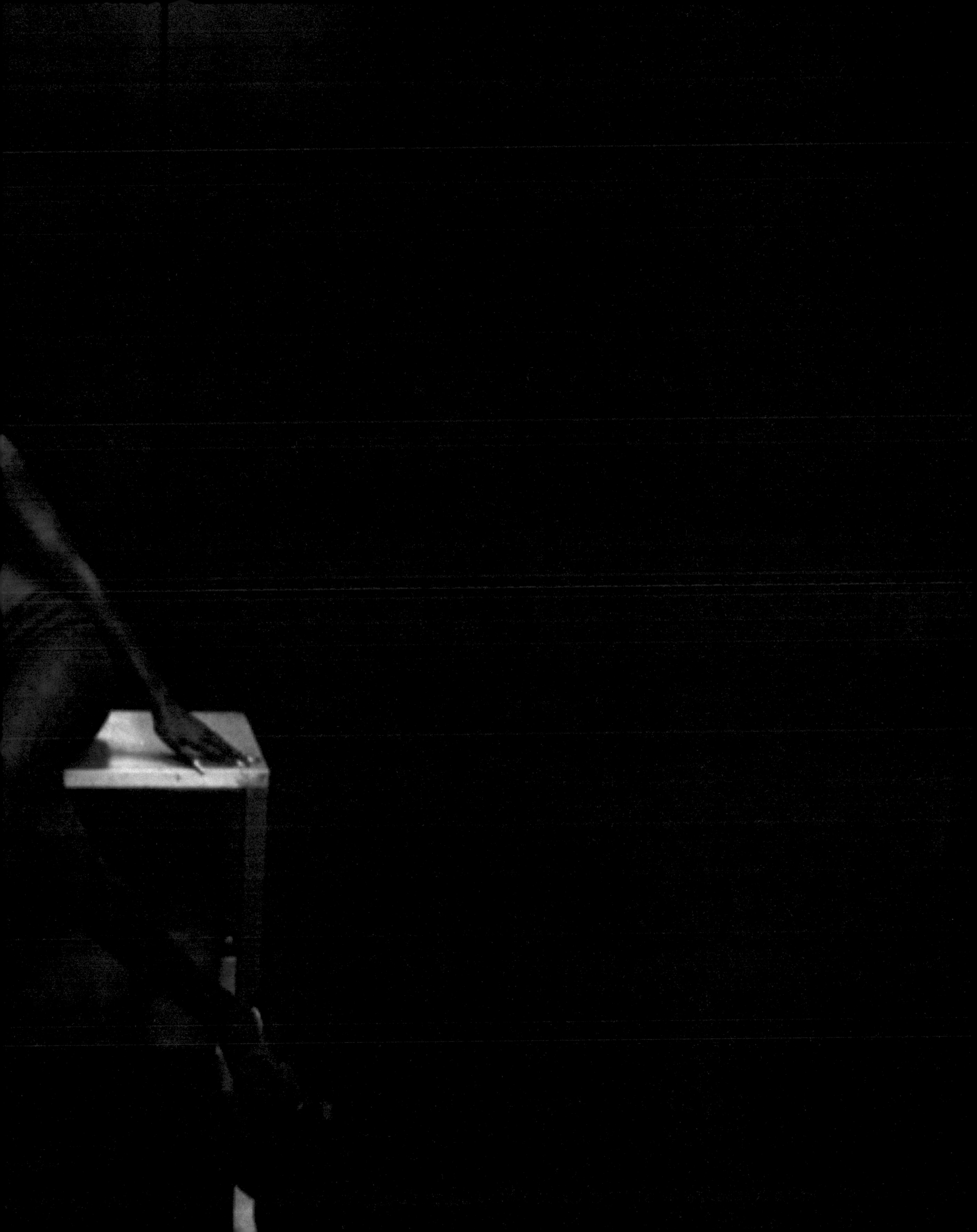

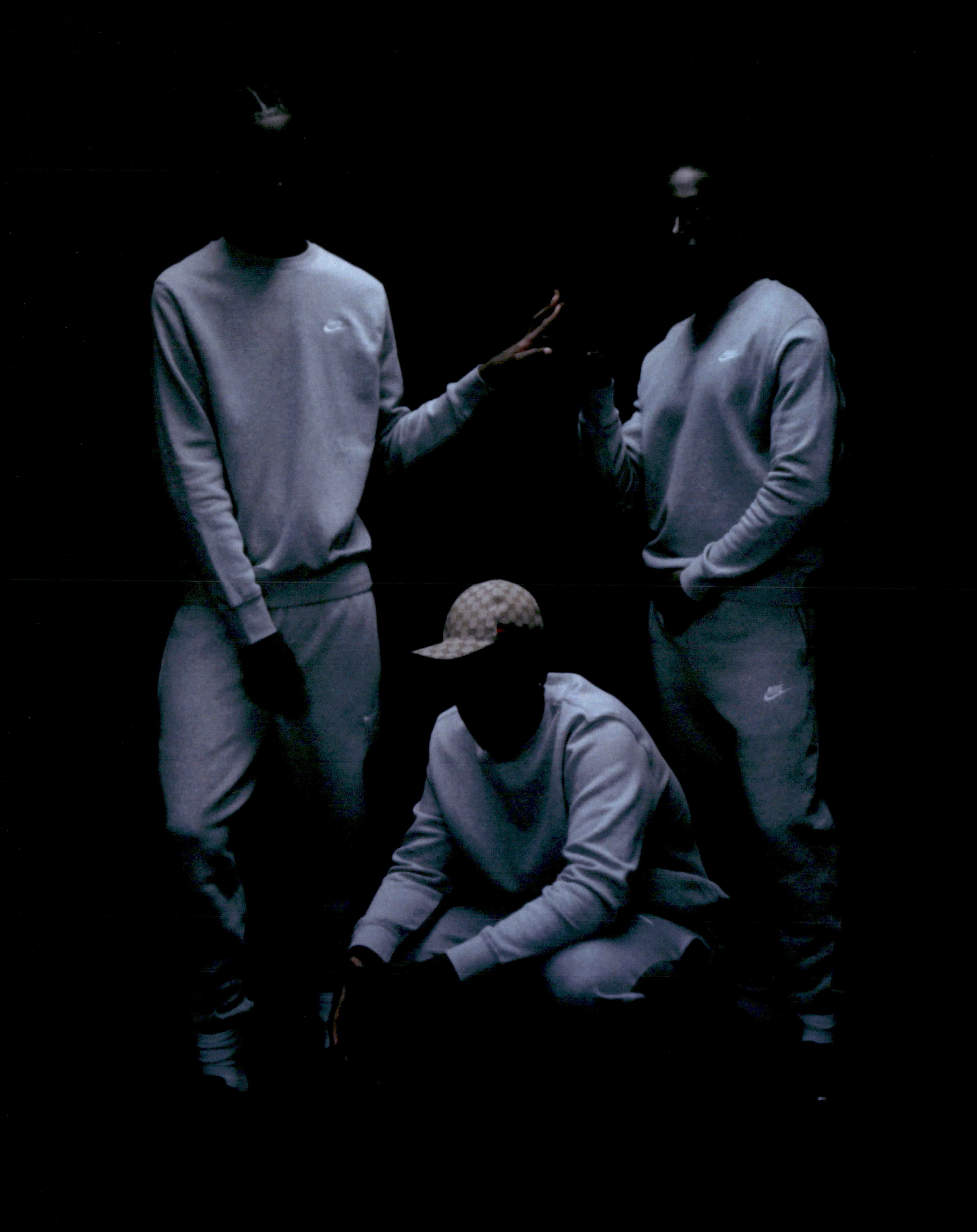

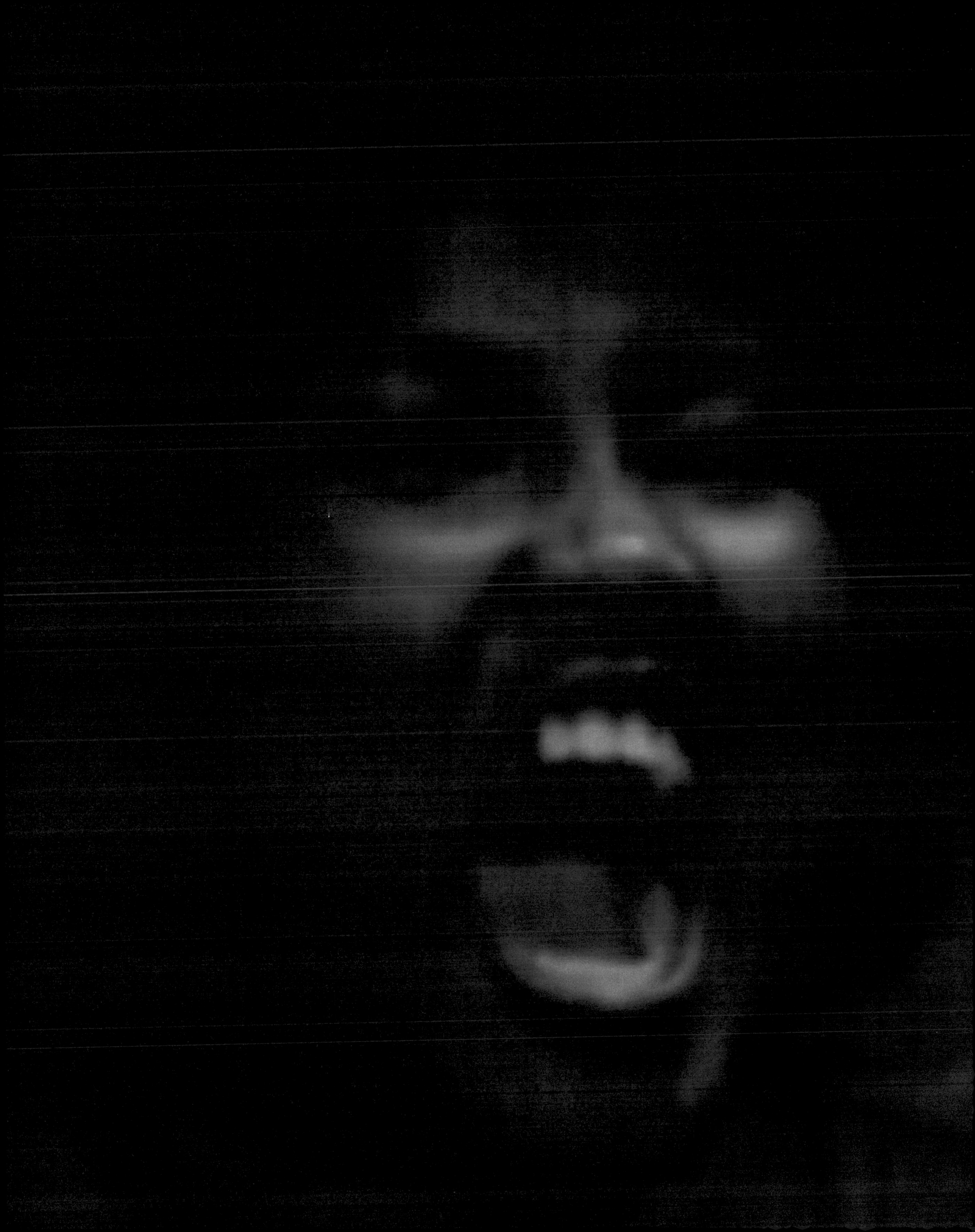

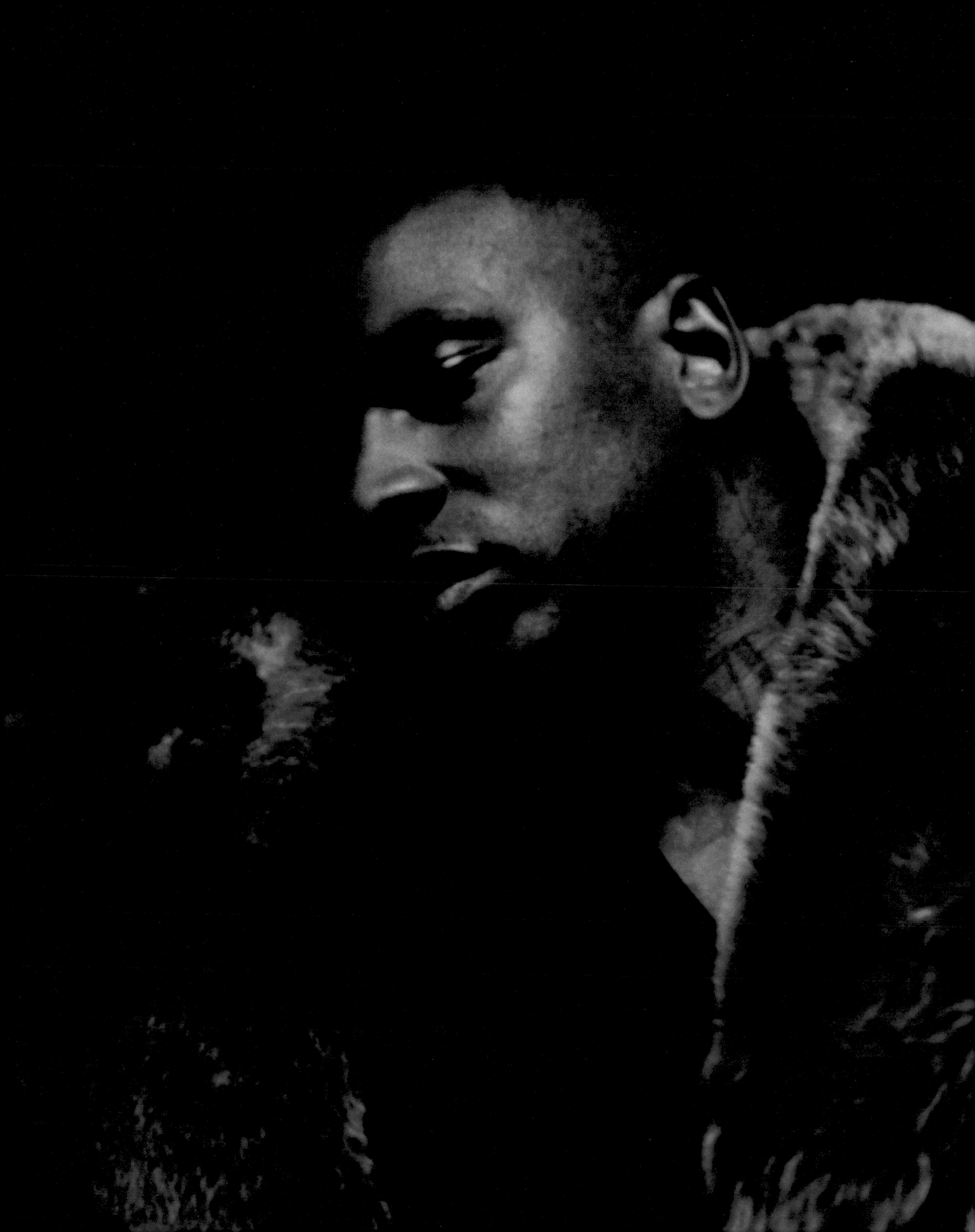

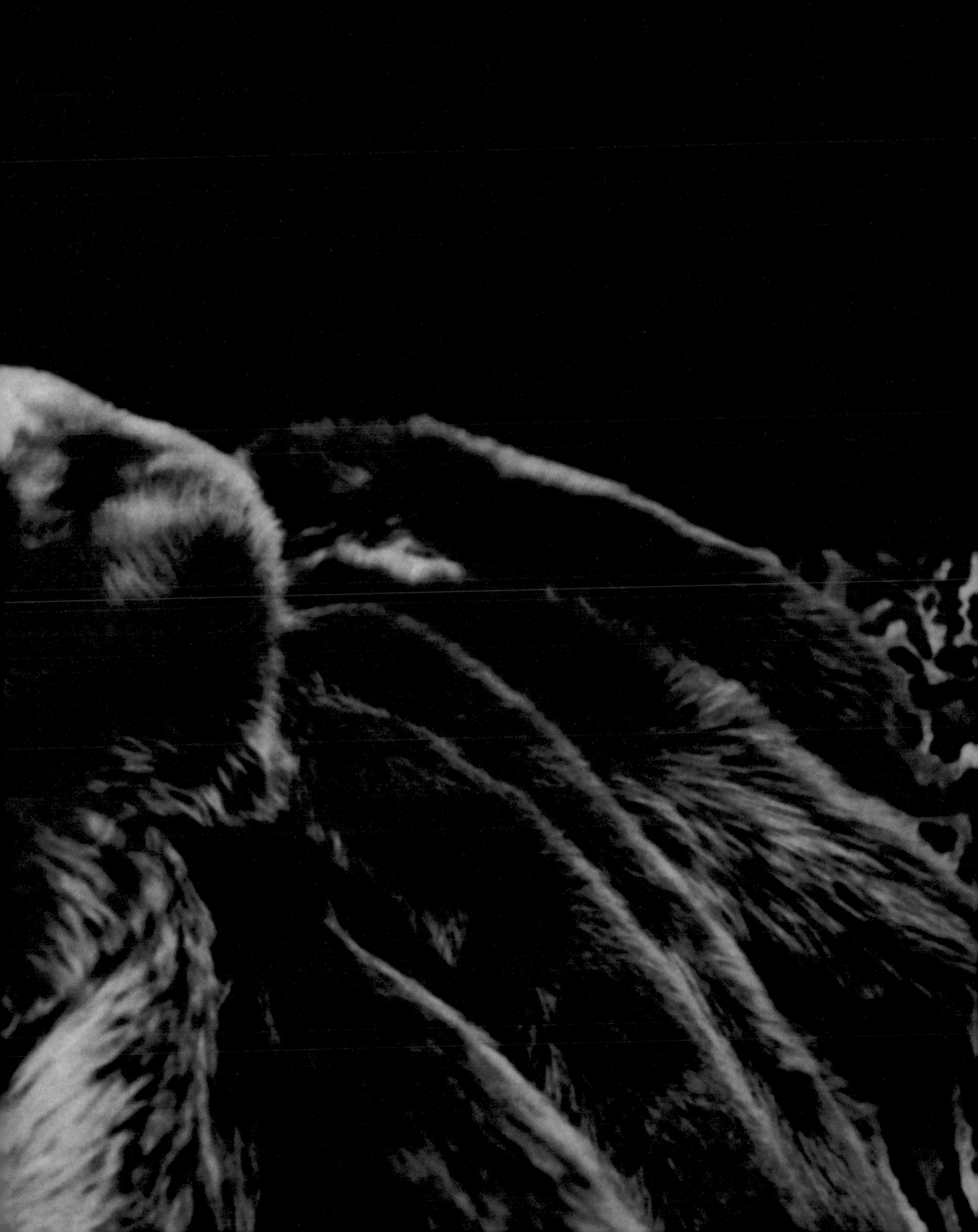

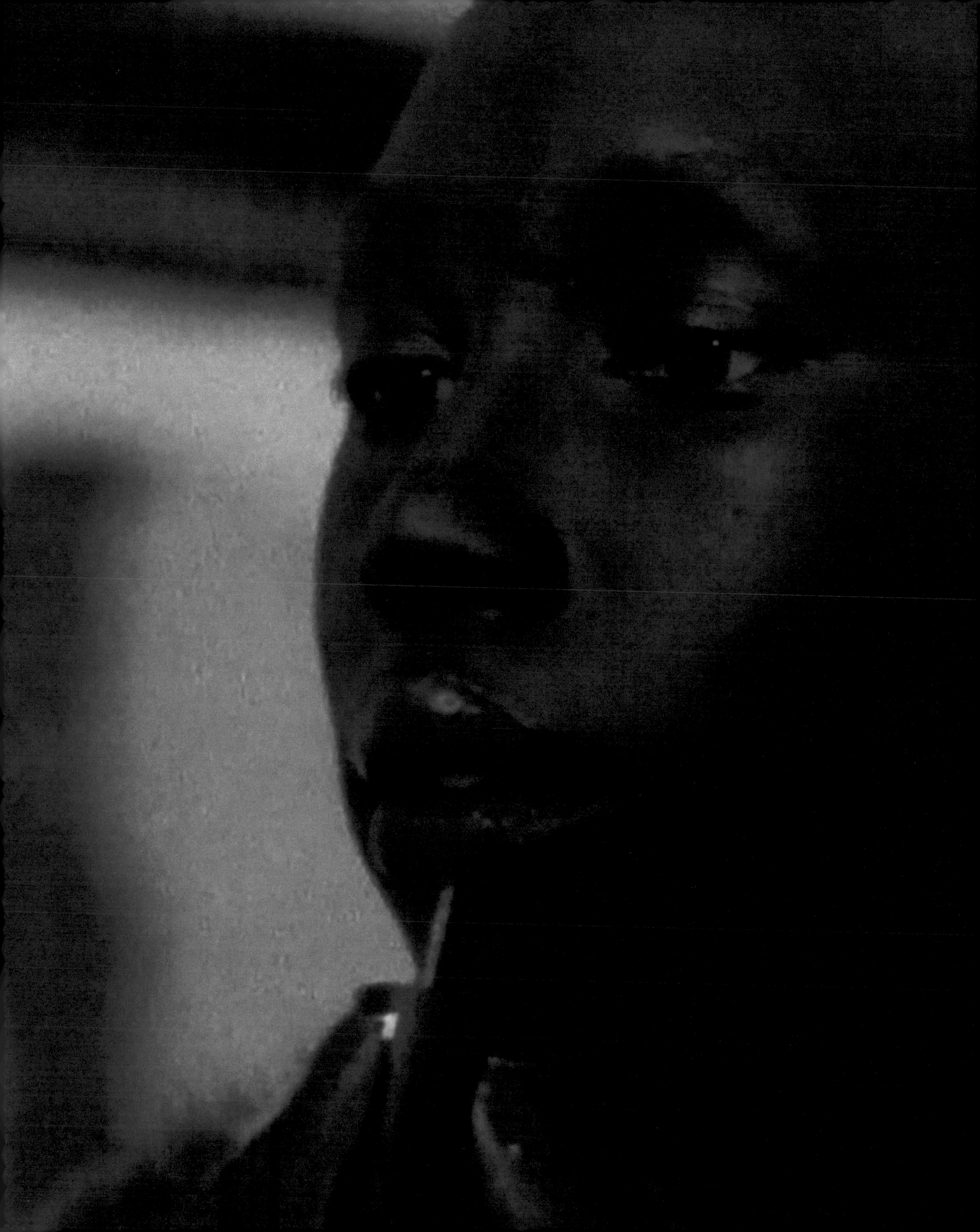

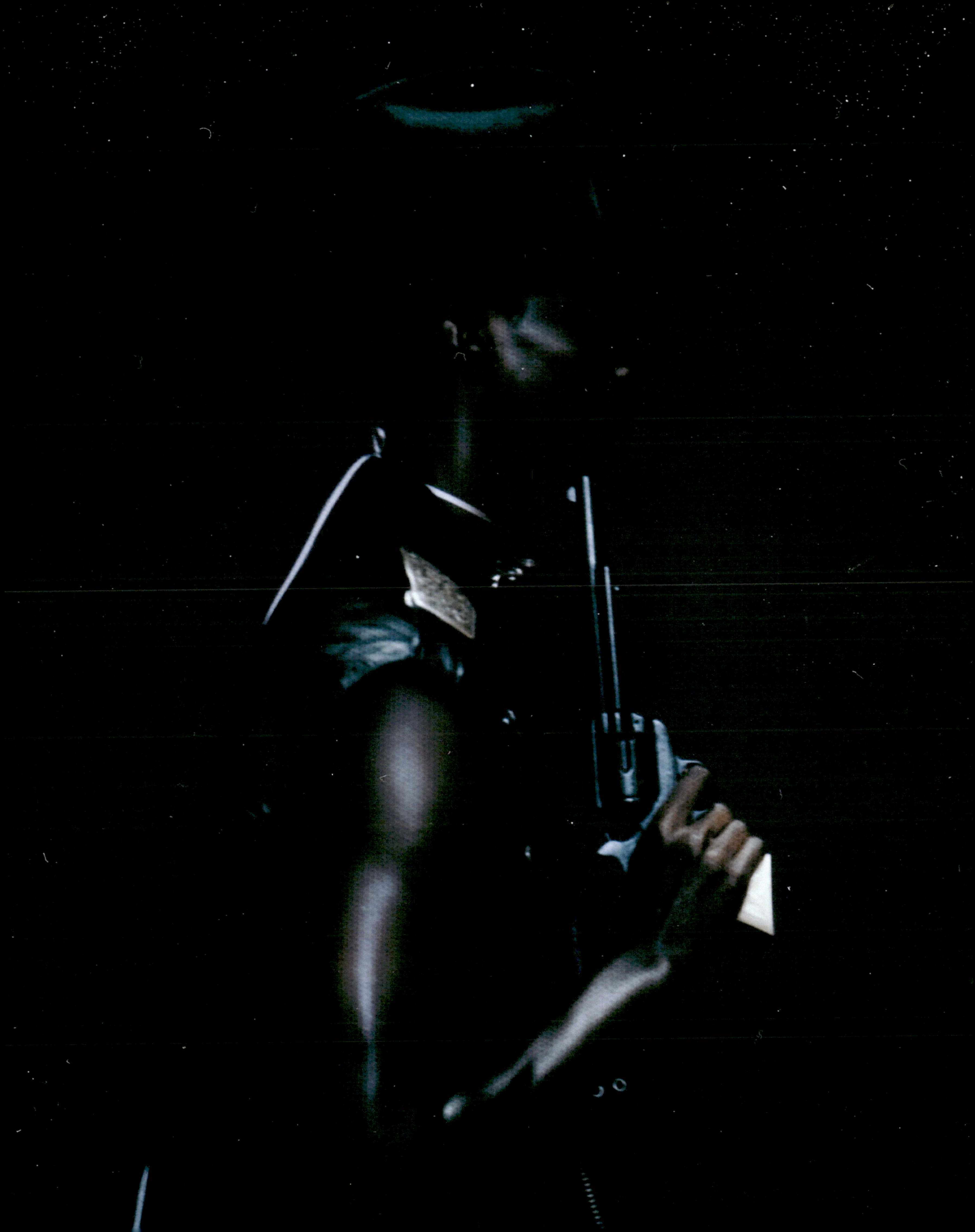

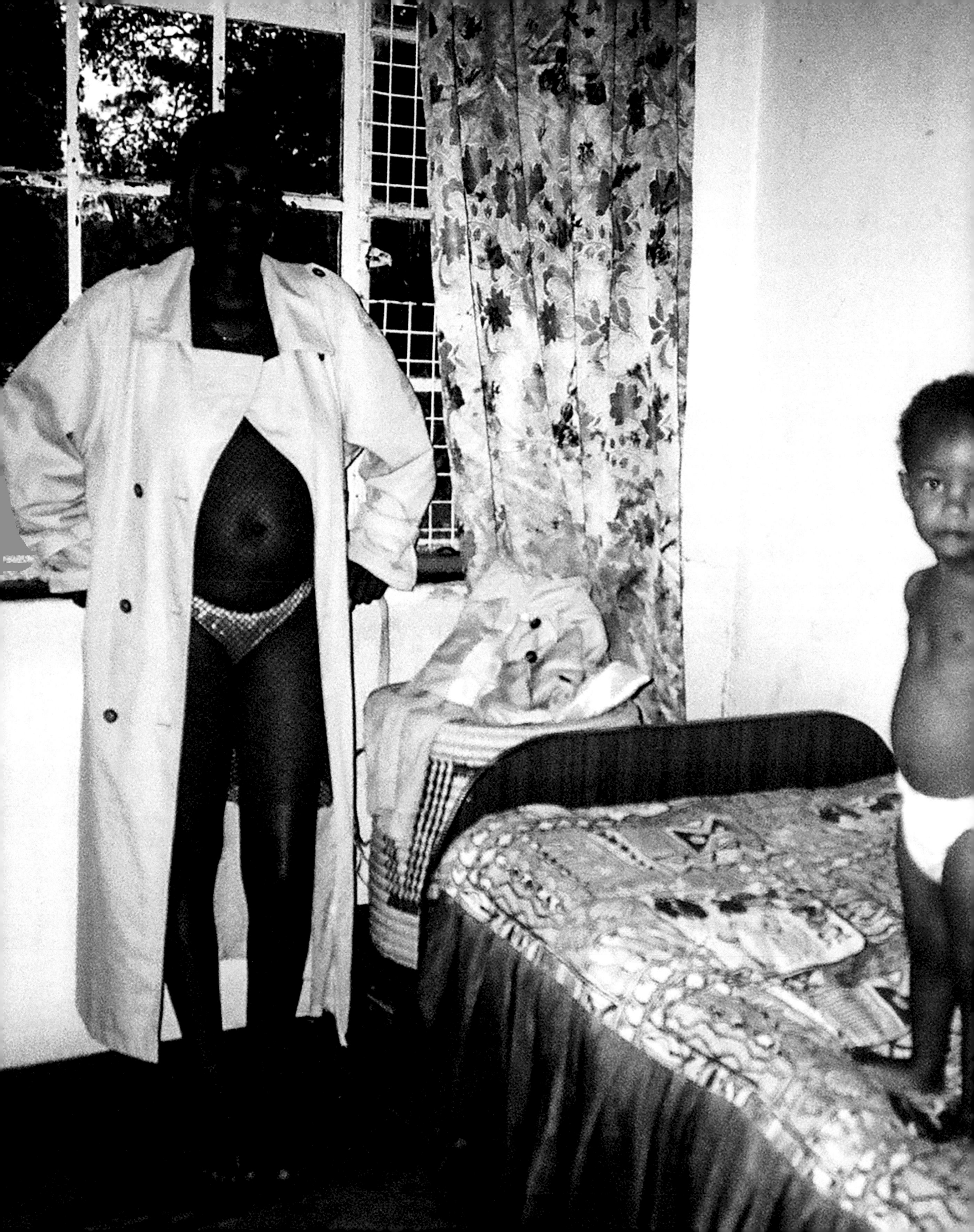

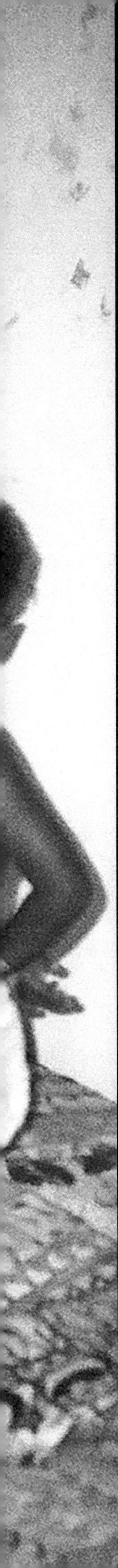

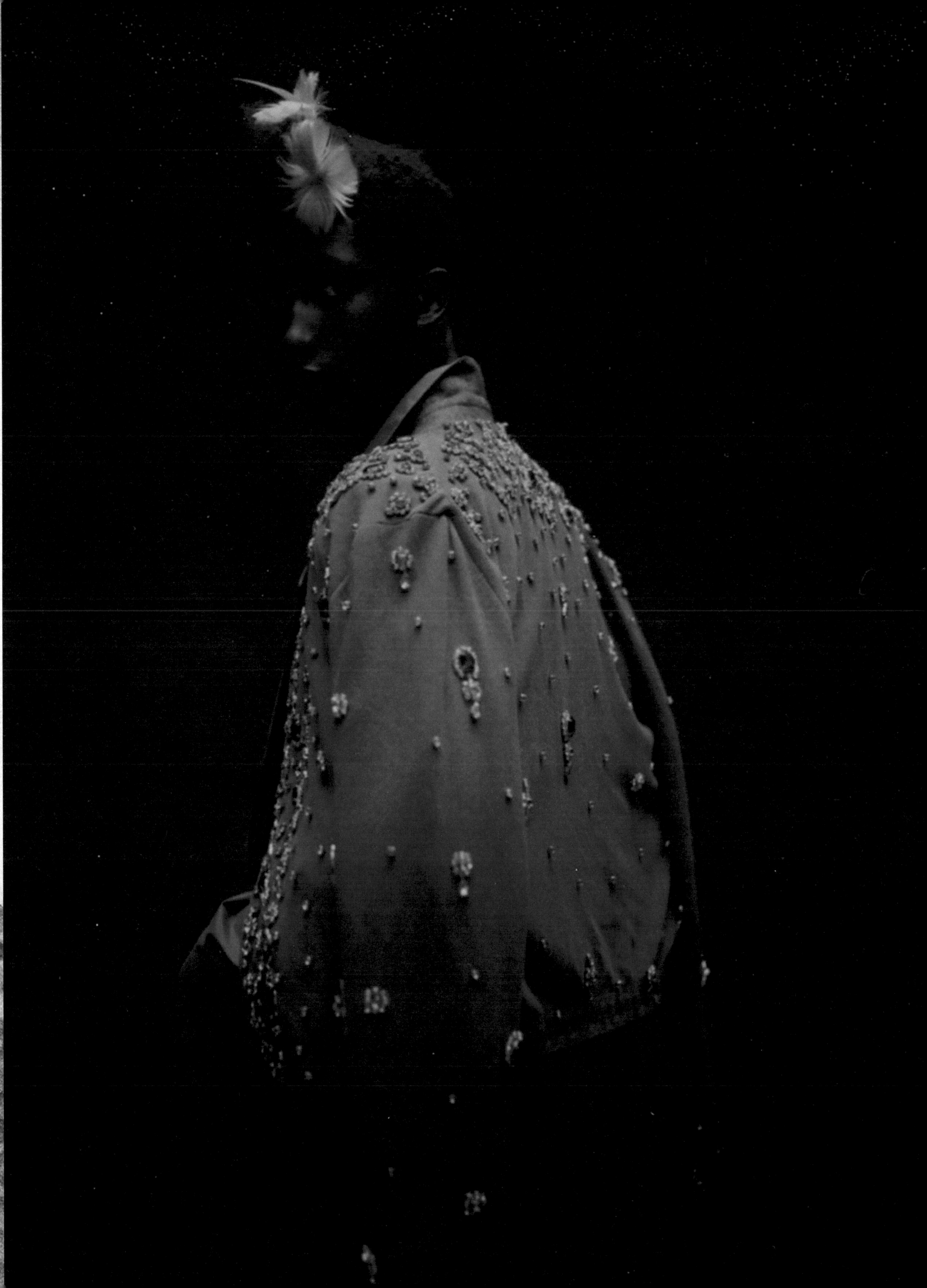

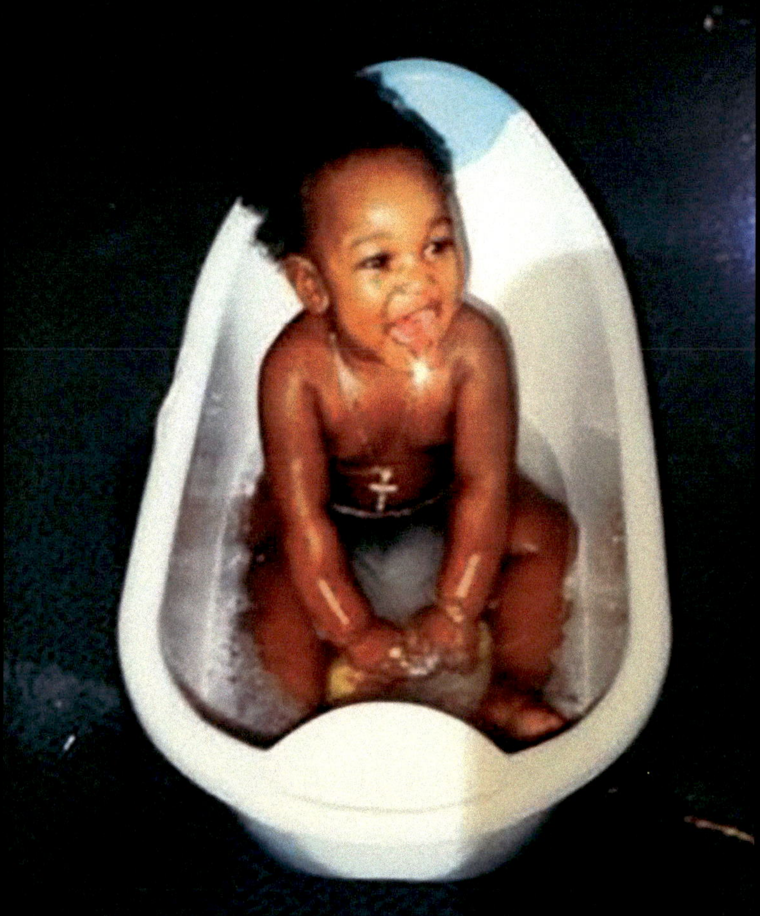

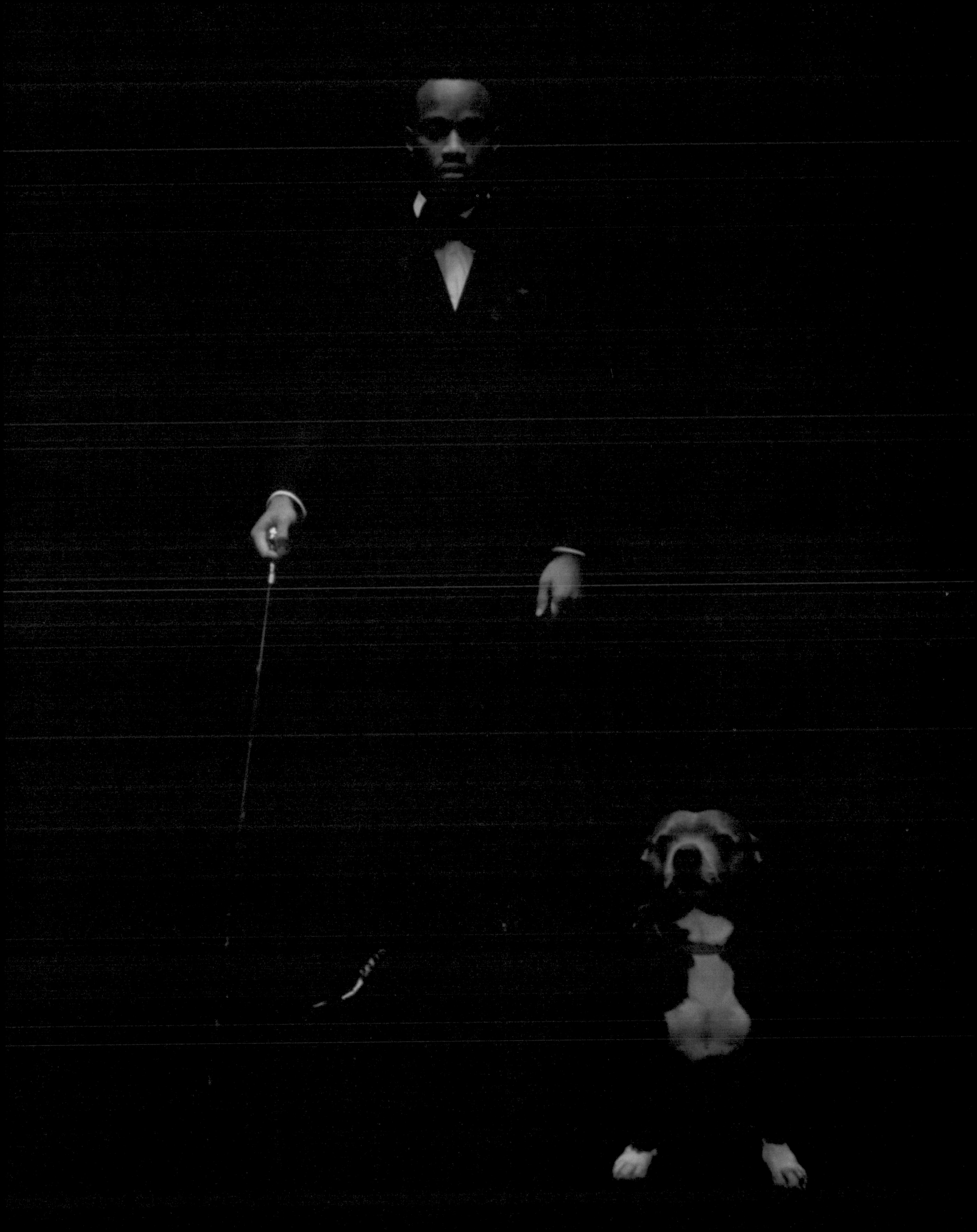

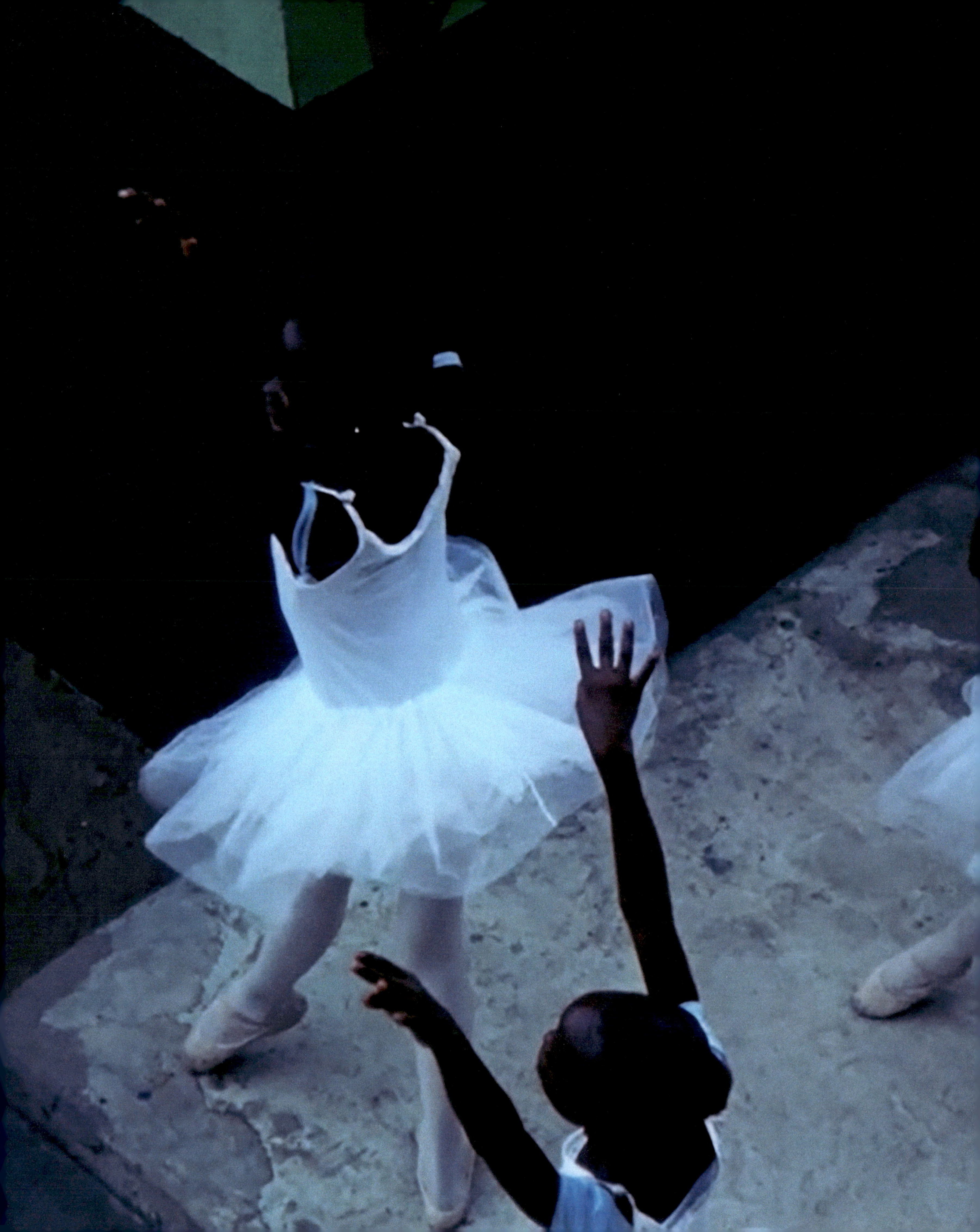

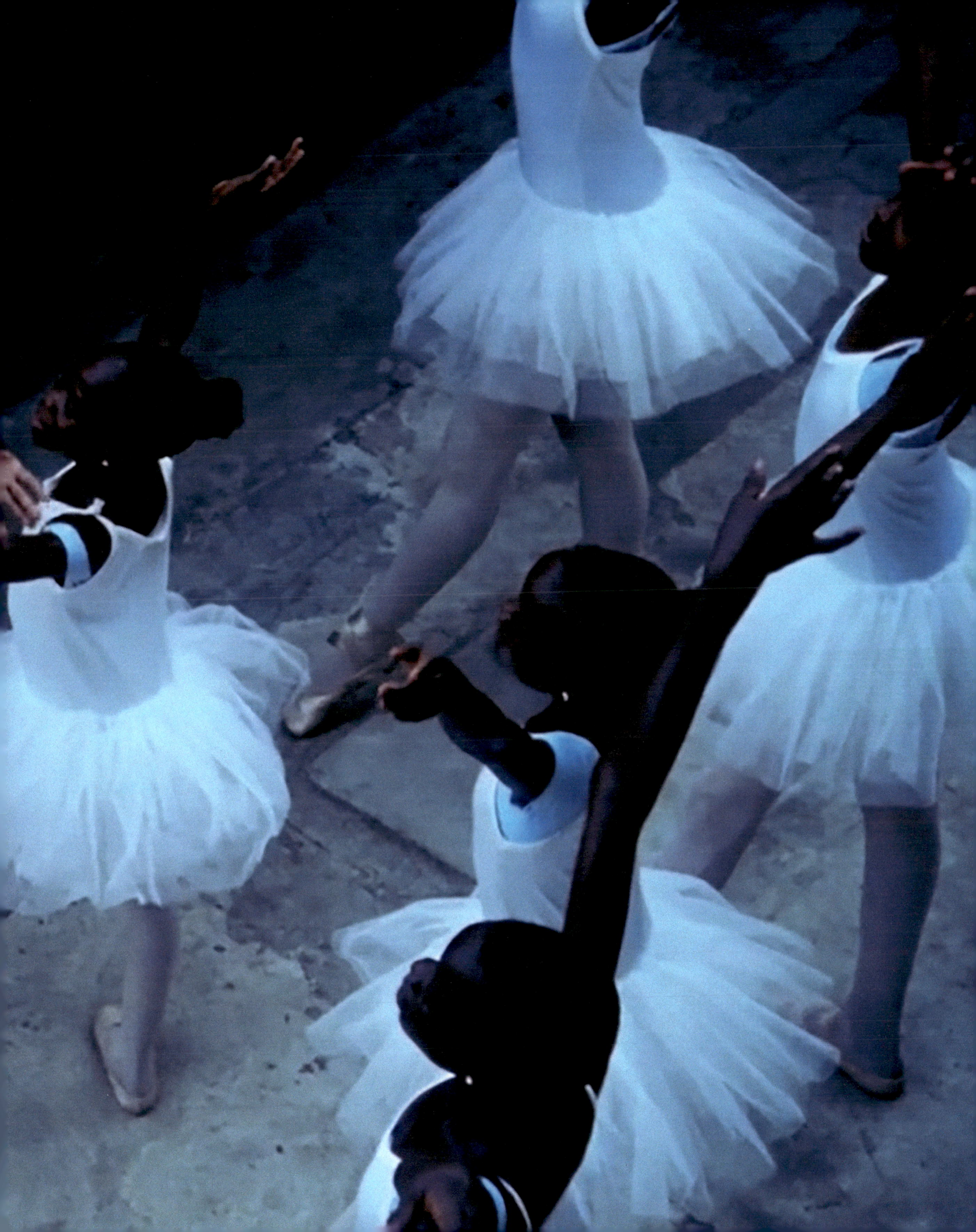

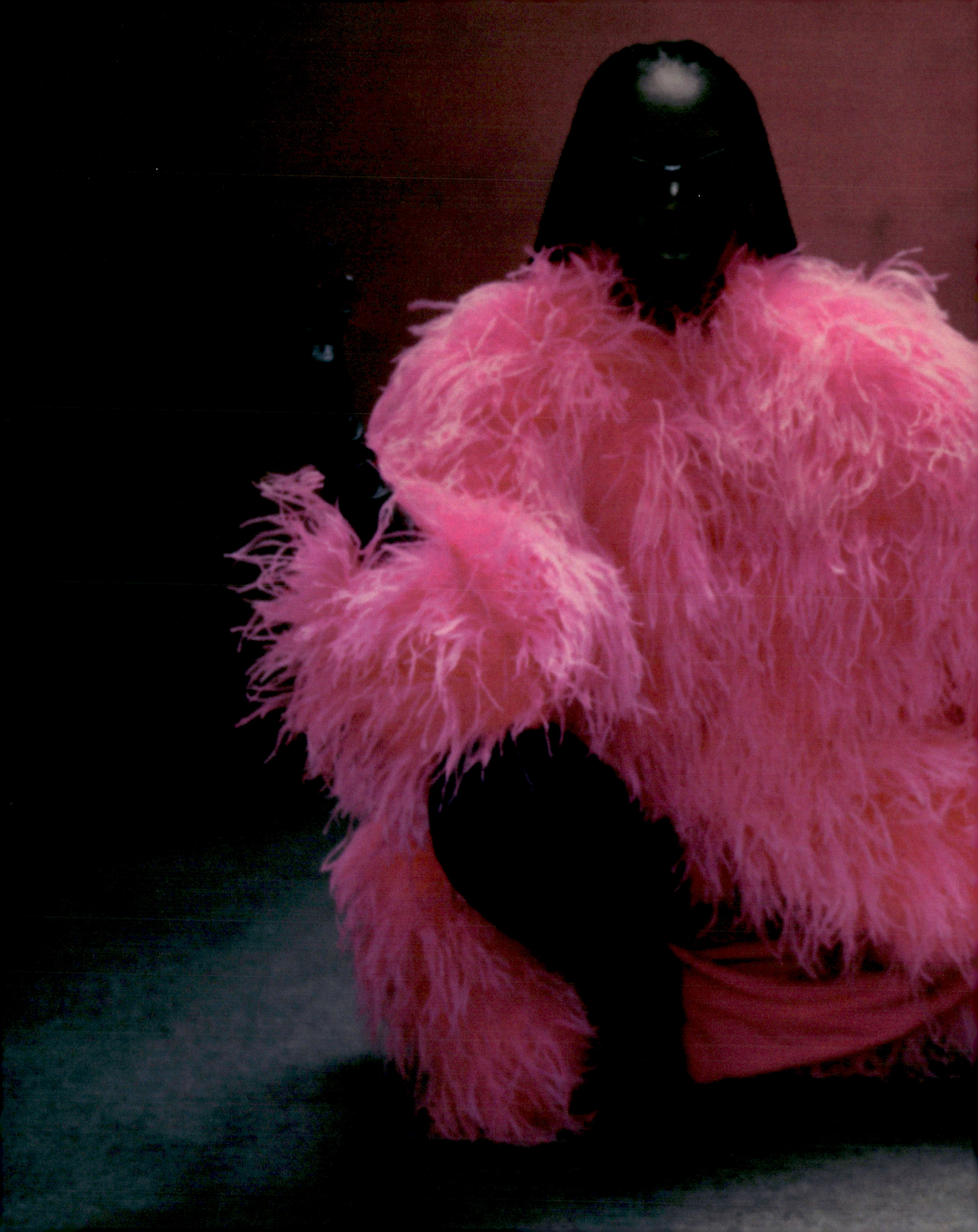

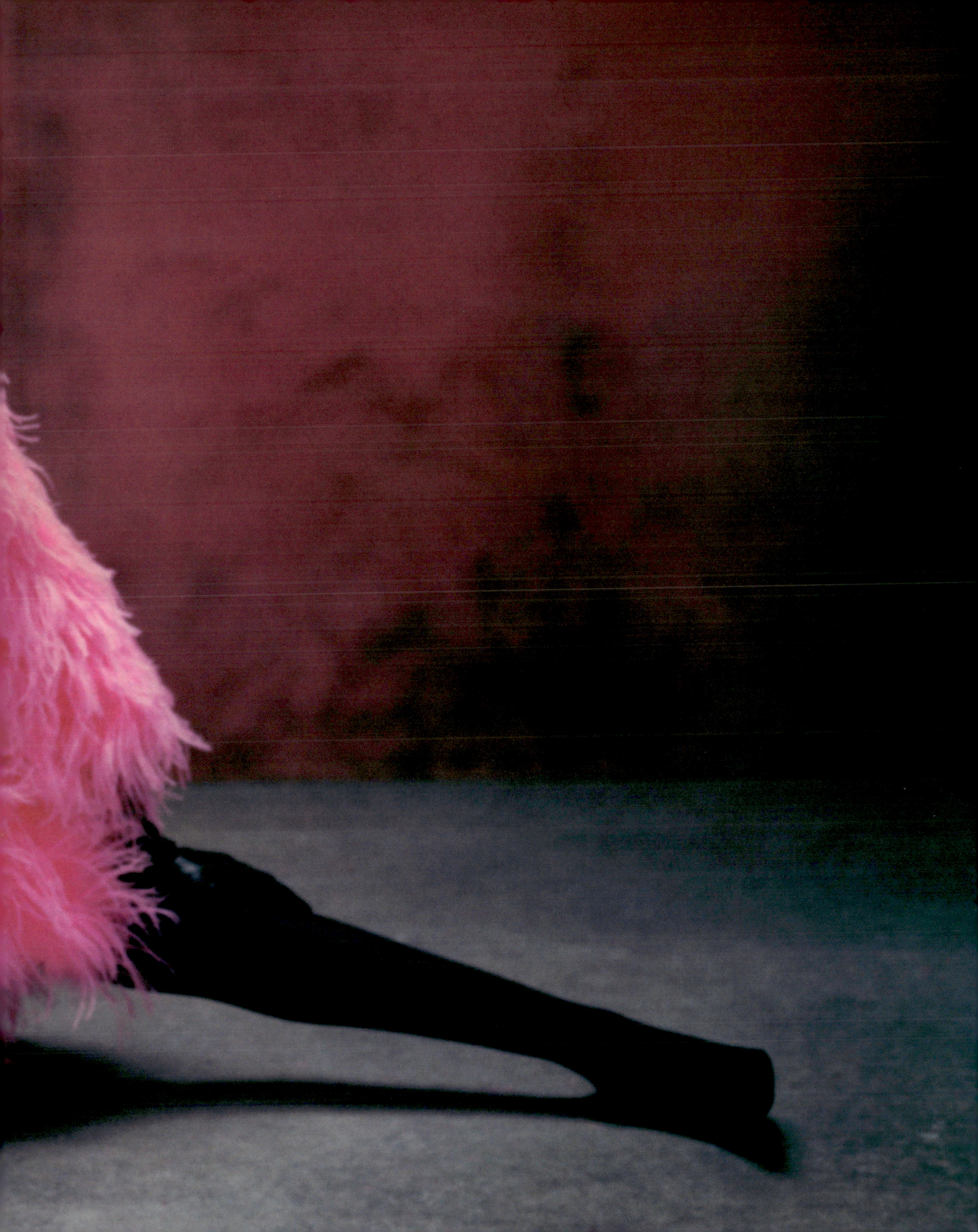

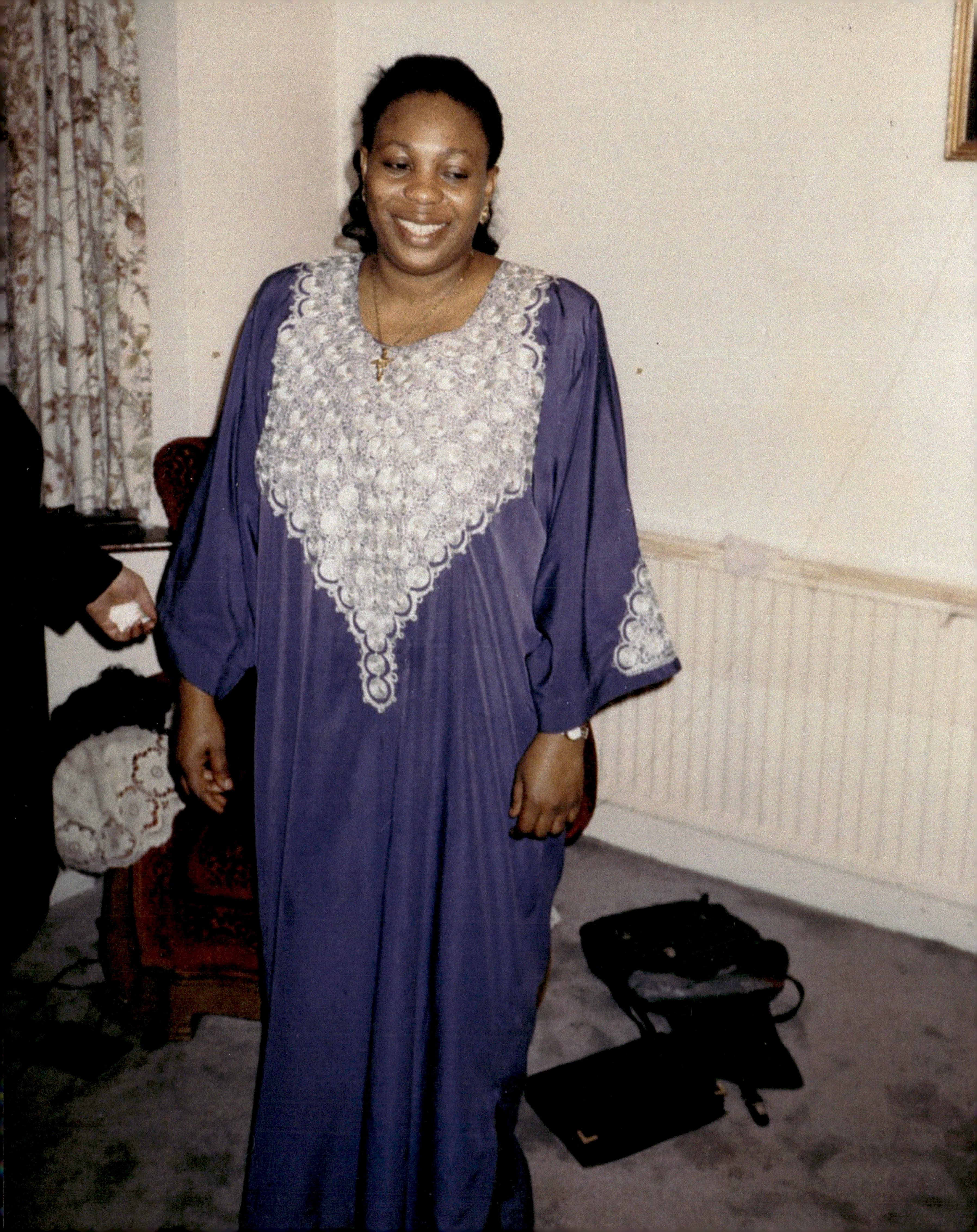

BY ARI CHANOUX

Mumsy,

It was never mine
Always ours
It was never a second
Always hours
You gave me it all and you want nothing in return
I could never believe in karma
Because by now you'd have wings
My angel
Guide me
Protect me
Until you no longer can
And then I promise
You'll have made me a better man.

SAMUEL ROSS

A generational savant who frames beauty through tension. Gabriel's practice follows the cadence of a purist's pursuit.

From subject, to study, to posture, sonics, and cinema, there are ephemera – unresolved issues, almost of the hero's journey – projected within each frame.

Power comes to mind when considering his practice, his contributions across the cultural Zeitgeist, the fashion and art industries.

Yet it's not simply a matter of volume and aesthetics, it's the expansion of concepts into an ether that seems to have no clear boundaries, no restraints or maximum capacity.

Bodies tumble and sling across the skylines, amber eyes emerge through ink-blue sinkholes, and blackened pigment reflects light as if the body were embalmed in a sheet of black ice.

Beyond the strength of Gabriel's signatures, it seemed pertinent to open this address with a sense of brotherhood within Gabriel's optimistic spirit and pragmatic stance to the arts and his matter of traversing the industry.

There is a lineage of practitioners that comes to mind, formed over the past ten to fifteen years, colleagues who have reshaped a stifled, relatively linear sector deeply in need of reconstruction.

There's also a lineage of artists who have produced almost half a century of contributions relating to the arts through the lens of our African diaspora.

Gabriel has contributed to both, and will without a doubt continue to shape future projects with power, cadence, and intensity.

CIESAY

Gabriel Moses, son, brother, friend, God-fearing, prolific, humble, determined, and ambitious – a few words to sum up the creative force I'm glad to call a friend.

I met Gabriel at a pop-up I had a few years ago. He introduced himself and said he wanted to work on a project with me. I was very impressed by the level of work he had done at the time, and immediately took a liking to the way he carried himself and his confidence. We worked on a project that ended up being shelved, but that did not deter us from continuing to work together. He soon approached me with the idea of becoming his manager. I was hesitant at first, because I had no idea how to do that, but I just really believed in him, and saw something special. He made me want to try and do it, so I became his manager. It's been amazing to watch Gabriel grow as an artist and as a person, and to continue to see his work and identity develop in real time.

Gabriel has cemented himself in a short time and showed everyone that he's a force to be reckoned with! I will continue to watch and be amazed by everything he does.

MATTHEW WILLIAMS

Memory is kind of blurry on how and where we met, but one of the first things Gabriel did was a video for my 1017 ALYX 9SM runway show, and he was probably not even twenty at the time. And I just remember how chill he was, and how amazing his work ethic was. He always has good energy around him and we instantly connected. It's been amazing to watch him grow and find his own voice, his own vision, push his creativity. And every time I see his work, project after project, year after year, I get more and more impressed by the leaps and bounds he is making in his own progress. And now there is a whole crew in his generation that is super inspiring, ranging from different artists, image makers, designers, musicians, etc., and they all just push each other, working collectively, creating a whole new world for themselves and generations to come. Impressed by the guy big-time, and can't wait for the day we go back to the studio and work on something new together!

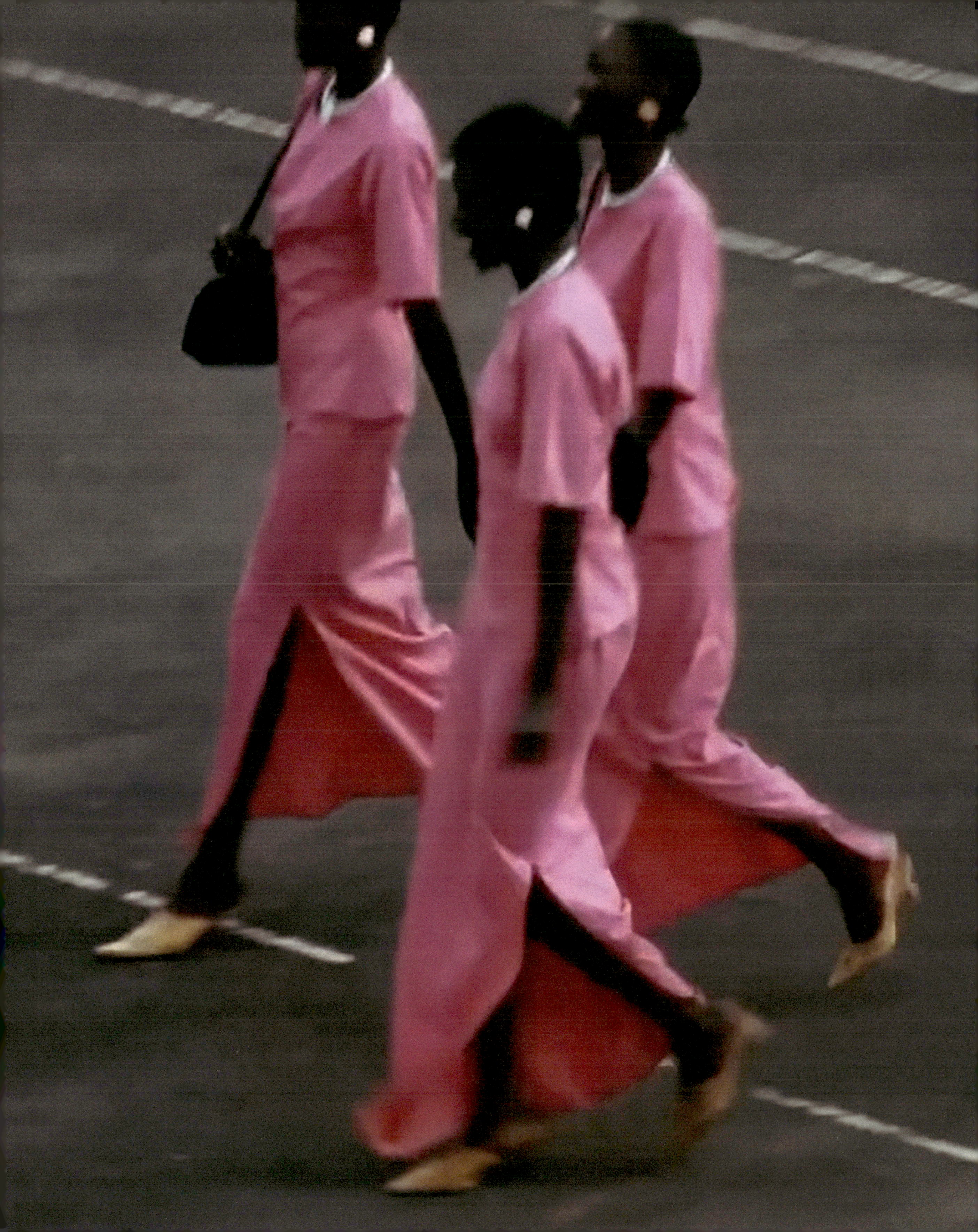

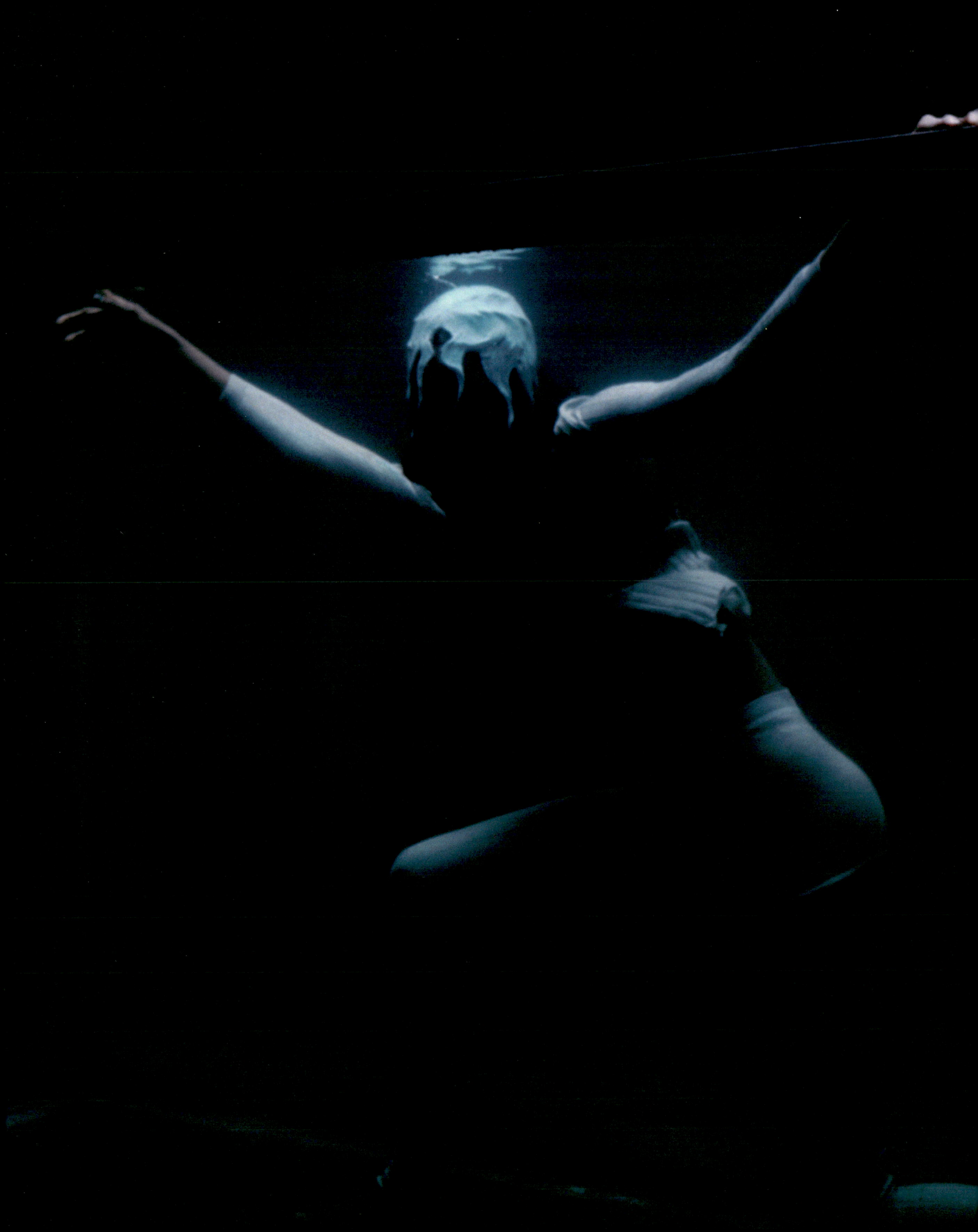

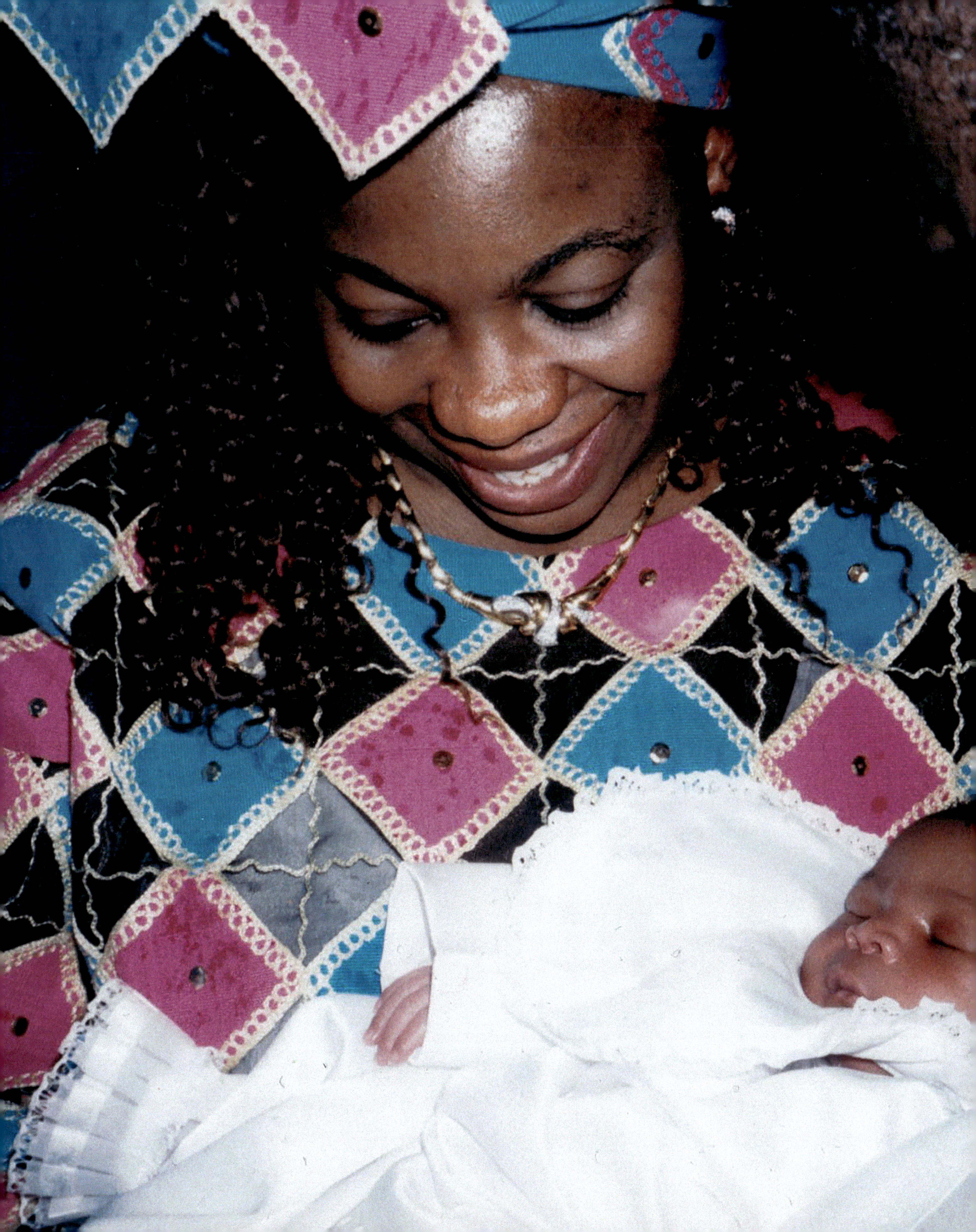

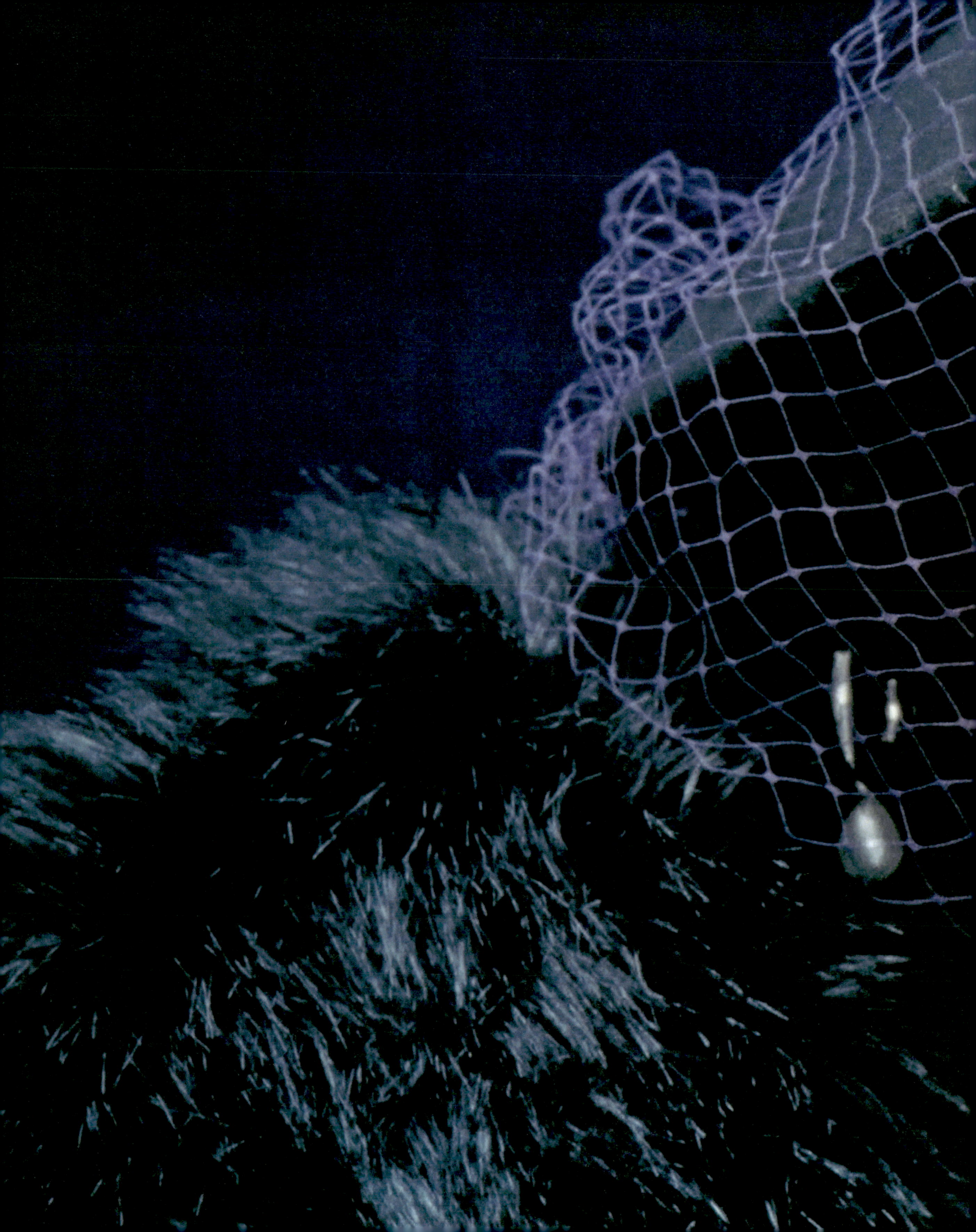

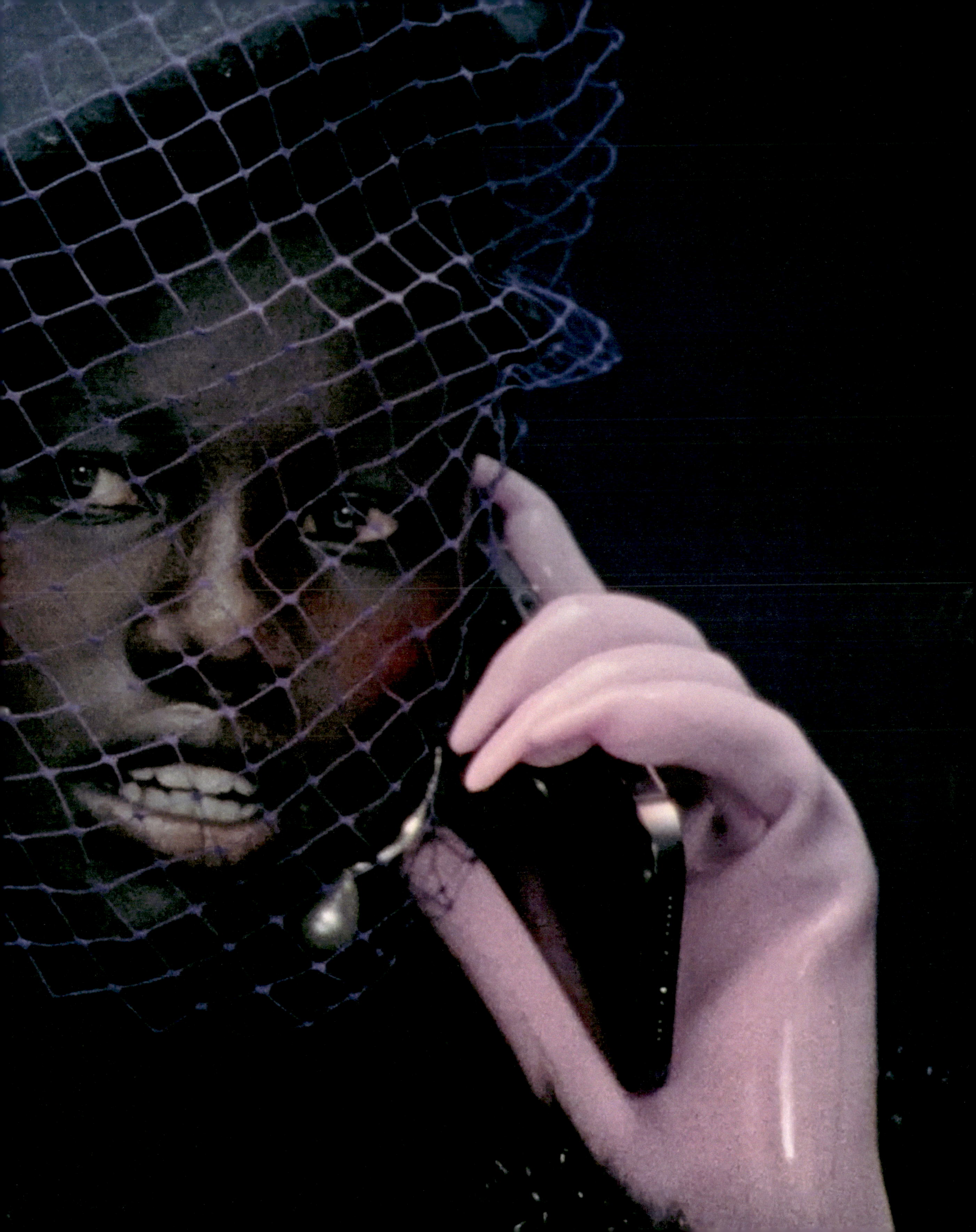

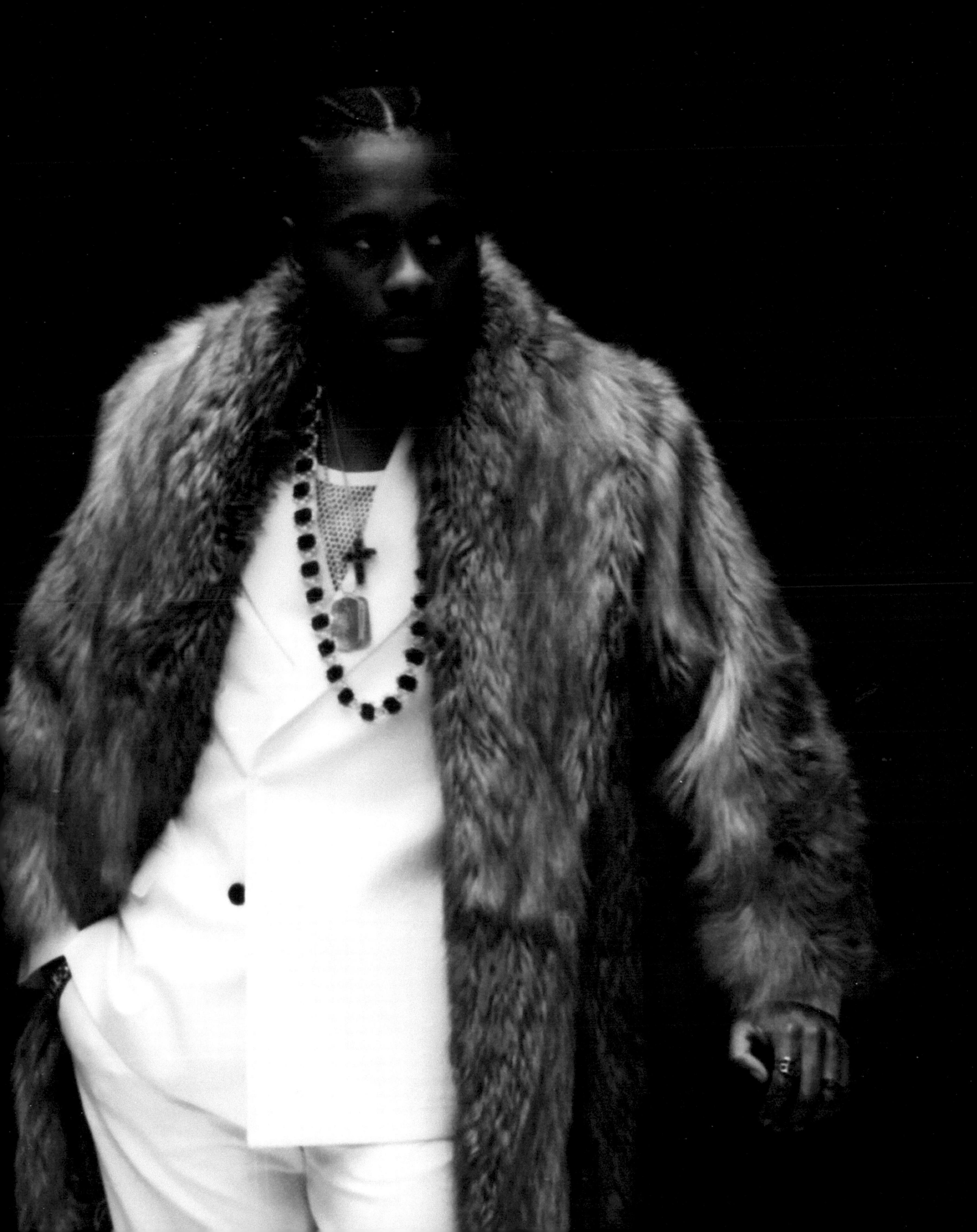

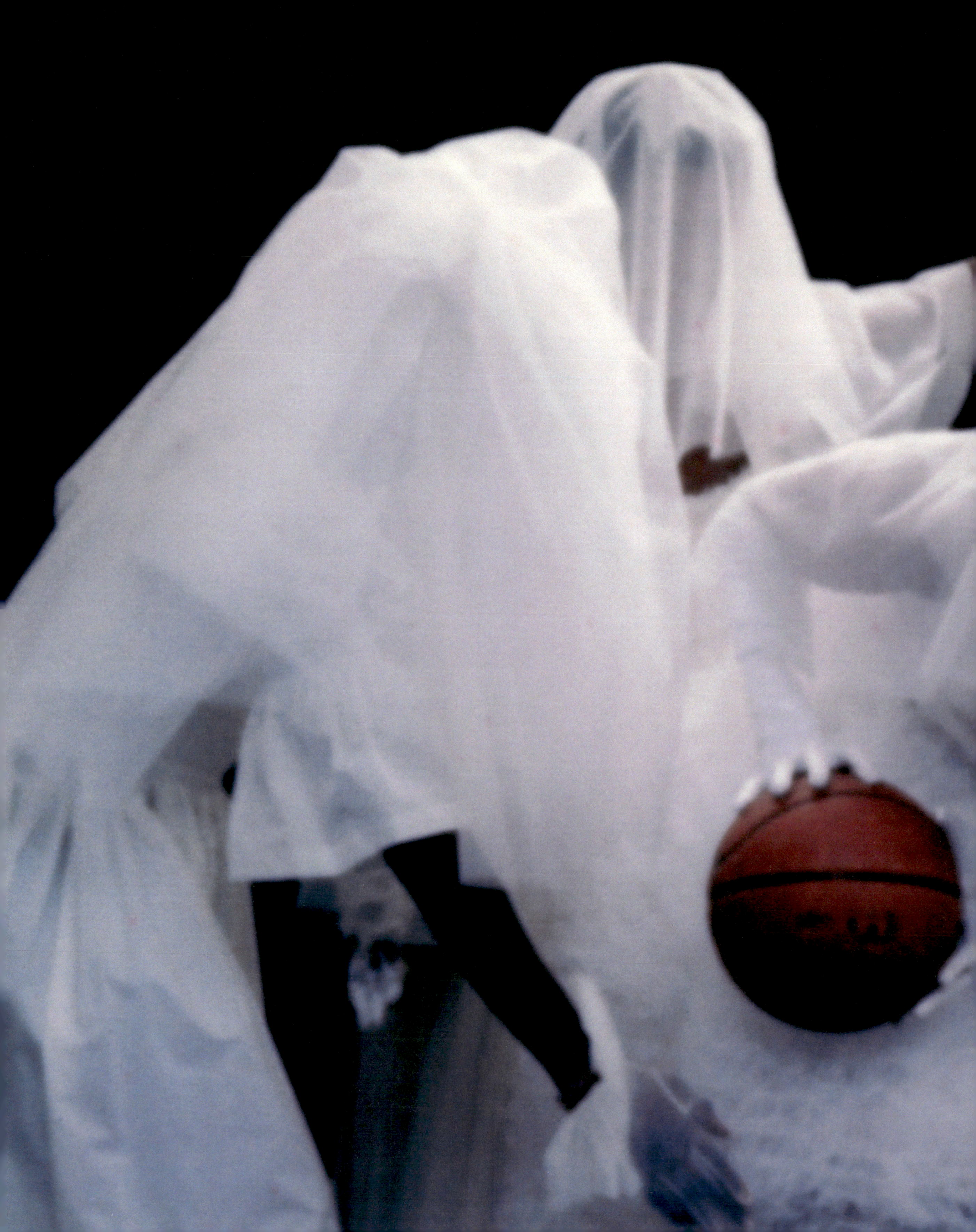

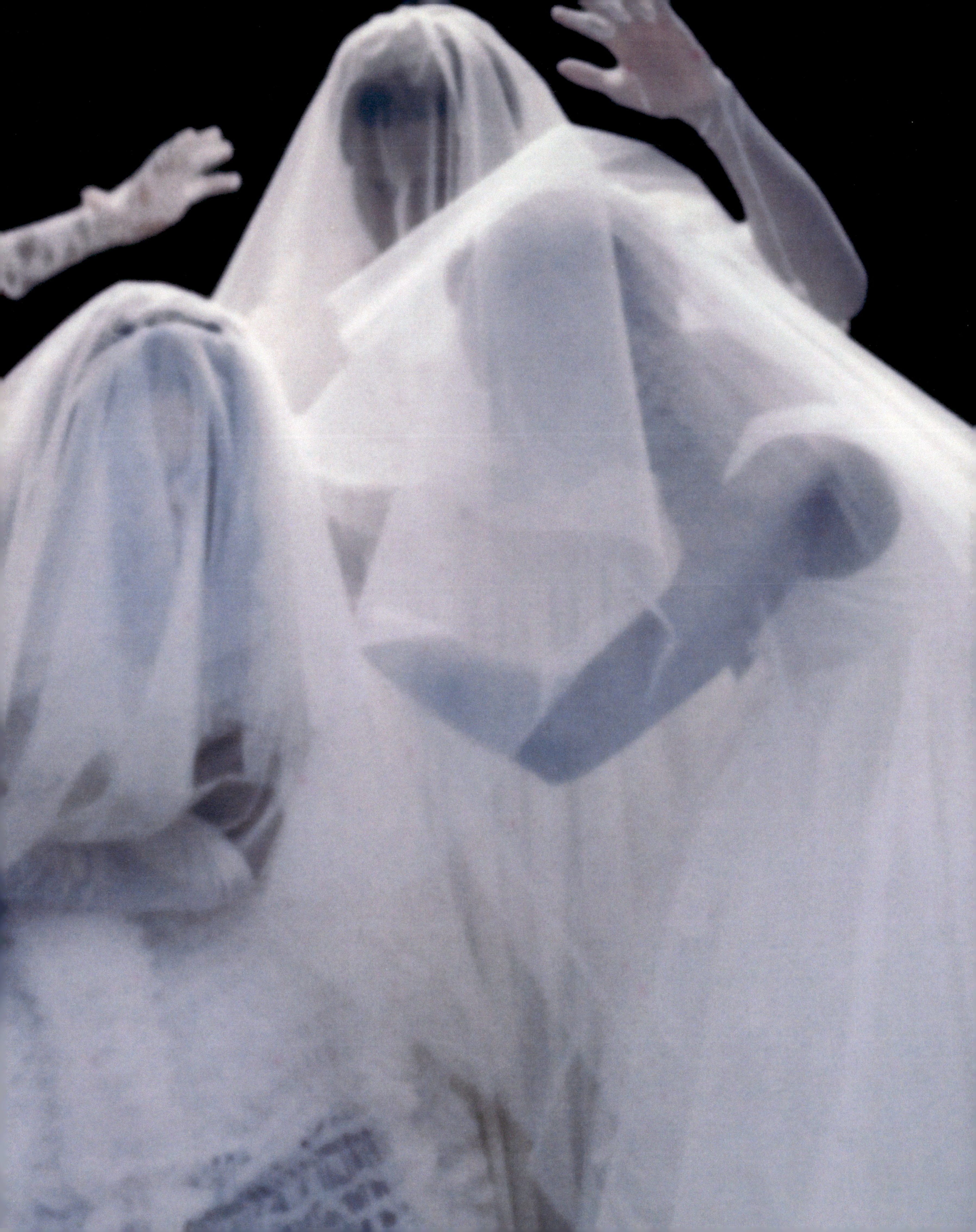

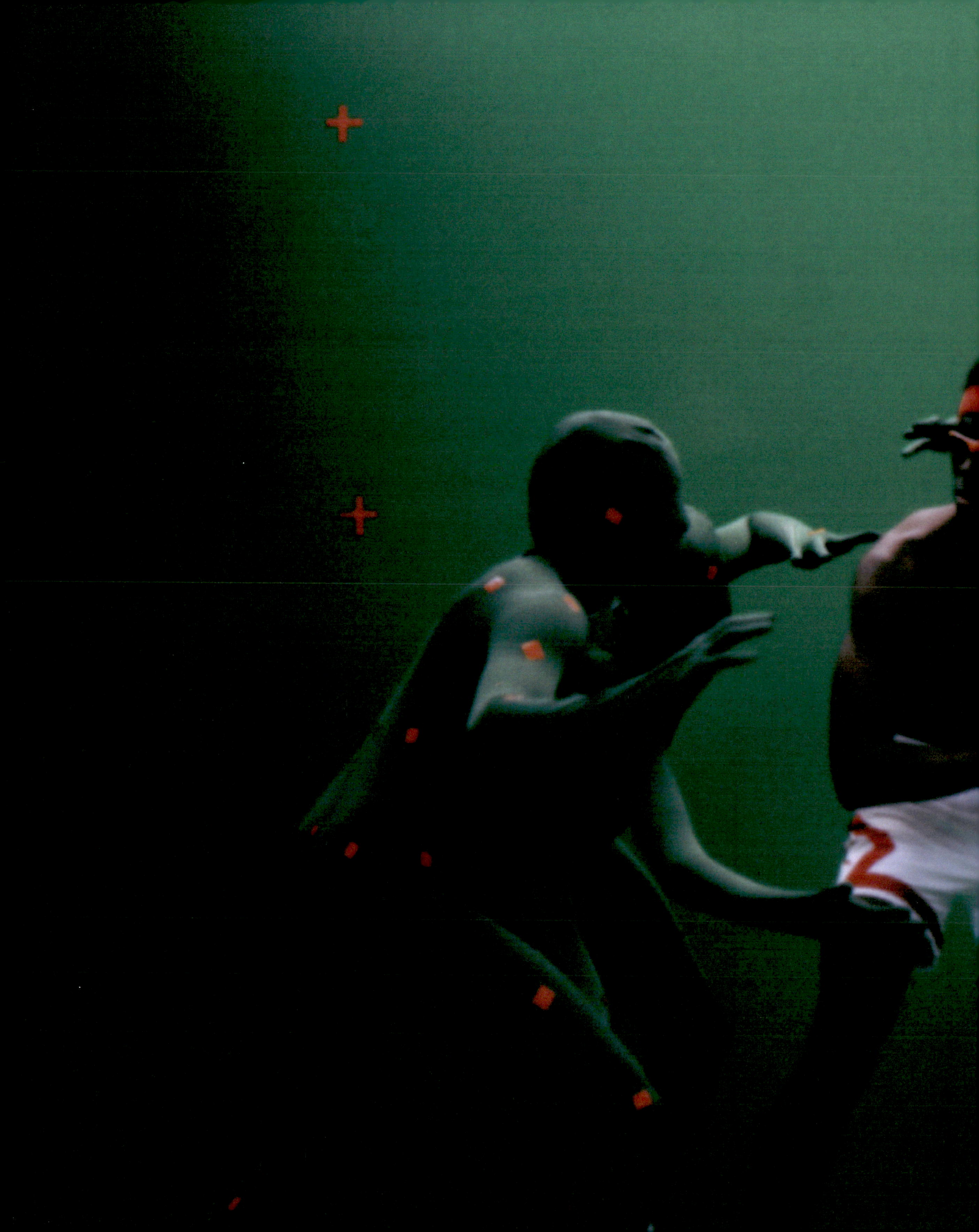

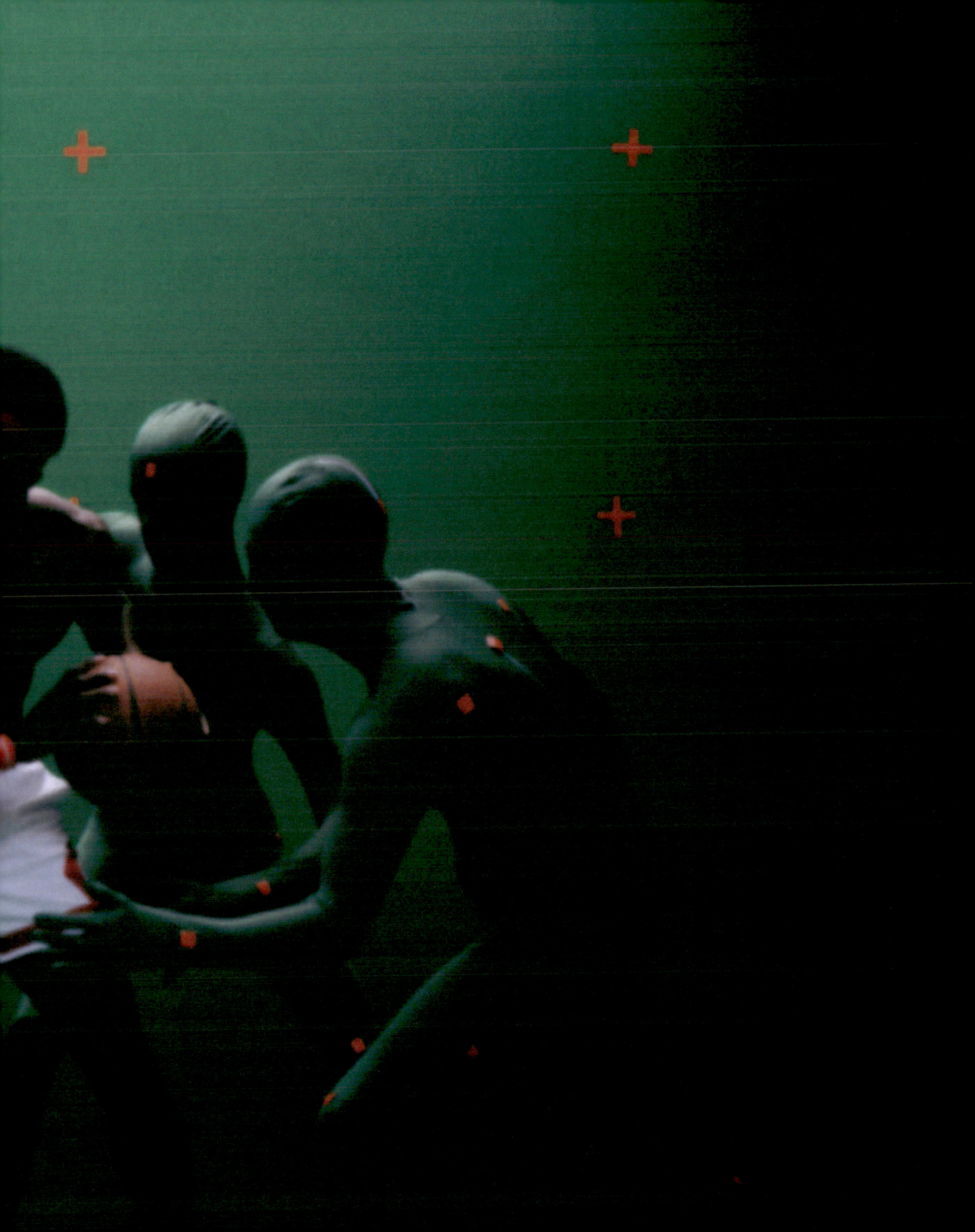

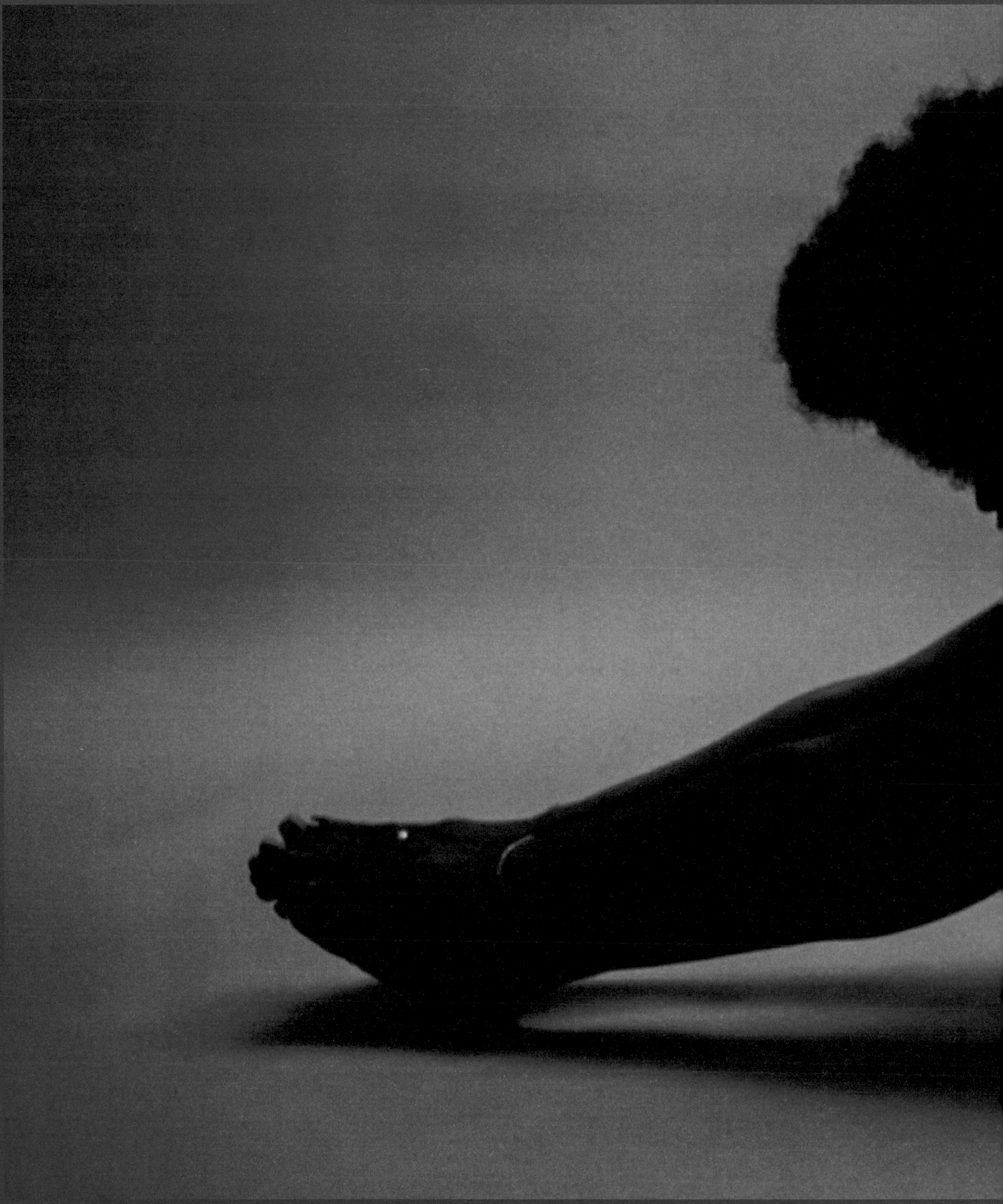

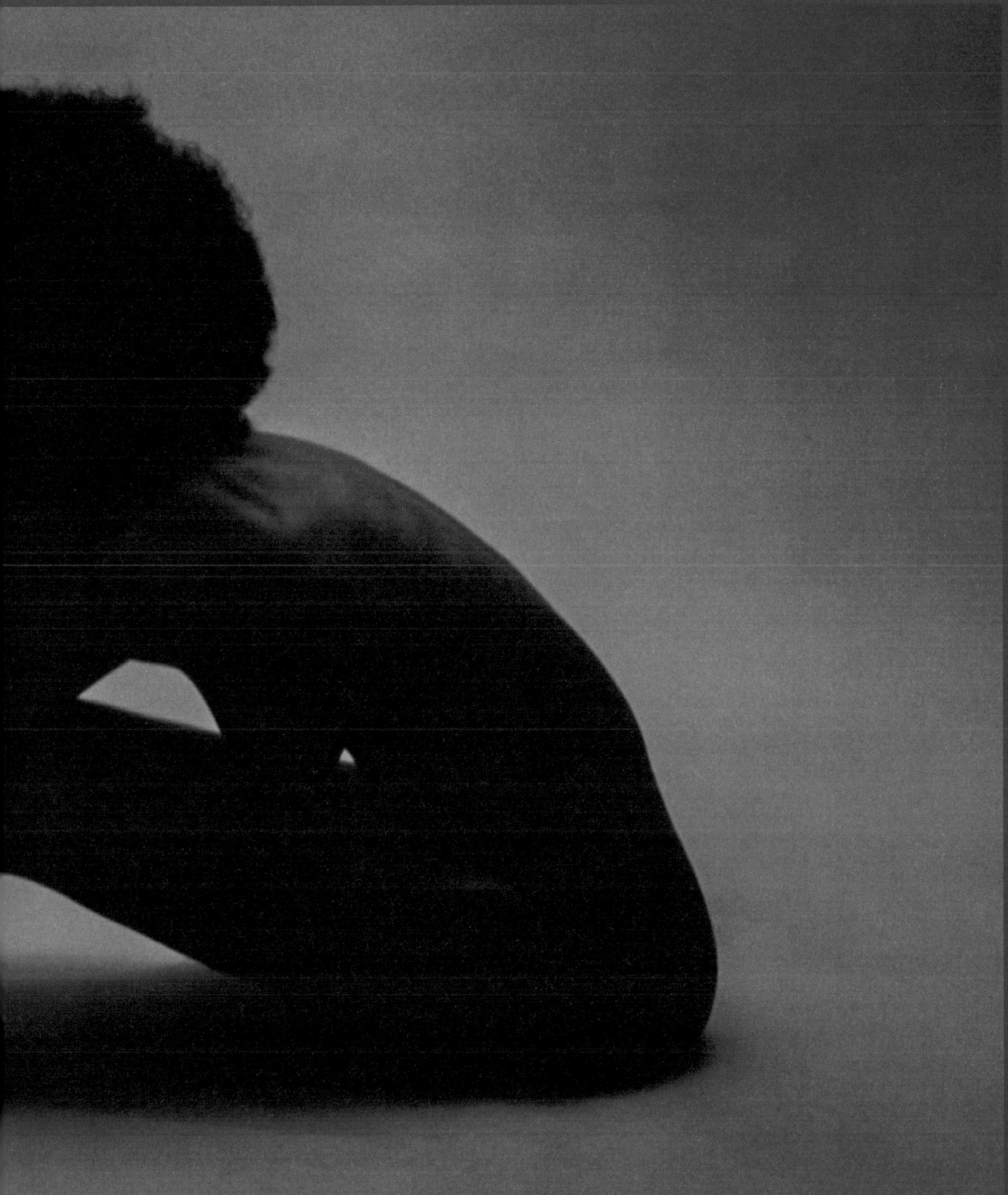

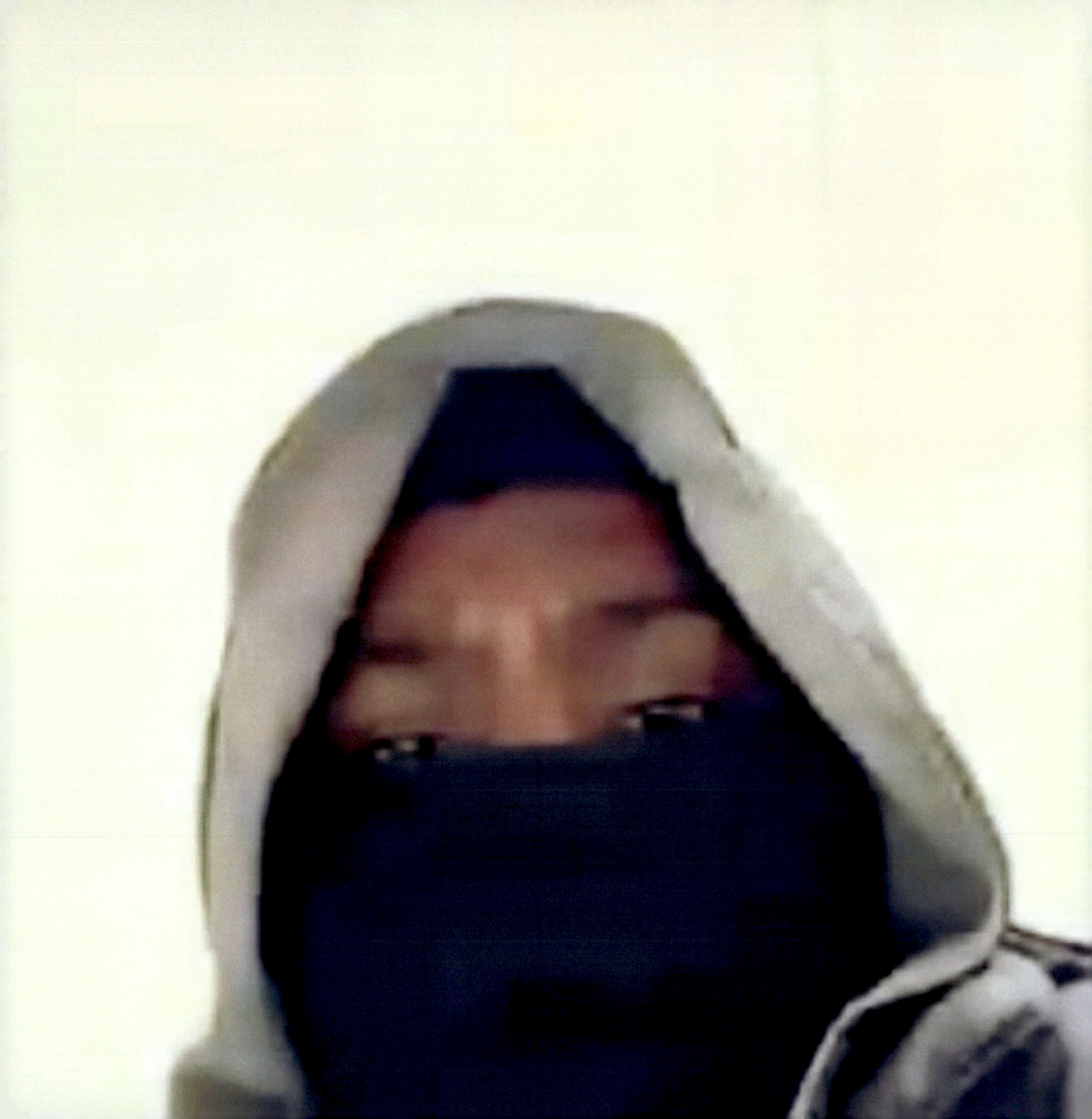

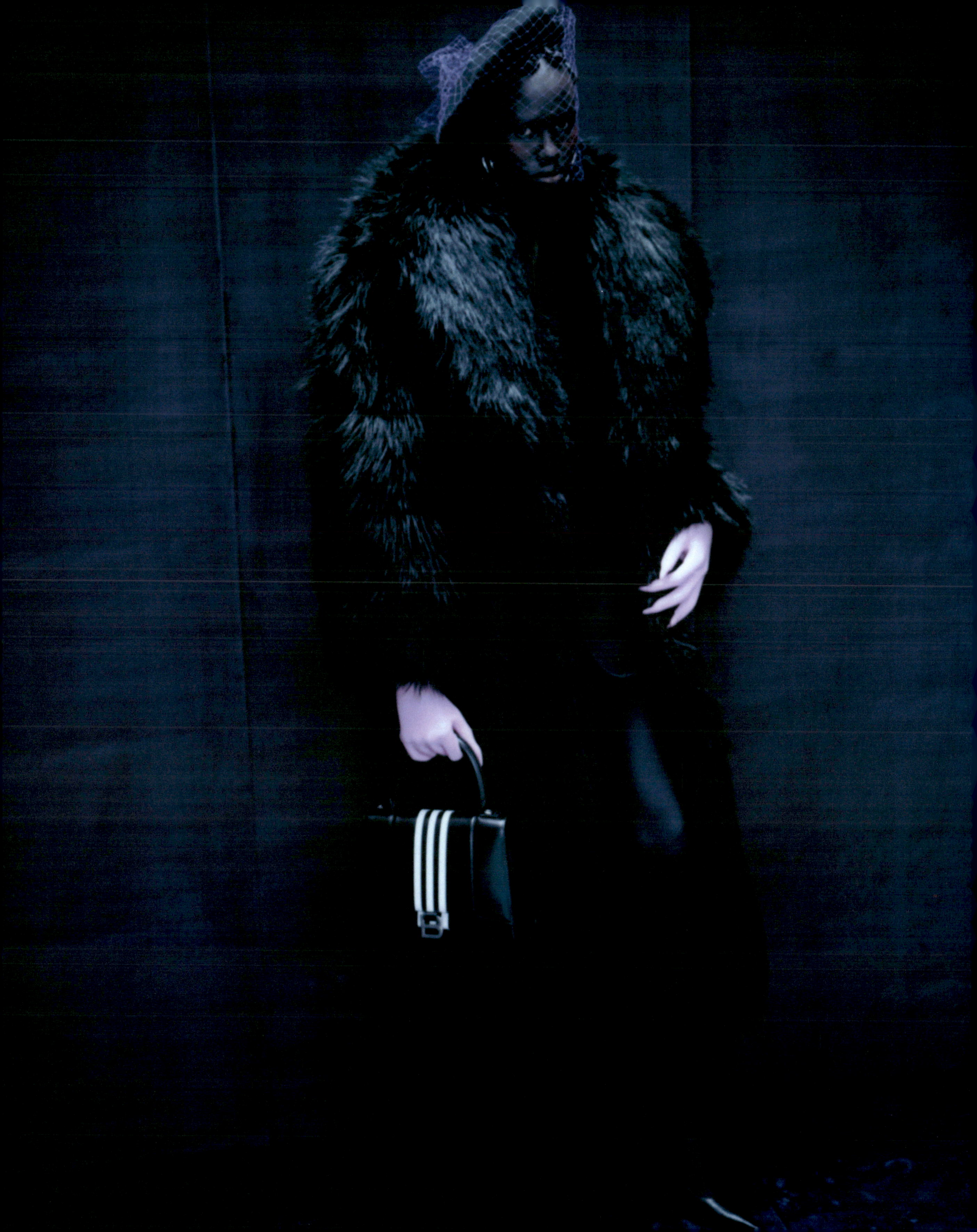

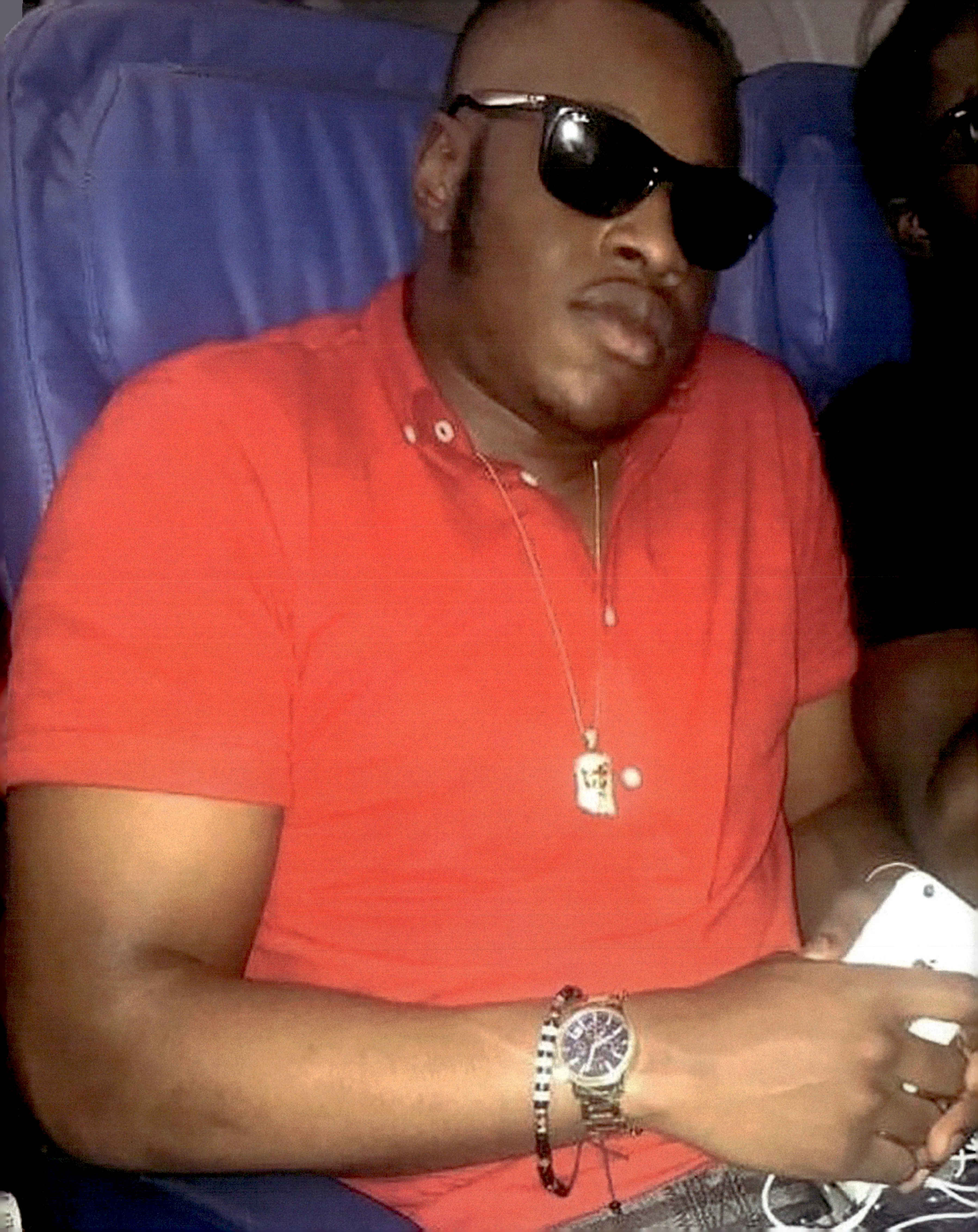

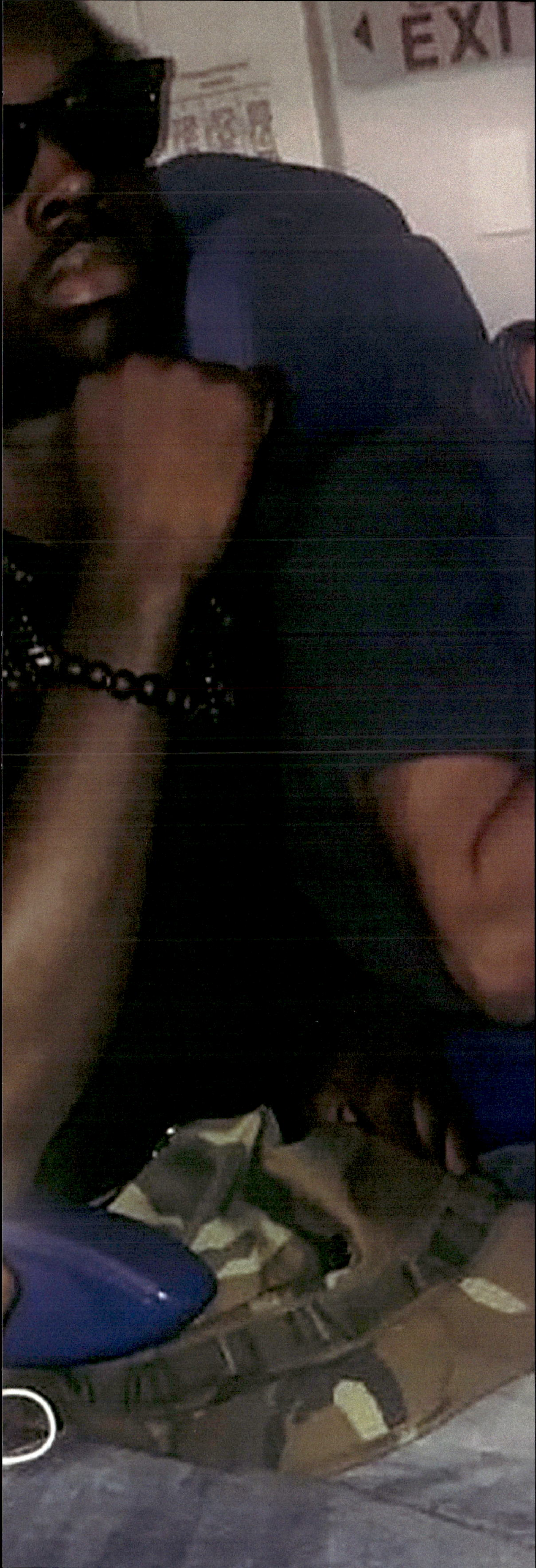

里賈納

L'HOMME NE PEUT VIVRE QUE DE PAIN

REGINA

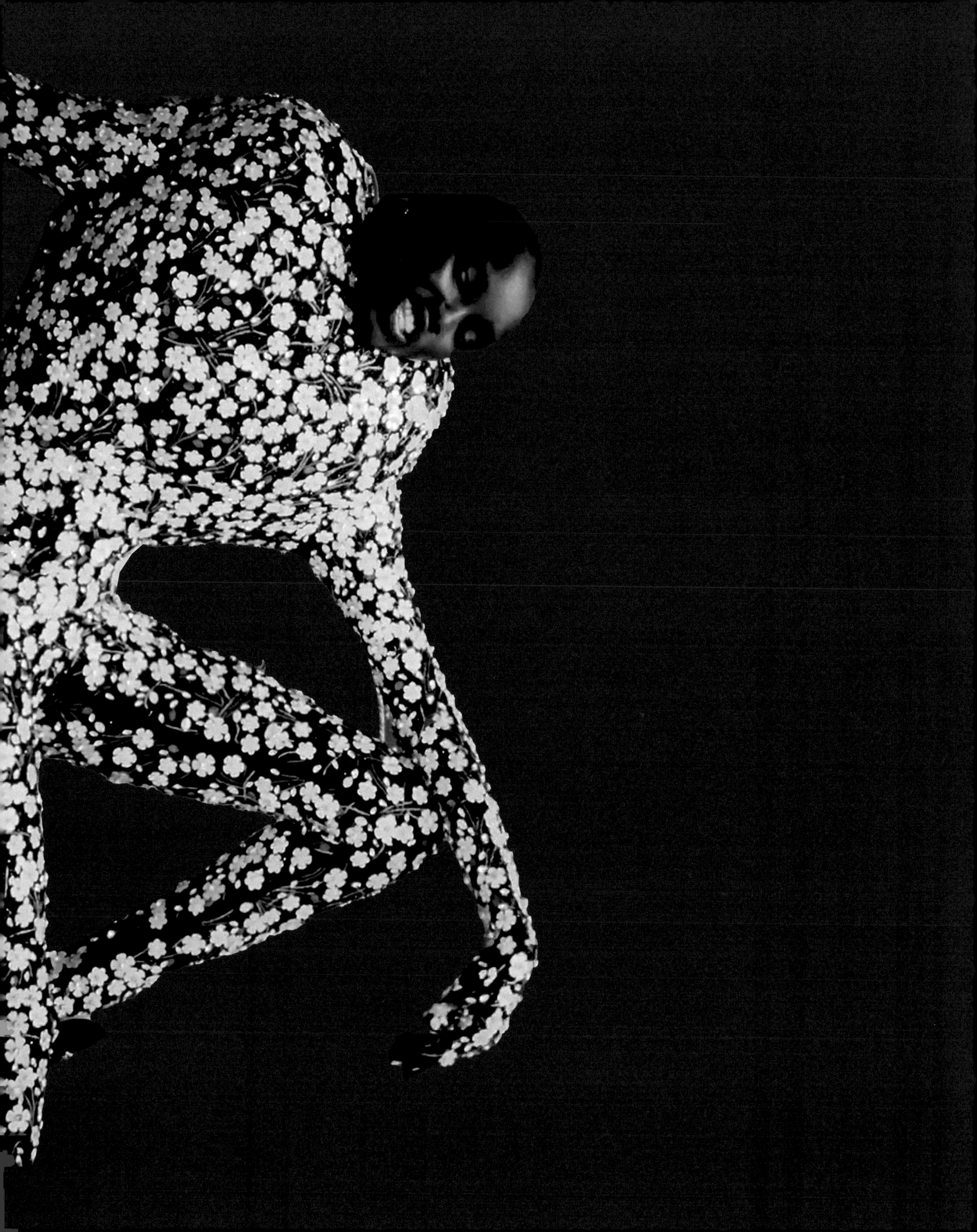

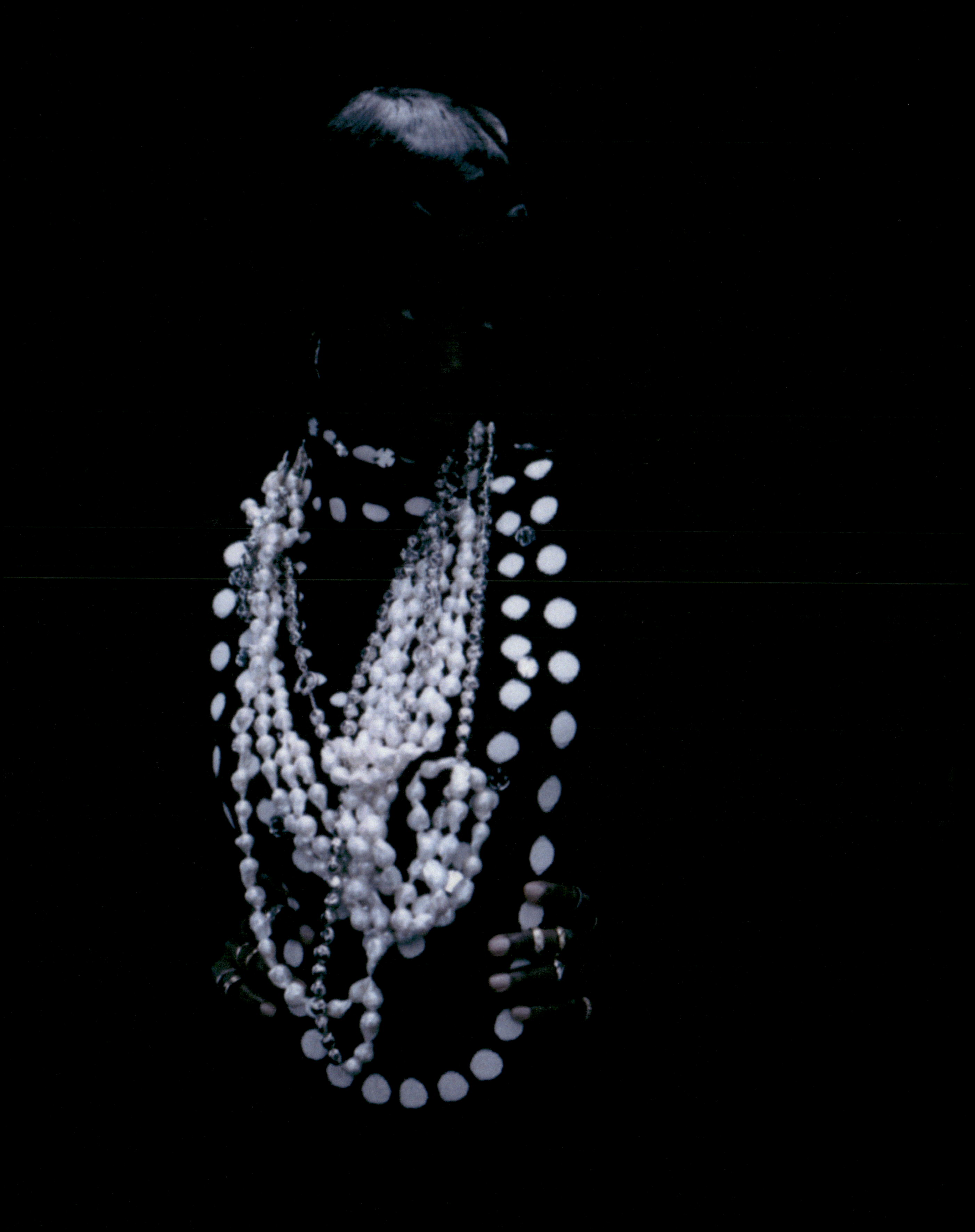

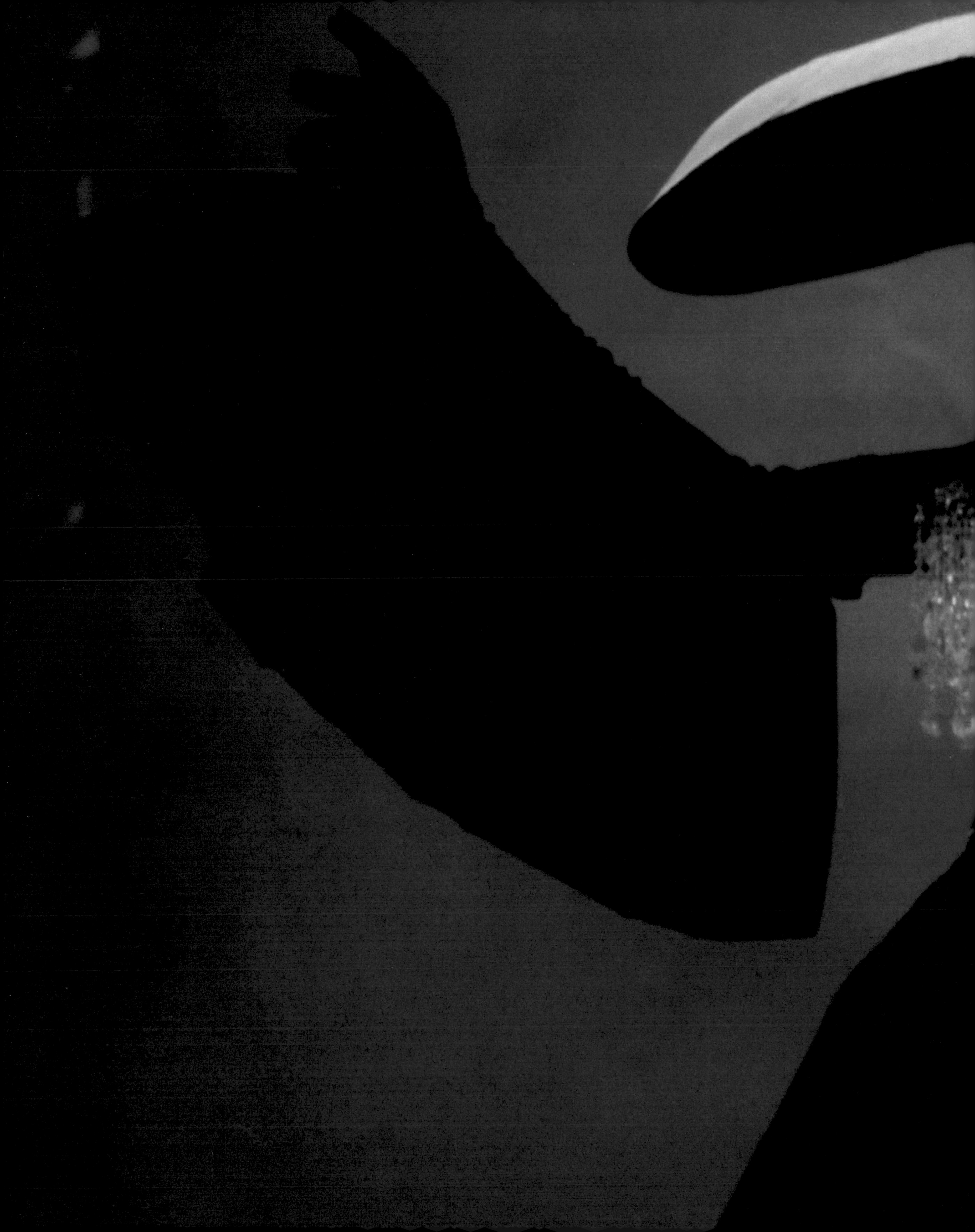

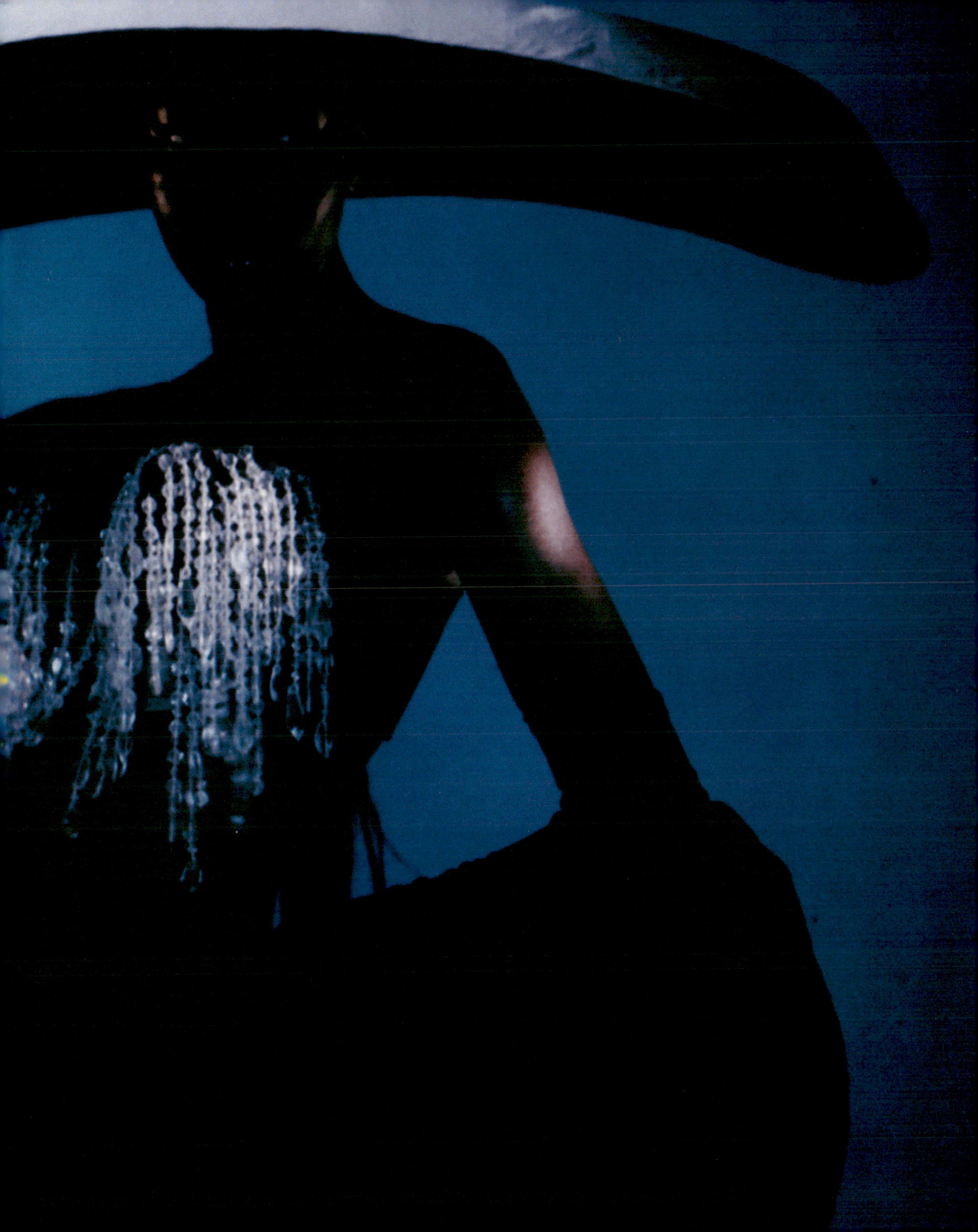

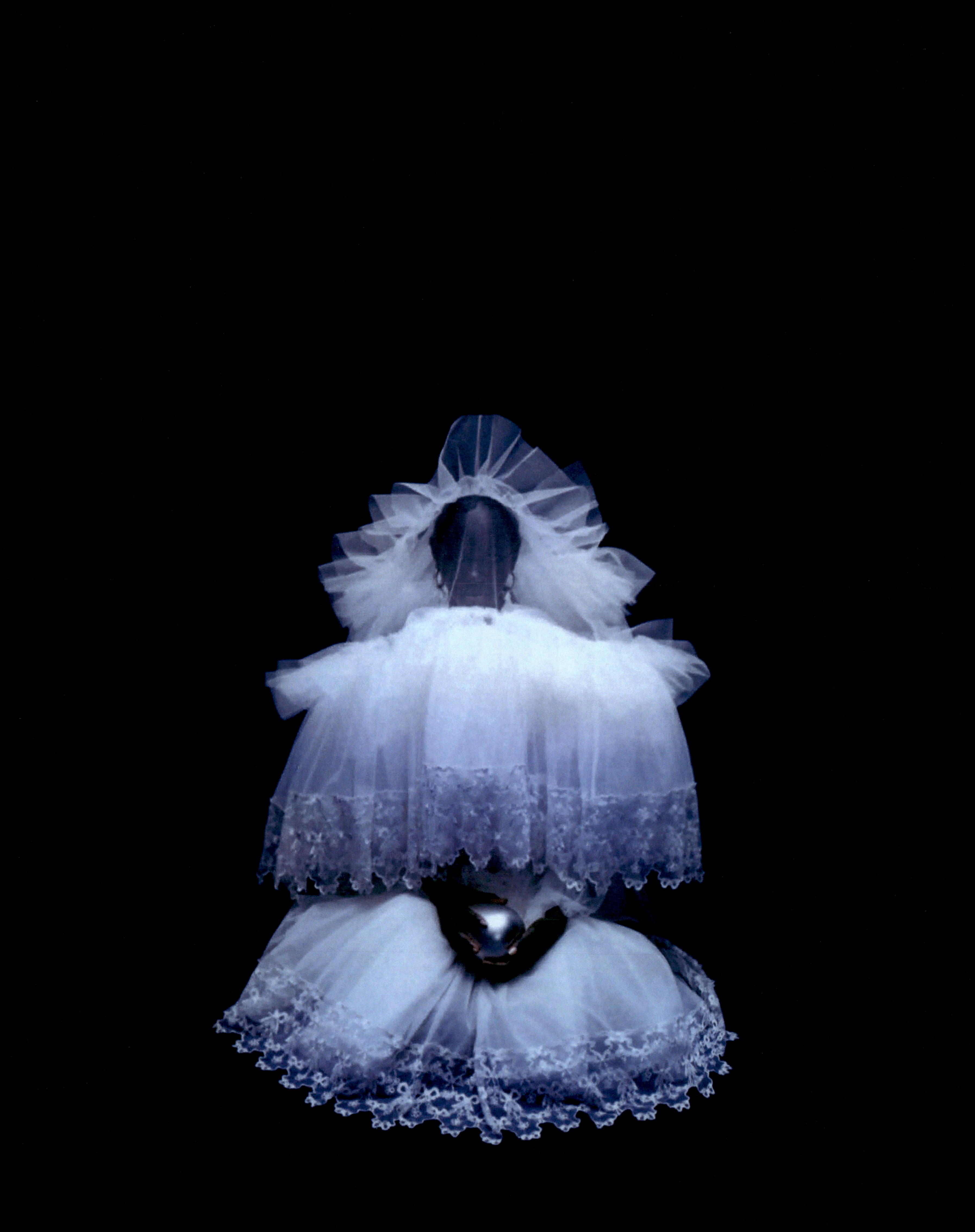

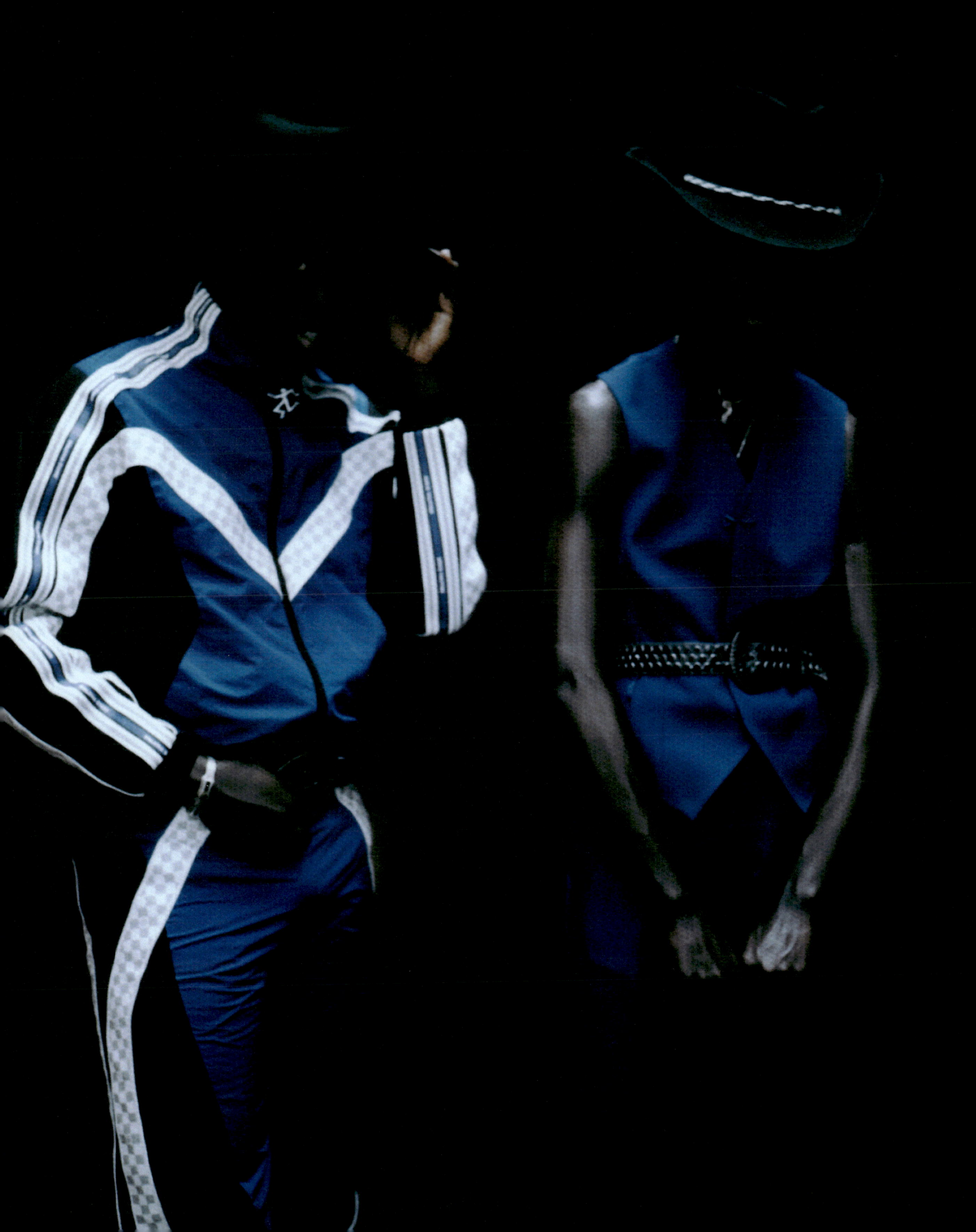

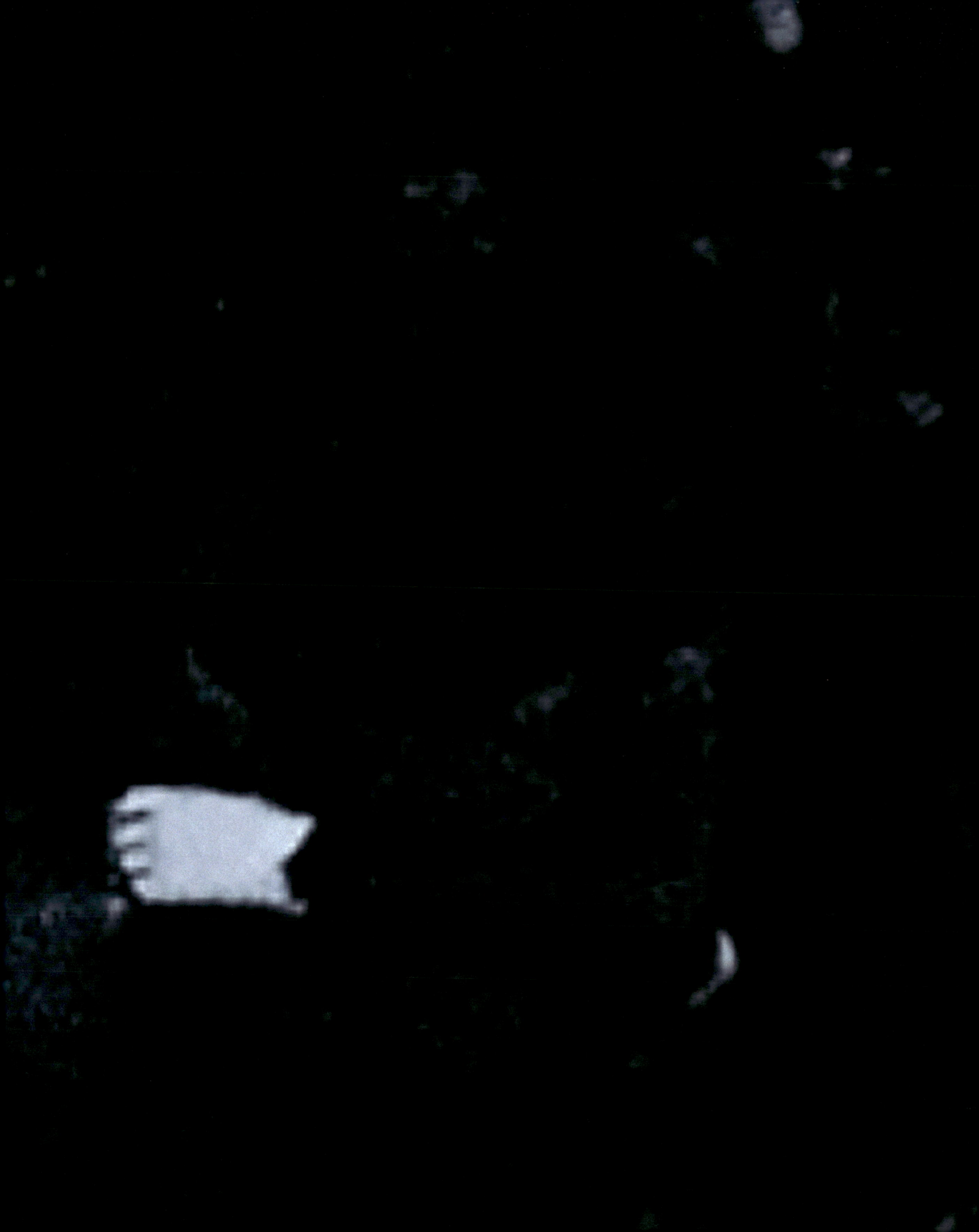

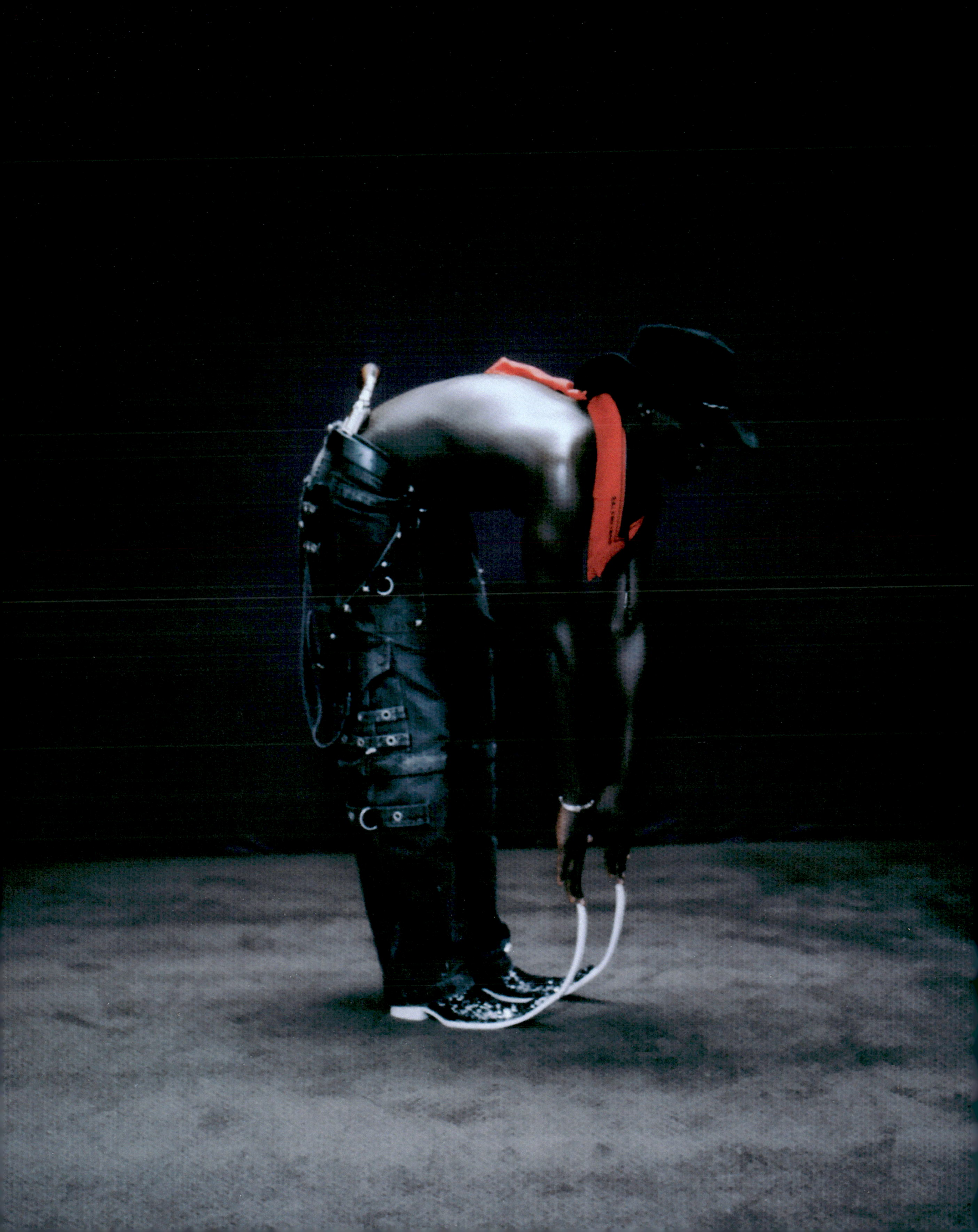

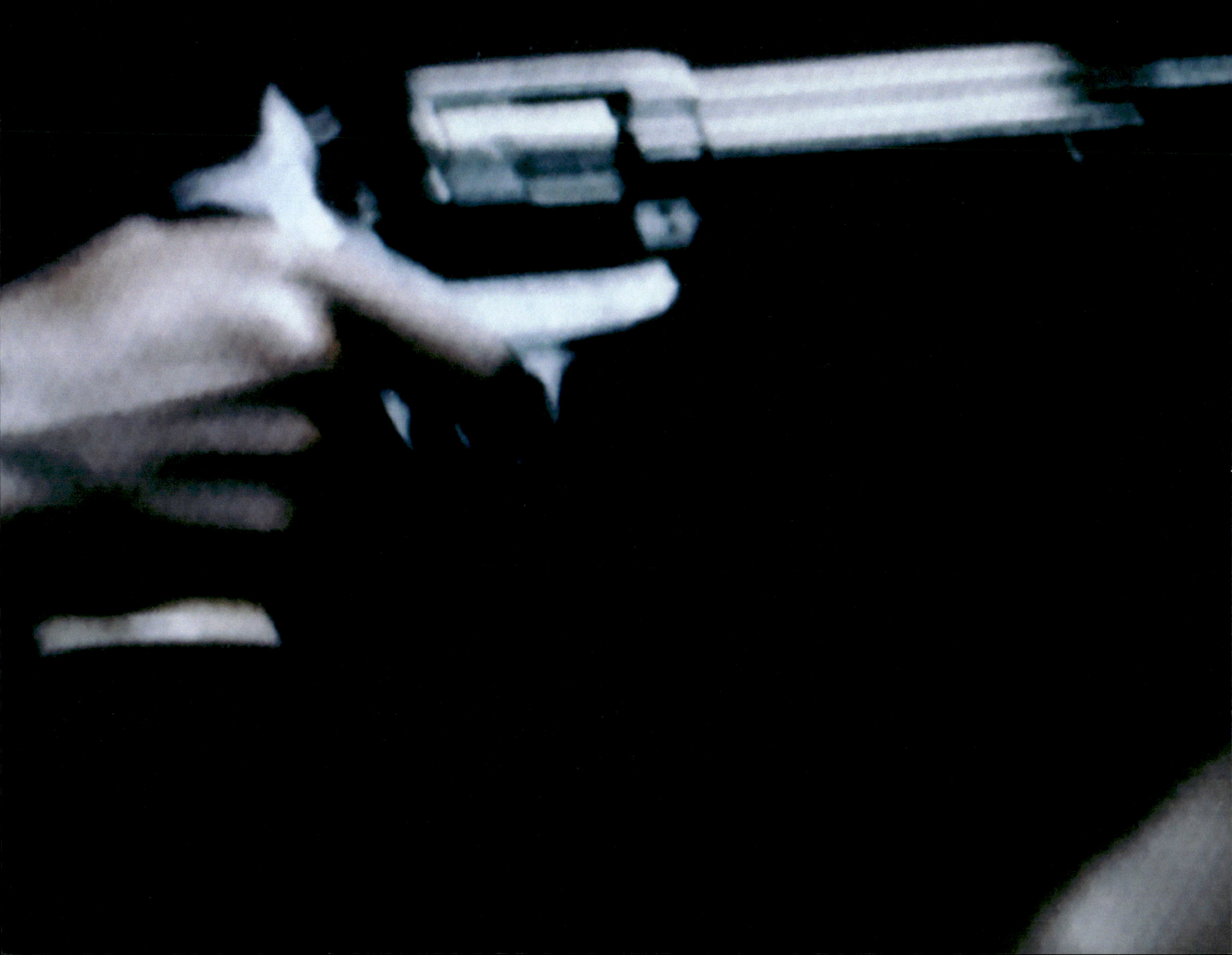

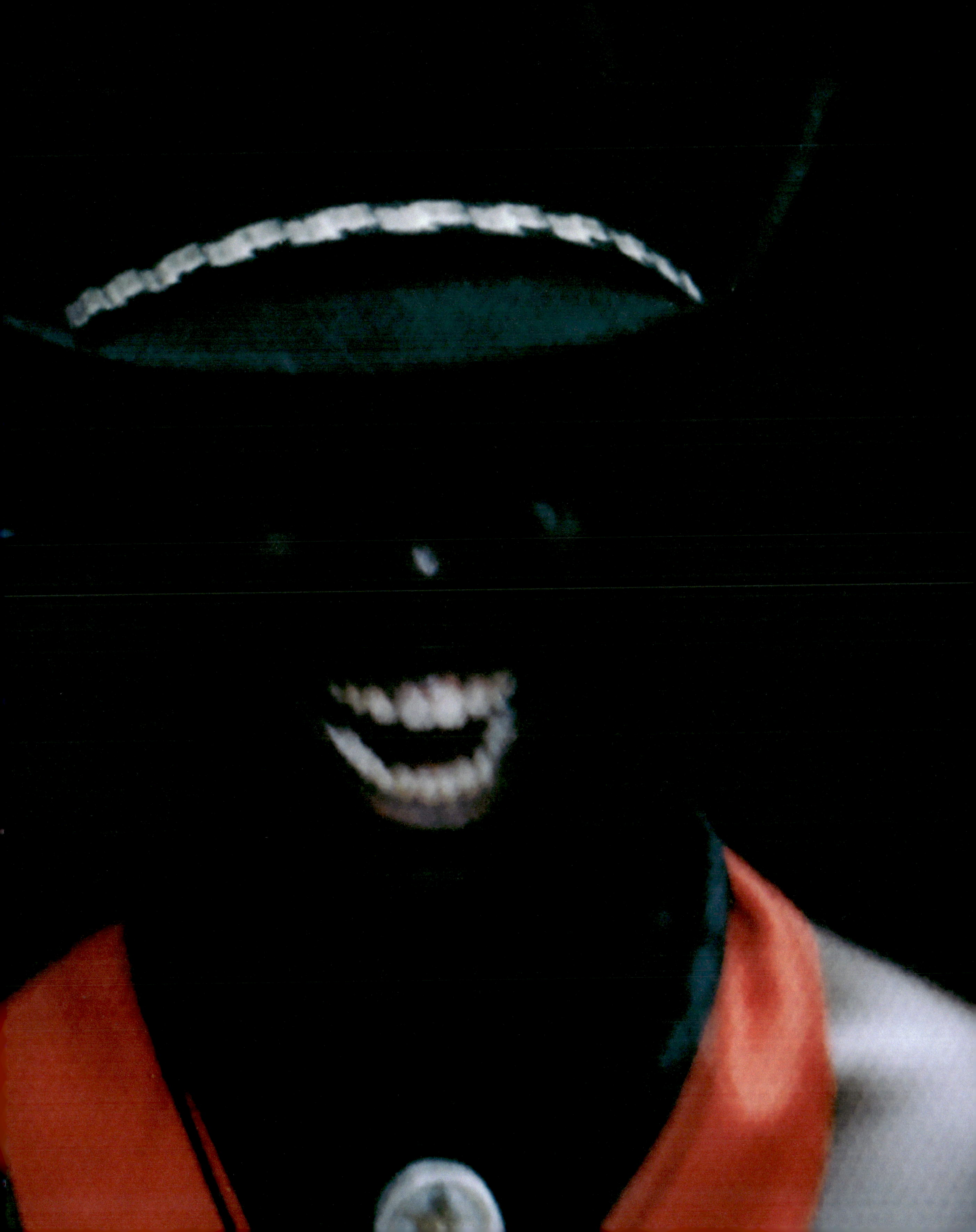

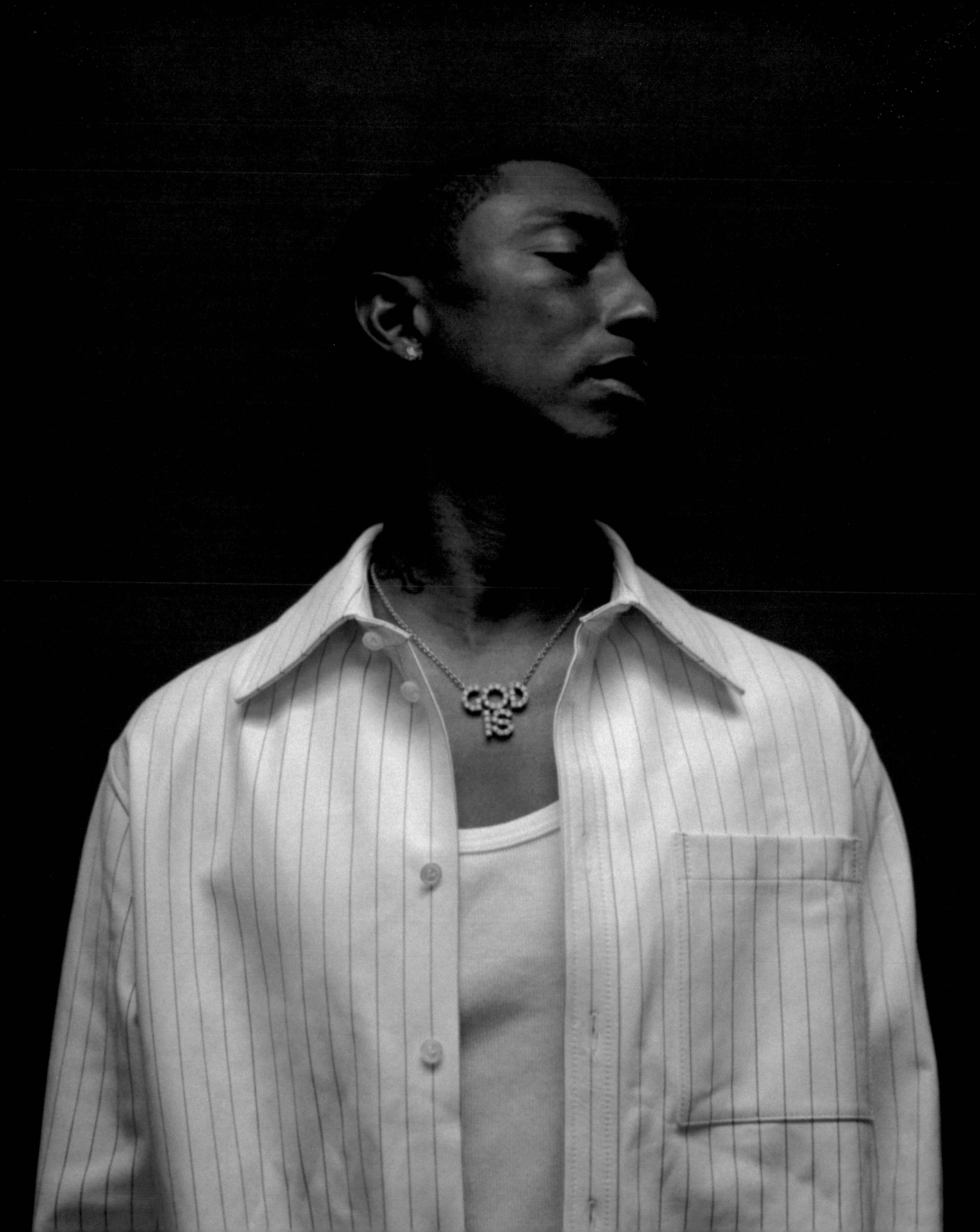
GOD
IS

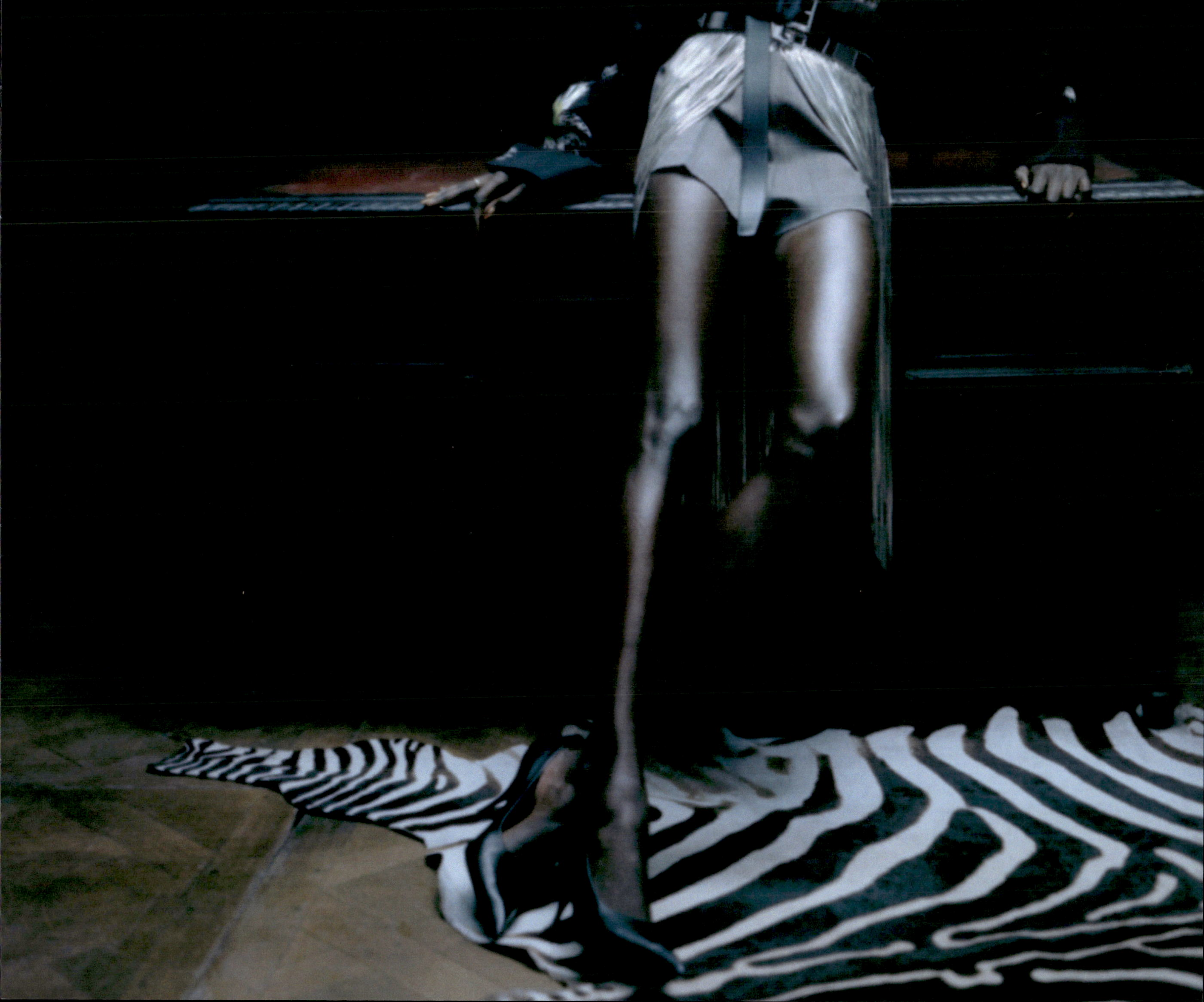

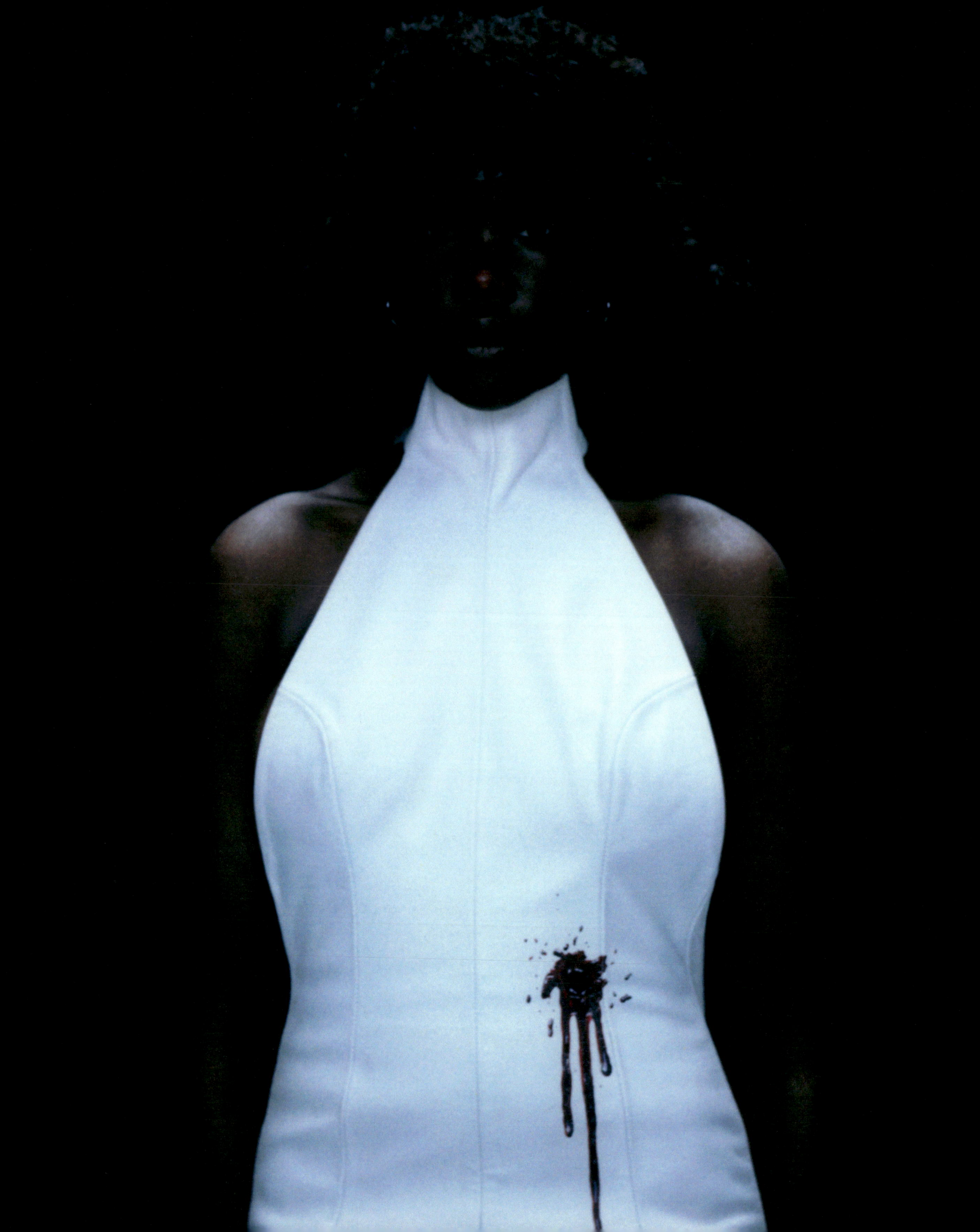

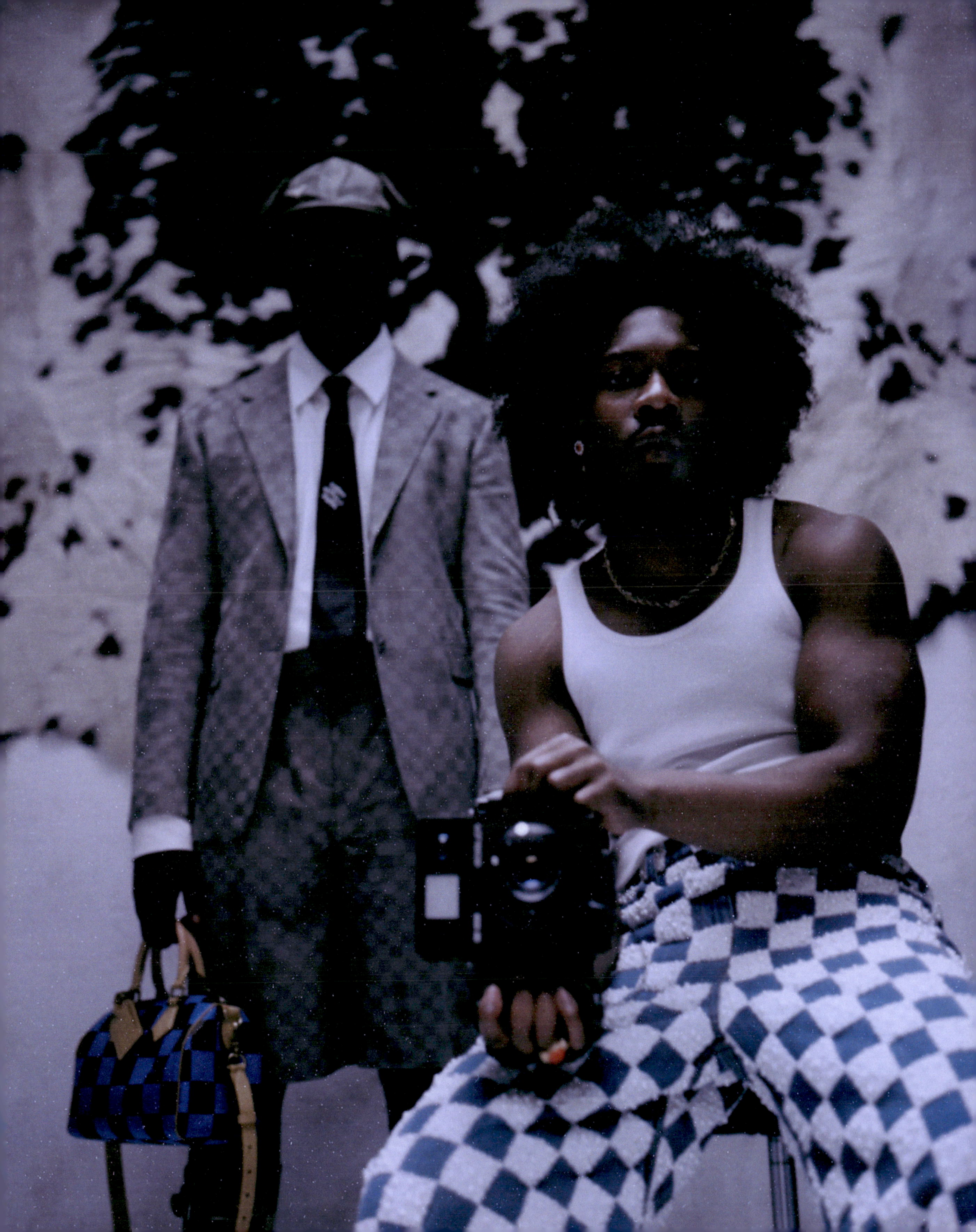

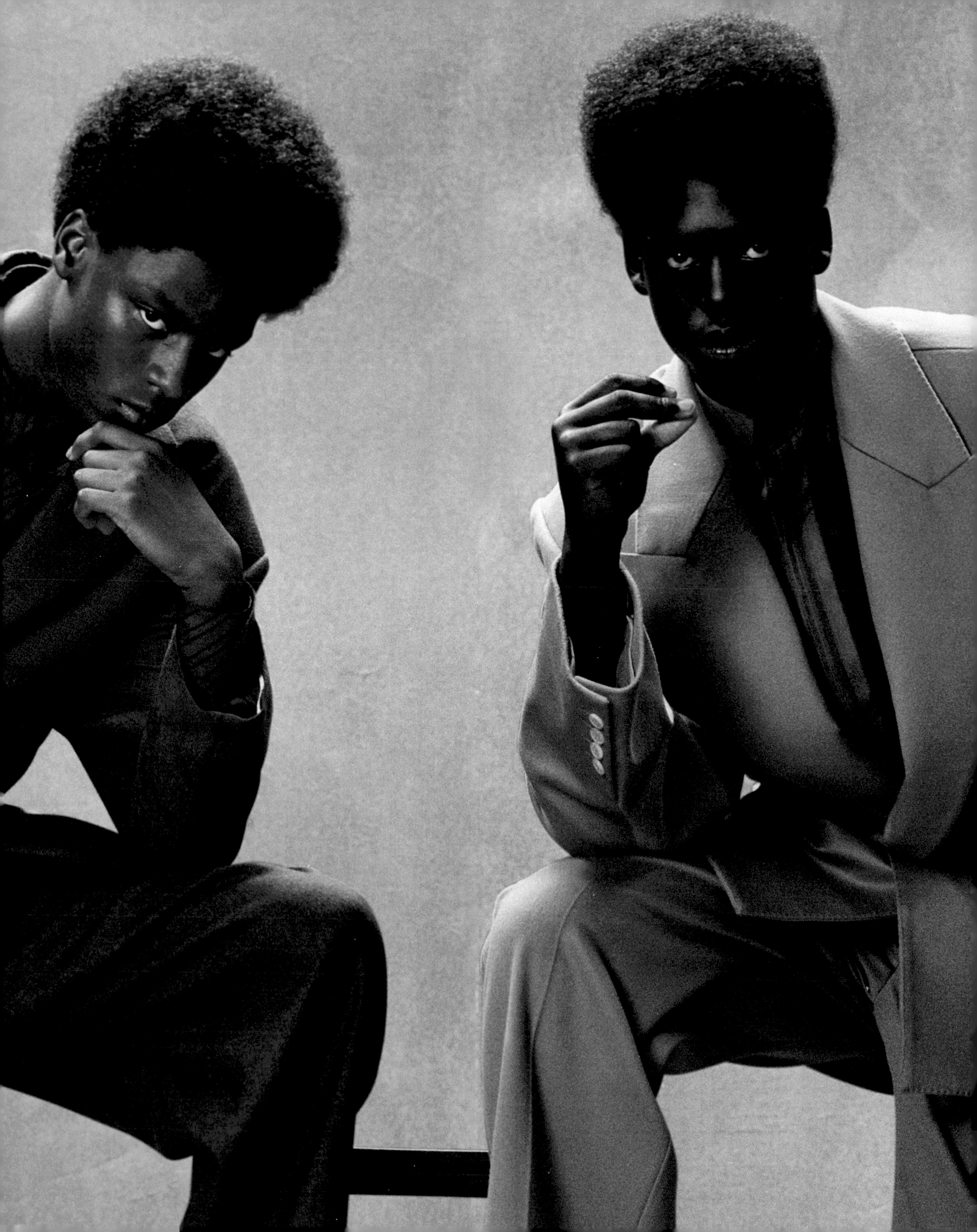

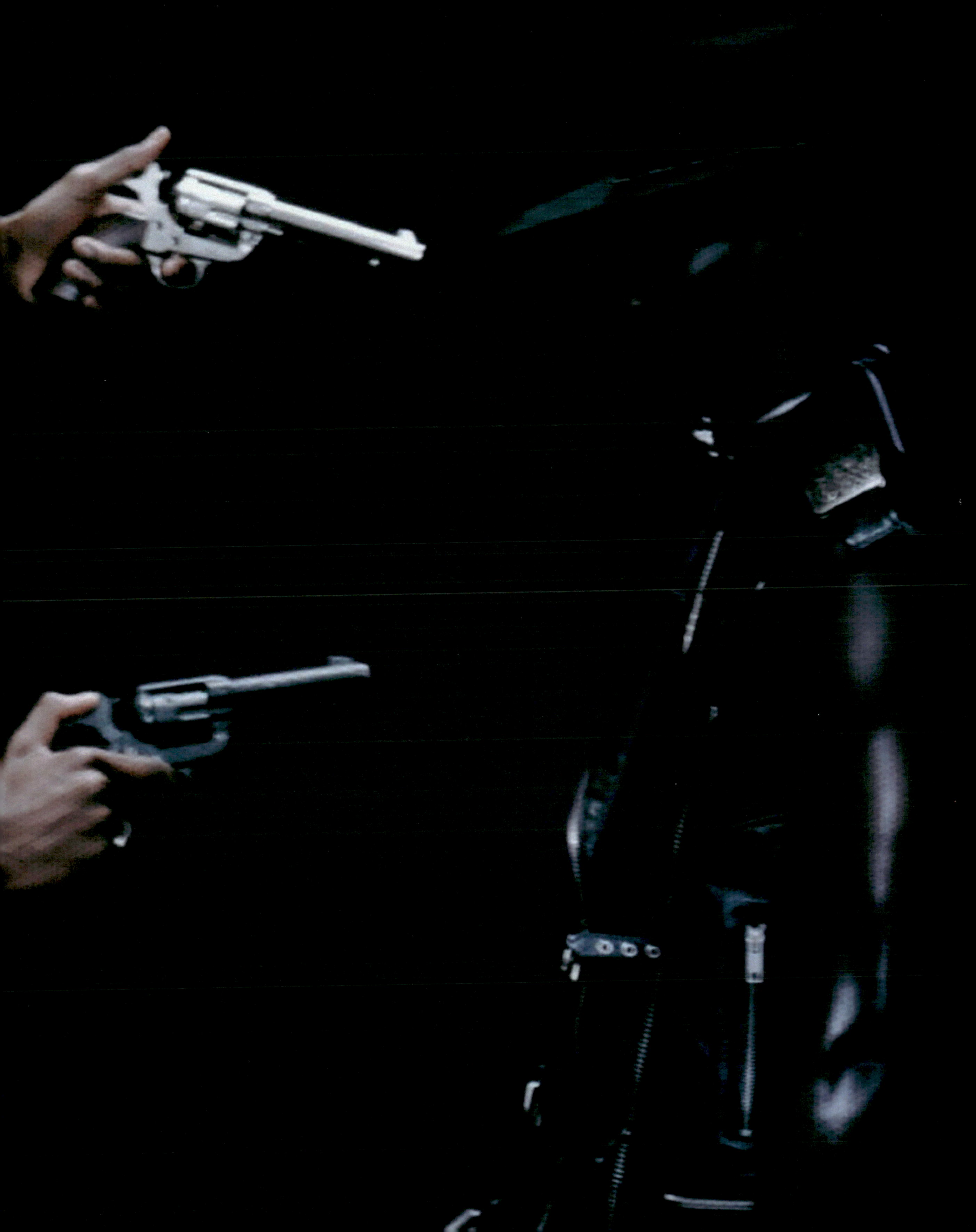

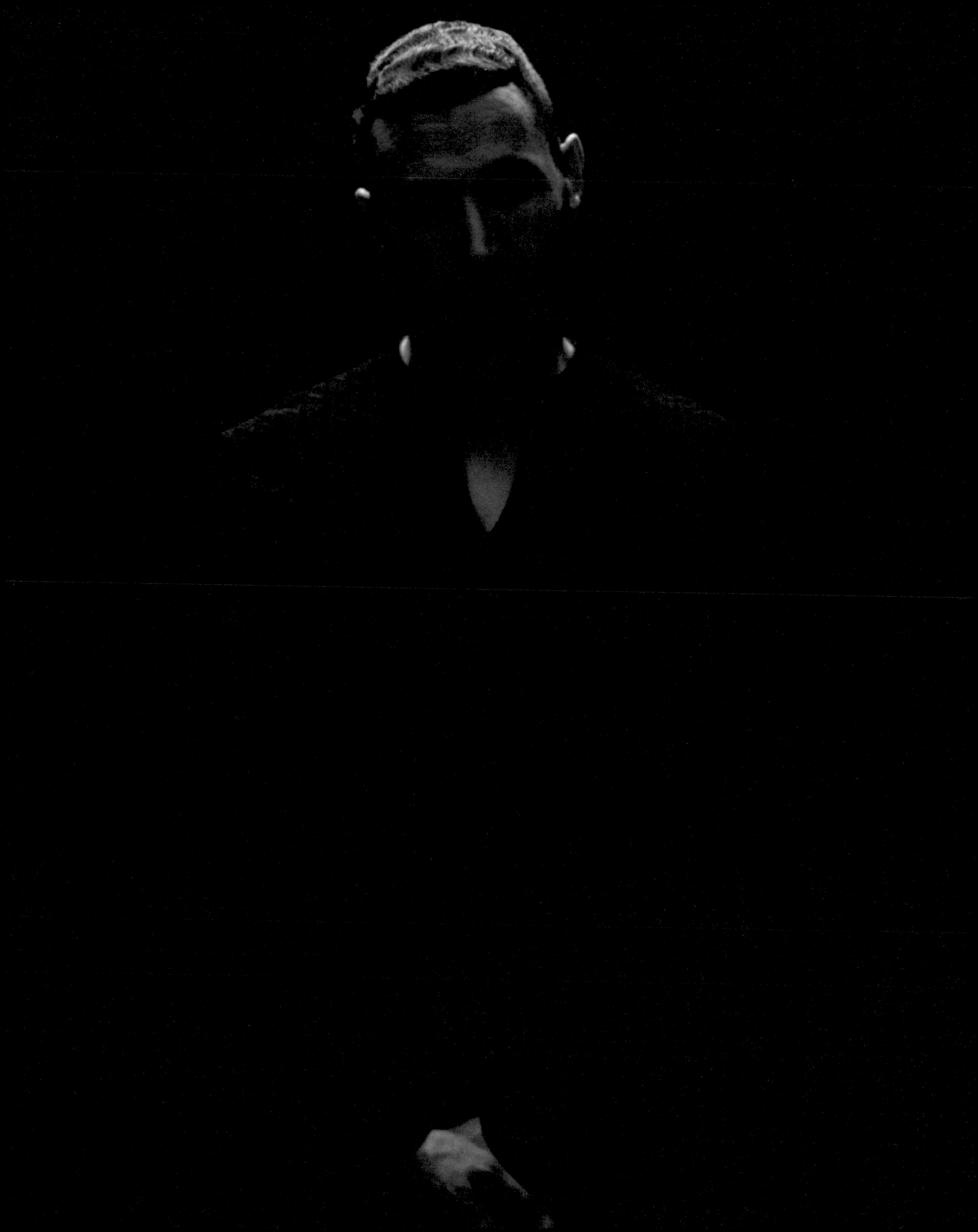

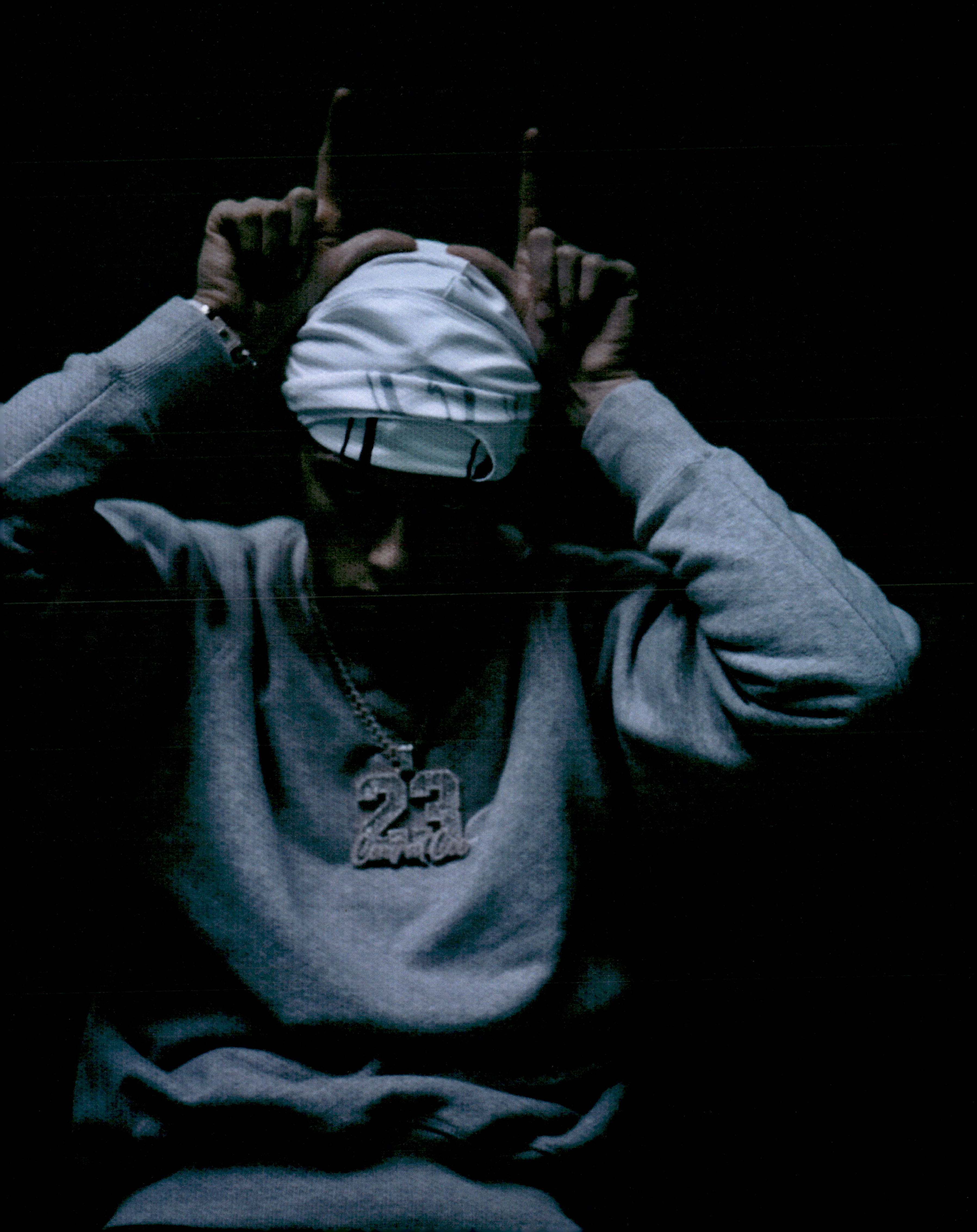

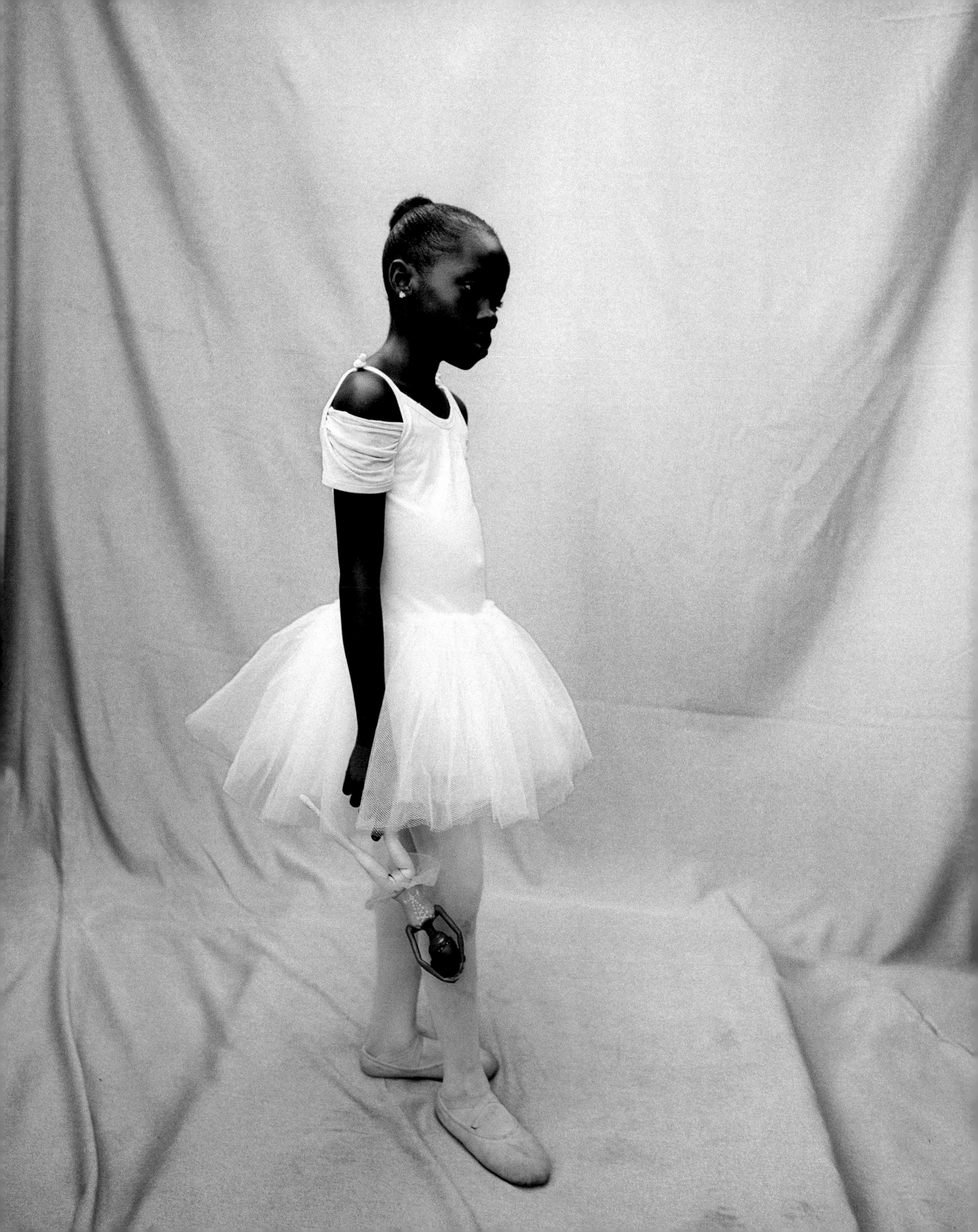

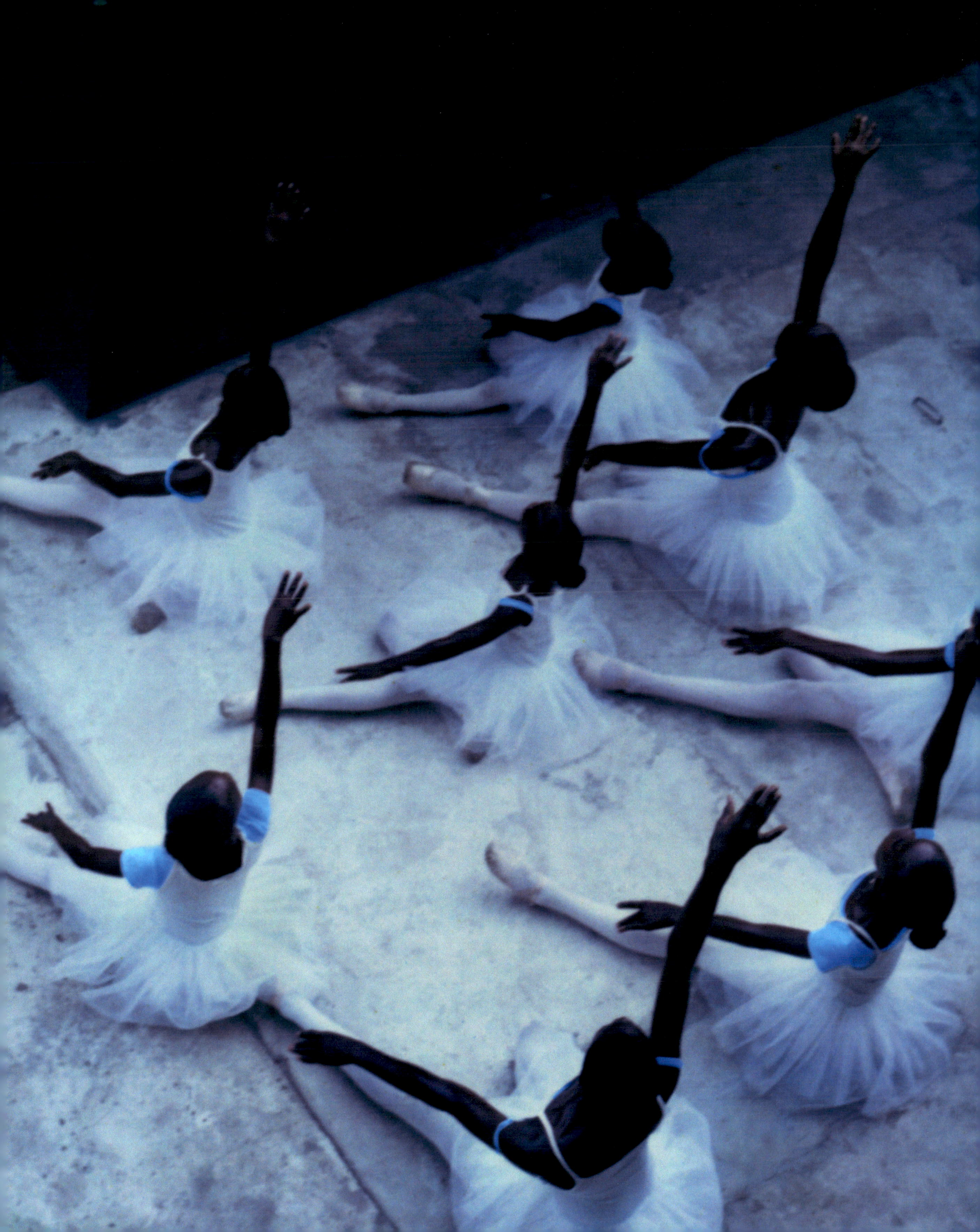

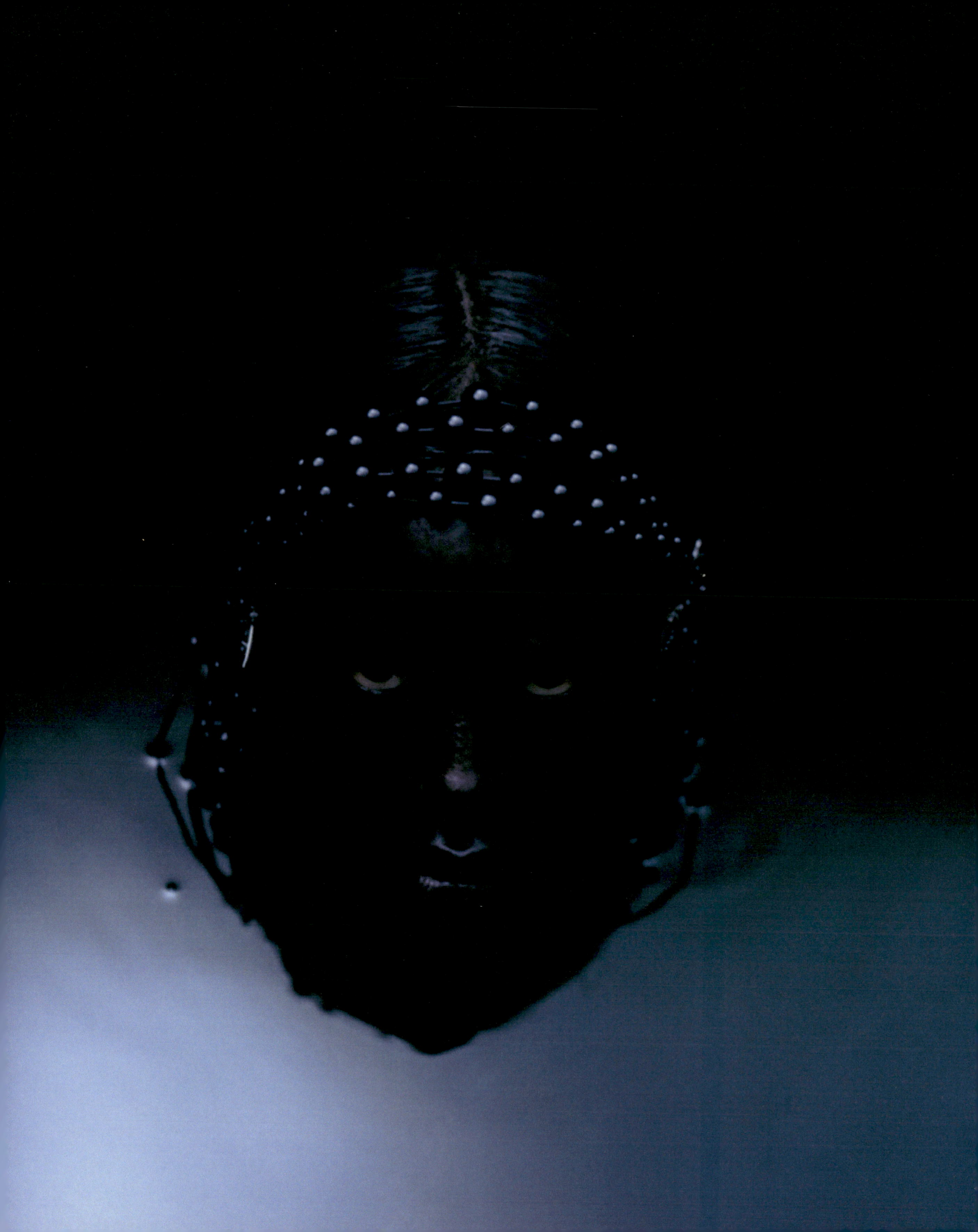

In Conversation: Nick Knight & Gabriel Moses

Interview by Katja Horvat

September, 2023. London.

K *(Katja Horvat)* Let's first get this out of the way; pictures or photographs?

G *(Gabriel Moses)* I would say pictures, that has somehow always stuck. If you ask my friends, they would still describe me as a cameraman who takes pictures, so...

N *(Nick Knight)* I've been slightly stuck with the term photographs and photography for a while now, because what we do isn't really just photography, it's more complex than that. Photography is still defined by a certain set of parameters which work if you look at the masters back in the day such as, let's say, Eadweard Muybridge or Robert Mapplethorpe, and so many others, they perfected their art, their skills, within a frame.

And then as the industry and disciplines progressed, we got Photoshop, we got 3D scanning, etc., and all these things changed the notion of what used to just be a photograph. We are creating moving images now. There is sound, there are all these effects, so I feel like it seems strange to limit ourselves by saying we're just photographers, or that something is just a photograph.

One of the things I was going to ask you actually, sorry to leap in with my own agenda here, but Gabriel, you do sculpture, you do film, you are an image maker.... Where I am going with this is – is your sculpture imitating your pictures or is it your film?

G I'd say a lot of my references, especially for moving images, are still life, or even moments from my life or from my community. I feel like a picture is always a starting point for a lot of my work, so in terms of some of my video stuff, there's re-creation of moments in time or history, you know. The same thing with some of my sculptures. The first sculpture I did, and that you would have seen at my exhibition, was one of my friends I've known since I was a kid, and it's an image I actually shot and recreated in 3D.

N It's sort of interesting to ask: are we doing sculptures that look like our pictures or are we doing sculptures which have their own aesthetic and have nothing to do with them? Starting out, my sculptures were sort of just feeding off of my existing work, but now I want to look at them in a different way, I don't want them to emulate my photography.

K Both of you are rather complex within your frame and visual language. How do you decide which idea is worth making a reality?

G I will generalise now and say it's a feeling I get, as we all do. When I look at an image and it feels correct to me, then I'm happy. I've always looked at my art as my perspective, and everyone has his own perspective, but as an artist my job is to produce my perspective in such a way that you see my world, and if people connect with that, then that's amazing – if they don't, then that's also fine. So when working through sculpture or image, once I reach the feeling of content, that means I've got there. I got it. And I just have the confidence and faith that it will translate to the public as well. But also, my work is not meant for everyone. I feel like art isn't supposed to serve everybody. People that connect with me, they're my audience.

N I guess that makes me want to ask you why are you doing what you do? I'm asking that because it's a strange career. Of course we can say "Well, you know, because I want to take pictures or because I want to earn money, because I want people to know my vision," all those sorts of things. But it doesn't really explain why we do it or what we're getting from it. My point is that when I'm working I'm not necessarily looking for happiness. I'm not trying to make myself happy by working. It's more a sense of fulfilment or like you're solving a puzzle that's within you, that nobody else can solve and isn't for anybody else in a way, just for yourself.

G I really fell into it. But one thing I would say is as a child I always had a wild imagination. Academically, I was not the best at performing, but when it came to things like English or when you were allowed to write your own stories, that's where I would excel. So I always found that I had an imagination that maybe goes beyond what's considered normal. Or when watching TV – I'd imagine how the advert should've happened, I'd always just imagine. Then when I started and just got into the flow of creative work, I liked the idea of taking something from my head, and now it exists. And that's one of my favourite things about what we do. It's the idea that if I say I want people flying, we can make that happen, and that exists as an image that lasts longer than me and you. I feel like there is beauty to that, to be able to imagine something and just bring it to life.

K I am wondering, what is the main thing you are looking for in an image though?

N It's quite a straightforward answer because I've been thinking about this for quite a long time. Creating pictures is like creating a melody. I'm looking for some sort of visual harmony in it. It's almost as real as that. I can almost hear my pictures. When they work, it's like a harmonious chord, or a melody that makes sense and has a feeling of completeness to it.

G I'm very into making sure that the little details in an image come together to make that feeling that I spoke about earlier. And for me that comes from everything, from all the details in an image to how I operate/move on a shoot. From the very beginning I knew the importance of creating a good environment on your set. If everyone is feeling good and working collectively, then we for sure are getting a better image. I've become very obsessed with the idea of being able to control conditions, because so many of the great photographers that I look at, like you, Nick, or Paolo Roversi or Jean-Paul Goude, they'd shot so much and it all felt in the same world. To be able to do that, you have to be able to control conditions. Whether you're shooting in London or New York, so many factors are going to contribute to how a shoot goes.

N Studio is a really special place. I think it's in part because when we go in to take a picture, we have to be aware of everything. I'm sure it's the same with you, when you start a session and you get yourself into a mental state where you are super aware, super sensitive to everything, which of course is a good thing, as an artist has to be super sensitive, but the problem is you're sensitive to the good and the bad. I used to do a bunch of weird stuff and make all these routines for myself, playlists, to get focused, to get in the right mood. Music is such an important part of my getting it right – a lot of my old mixtapes are quite funny to listen to now 20 years on. . . . Anyway, I create the mood with the music, but I would only use 10 to 15 seconds of each track, which for me was fine, but for everybody else in the room it was a nightmare, but I just didn't want to install one mood. I wanted to keep people on their toes, all until one shoot with Gisele Bündchen back in the day. Somehow for her to get into the mood was the exact opposite. She wanted one song, so for 5 days straight we would listen to Mary J. Blige, "Family Affair," on repeat!

Apart from music, I would also often walk around the studio, over and over again. You're waiting for maybe 2 to 3 hours for hair and makeup to be done, and what do you do with yourself in the meantime? It's the worst time of the shoot, the waiting. You sit there and overthink. It is almost impossible to relax. I usually can't do anything about it. I can't quell my anxiety or fear. I can maybe imagine what the image is going to look like, but I've got to wait until I have a model in front of my camera to see if that's the case. So I'm basically just there, passing time in the most uncomfortable way possible.

G And it's funny because you wait for so long, and then when everyone is finally camera ready, now it's like you're in a theatre where everyone's watching your every move, it's mad.

N Exactly. An awful fear of performance can set in. Even though you're only performing in front of 10 to 20 people, even if it's just in front of 2 people, they're people you care about, whether it's your friends, the model, or the client, they're people you care about. It's scary because we can't predetermine what we're going to do. We're not like musicians who can go and sit in the studio and work out the chords, just rehearse it until it's perfect. We're doing spontaneous creation, so there's no practice. You never know what it's going to be, and I also never draw out. I never storyboard. I just go in there and wait to be inspired. But it's the most nerve-racking thing because A., I don't know how I do it. I've no command of what I have to do to get an image worth seeing. And B., you never know what's going to happen. The model could do something you never expected. They could move in a way that you didn't consider, and you've got to be open to that. So you can't go in there thinking, I'll get them to do this, they'll sit there and we'll move that, it'll be this lighting and that sort of stuff. Obviously you've got to have an idea. . .

G You've almost got to be a fly on the wall at the same time.

N You really need to have an open mind. It's funny, because often I sort of think, "Okay, let me do something completely different so it doesn't look like another picture I've taken before." So I've tried everything, I even tried giving the model the camera one time. Otherwise you end up ploughing a furrow that gets narrower, so you have to keep on expanding that, letting go, not being in control, and allowing randomness and chance to get in. I think it's sort of important, that whole idea of what part of our brain we use when we're creating an image, because it's not a conscious thing. The surrealists were big on dreams, talking about them, writing them down, and recreating them. And I think the interesting thing is that when we dream we don't have social restrictions. We don't have the taboos society puts on us. We're free to basically do whatever the dream tells us. And what we should be taught is getting in contact with that part of our brain, because it's very hard to teach photography to anybody, actually physically teach it. How do you say, "Well okay I'm going to teach you how to make a better image," other than the basic stuff, expose your film correctly. It's very hard to make people more perceptive or more intuitive. We're taking pictures we can't yet see. I take pictures I can't see. It hasn't happened, and when we hit the shutter it's about to happen. You're basically predicting it each time. But actually the split second it takes for you to want to hit that shutter, that's the moment, and you hadn't seen that before, how could you?

G I've got a question. For me, all I've known in terms of fashion photography and shoots is having to shoot a million looks in a couple hours, in a day. When you were shooting back in the day, shooting editorials would go across days. How do you feel about that, you've seen both sides?

N It's something we need to re-address, the balance. I would like to base how many pictures I'd take a day on what Irving Penn once said, and that is 2. So in my opinion, that's about as much as you should be doing a day, 2 final shots.

G I hear that.

N It doesn't happen, but that's the level it should be. Taking it back to Richard Avedon and Irving Penn, they were taking 2 weeks to do an editorial of 10 pictures, or a month. So that's the difference, and I think if there's any re-addressing to be done in the industry, they need to understand that. Understand that people like you or me, or any other image maker, need time! The time to look and experience. The time to make corrections, changes, investigate, etc. If you ask someone to take 30 great pictures in a day, you won't get 30 great pictures. You probably won't get any great pictures. Okay, you might get one, if you're lucky. But these days, we're just not given the time to really get into the zone.

G Exactly. The pace that is set is working against us.

N It's like saying to somebody, "Write 30 songs in a day." It's the same thing. But generally, I tend not to go above 10 images per day.

G Fast-food imagery is almost what they want. But I'm very much on taking my time and slowing the pace down because at the end of the day my job is to create the best image possible. We can't rush for the sake of changing a look. I always tell people that images last forever, we need to come correct and handle it with precision. Rushing won't get us there.

N When I used to shoot with John Galliano for Christian Dior back in the 1990s we would shoot for 5 or 6 days. On the first day, we wouldn't produce anything. We would just look, try things, play with the lighting, then do the hair and makeup, redo it, do it again, another model would come in, we'd try it on somebody else. Also, sometimes you'd produce nothing day 1, nothing day 2, nothing day 3, nothing day 4, and you'd produce everything on day 5.

K I think that generally speaking, the last day as a whole is always the best, as everyone is attuned and somehow comfortable with each other, not always, but most of the time. That one magical image has lots to do with luck and everything falling into place, but to think of a whole shoot, all my bets are usually on the last day.

N I agree, especially when it comes to images Gabriel and I make, and the environment we create, but to think from a perspective of other photographers like, let's say Danny Lyon or Robert Frank, they only have one frame and they are either gonna get that shot or not, with each second their environment would change. There are many approaches to image-making. Robert Frank was drifting around, taking pictures on the streets of America. Obviously you can see their contact sheets, but it's just the one frame and the frame after is different, the frame before is different. It's just that one thing. But if you're being put in a situation where you're saying "Create a world with this vision of ours" etc., you need to find it, and you need the space and support to be finding it. If you look at the Diana Vreeland interview, she talks about going to Japan for a month with Richard Avedon to do one editorial of 10 pictures. Of course the pictures were beautiful, and that's what you want. It doesn't always have to be a month, but you know what I mean.

K Time is money, and we all know the limitations of budgets on shoots, so sadly it all just comes back to that most of the time. Anyhow, let's talk a bit about how the narrative of one's work changes depending on where it is shown. In a magazine it feels different than it does when we see it on our phones, and then once these images are placed in a museum or gallery environment, well then they almost take on a completely new life . . .

N It's funny how the place you show work really is important. And I never wanted to do that. I never really wanted to do exhibitions of my work. So for about 30 years I didn't do an exhibition. I was in group shows occasionally, but I just never wanted to do the big retrospective kind of thing, because I thought, I like people seeing my work on the side of a bus, or on the back of a magazine when they're waiting to go to the dentist. I like the fact that they don't have to know who I am, that they just have to see the work and enjoy it. And a lot of the work we do goes on billboards people are seeing when they're walking down the street on their way to the grocery or to pick up their kids from school or whatever. They walk past it, and it becomes part of their life without a commitment to the work, just something that's a part of the colour of the world around them. So I prefer that way of communicating with an audience. I was always very standoffish and shy and not willing to have a one-man show because I thought it would just be people who kind of like my work, and that's nice, but do I need that? It also takes a long time to put on a show. I'm sure you know that. Anyhow, one day an invitation from South Korea came through, and after some time I just gave up and thought to myself, it's time, it's time to put on a show, at least try it. So I did it, and funnily enough, I really enjoyed it. I really enjoyed creating a path through my work by showing a film here and a picture there, a bit like you did, Gabriel, at your show. It was a journey. You took your audience on a journey through your mind and desires. It wasn't just the best pictures you've ever done, that's not interesting. It's interesting when you take people on a journey and it becomes something they can't do without going to that space and seeing it. They can't just get a book of yours and look through it, that's another journey, but the journey you create in a space is unique. Consequently, like most things in my life, I realised I was completely wrong and I should consider exhibitions, and really consider putting work into different spaces.

G My first exhibition was a big learning experience for me. And before then I felt the same as you, I was not keen on exhibiting my work in a gallery space, and limit it, in a way. I always preferred the idea of just making images and putting them out into the world straightaway. So the idea of creating a presentation of how you/we see the world for people to be able to visit and look through, was a new challenge for me.

But my biggest takeaway and what put things in perspective was the people that came and saw the show. Just the idea that someone would plan to come see my work. They would leave their homes, they would bring their kids, people came on dates. The response really surprised me, and how many people showed up. Especially as I've come up in an Internet era, where I can just throw something on Instagram and you feel the love in that way, but then to have that physical interaction. Even at the opening, and you saw how that was, the turnout – I couldn't have expected that. Even when I'd pop in on random days, I'd see the effect it had on people in real life.

K But there is just something about the physicality of an image, even if it's the same image we all saw on social media before. Once you see it in a different scale, right in front of you, with other images, videos around it, it takes on a whole new life. Also, exhibitions bring in a broader audience by default, some of which are familiar with your work from before and they are there because of it, but then there are some who just happen to be there and that space you created is their first interaction with you and your work.

G Exactly, there were so many people at my show whose first

interaction with my work was that actual space. People who are not into fashion or art somehow ended up there, and these people, those reactions, were the best for me, they were the most sincere. I always loved that, the idea of showing my work to someone who is from a different world. People that are into art and fashion have a certain way of thinking, certain parameters of what even qualifies as art. But, to go off Virgil, you can call art whatever you want. Even if I just put a trashcan in a white, pristine space, if I see it as art, it's art.

N There's something very interesting about being with people when they see your art, because you're right. You grew up in this Instagram, straight online approach, which differs from my situation, but actually physically being with people when they see your work is a different game. The problem I've always had though, is that when I take a picture and it goes out, even when at first you're happy with it, when you see it again, you think, ah, it should've been better. It's a bit like seeing a deforming mirror. You see all your worst bits. So for ages not only would I not have an exhibition, but I wouldn't put any of my work on the wall, especially not in my house, I'd never have my pictures up because I didn't want to keep being reminded of what I could have done differently.

K It's a very relatable feeling, but let's just apply the idea of time on it – you were a different person when the work was being created versus when the work is then done or shown. Seeing it later is like coming back to the old version of you, which in that moment in time thought the image was good enough. But is there an image you both favour over any other image that you've taken? That one shoot that is just fundamentally you/yours?

G Yes, for me it is the top shot of the ballet dancers from *IJÓ*. I think it is by far one of my favourite images, but just because I know what it means in the future. I took that image for my future daughters, my nieces, every other person's daughters to be able to see. That school at that moment was so special, because ballet isn't something Black girls have grown up believing they can do, especially as a group. Then to see a group of 15, 20 young Black ballet dancers in a country like Nigeria, was a magical moment. To be able to document that was amazing, and I was excited to work with these kids, all super talented. Even to go home for the first time since I was 4 years old, so there were so many moments in a city close to where my grandma was raised. It was so loaded, and I know this image is going to travel for decades. It also just represents so much for me and to me. It really is a moment in time I will never forget.

N As much as I love the poetics of that, I just see my work more as an ongoing conversation. I always think I'm just starting because I haven't really gotten to where I want to be. So I just think, the next one will be it, the next one will be the one.

G But I guess that's what contributes to the longevity you've had. That idea of chasing that next image. But one thing I admire is that even though there's this chase for something new or something different, you've stayed consistent in your style from the very beginning. There are just different variations and ways to re-create yourself within a specific world.

K Pictures you take are an extension of who you both are as people. They are your language, and in each frame if we all just look closely we can see aspects of your life, your influences, but to conclude, let's turn this around. What sort of role does photography play in your day-to-day life? How does what you do change the way you go about your everyday life?

G Taking pictures, making films, it was the first thing that gave me a bit of a purpose in my life. I feel like it gave me tunnel vision, which was a blessing, because when you're surrounded by certain things it can easily go left or right. But pursuit of this gave me a clear vision of where I want to go, and what I want to do. That also separated me from a lot of my peers in general, it just gave me focus.

N For me, it was the only thing I was good at. I wasn't really good at anything else. I wasn't very good at photography either, but I was better at it than anything else I was doing. Parents' pressure stirred me for a little while back then. They wanted safety for me, they wanted me to be a doctor, so I was starting down that line, but it was quite clear that I wasn't going to end up being a doctor because I just didn't have the dedication for it, or interest. But it's funny, because I took up photography by chance. Picked up a camera one day, it was in the house, and said to my dad "Can I take this?" I went into my local town and started taking pictures of people, and I really enjoyed it. I just enjoyed that relationship that a camera gives you. A camera almost gives you licence to do anything, it's a passport into the rest of the world. If you've got a camera, you can go up to anybody and say "Can I take your photograph?" If you were a doctor, what would you do? "Hi, can I take your blood pressure?" It doesn't work. (Laughs)

So photography is such a great medium because it takes you anywhere. Anywhere you want to go, you have a passport to be there. Whether it's photographing people you bump into on the street or landscapes, it's a reason to go there. I can go anywhere to do it. I didn't really decide to do photography, it was never a career plan. My parents didn't know anything about the arts at all, nothing, and so they just wanted me to have a steady job, a respectable kind of job. But with photography, it's the only thing that has always felt exciting and new to me. It's that one thing I know I can do, and I'm not trying to say I can do it brilliantly, but I can do it, and the more I do it, the more interesting it becomes. Sometimes I still think, "Would the world have been a bit better if I were a doctor? At least I could have cured a few people of pain, broken bones, and stuff." But other than that, I think all the things that we do are brilliant. It's such a great art form, and I am happy this is the path we are both sticking with.

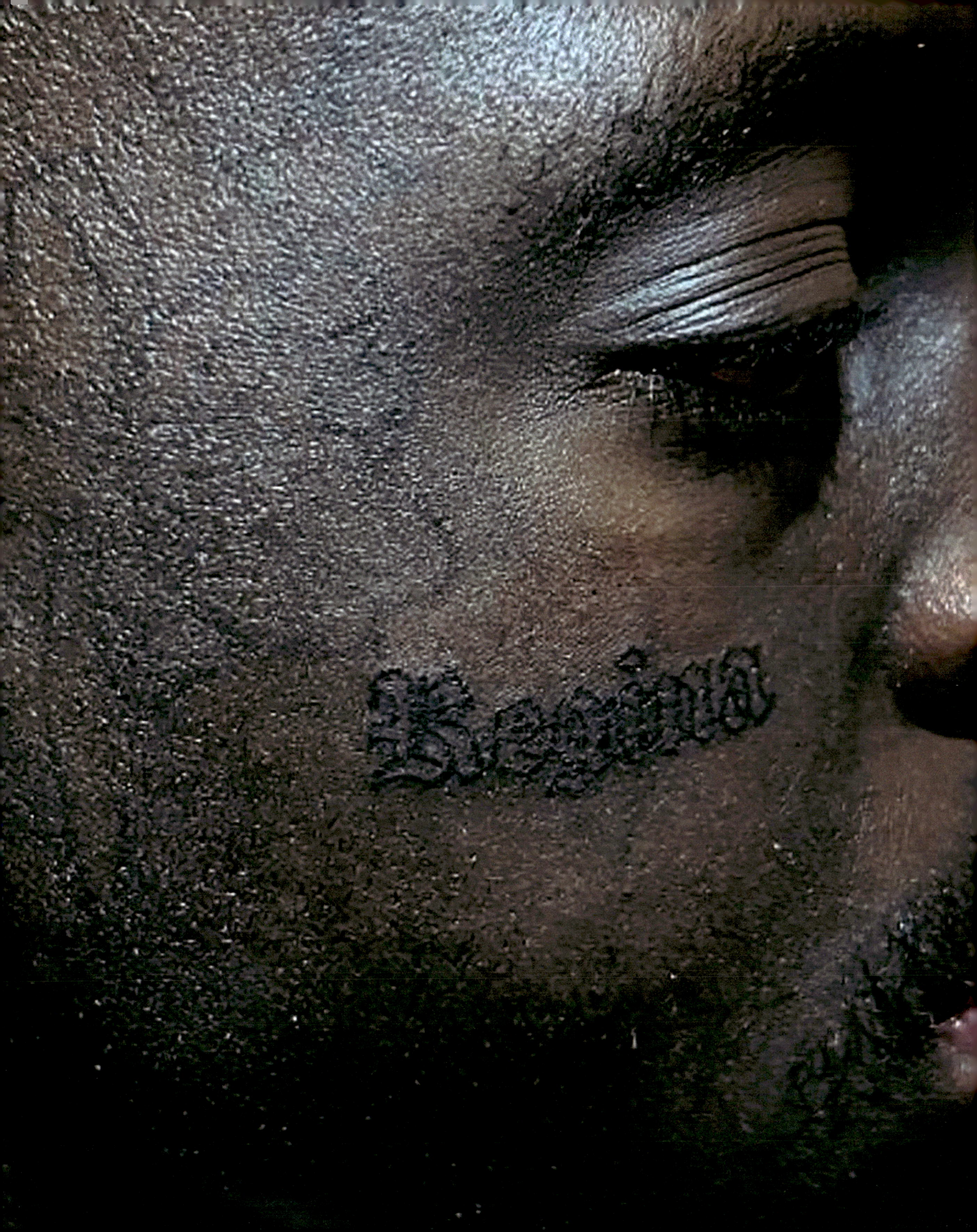

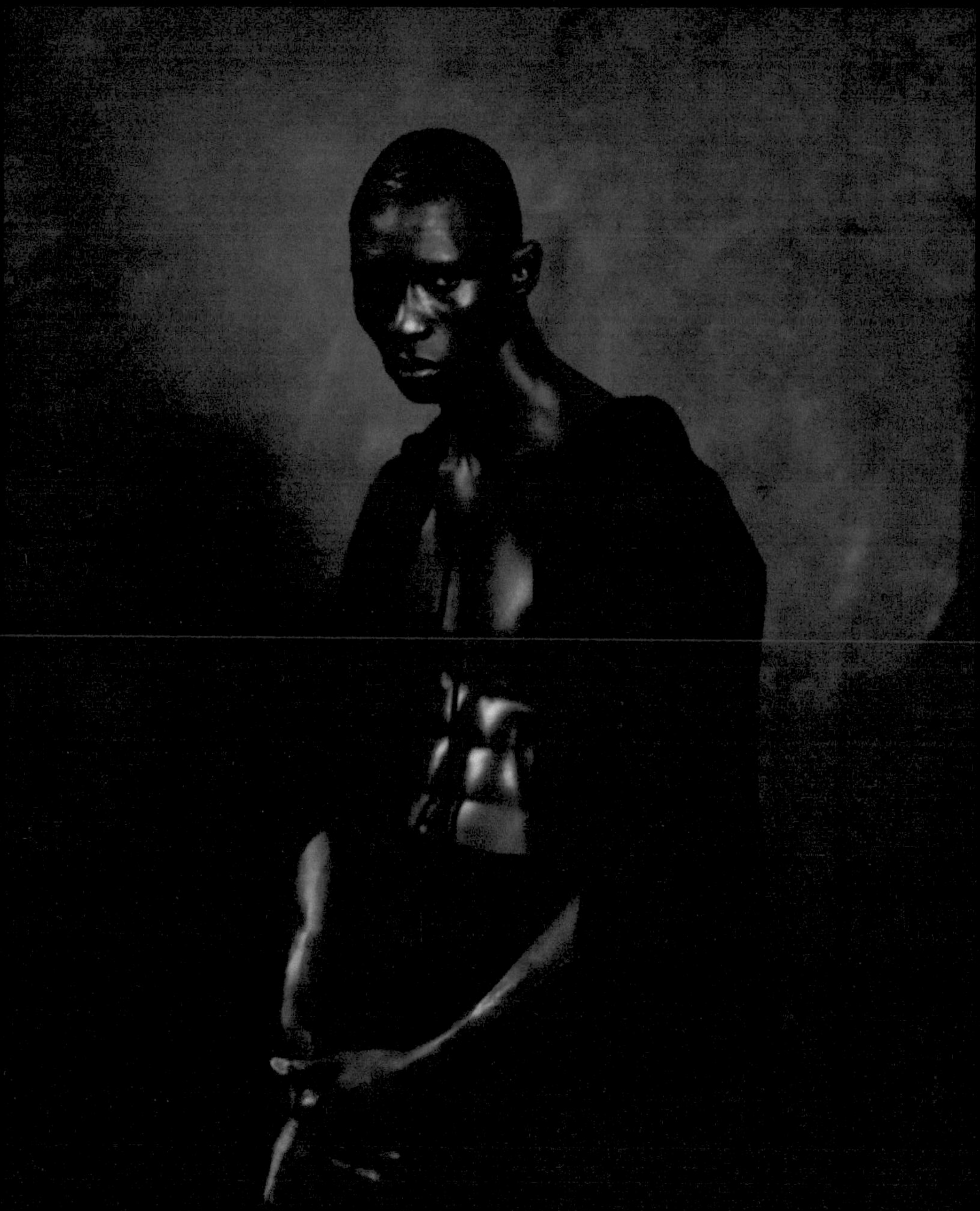

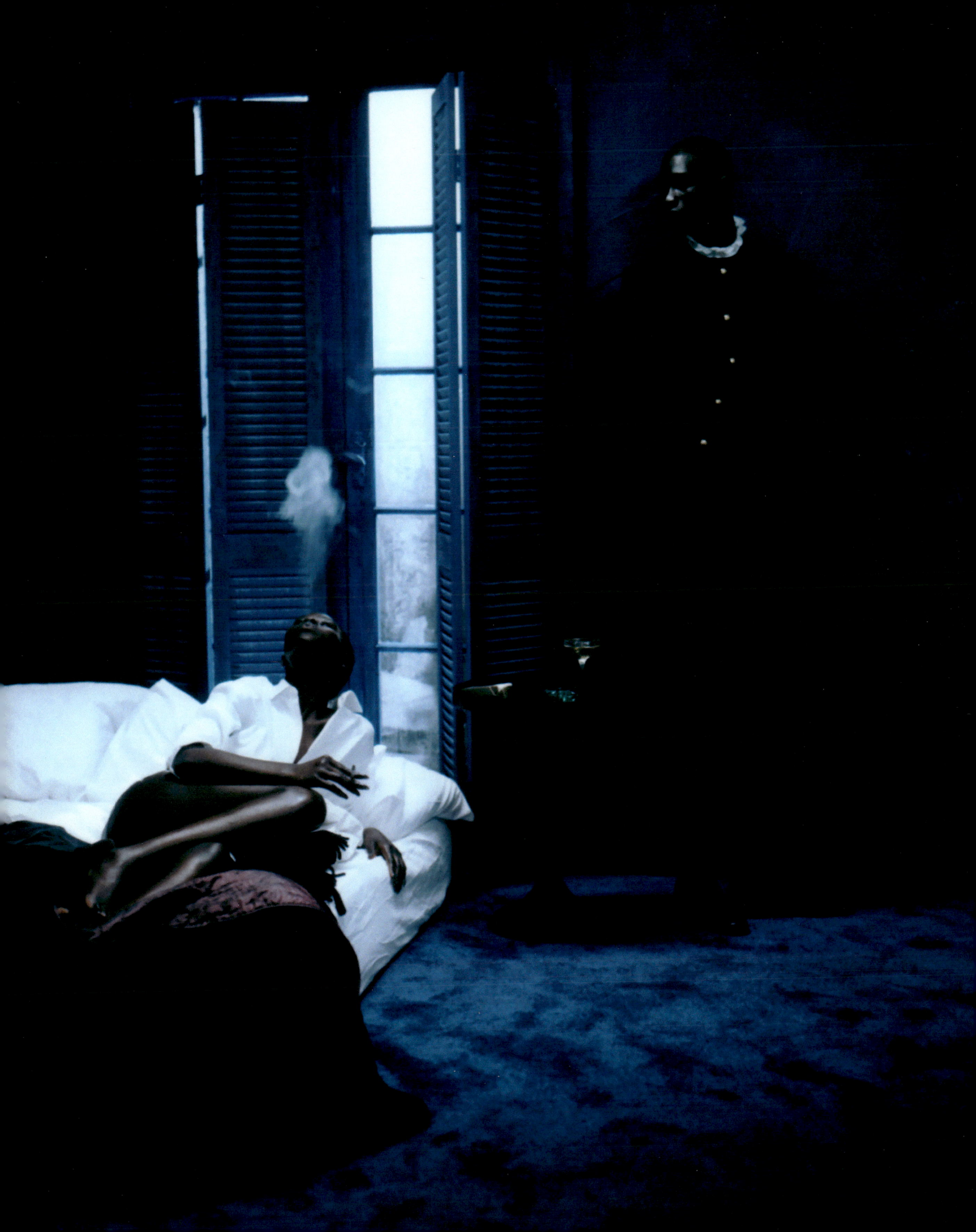

Good Afternoon mandem

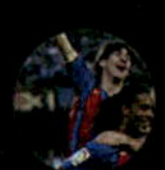

" Trust in the LORD with all your heart, and do not lean on your own understanding " proverbs 3:5

❤️ +3

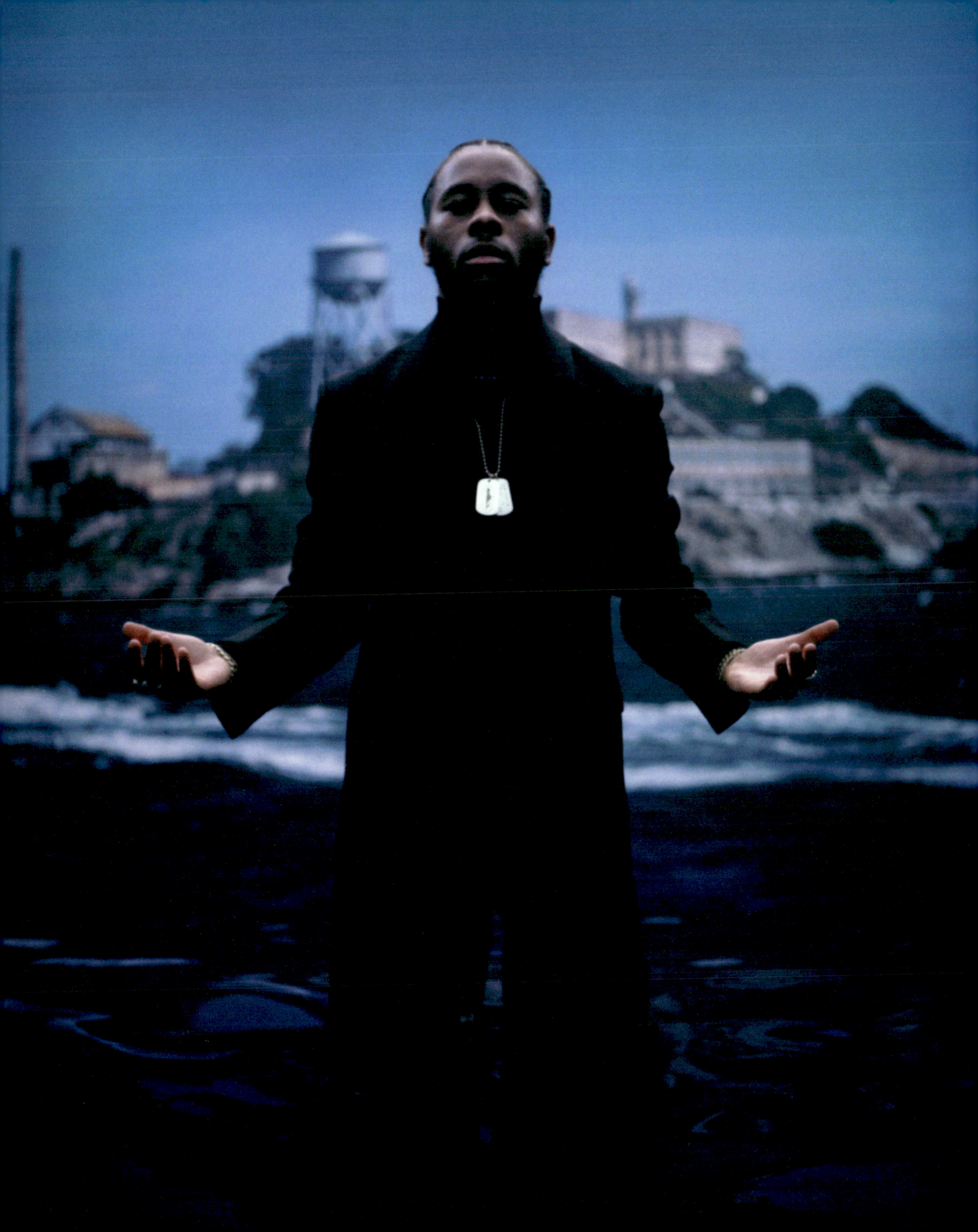

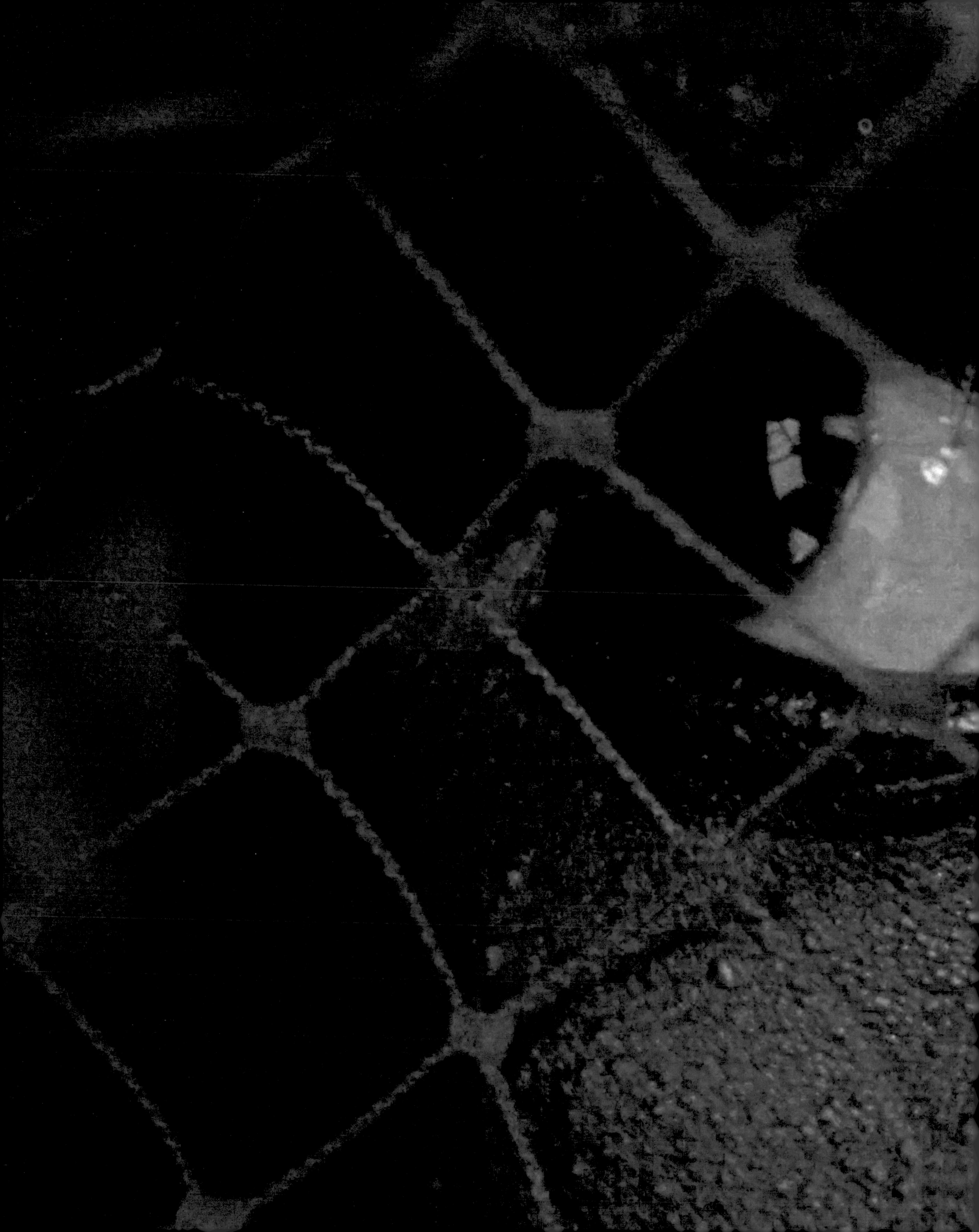

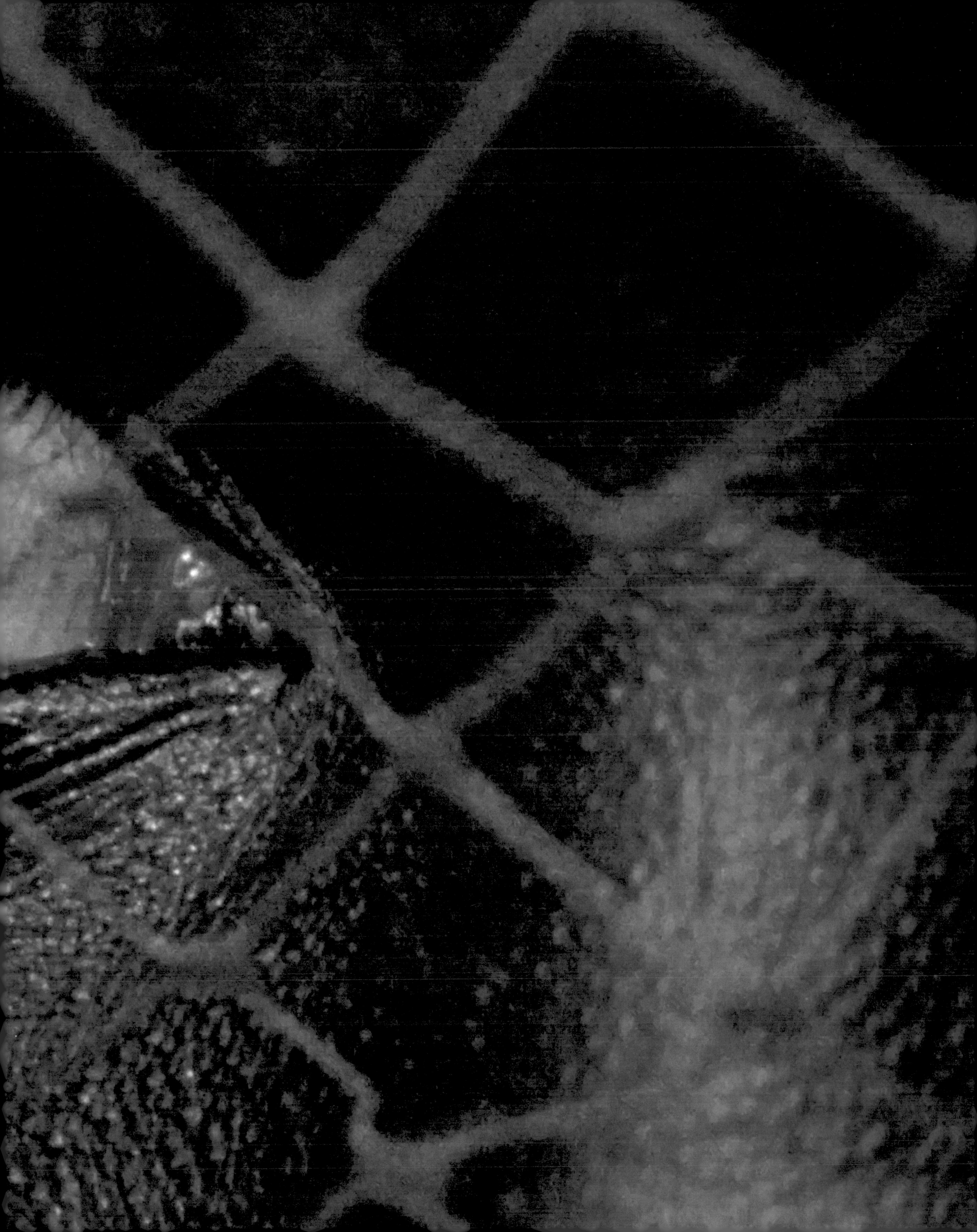

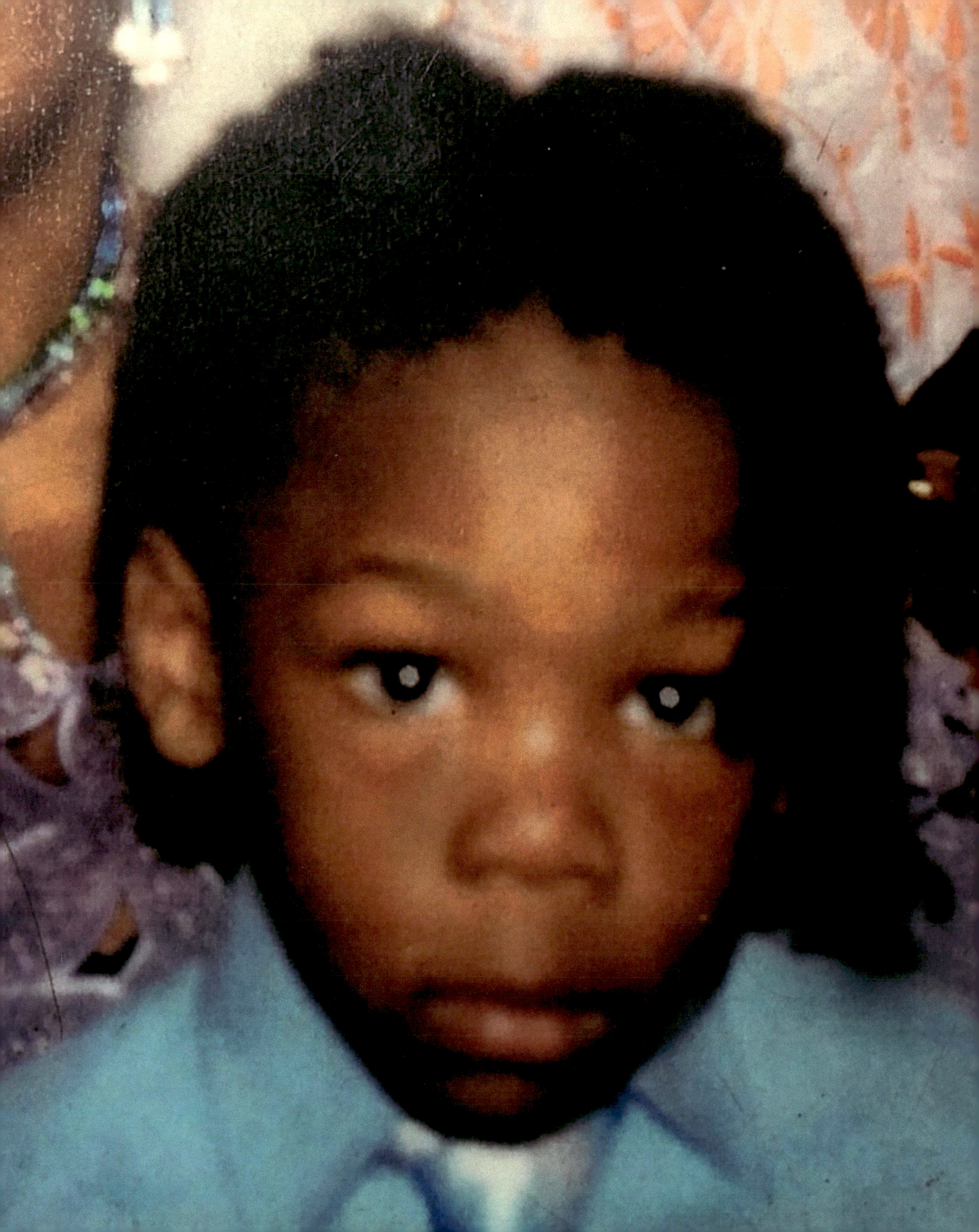

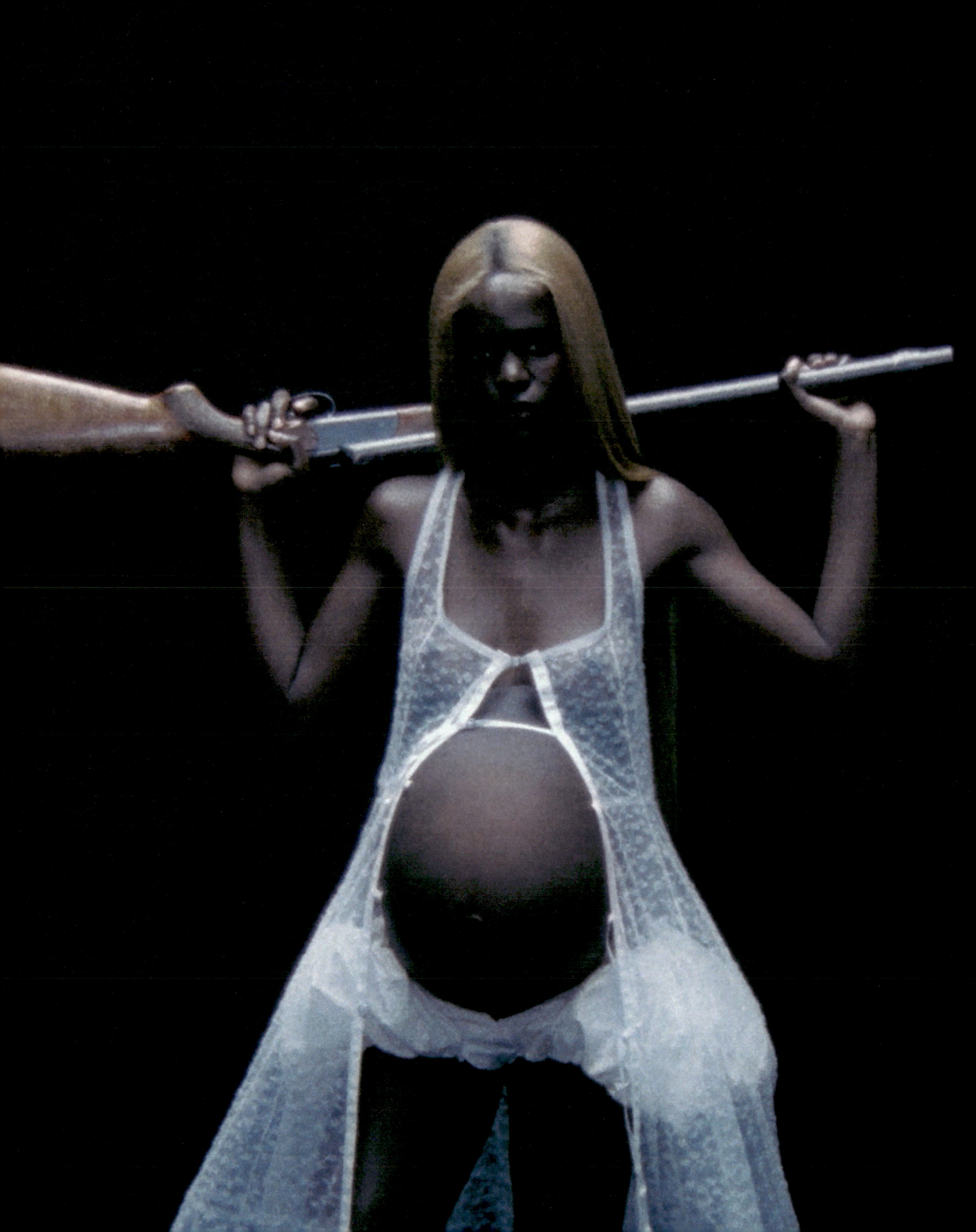

G

Gabs telling kids they gotta want it enough on Insta live

❤️

K E A T O N 1 N I N E 🐍

again?

❤️

nbapluto15

Yep

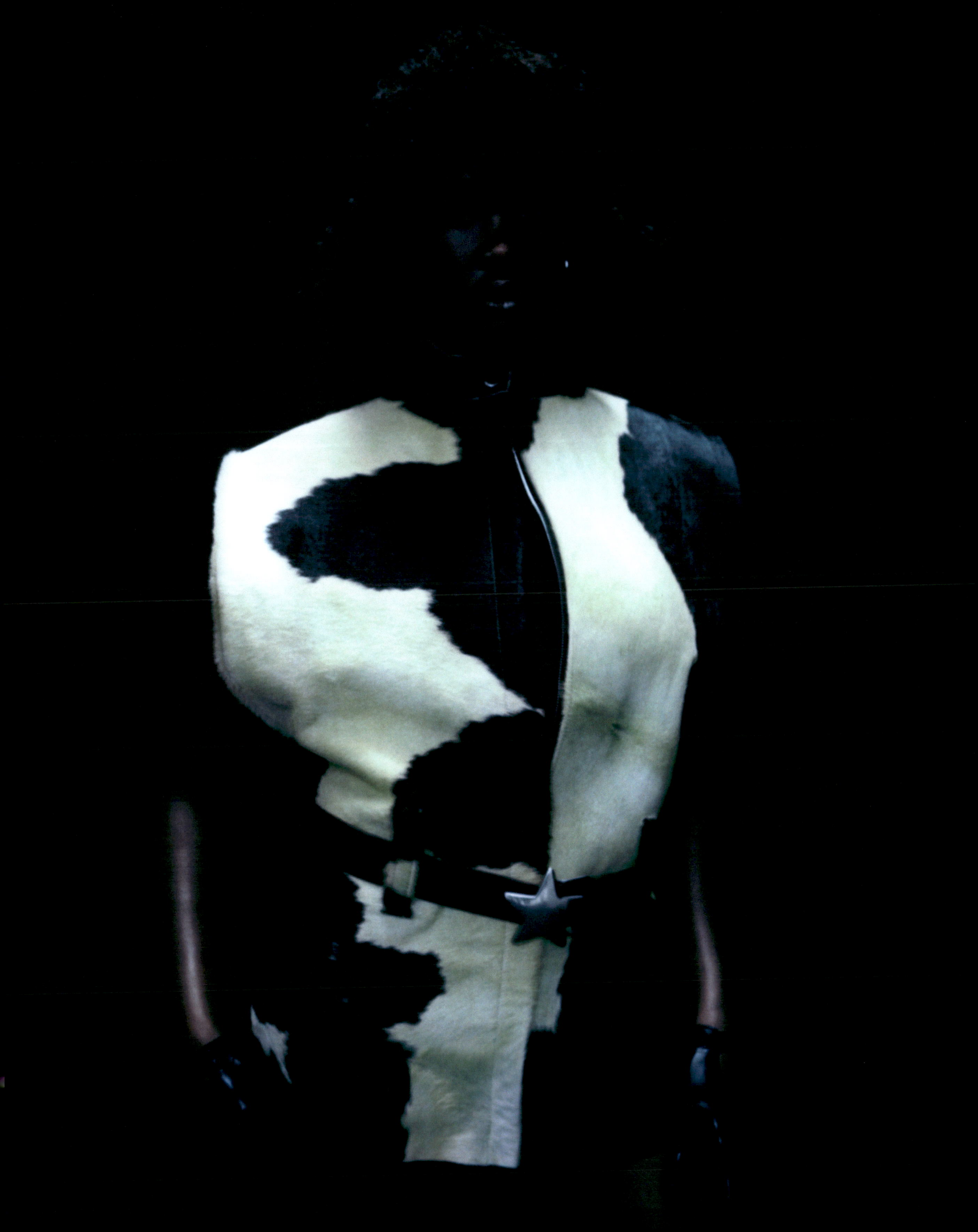

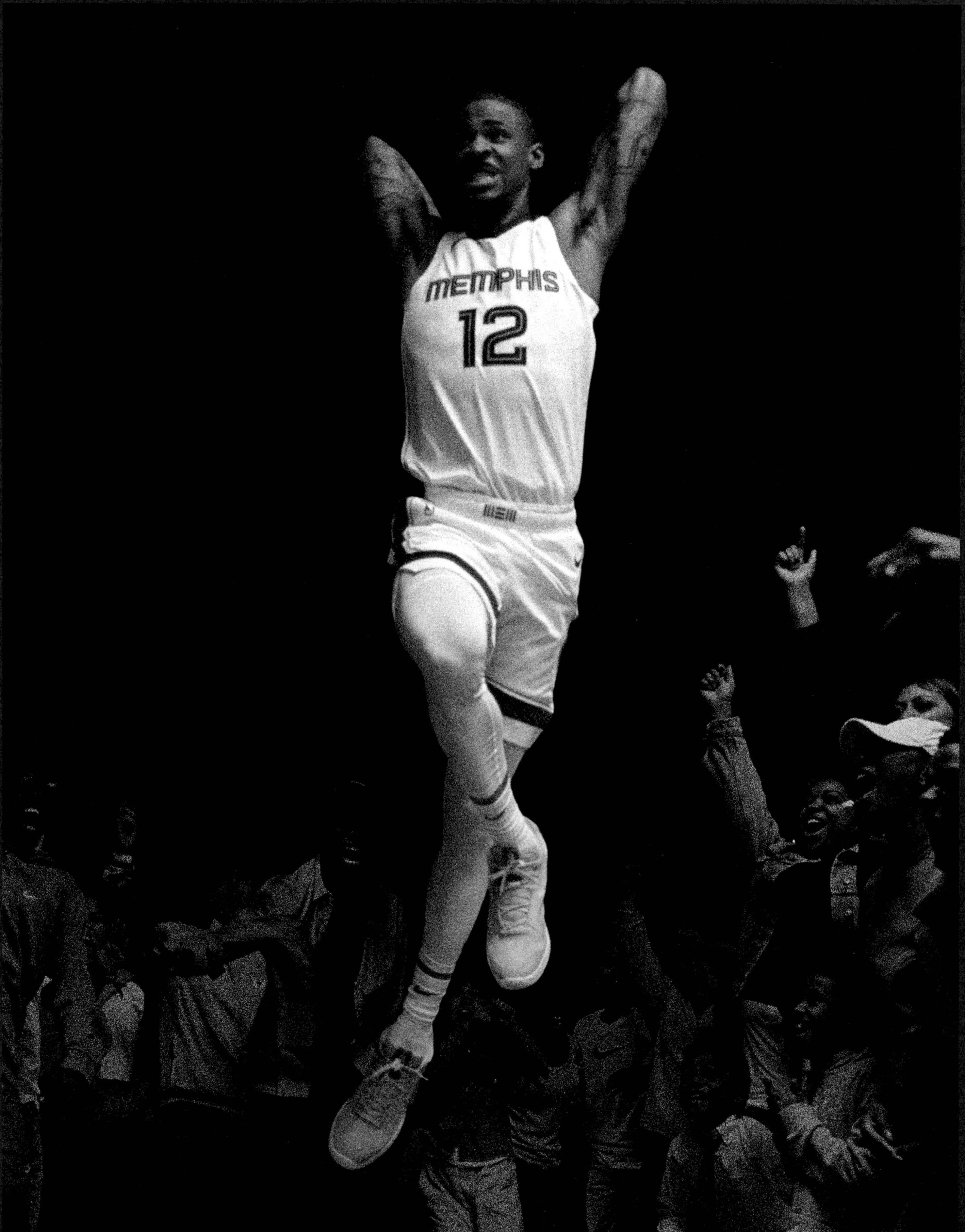
MEMPHIS
12

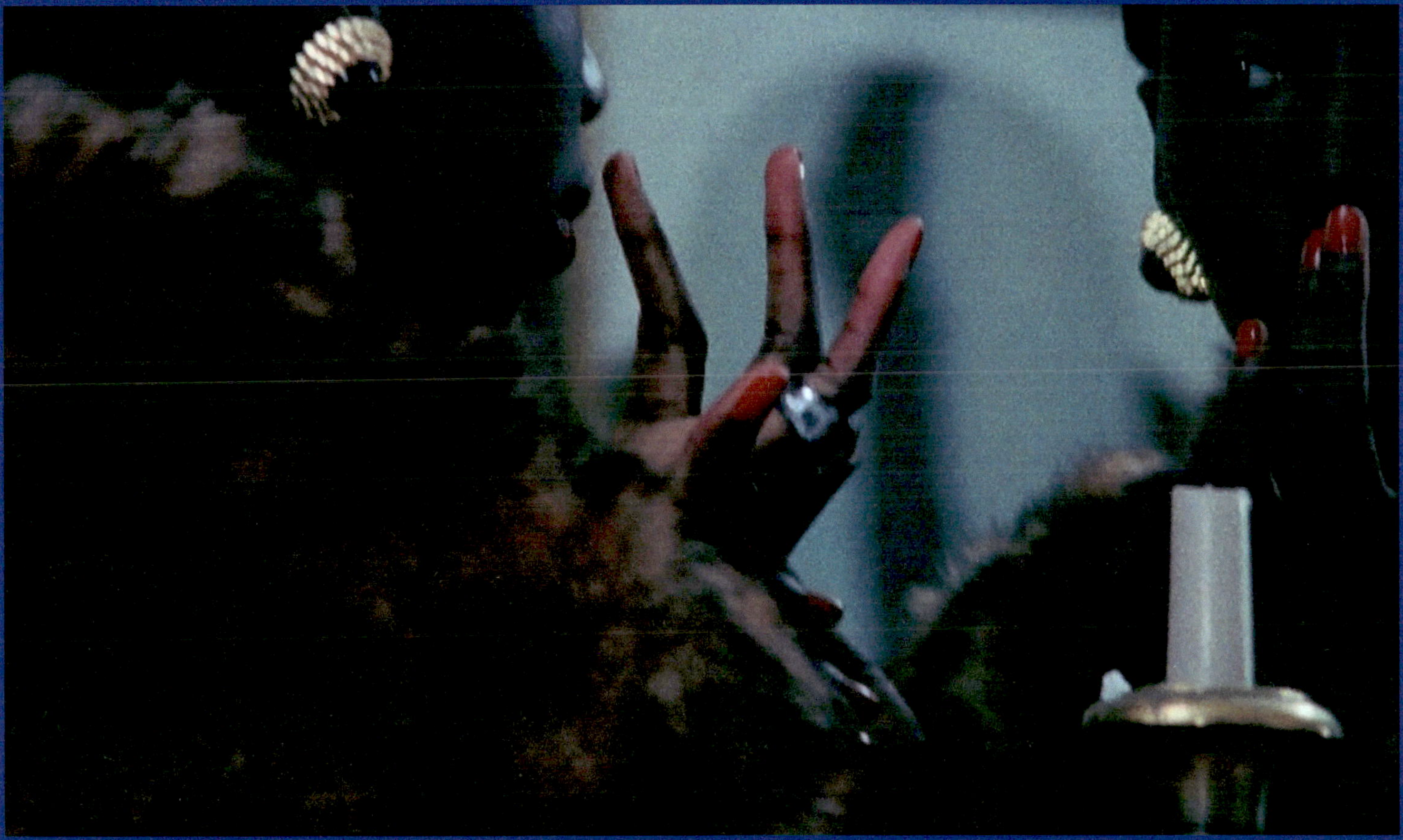

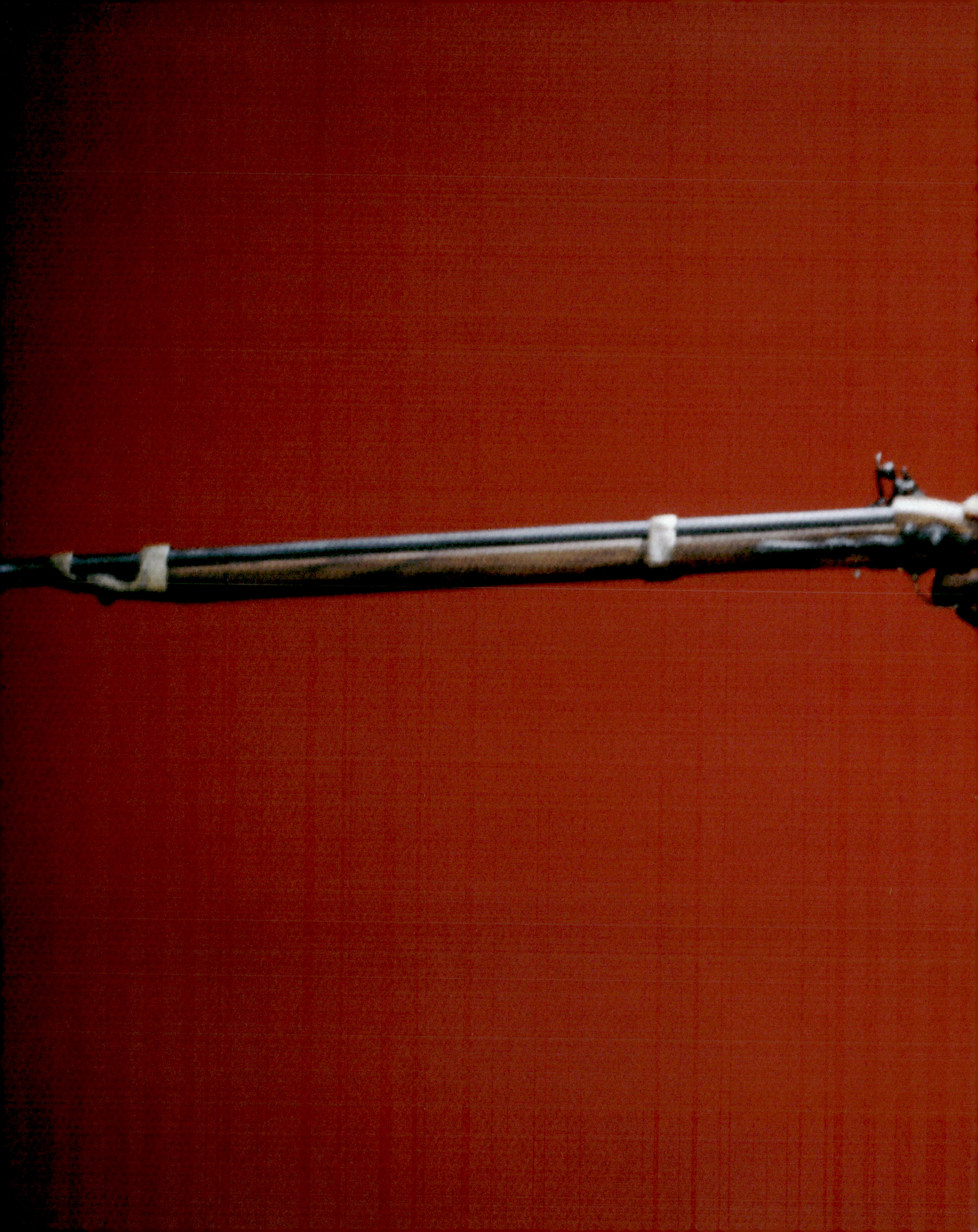

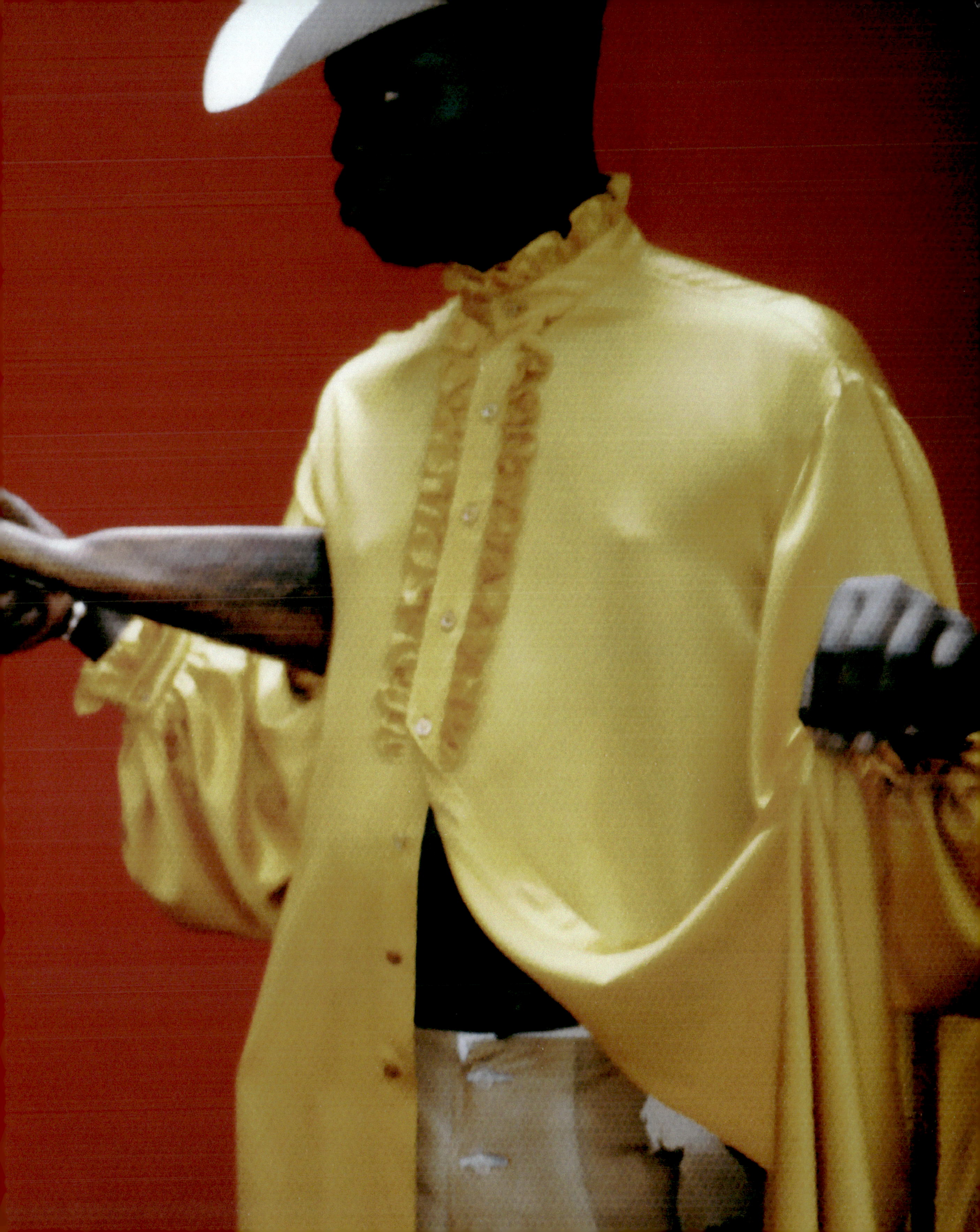

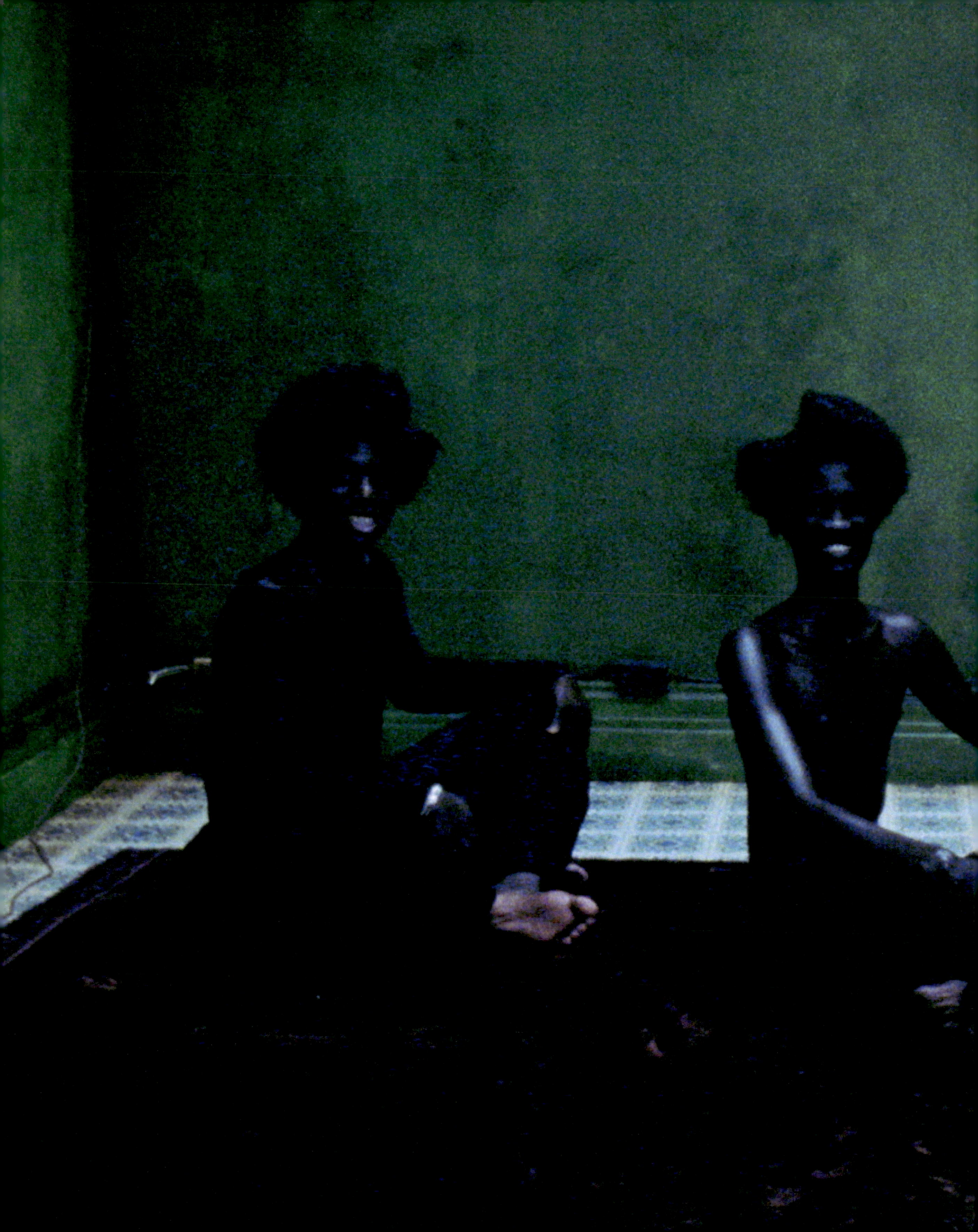

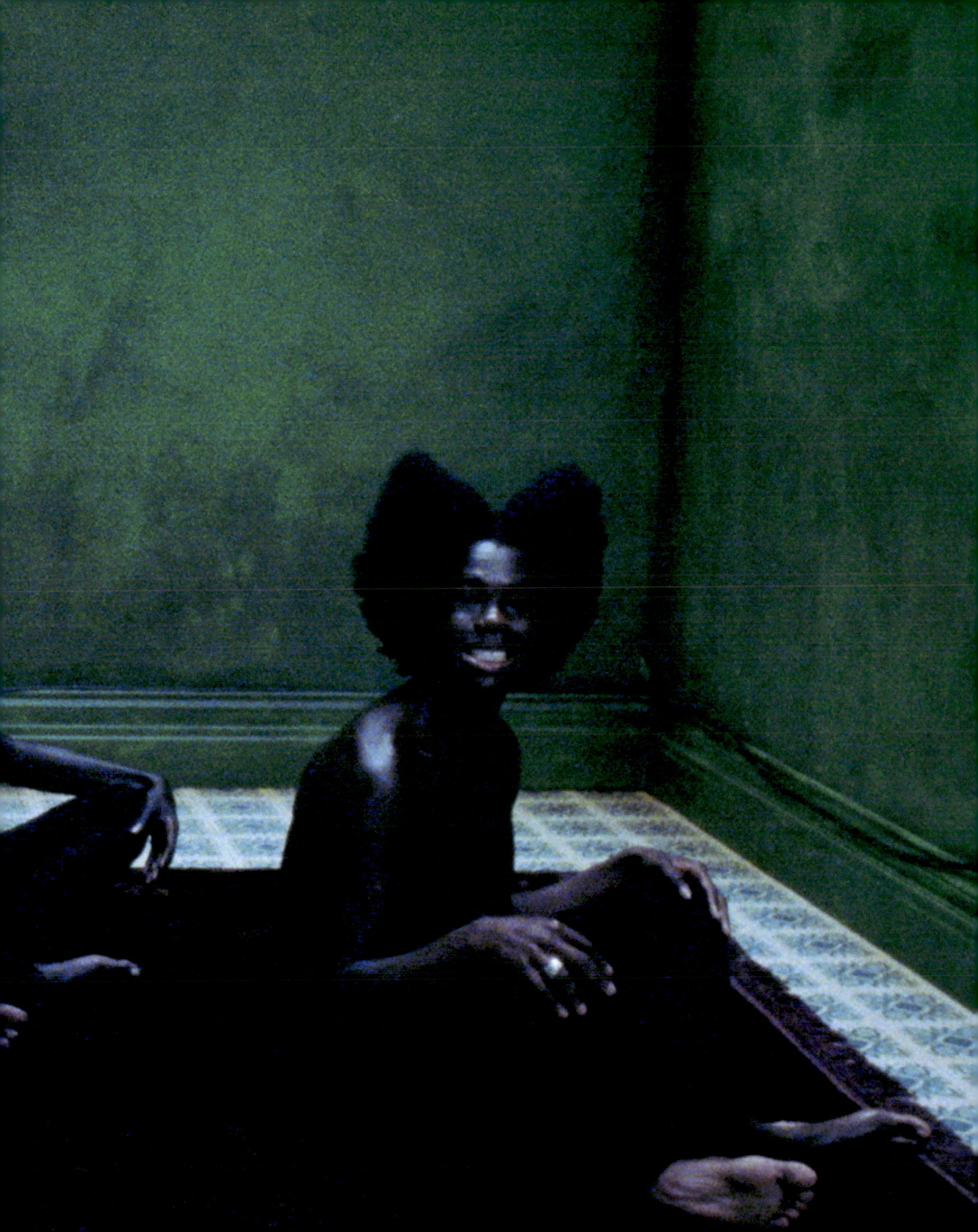

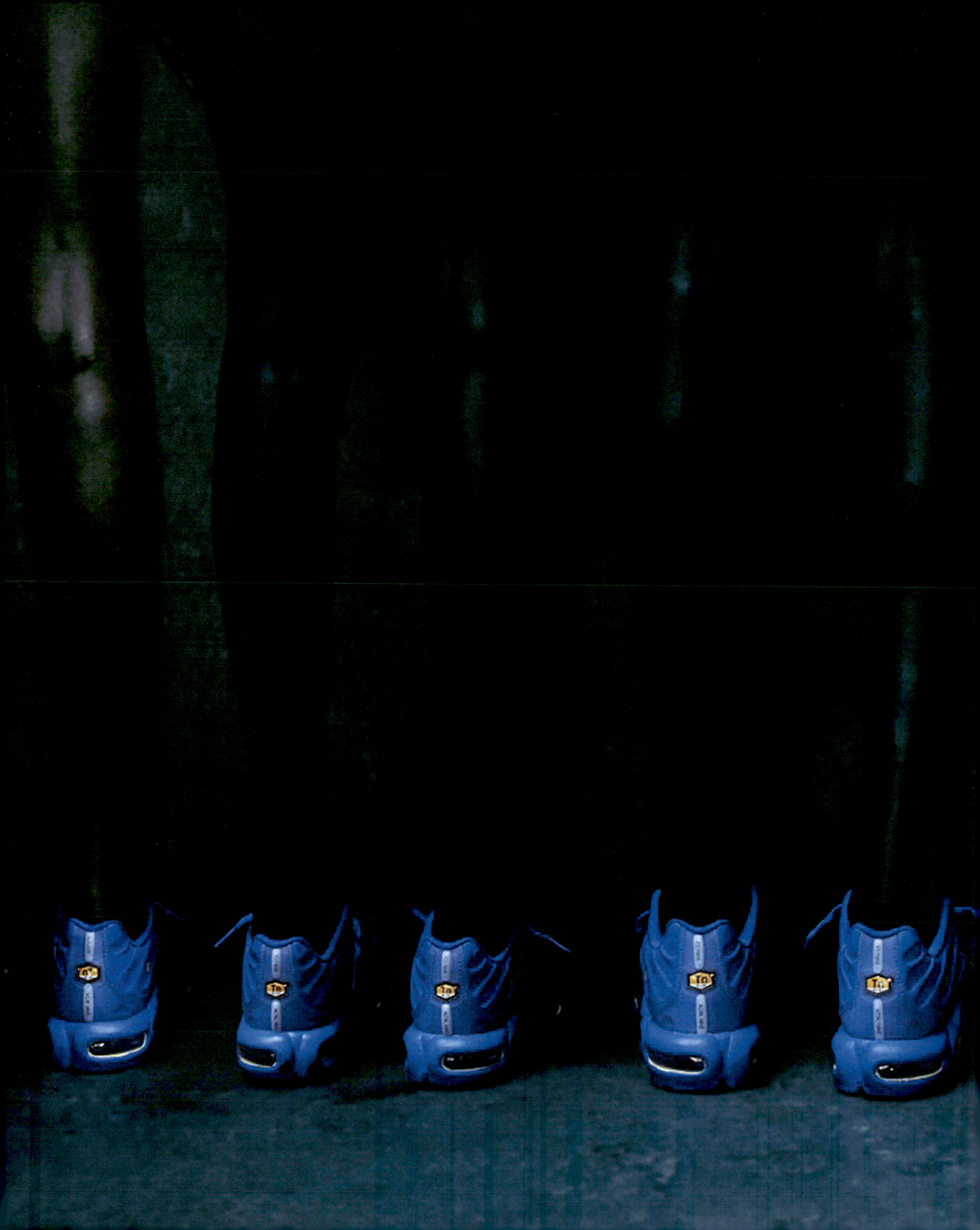

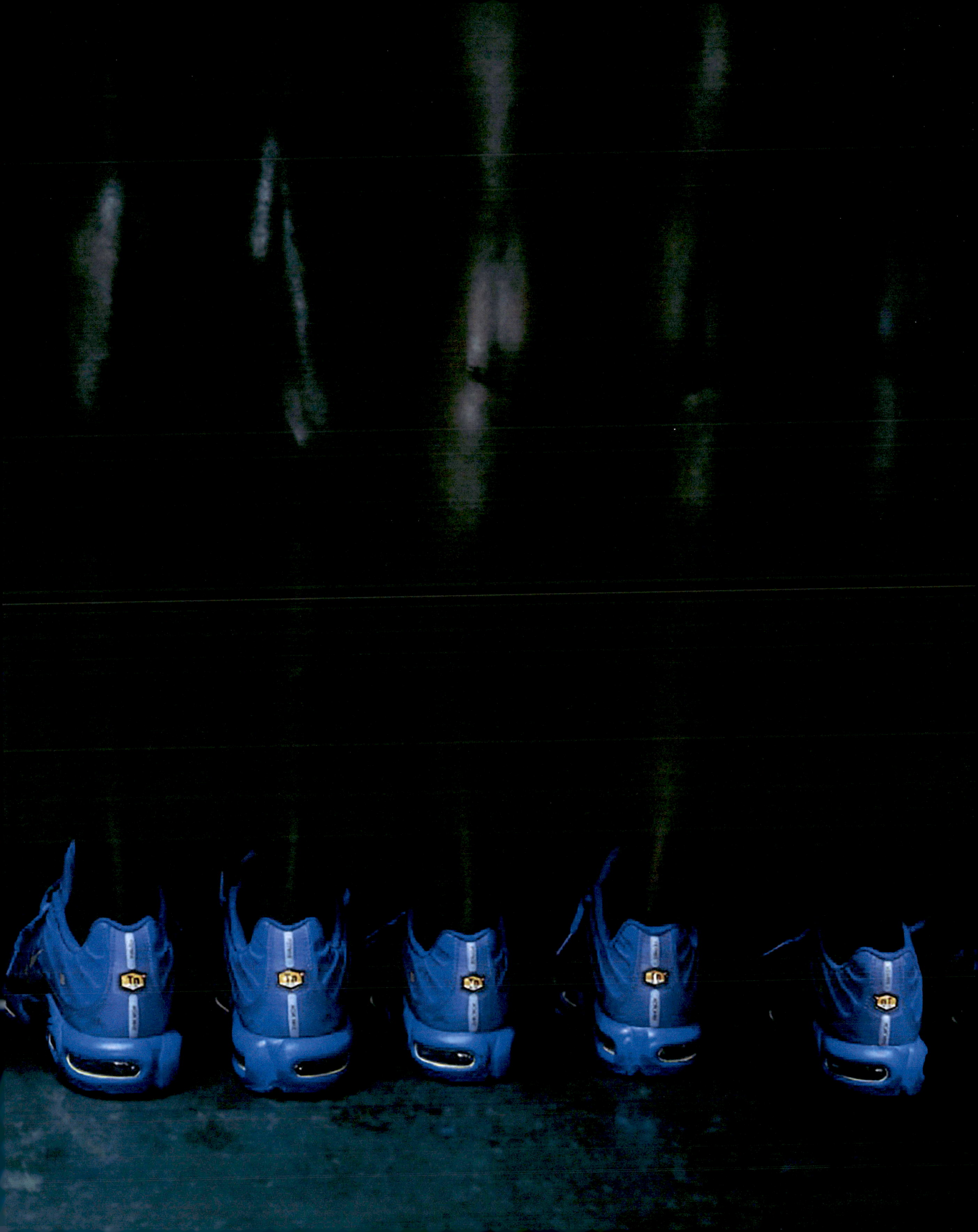

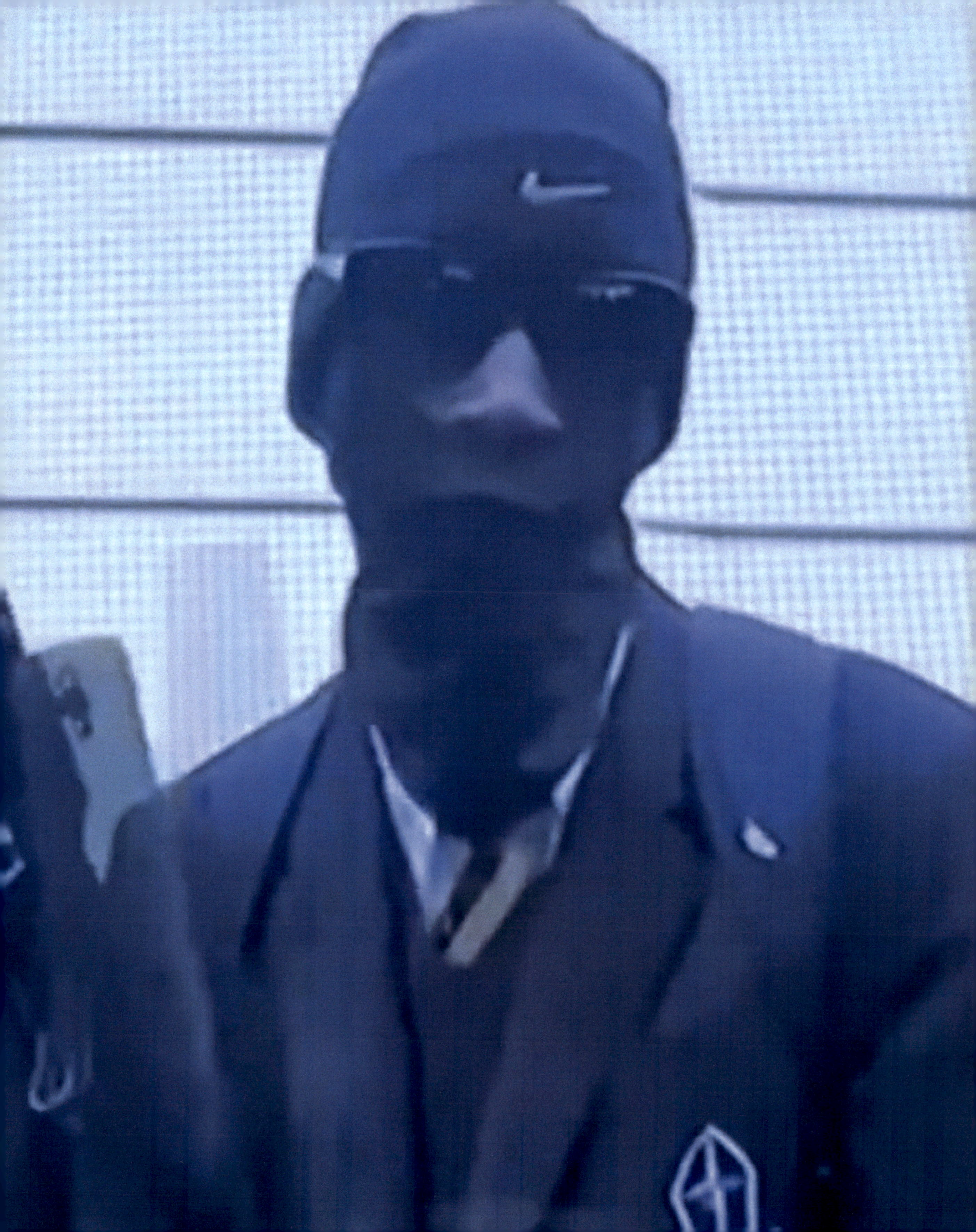

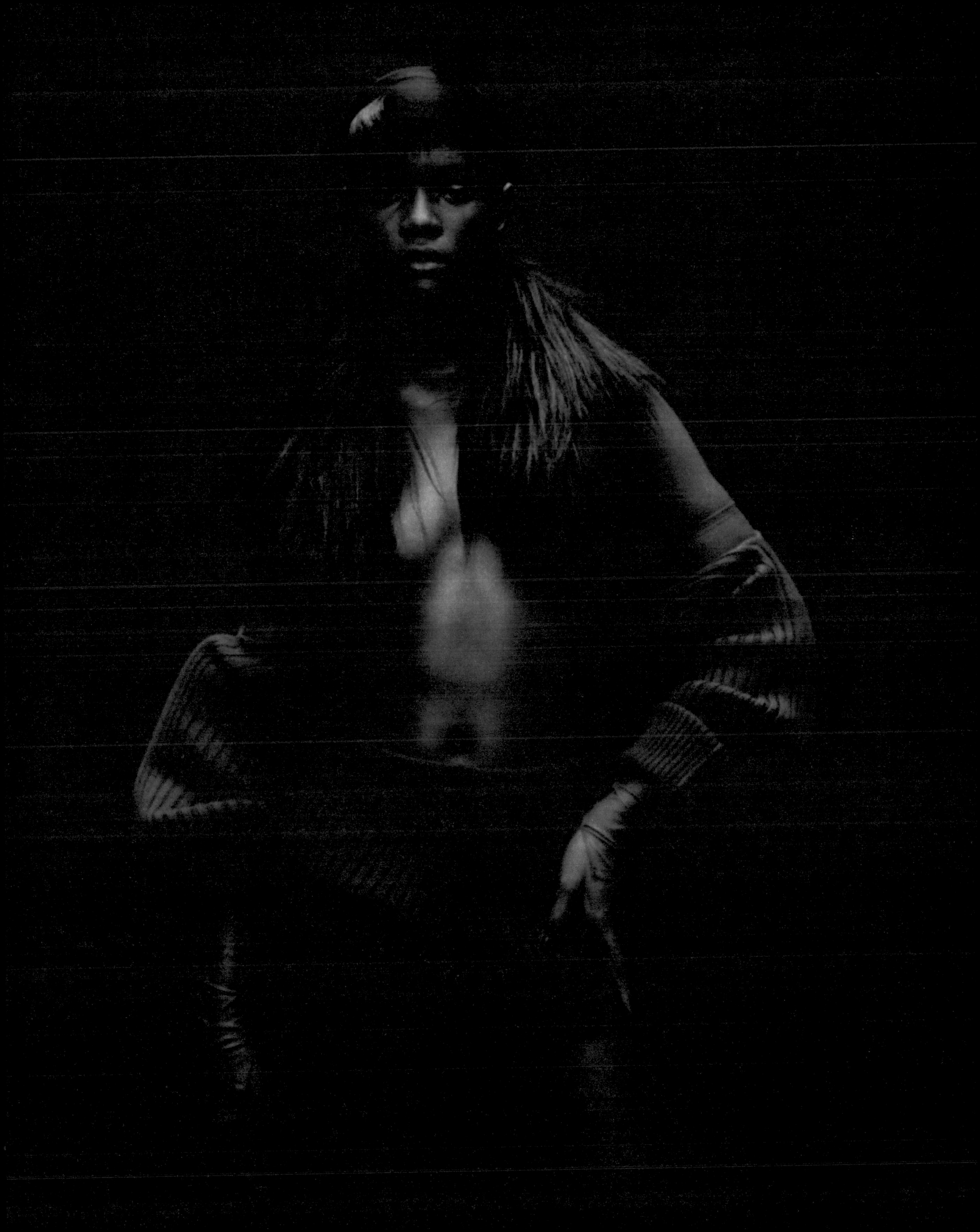

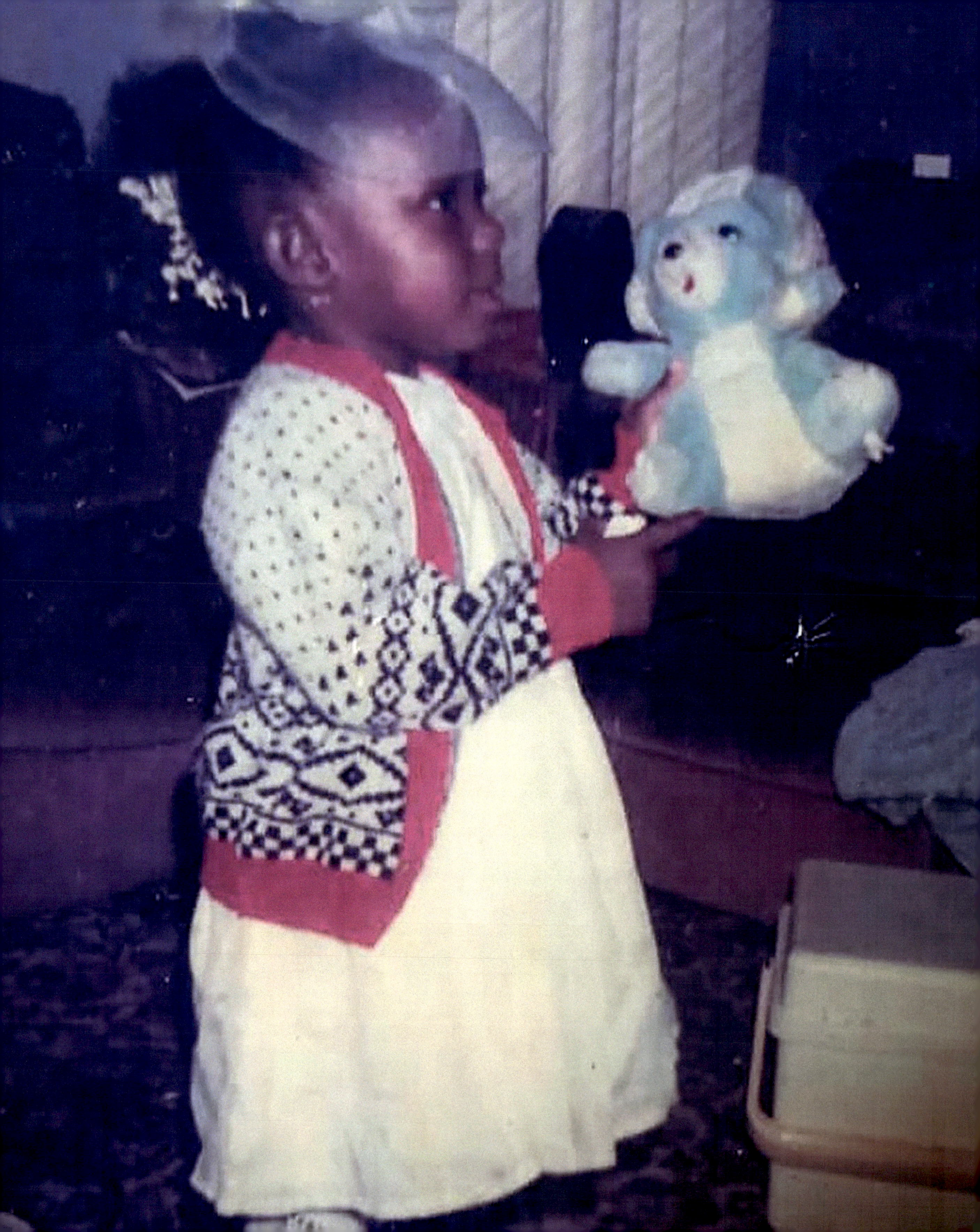

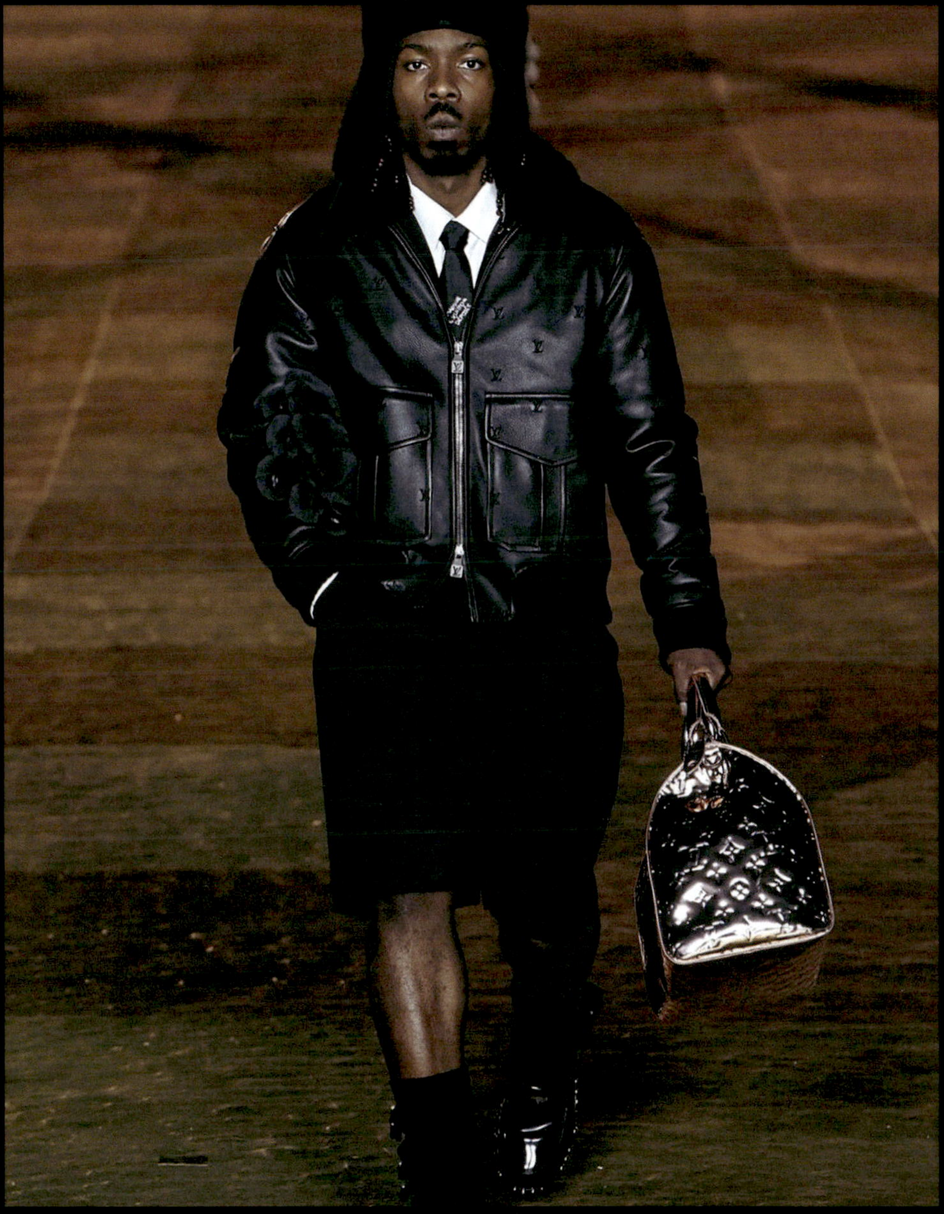

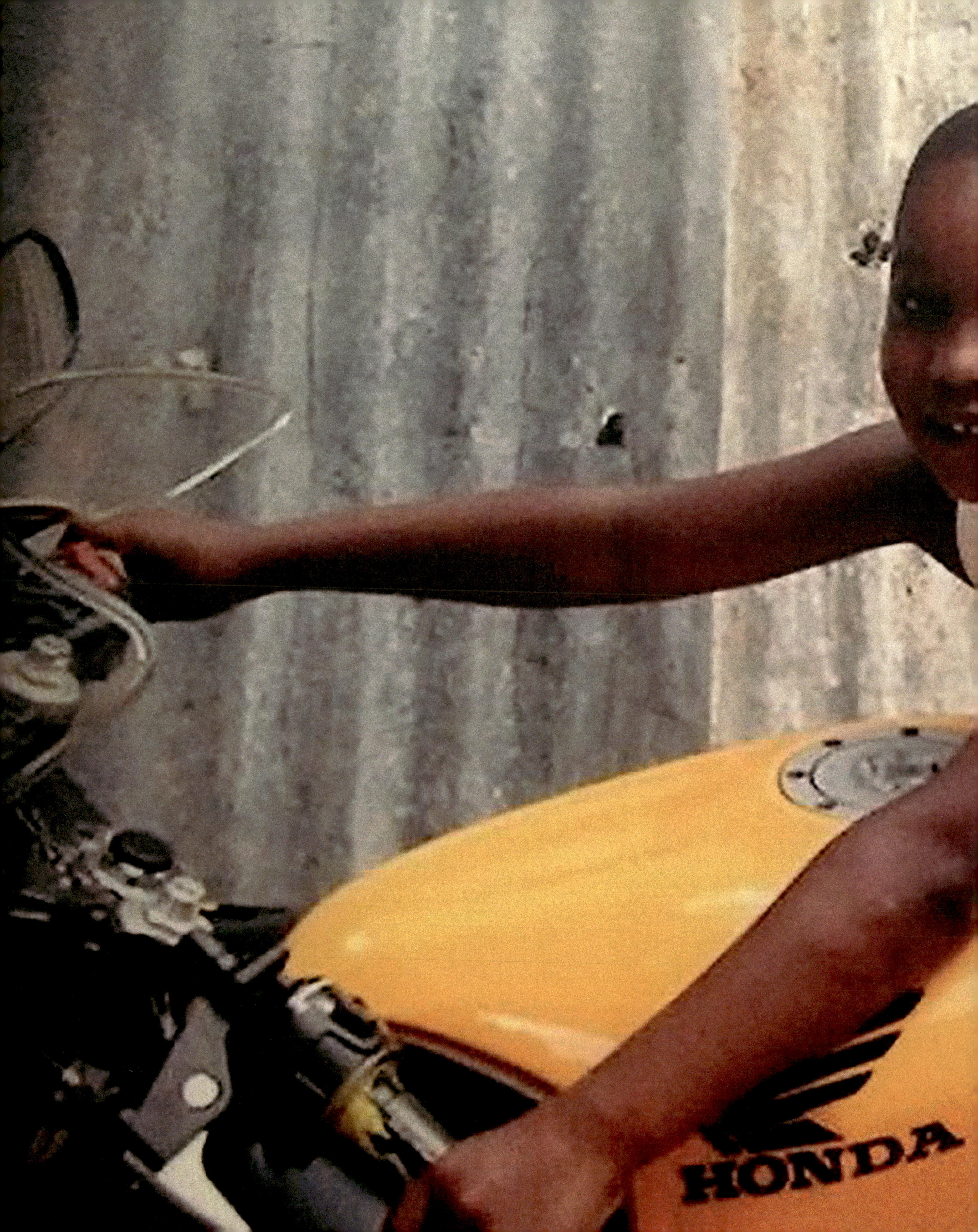
HONDA

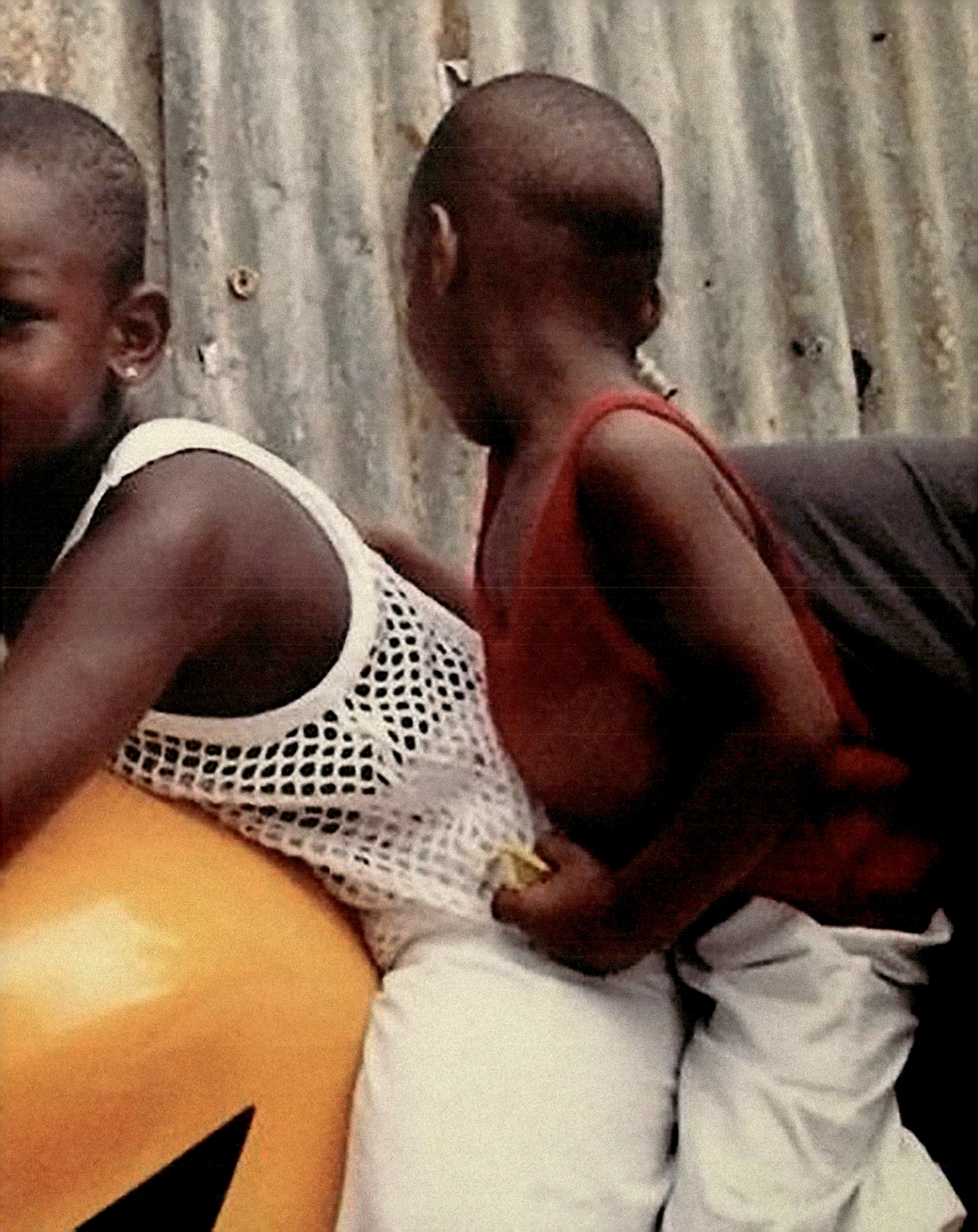

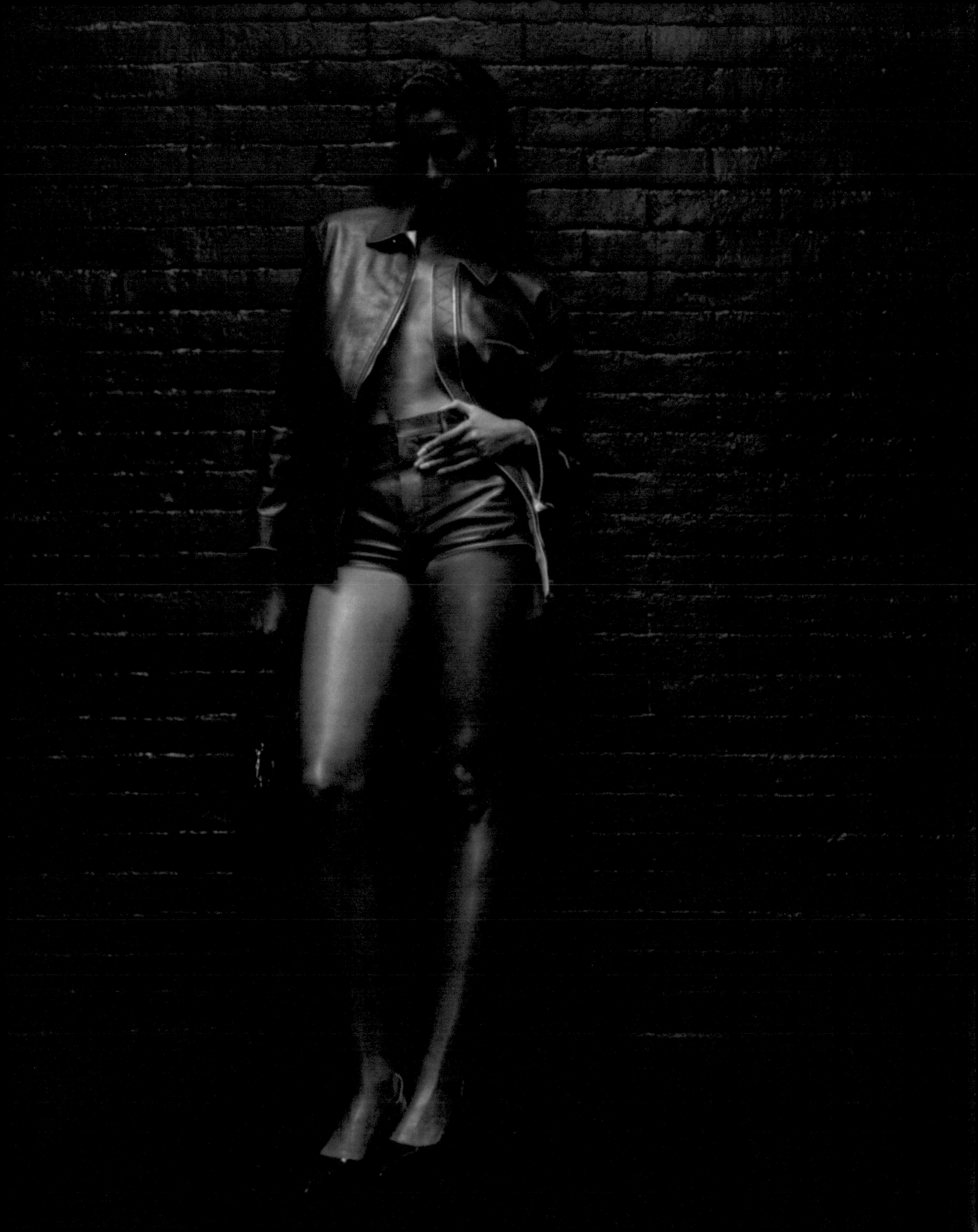

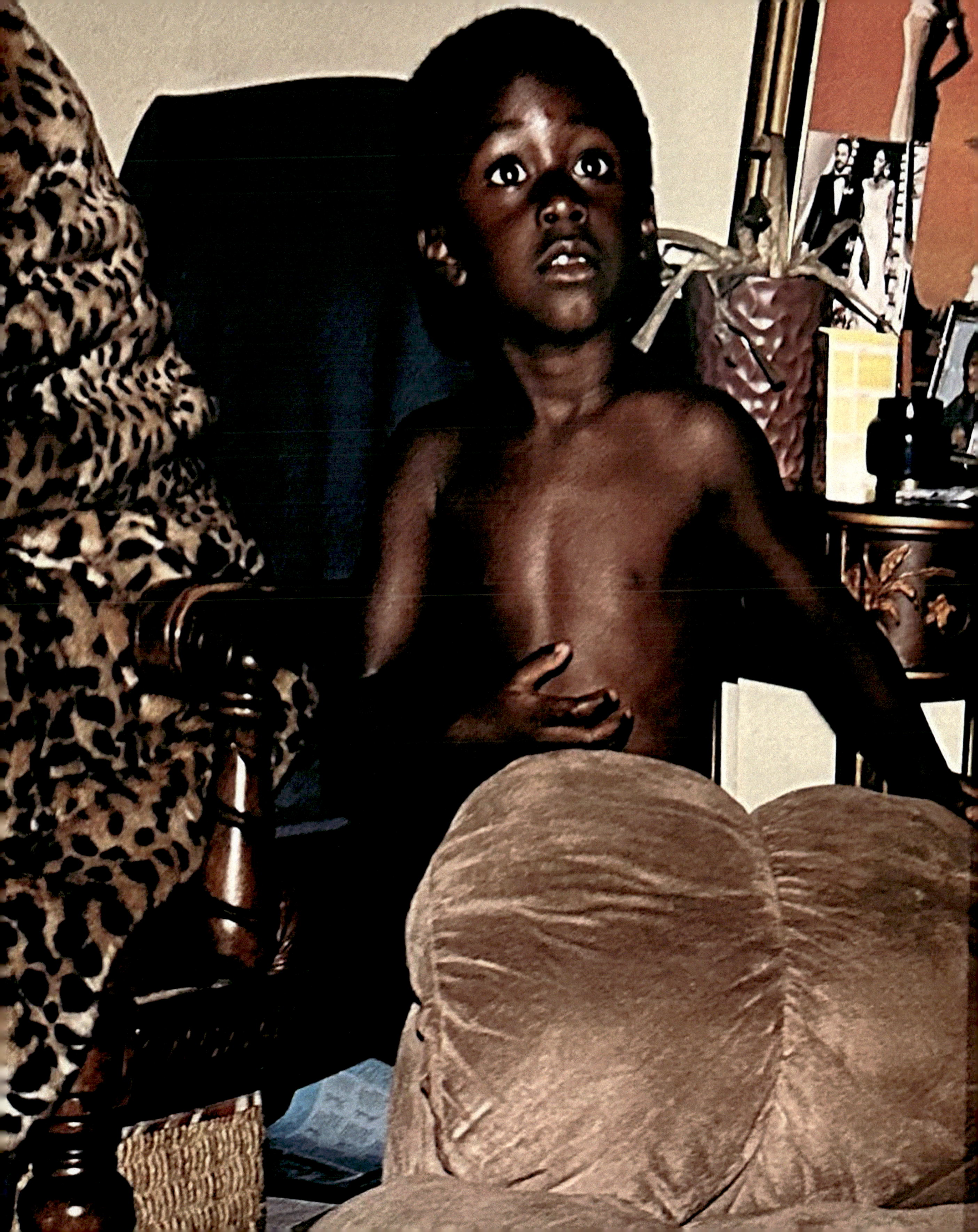

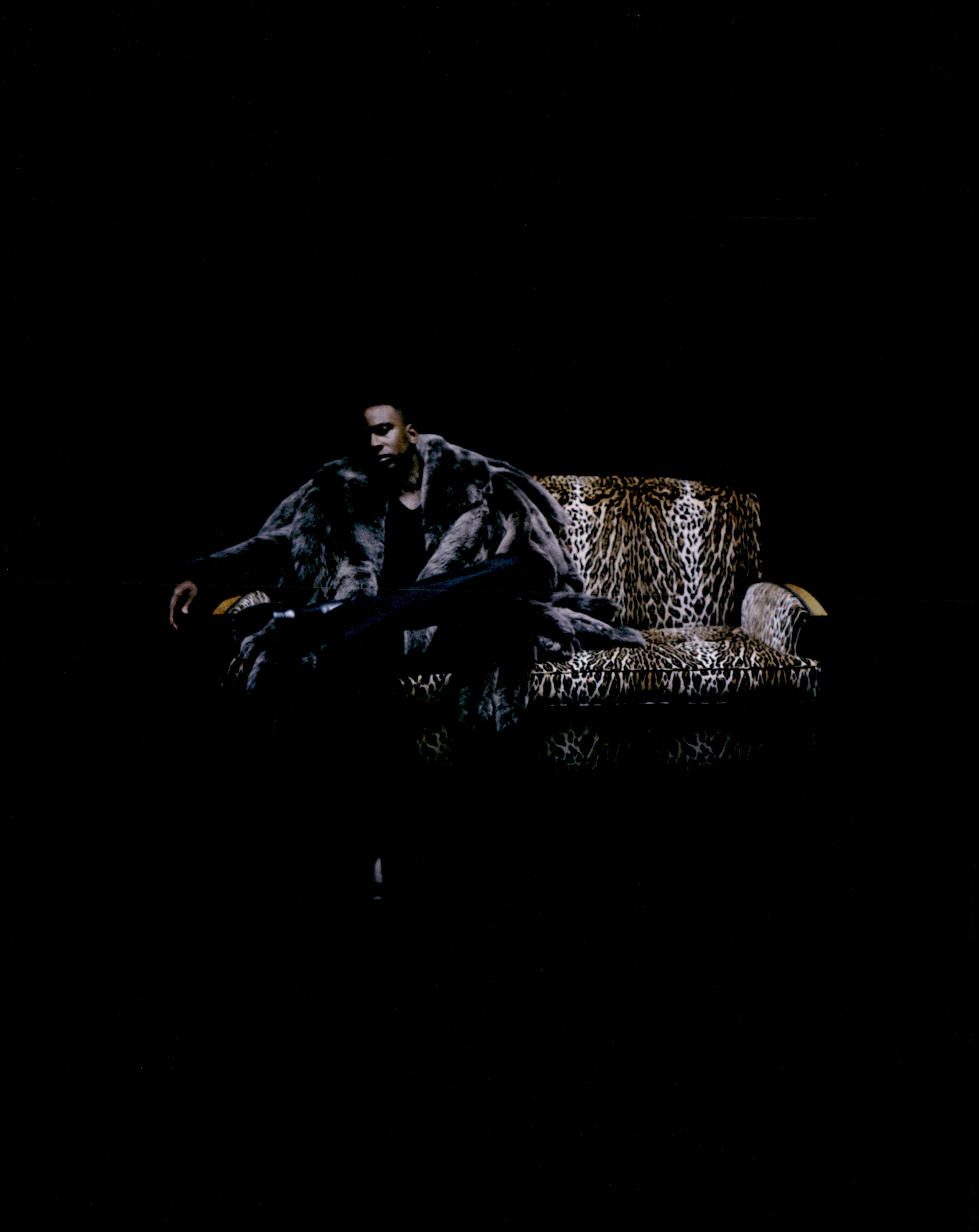

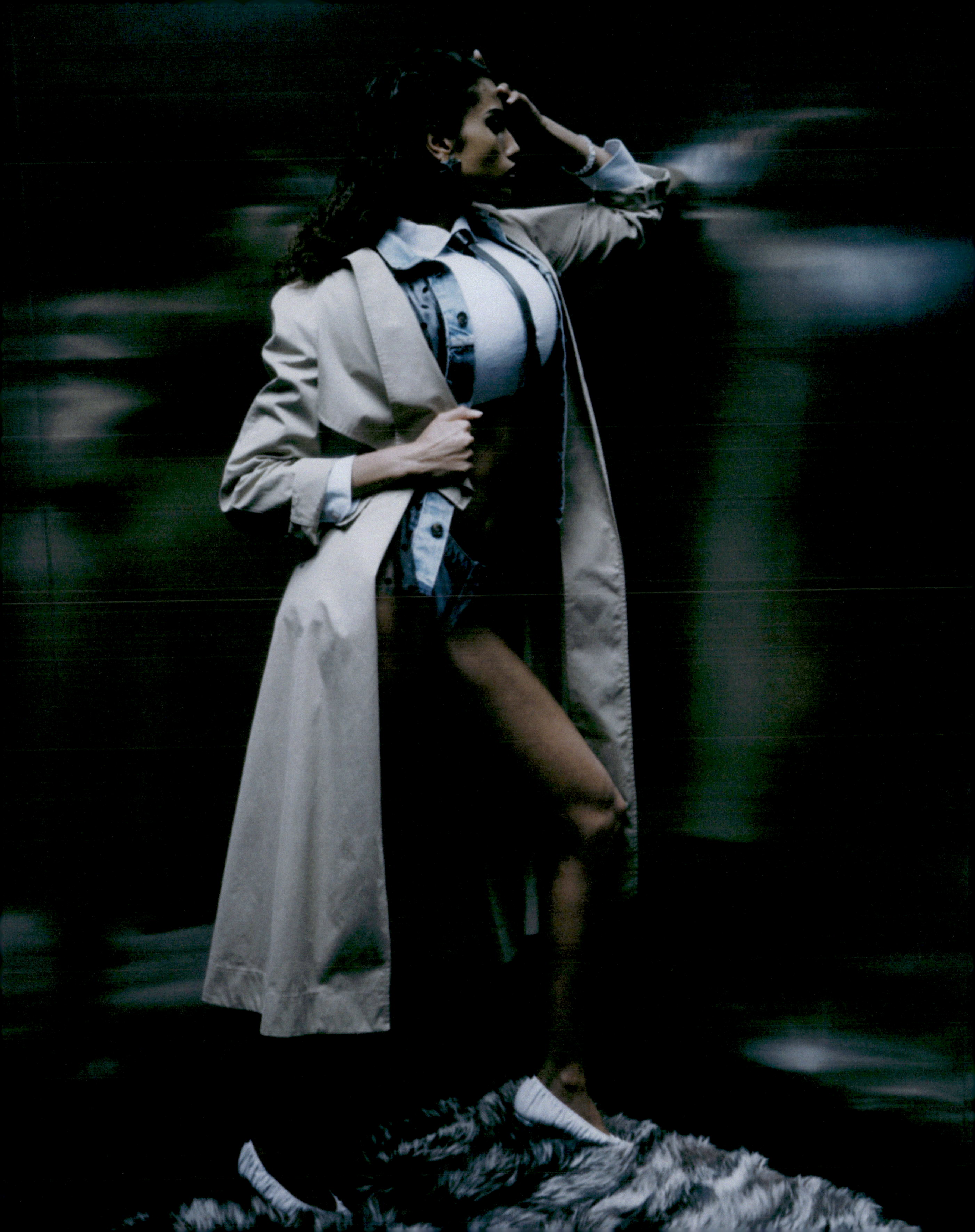

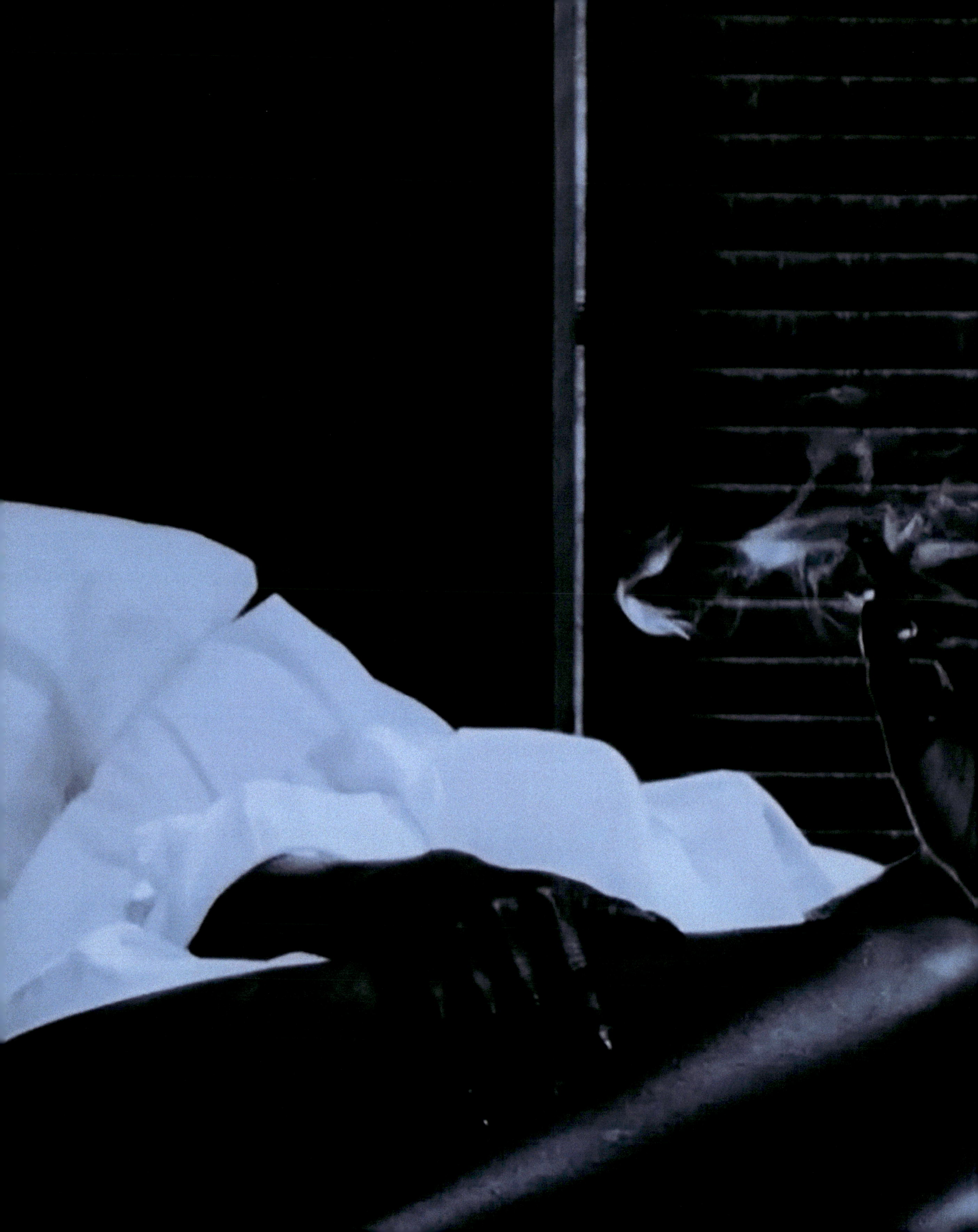

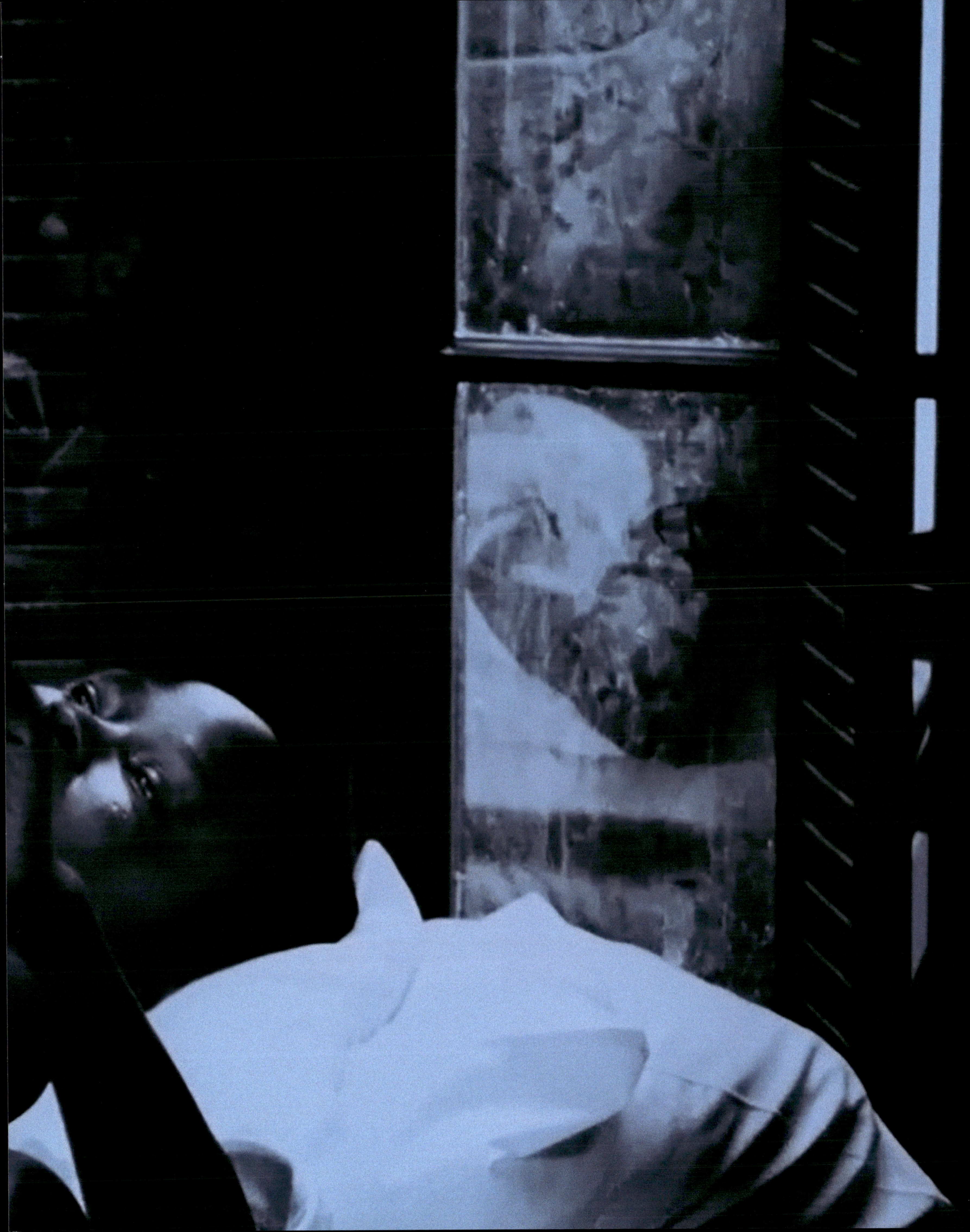

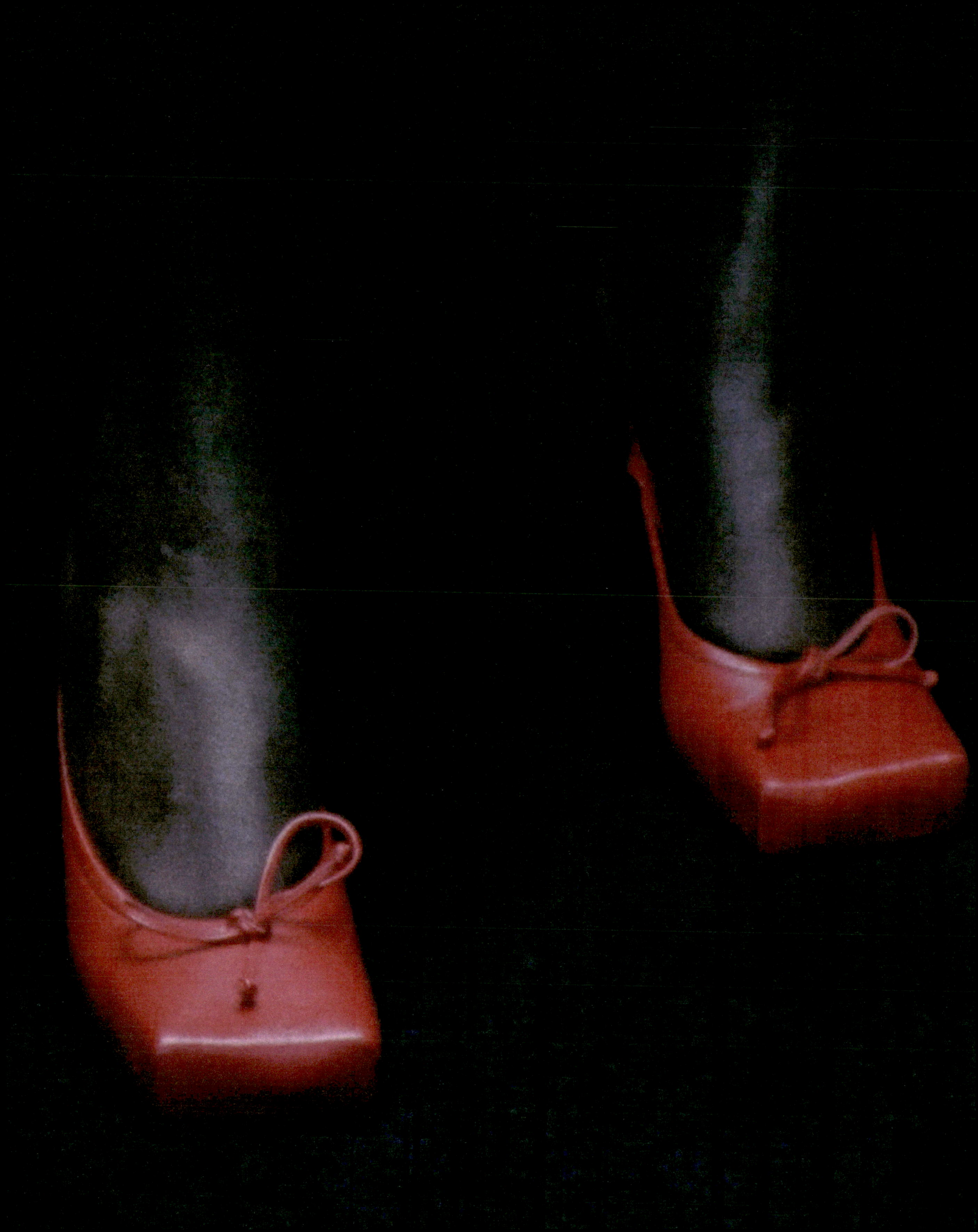

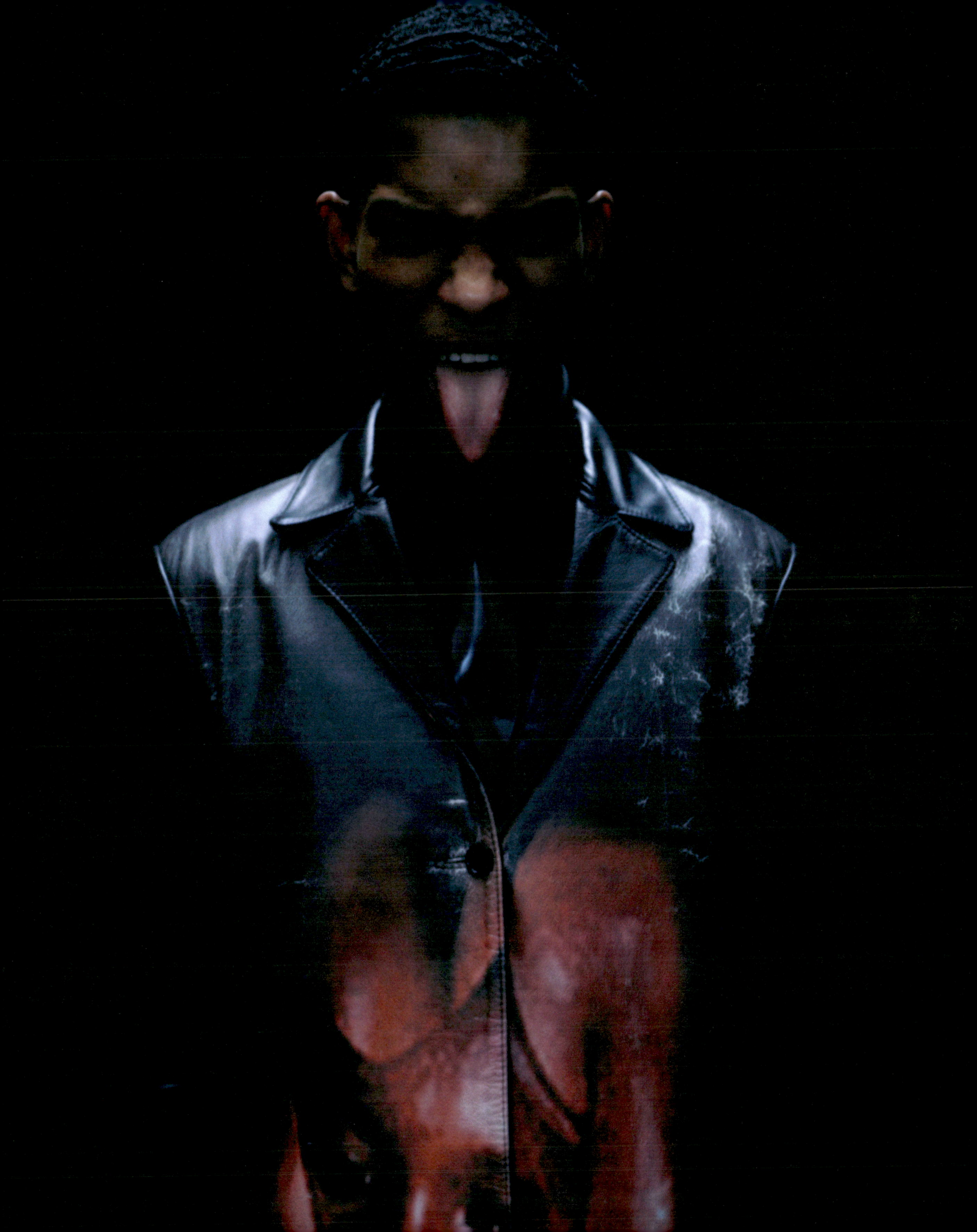

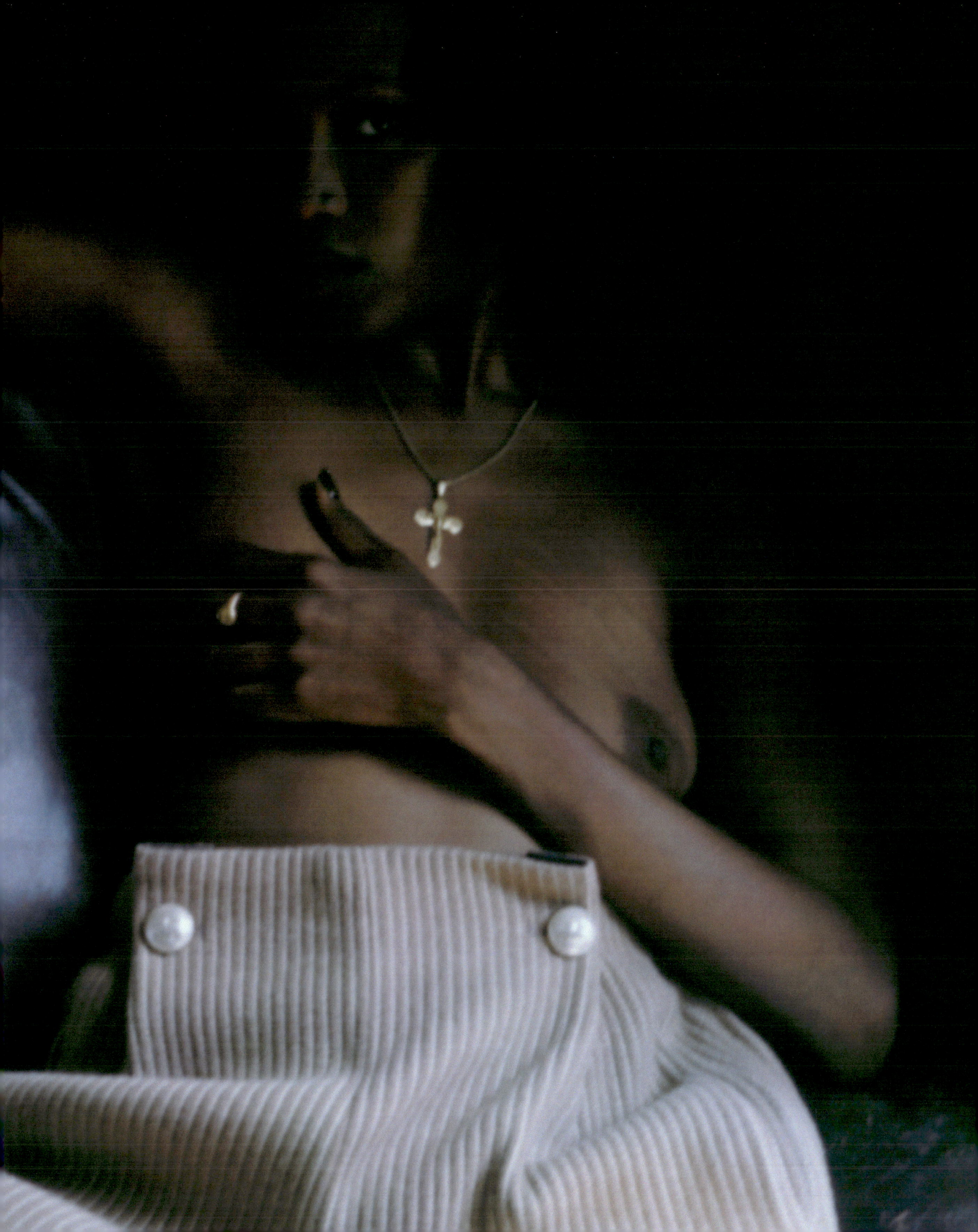

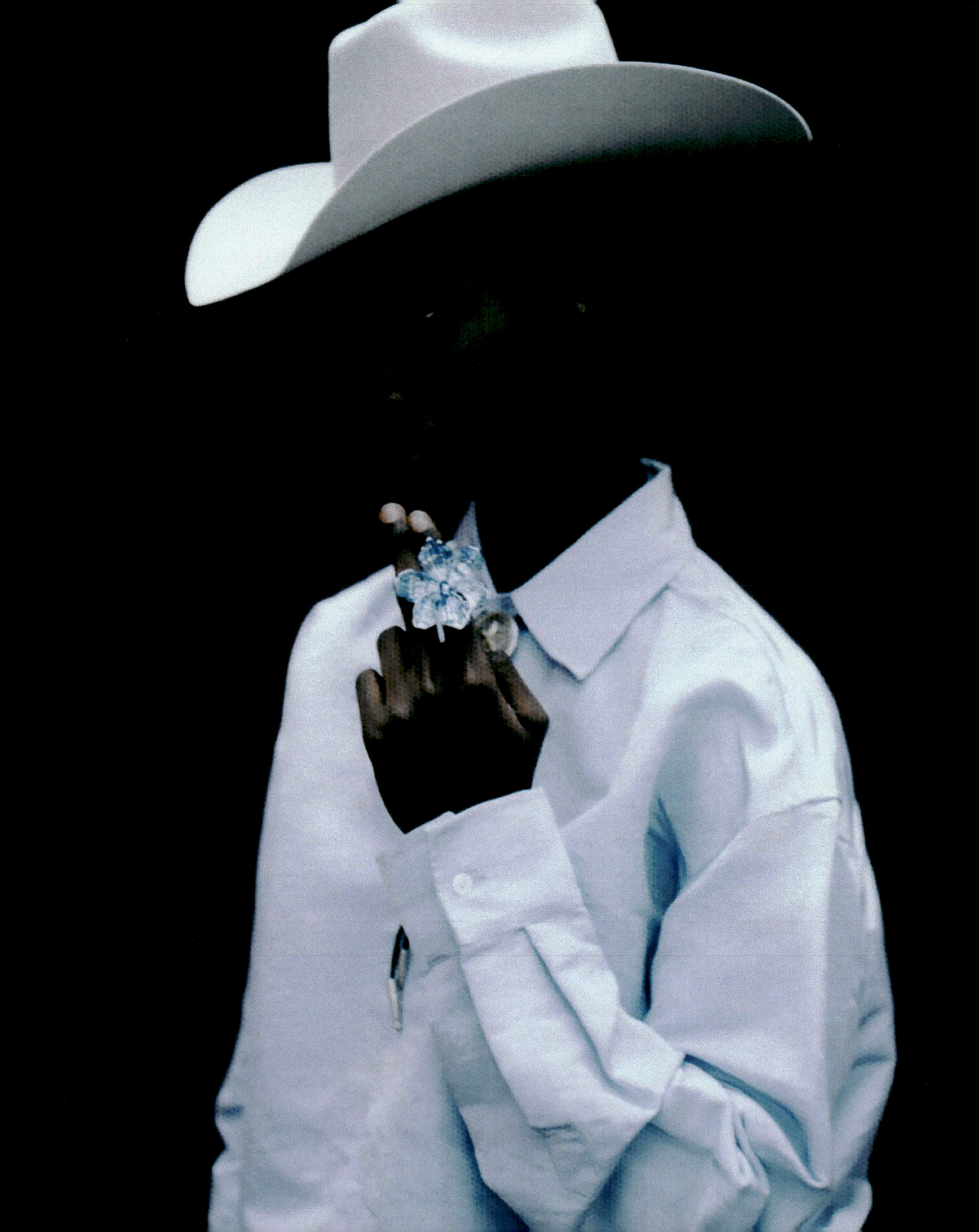

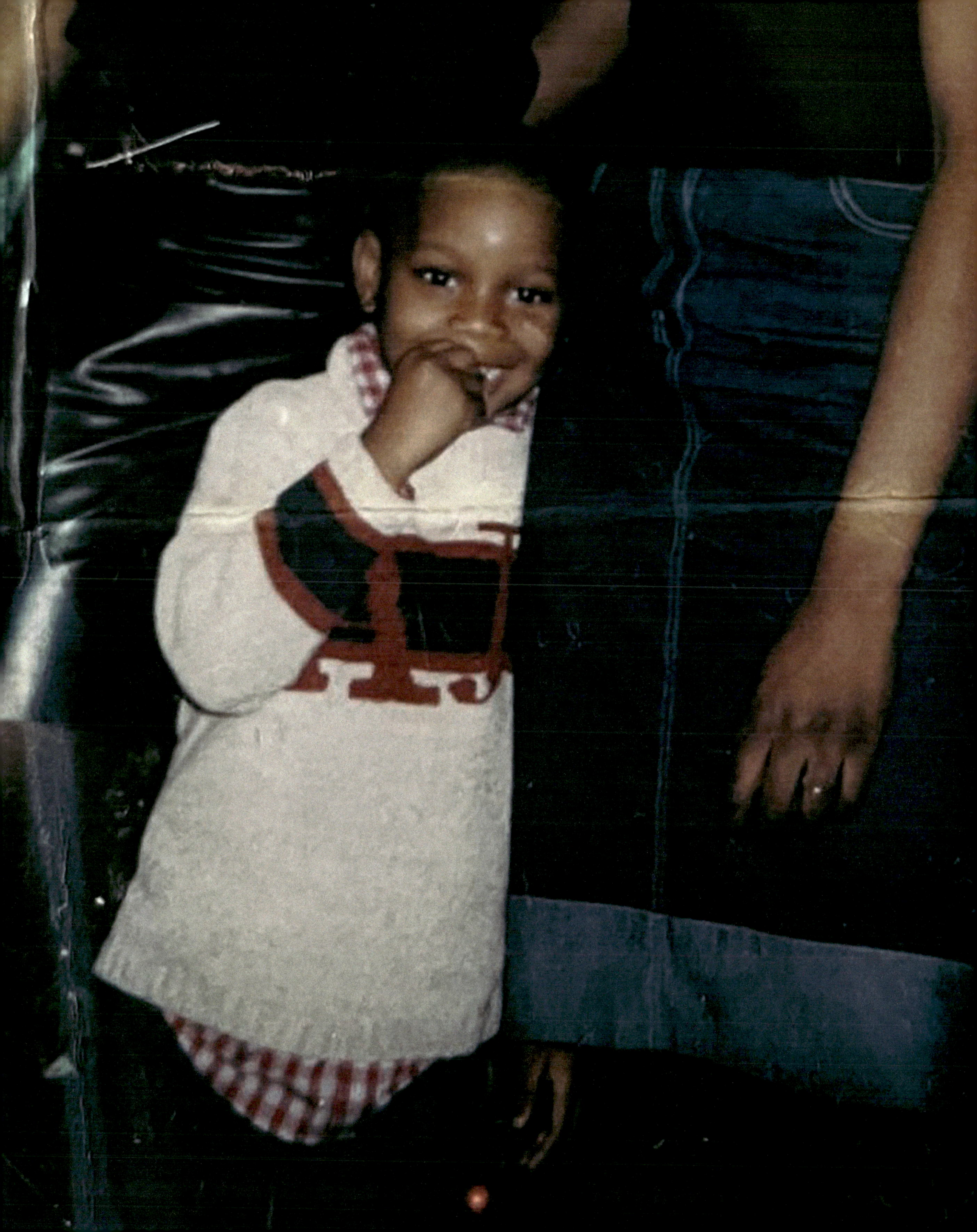

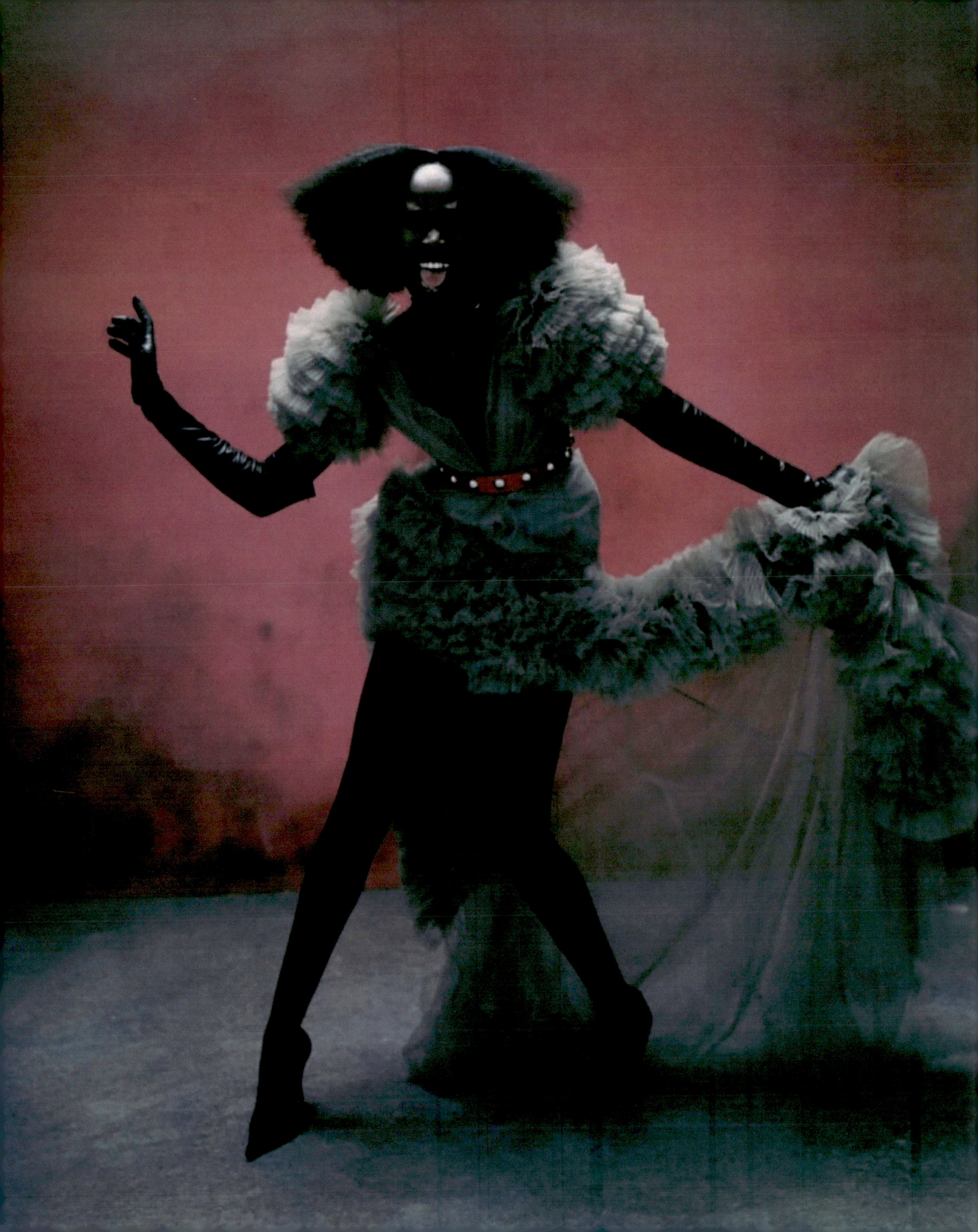

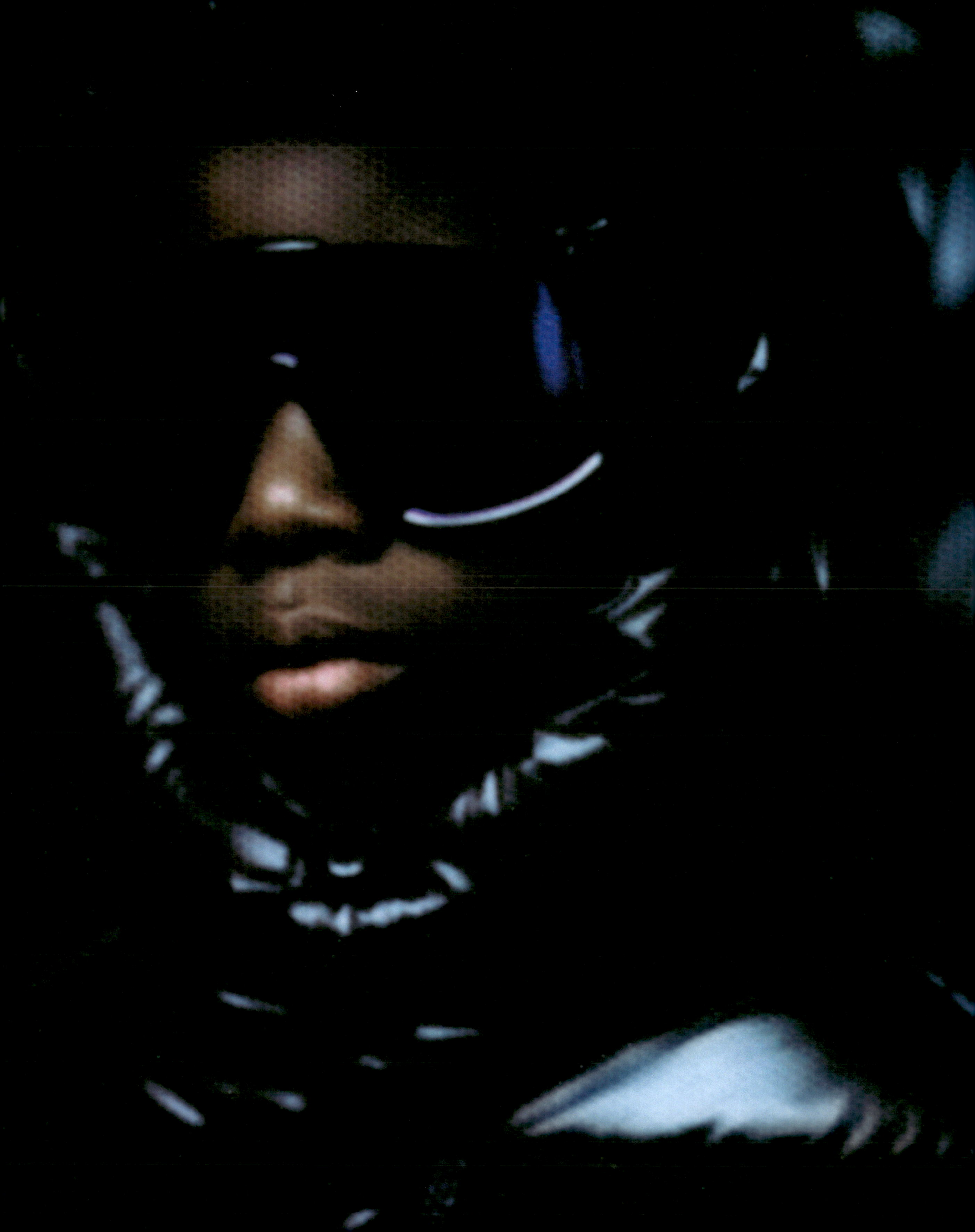

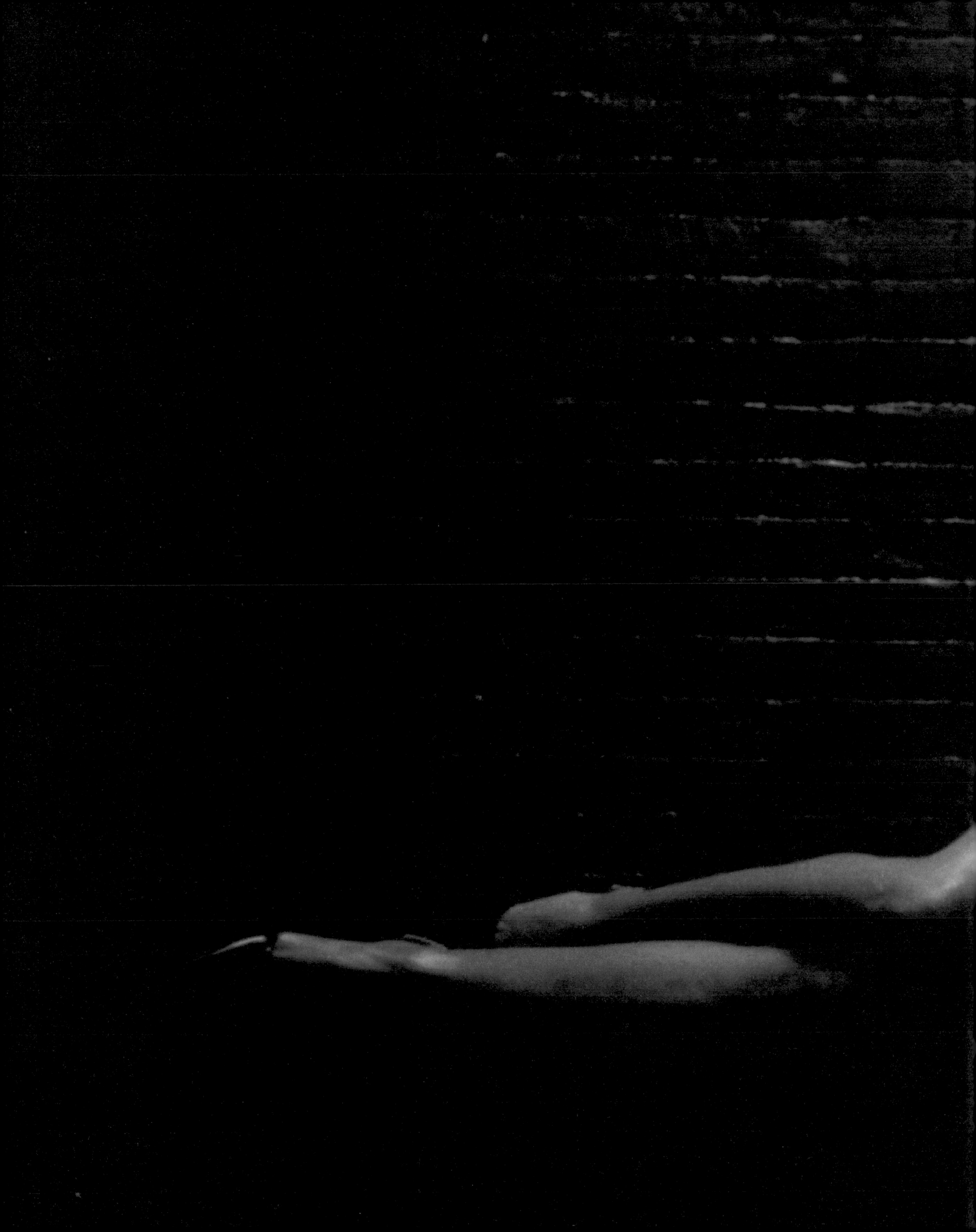

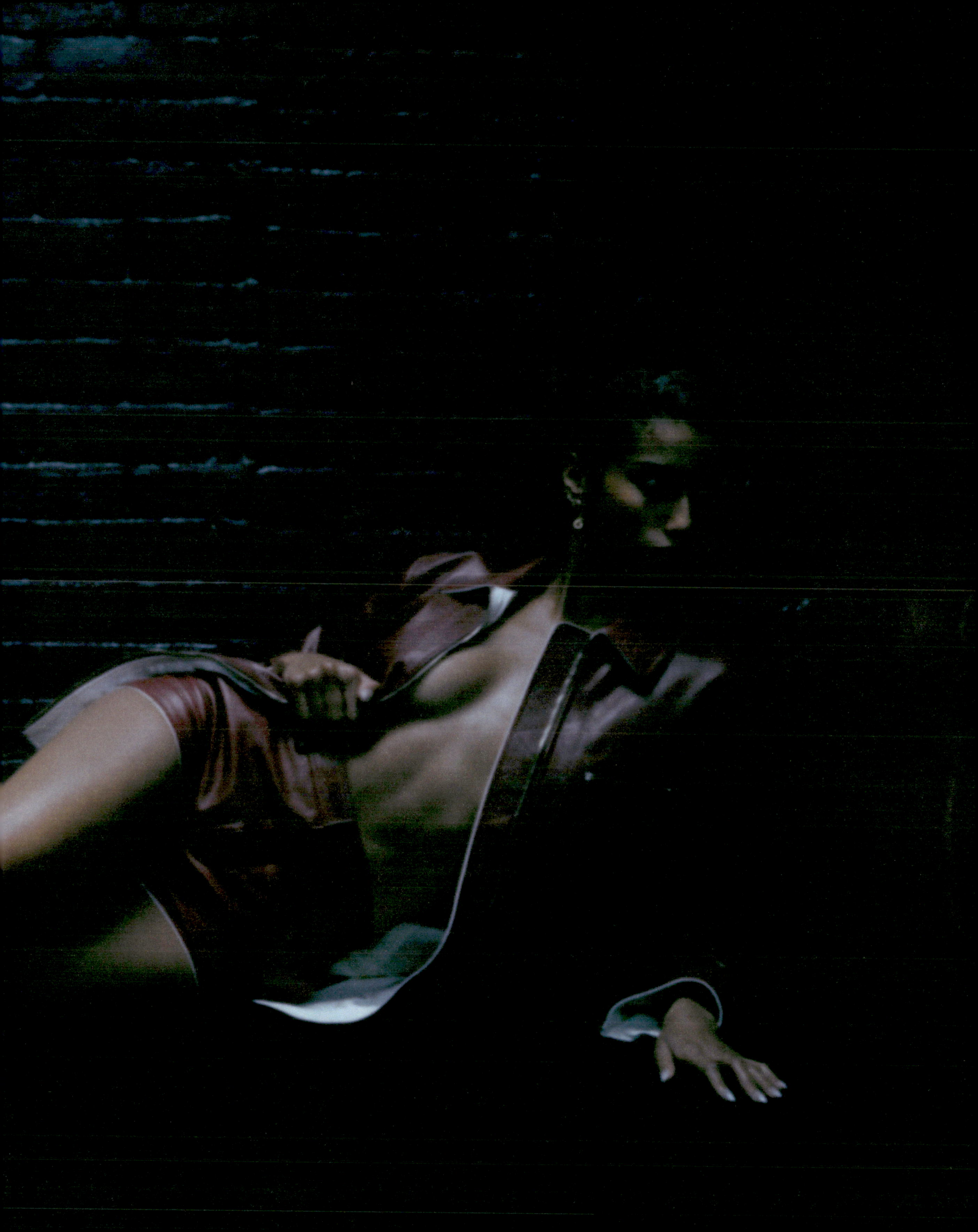

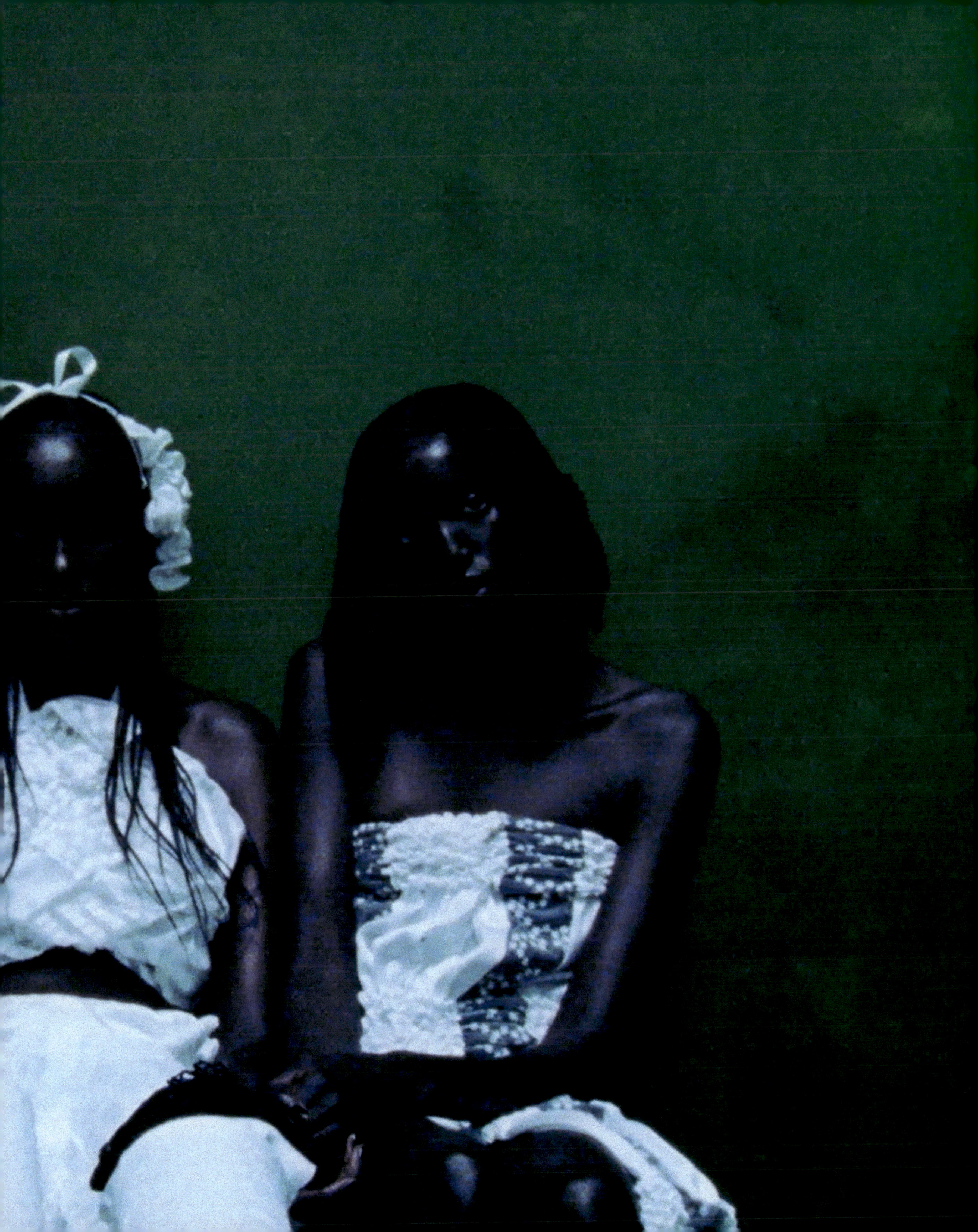

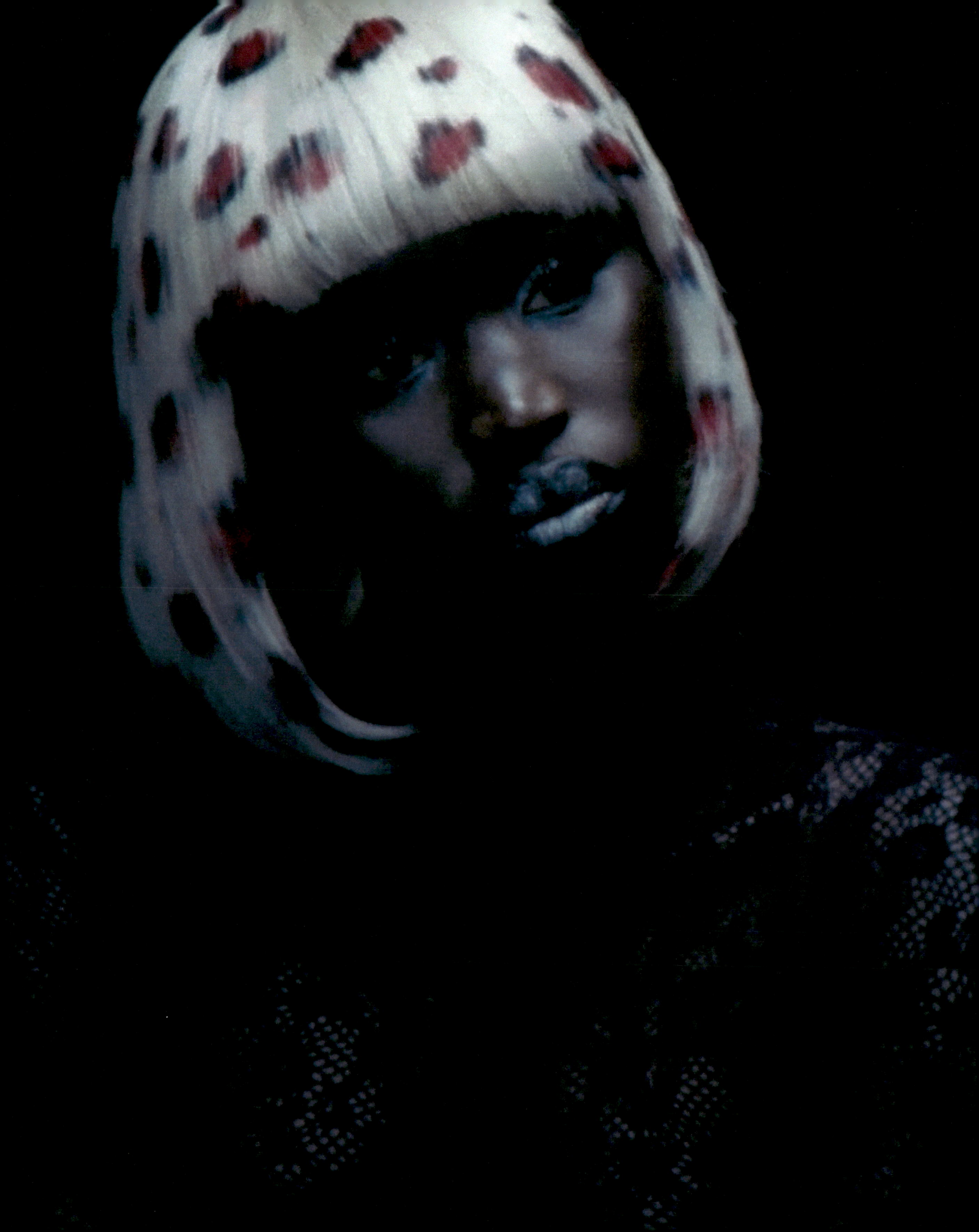

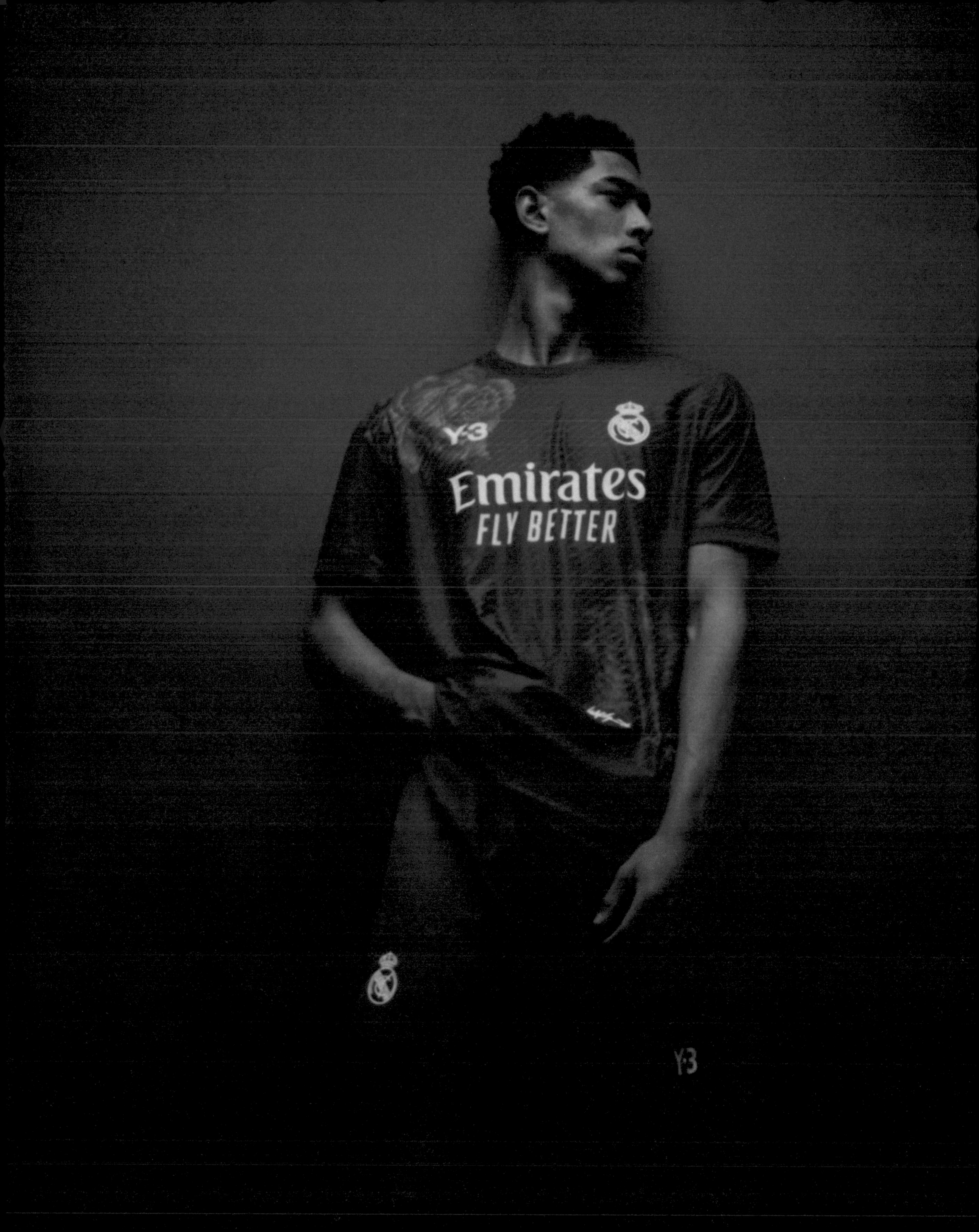
Y-3
Emirates
FLY BETTER
Y-3

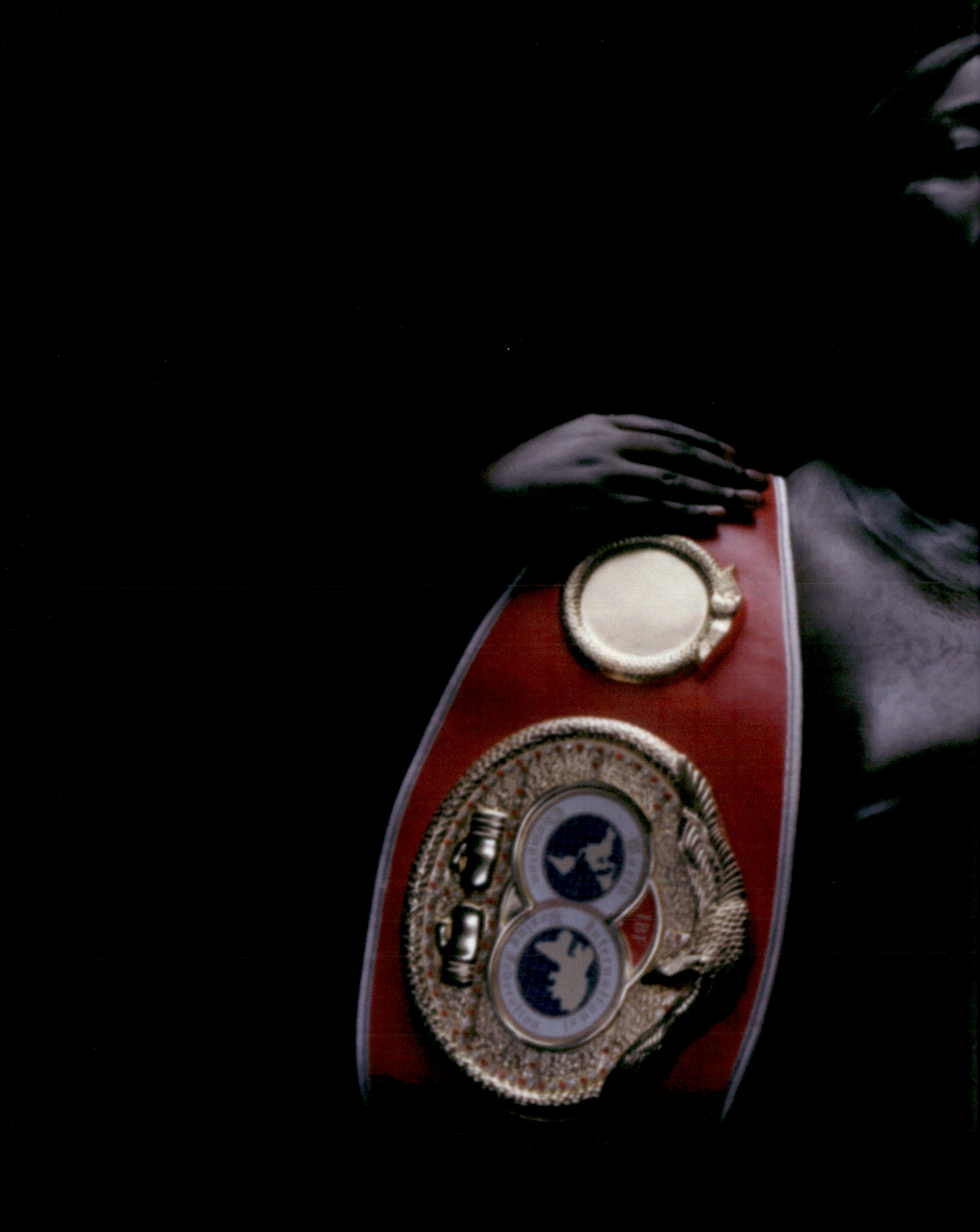

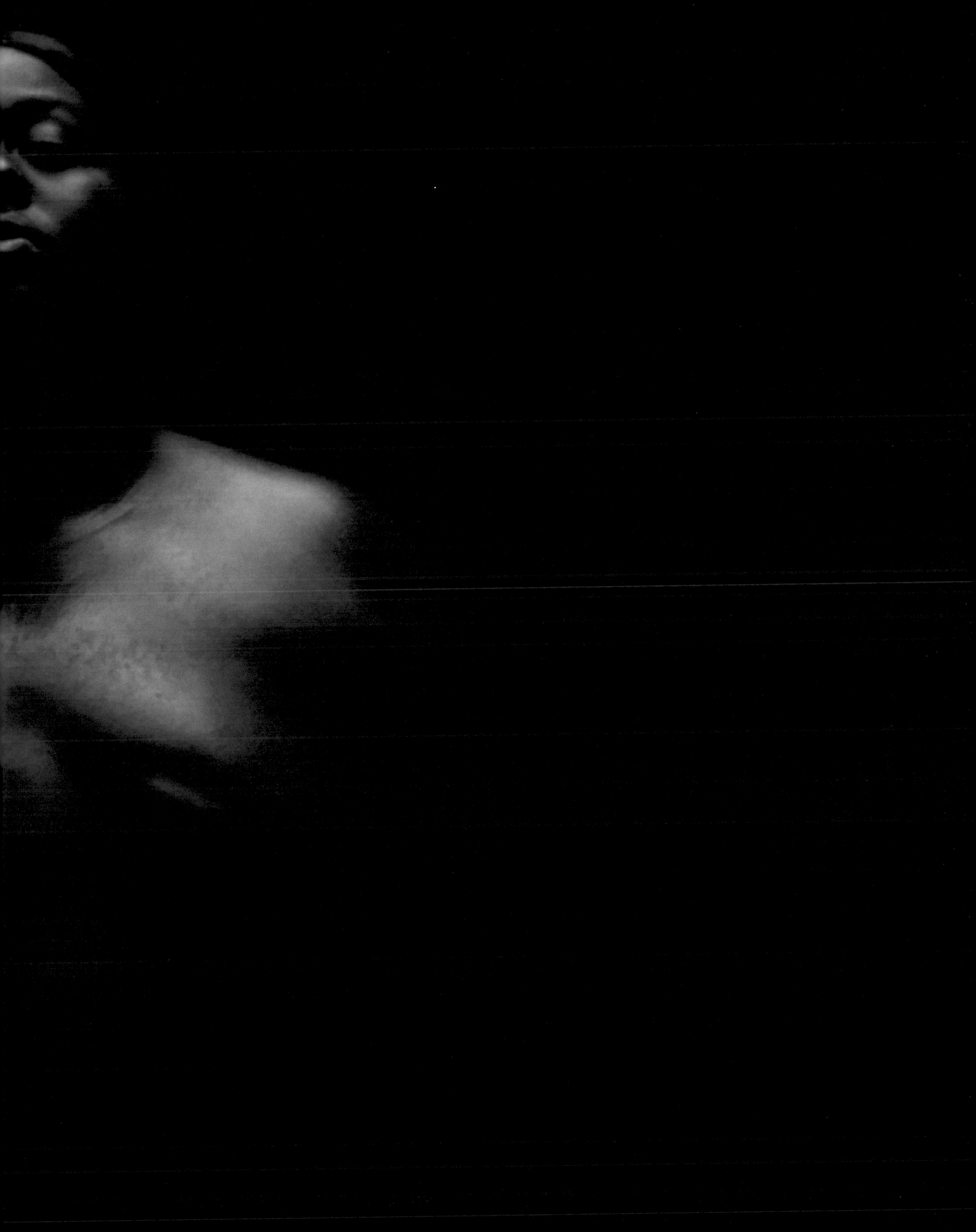

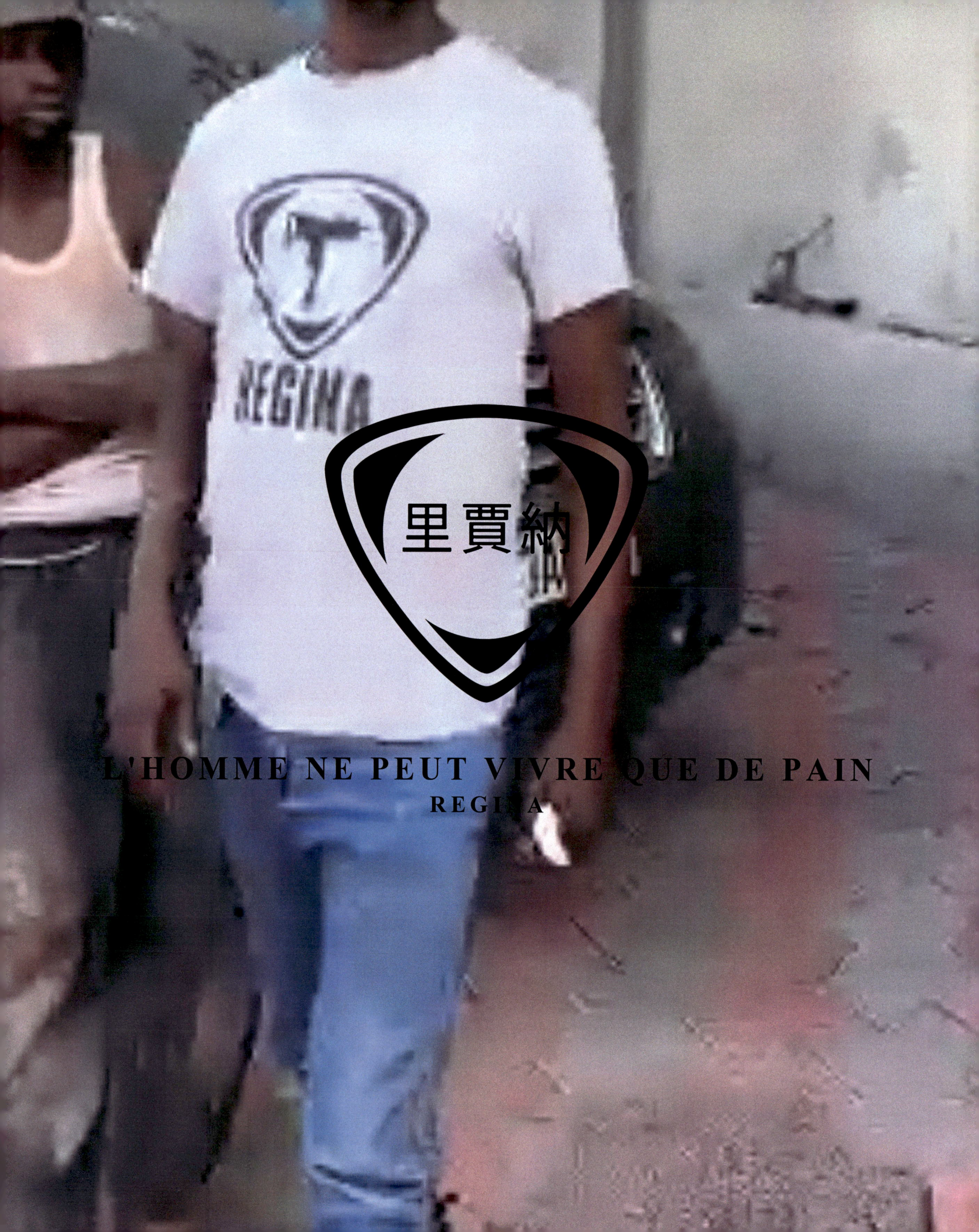
REGINA
里賈納
L'HOMME NE PEUT VIVRE QUE DE PAIN
REGINA

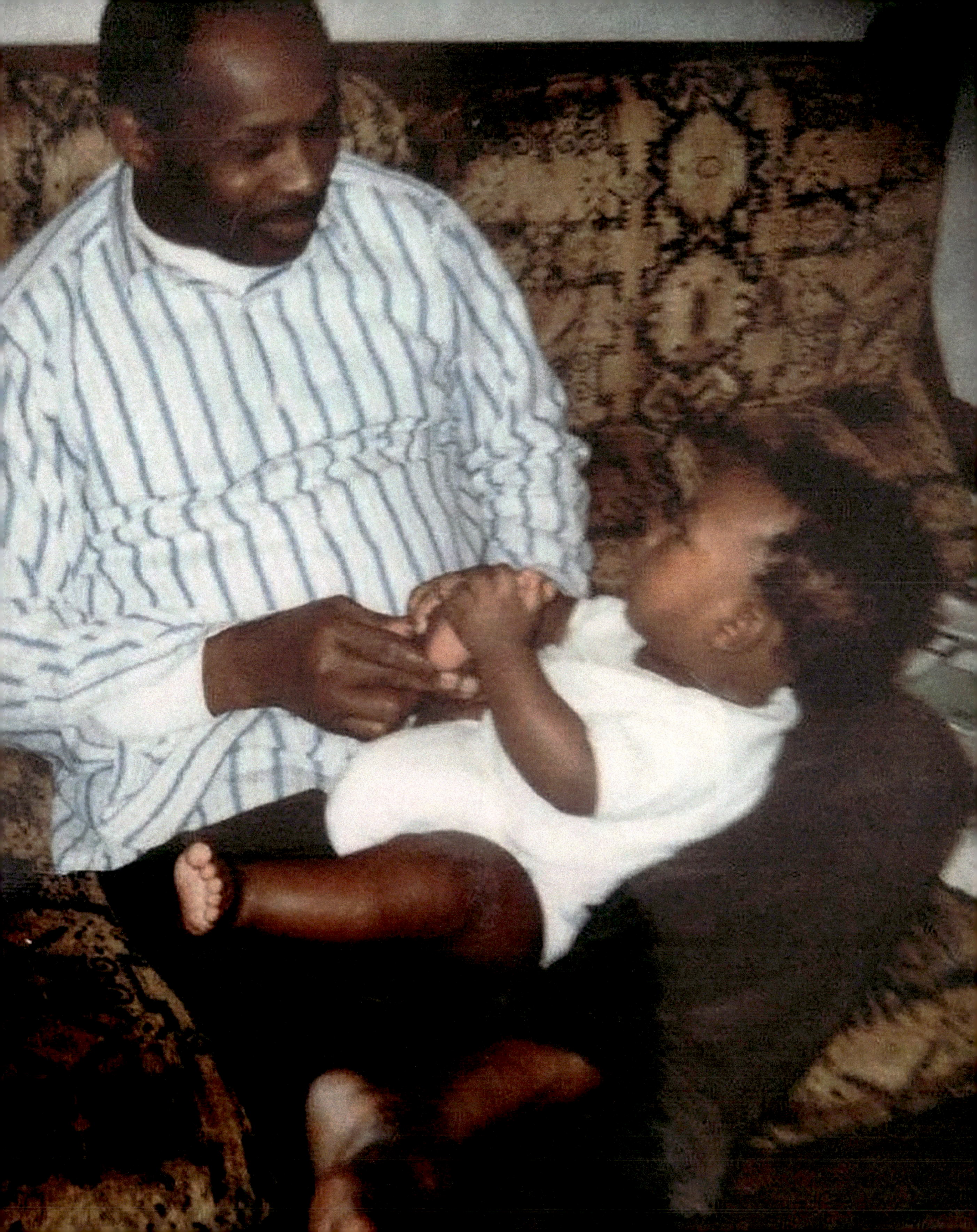

Page	Publication	Year
010	REGINA	2024
012	REGINA	2024
014	REGINA	2024
016	POP MAGAZINE	2024
018	NIKE AIR MAX DN	2024
020	REGINA	2024
022	HARPER'S BAZAAR	2023
024	REPLICA MAN MAGAZINE	2022
026	VOGUE ITALIA	2023
028	REGINA	2023
030	DAZED	2022
032	ARENA HOMME	2023
034	REGINA	2024
036	ARENA HOMME	2022
042	REGINA	2024
	VOGUE ITALIA	2023
044	REGINA	2024
	STAR SIGN BY FRANK DORREY	2022
046	ANOTHER MAGAZINE	2024
048	REGINA	2024
050	HARPER'S BAZAAR	2023
052	ANOTHER MAGAZINE	2024
	REGINA	
054	REPLICA MAN MAGAZINE	2022
056	REGINA	2024
058	ARENA HOMME	2022
060	ANOTHER MAGAZINE	2024
	REGINA	
062	REGINA	2024
064	REGINA	2024
066	BODIES MOWALOLA	2023
068	REGINA	2024
070	VOGUE ITALIA	2023
	POP MAGAZINE	2024
078	BIG! BY FRANK DORREY	2023
	ANOTHER MAGAZINE	2024
080	IJÓ	2021
	DAZED	2022
082	BODIES MOWALOLA	2023
084	REPLICA MAN MAGAZINE	2022
086	DAZED	2021
	REGINA	2024
088	DAZED	2022
090	DAZED	2022
	RE-EDITION	2021
092	DAZED	2022
094	REPLICA MAN MAGAZINE	2022
096	Y3	2024
	REGINA	2023
098	POP MAGAZINE	2024
	REGINA	
100	ACW NIKE	2023
102	REGINA	2024
104	ANOTHER MAGAZINE	2023
106	REGINA	2024
108	MONCLER	2022
110	POP MAGAZINE	2024
112	REGINA	2022
	HOLIDAY MAGAZINE	
114	REGINA	2022
	THE FACE MAGAZINE	
117	ARENA HOMME	2023
118	NIKE AIR MAX DN	2024
120	DAZED	2023
	LOUIS VUITTON	2024
122	REGINA	2023
	ANOTHER MAGAZINE	
124	ANOTHER MAGAZINE	2023
126	REGINA	2024
	ANOTHER MAGAZINE	2023
128	032C	2022
130	HARPER'S BAZAAR	2023
	REPLICA MAN MAGAZINE	
132	BYREDO	2023
	ANOTHER MAGAZINE	2024
134	REGINA	2024
136	IJÓ	2021
138	HARPER'S BAZAAR	2022
140	REGINA	2023
145	BYREDO	
146	VOGUE ITALIA	2023
	REGINA	
148	T MAGAZINE	2022
150	DAZED	2023
152	DAZED	2023
154	DAZED	2023
156	HOLIDAY MAGAZINE	2022
158	REGINA	2022
	T MAGAZINE	
160	REGINA	2024
162	REGINA	
164	DAZED	2023
	VOGUE ITALIA	
166	HARPER'S BAZAAR	2022
168	T MAGAZINE	2022
	REPLICA MAN MAGAZINE	
170	HUMAN RACE	2023
	REPLICA MAN MAGAZINE	2022
172	REPLICA MAN MAGAZINE	2022
174	OFFICE MAGAZINE	2022
	POP MAGAZINE	2024
176	BODIES MOWALOLA	2023
	ARENA HOMME	
178	SIXTEEN JOURNAL	2022
	REPLICA MAN MAGAZINE	
180	GQ	2022
	THE FACE	
182	IJÓ	2021
184	VOGUE ITALIA	2023
190	ARENA HOMME	2022
	ARENA HOMME	2022
192	DAZED	2023
194	T MAGAZINE	2023
196	REGINA	2024
	REGINA	
198	BODIES MOWALOLA	2023
200	NIKE BASKETBALL	2022
	HARPER'S BAZAAR	2023
202	REPLICA MAN MAGAZINE	2022
204	DAZED	2022
206	ACW NIKE	2023
208	REGINA	2023
	REGINA	
210	REGINA	2023
	LOUIS VUITTON	
212	REGINA	
214	POP MAGAZINE	2024
	HOLIDAY MAGAZINE	2022
216	032C	2022
	POP MAGAZINE	2024
218	ARENA HOMME	2022
220	REGINA	2023
	BODIES MOWALOLA	
222	HOLIDAY MAGAZINE	2022
224	REPLICA MAN MAGAZINE	2022
	REGINA	
226	HARPER'S BAZAAR	2022
	MONCLER	
228	POP MAGAZINE	2024
230	DAZED	2022
232	REGINA	2024
	Y3	
234	REGINA	2024
236	REGINA	